WHAT CAN
YOU DO WITH A
LAW
DEGREE?

Other Books by Deborah Arron

■ ■ ■

The Complete Guide to Contract Lawyering

*What Every Lawyer and Law Firm Needs to Know
about Temporary Legal Services*

with Deborah Guyol

NICHE PRESS

■ ■ ■

Running from the Law

Why Good Lawyers Are Getting Out of the Legal Profession

TEN SPEED PRESS

See the back pages of the book for order information.

WHAT CAN YOU DO WITH A

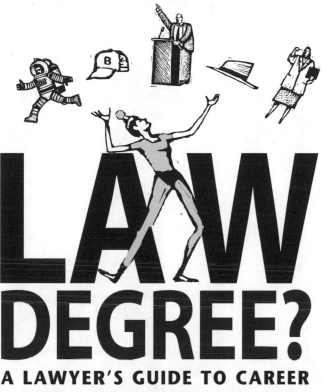

LAW DEGREE?

A LAWYER'S GUIDE TO CAREER ALTERNATIVES INSIDE, OUTSIDE & AROUND THE LAW

...

DEBORAH ARRON

NICHE PRESS

SEATTLE WASHINGTON

Deborah Arron offers keynote addresses, lectures, seminars
and workshops for lawyers and law students on career
choice, job hunting, and client development. Interested
sponsors may contact Ms. Arron at (206) 285-0288.

Published by:
Niche Press
PO Box 99477
Seattle, WA 98199
(206) 285-5239
nichemj@aol.com

Library of Congress Cataloging-in-Publication Data
Arron, Deborah L., 1950–
      What can you do with a law degree? : a lawyer's
guide to career alternatives inside, outside & around the
law / by Deborah Arron.
          p.   cm.
      Includes bibliographical references and index.
      ISBN 0-940675-46-3 (alk. paper)
      1. Law—Vocational guidance—United States.
      2. Lawyers—United States.   I. Title.
KF297.A875   1997
340'.02373—dc21   96-49539
                                                            CIP

Copies of this book are available at quantity discounts.
Please contact the publisher for further information.

Designed and typeset by Elizabeth Watson

Printed in the United States of America

ISBN 0-940675-46-3

Acknowledgments

This book has evolved, and continues to evolve, as a direct result of the personal experiences and insights of countless lawyers and law students, law school career services professionals and career consultants. Among these, I'd especially like to thank:

Deborah Hirsch, assistant dean for career services at the University of Houston School of Law, whose practical innovations regularly establish new benchmarks in career development services for lawyers and law students;

Career consultants Ron Fox, Cheryl Heisler, Celia Paul, Sheila Nielsen, Joan Bibelhausen and Leslie Messman for their continuing support;

Deborah Guyol, for her ability to add a little protein to tired paragraphs;

Naomi Weissman for her research assistance;

and, as always, my husband Mark, for perfect attendance.

Foreword viii

PART A Successful Career Development 1

   1 Asking the Right Question   3
   2 Three Steps to Successful Career Transition   6
   3 Understanding Today's Workplace   11
   4 Is This Plan Realistic for You?   16

PART B Coming to Terms with Change 21

   5 The Roots of Dissatisfaction   23
   6 Distinguishing Burnout from Dissatisfaction with Your Work   40
   7 Accepting Your Natural Resistance to Change   45
   8 Reasons to Maintain the Status Quo   50
   9 Overcoming Barriers to Change   54

PART C Self-Assessment 57

  10 Why Self-Assessment Is Essential   59
  11 What Is Self-Assessment?   65
  12 Self-Assessment Exercises   76
  13 Transferable Skills Analysis   89
  14 Creating Your Ideal Job Grid   96

PART D Research 113

  15 An Overview of Alternative Careers   115
  16 Working with Your Ideal Job Grid   122
  17 Researching Your Options   127

PART E Being Realistic about Transition 135

  18 Is This the Right Time for Change?   137
  19 Improving Your Financial Situation   140
  20 Finding Stepping Stones   148
  21 Filling the Gaps   157
  22 Adjusting to the Prospect of Leaving the Law   163

PART F Implementation 167

   23 Three Keys to a Successful Job Hunt   169

   24 Focusing on the Employer's Needs   171

   25 Overcoming Objections to Your Background and Experience   179

   26 Marketing Techniques   190

   27 Résumés and Cover Letters   207

   28 Pursuing Your Goal   227

   29 Reaching Your Goal   234

   30 Steps to Take If You Leave the Profession   244

Afterword 249

APPENDIX 1 Could There Be a Lay-Off In Your Future? 251

APPENDIX 2 Resources Targeted to Lawyers & Law Students 257

   Nonprofit Career Programs for Lawyers · The Changing Legal Profession · Books on
Stress and Burnout · Alternative Work-Schedule Resources · Changing Location ·
Job-Hunt Resources · Job Announcement Resources · General Legal Career Resources

APPENDIX 3 Other Helpful Resources 267

   Understanding Change · The Changing Workplace · Confronting Burnout ·
Financial Change · Alternative Work-Schedule Resources · Self-Assessment Books ·
Career Counselors · Testing Resources · Job Search Resources · Job Search Tips for
Older Workers · Résumés & Cover Letters · Job-Finding on the Internet · Overview
of Other Jobs and Careers · General Research Resources

APPENDIX 4 Job Options for Lawyers & Law School Graduates 281

   Alternative Dispute Resolution · Arts & Entertainment · Bar Associations ·
Communications · Consulting · Corporate, Business & Banking · Counseling ·
Education · Entrepreneurial Ventures · Environmental · Ethics · Foundations &
Nonprofit Organizations · Government · Healthcare · Legal Information Science ·
International · Judiciary · Labor Unions · Law Enforcement · Law Firms · Lobbying &
Public Affairs · Publishing · Real Estate · Sports · Technology

APPENDIX 5 Selected Job Descriptions 363

Indexes 381

   Subject Matter Index 382

   Index to Directories 386

   Index to Organizations 388

   Index to Websites 389

Foreword

Most of you will recognize this classified ad for what it is: a piece of fiction. Even so, there's probably a part of you that deep down wants to believe it could be real. "I'm a lawyer," you say. "I've paid my dues. There has to be *someone* out there who recognizes my value."

I found myself saying the same things, and indulging in the same desperate fantasies, before I closed my law practice in 1985. Back then, I actually imagined myself running into a colleague who would offer me a well-paid position that would relieve me of everything I disliked about my law practice, but provide unlimited opportunities to express myself in the ways I loved. Like most fantasies, it never materialized. I had to construct my new career on my own—one brick at a time.

Many—maybe most—of you have picked up this book in the middle of a similar career crisis. Maybe you're facing unemployment or retirement, or graduating from law school with no clear career path ahead of you. You may be wondering if you want to return from parental leave or whether part-time work is the answer. Others of you may be bored; still others may be feeling too burned out to drag yourself to the office each morning. When you're experiencing so much confusion and discomfort, you're entitled to some concrete answers. Right?

On its own, no book can provide that, and you won't find any easy answers or quick career fixes in this one. What you will find is a pragmatic, effective approach to career development, and a multitude of job-finding techniques, that have been successfully tested by thousands of lawyers and law students. By working through sections of this book, you'll learn how to emulate the many practitioners and law school graduates who have found rewarding work inside, outside and around the law and how to avoid the self-defeating patterns that lead to unemployment, under-employment or just being unhappily employed.

As we move into the 21st century, every lawyer should expect rocky career roads ahead. The combined forces of technology, competition, politics, aging and apathy are shortening, or threatening to shorten, what have traditionally been considered bullet-proof careers. Lawyers are facing the kind of occupational dislocation that has already sent banking, manufacturing, retailing and the travel industry into tailspins, and nearly toppled corporate giants like IBM and Chrysler.

Because of that, I hope you'll retain this book as a career development tool, taking it down from the bookshelf for help at your next crossroads. And please let me know if its suggestions help you find rewarding work. Others will be inspired by your story. Write me c/o Niche Press, PO Box 99477, Seattle, WA 98199, or e-mail me at dlajd@aol.com.

Deborah Arron, January 1999

SUCCESSFUL CAREER DEVELOPMENT

Asking the
Right Question

"Stop looking for other people to supply the solution. You are the solution.
If you're not, there is no solution."

—Michael Ventura, author

■ ■ ■

What *can* you do with your law degree?

The short, honest answer is: anything you want to do. Your choices are as vast as your imagination and perseverance can make them.

"Come on. Be realistic," I hear you saying. "What companies consider a law degree an attractive credential? What jobs pay as much as practicing law?"

Having assisted lawyers and law students with their career development for ten years, I've learned that these are the wrong questions to ask. Making a list of the realistic options for someone with a law degree is—without qualification—an ineffective way to build a career. Success stories are seldom motivated by realism.

> What can you do with your law degree? Anything you want to do.

Take Mike, for example. He didn't do the impossible—transferring his experience as a small firm personal injury lawyer into a position as in-house counsel for a high-tech company—by limiting himself to the realistic options for someone with his background. He did it by repackaging his skills, becoming knowledgeable about emerging corporate law issues, joining the right organizations and continuing to make contact with those working in the field until he landed the job.

Similarly, Dace didn't become the first underwater diver planner for the Grand Cayman Islands by looking at a list of realistic options. She converted her passion for scuba diving and her experience as counsel for the Seattle City Counsel into a position where she examines the coastal waters, figures out what needs to be protected, and drafts and enforces new environmental legislation.

Then there was Barrie, a Vanderbilt Law School student who became executive director of the Tennessee Bar Foundation immediately upon graduation from law school. The job wasn't posted on a list at her school; it wasn't her law school education that impressed her new employer. She succeeded by acknowledging her love of administrative work rather than the practice of law, and by concentrating her job search on those types of opportunities in the legal profession.

"Okay," you say. "I get it. If I want work that's right for me, I shouldn't limit myself to the obvious choices. But I just want something that will be better than what I have now. Tell me where those jobs are." Wrong question again. It's just as futile to define your search in terms of avoiding the detriments of your current job. More often than not, you'll find yourself missing the positive aspects of your previous position in the next, while new problems you never imagined will replace your old complaints.

In my work as a career consultant, I see lawyers at their most vulnerable. Some clients practically whisper their questions to me. They've spent so much time keeping everything inside out of a fear of losing their job or their clients if their doubts are discovered that being forthright now is just too threatening. Others are too depressed to ask many questions at all, having achieved all the accouterments of success only to feel trapped by "golden handcuffs." As their lifestyle has expanded to equal or exceed the money they earn, the combination of steep mortgage, car payments and private school tuition for their kids, and the unspoken expectations of their families and friends, has made them believe change is impossible.

Here's my challenge to all of you: Whether you're unemployed, under-employed, or unhappily employed, the best way to capitalize on your legal education and experience is to start asking the more provocative—and ultimately more practical—question: "What do I *want* to do next with my law degree?"

Your law degree and any subsequent professional experience you've gained are valuable credentials in a competitive job market. Contrary to what you may believe about yourself, merely having succeeded through law school—last week, last year or 20 years ago—tells the world you are a competent, intelligent and responsible person who attains goals you set for yourself. You're someone who commands respect.

For some of you, this notion may come as a shock. Rather than feeling successful, you feel like a failure because:

► You didn't graduate at the top of your class.
► You didn't get an invitation to join a highly-rated law firm.
► You aren't now practicing law in a prestigious firm.
► You haven't found a job within the legal profession.
► You didn't recognize the signs that you were going to be laid off.
► You aren't a super-lawyer, super-parent and super-person.
► You can't imagine practicing law for the rest of your life.
► You can't seem to get your work done, or done right.
► You don't love your work.

Don't assume because your law school classmates earned better grades, or because they now win more cases, earn more money, or look forward to their work-day while you dread yours, that you have failed. That fatalism is counterproductive. Other lawyers' success and satisfaction is only a sign that they're in the right place and you're not. You are a bright, accomplished person whose feelings of failure and frustration will vanish when you move to an environment more suited to your strengths and interests. It's as simple as that.

So, let me ask you now: What *do* you want to do next with your law degree?

Three Steps to Successful Career Transition

"Work is something made greater by ourselves and in turn that makes us greater."
—*Maya Angelou, author and poet*

■ ■ ■

Although a law degree is a valuable credential and earning one tells the world you're worth paying attention to, it's not an automatic entree to any job or career. Putting your legal background to work for you requires serious effort—and a well thought out plan.

Think of your job or career transition as you would an important lawsuit. First you must develop the basic facts and research the law. To do so, you spend a lot of time, and often considerable money, learning as much as you can about the client, the event, the damages, the witnesses, and the position of the other side. If you pursued the lawsuit with any less enterprise, you could plead the wrong facts, omit essential facts, ask for the wrong relief or seriously misjudge the merits. You might even be barred from doing anything to remedy your mistake.

> Think of your job or career transition as you would an important lawsuit.

Job or career transition follows a remarkably similar pattern. Compare the first step—self-assessment—to your first actions after taking on a new case. To initiate a case, you learn about the matter from your client's perspective, and focus on the relief you could get considering the facts in the light most favorable to your client. Similarly, in the self-assessment stage of job or career transition, you focus on what's right for you—not on what opportunities might be out there—by analyzing your preferences and figuring out what motivates you in the workplace.

Some of you may worry that if you start to ponder your likes and dislikes, you may find that you won't be satisfied by the law, or that you'll have to move to a different city, or forfeit your comfortable lifestyle. Worse yet, you worry that you won't achieve the success you feel you deserve if you pick a field that appeals to you instead of the one you've trained for.

I understand your fears, but consider this: Although it's scary to limit your quest by declaring your preferences, the paradox is that you actually create *more* opportunities than you miss by choosing a direction that suits you. Employers and career consultants agree that job seekers who narrow their search to something that excites them are more successful in securing employment than those who are willing to take anything that comes their way. "People who offer themselves as a kind of jack-of-all-trades are generally unsuccessful in their job hunt," says management consultant and former practicing lawyer Larry Richard. "Employers are interested in somebody who has enthusiasm and motivation, and who has formulated a game plan. They believe that a goal-directed person will apply that same single-mindedness to their businesses."

Once you've identified your preferences through self-assessment, you move to the second step: researching the employment scene to determine where you best fit in. I can't emphasize this point too much: You must define the specifics of the environment and type of work that will suit you before you explore the marketplace, rather than asking the marketplace to determine what type of work you can get. This is a difficult notion for many lawyers and law students to accept.

Although there are hundreds of fields for which your legal background might be helpful, that background alone will not get you employed. Not anymore. The competition is just too fierce. Nowadays, you also have to demonstrate a deep, personal connection to the work you seek. Anything less and you're just another faceless résumé. Thus, knowing what jobs or careers other law school graduates have pursued is irrelevant. You only need to know what jobs or careers interest you enough to pursue them with full commitment. You won't find that information by scanning generic career books or classified ads; you gain it by talking to people with experience in your areas of interest.

After you identify a suitable target, you can move to the third step, implementation, the process of actually getting the job. This is the stage at which you begin fine-tuning your résumé and cover letter, and mining job leads.

Postponing implementation until you've done sufficient self-assessment and research can really frustrate lawyers and law students. You have to be pretty bottom-line and action-oriented to make it through law school. With this orientation, self-assessment can appear too "touchy-feely" and research too time-consuming. Unfortunately, this go-getter attitude lands you in trouble when applied to your career. When you persist without thinking about where you are now, where you want to go and how to get there, you're more likely to end up in a worse environment

PLANNING YOUR TRIP

Career development resembles a road trip.

▶ First, you get your bearings; you evaluate where you are now and where you want to go. "Where you are now" is your background, your unique combination of strengths and preferences, and your credentials. "Where you want to go" is your vision of the future, the qualities you hope to find in your work, and the contribution you want to make.

▶ When you've identified starting and ending points, decide what the trip itself should be like. Do you find a flight on the Concorde tempting, trading speed for expense? Or are you more interested in country roads that allow you time to meander, explore and learn unexpected lessons? Perhaps you'd like to take a detour before heading for your ultimate destination by building a family, achieving financial security where you are, or taking a sabbatical or vacation.

▶ In other words, you must decide which road to take.

▶ Robert Frost recommended "the road less traveled." Cartoonist Gary Larsen suggests the "scary or weird" road. There are the roads everyone else can see, and the ones that are apparent only to you. In every case, though, the most exciting and rewarding trip is on your own road, one you've chosen and built for yourself.

▶ Sometimes, the only way to locate the path that's right for you is to start on a road with everyone else and then branch off. Don't be discouraged if it takes a while to find the right alternative route. Depending upon how boxed in you are, you may have to turn around, travel around a corner, or wade through the underbrush to find a meaningful road. You might also have to stay in one place while you construct a new thoroughfare.

▶ The last step, of course, is to start the trip. Do something that gets you on that road, and then persist in your journey. "Don't stare up the steps," says motivational trainer Zig Ziglar. "Step up the stairs."

than better. If you persist in searching for work without first gathering information about yourself and your potential markets, you may:

▶ Discover that you're an "aimless associate" who has secured "the same terrible job in two different buildings";
▶ Find yourself trapped by "golden handcuffs";
▶ Pigeonhole yourself in a specialty you didn't really choose;
▶ End up as one of the long-term un- or under-employed;
▶ Reach a dead-end, with no place to go for challenge and increased responsibility; or
▶ Bounce from job to job until your résumé establishes little more than your effectiveness in finding work.

The three steps to career transition work best when you add one more skill to your toolbox: You need to involve others in your efforts. "What helped me the most was a lot of support, but I wouldn't have thought that when I started," says human services consultant and former practicing lawyer Nancy Ashley. "I think of myself as a very independent person. I had gotten through law school on my own. Why would I need all these other people? But I'm certain I never would have accomplished my career change without all the support I received."

To some of you, asking for help is synonymous with admitting failure. You regard your independence and self-sufficiency as among your greatest strengths, and you may see those who rely upon others for assistance as weak and incapable. Acknowledging your dissatisfaction may also trigger less than sympathetic responses from family and friends. West Coast consultant Ava Butler has worked with attorneys who, when they tell their families how unhappy they are with being a lawyer, end up with the mother crying, the father screaming, and siblings looking at them with a "what-the-hell-is-wrong-with-you?" attitude.

Some of you also worry you'll jeopardize your job if you confide your plans to others. "I kept waiting for my clients to notice what a great job I was doing for them and invite me in-house or tell their business associates that I was a guy who should be working for them," says one lawyer who eventually left private practice for the corporate world. "But they didn't know I was dissatisfied and I was caught in the vicious cycle of feeling like I couldn't tell them I was because then they'd want to find another lawyer. On the other hand, I was always aware that they couldn't read my desires on my face."

Unless you convey messages to the contrary, the people around you will assume you're happy doing what you're doing. If you can't take the risk of telling other people about your goals, they won't be able to help you with job leads and contacts.

What do I mean when I say "support"? This simply involves asking for what you want—empathy, inspiration, financial resources, or referrals—from family, friends, acquaintances or business associates. You also need to identify others who have made successful changes and use their examples to find solutions to your own problems, or find support from those who are undergoing a similar experience.

If your family thinks you're crazy and you're afraid to trust your friends, you can seek moral support from private career counselors, your law school career services office or perhaps your bar association's lawyer assistance program. You might also form your own support group, take career development classes, join forces with friends in a similar situation, or contact non-profit organizations in your area that provide support to job-seekers.

Self-Defeating and Dangerous Career Strategies

▶ Trying to do something about your career only when you're unhappy with it.
▶ Waiting for opportunities to fall in your lap.
▶ Intellectualizing where to go next and how to get there.
▶ Hoping to fall into something interesting by being a generalist.
▶ Deciding at the outset that your next job must provide the same amount of money, or maintain the same level of responsibility or prestige.
▶ Believing that you'll only be hired to do something for which you have been formally trained or educated.
▶ Getting yet another educational degree simply to postpone your job hunt, or when it isn't a requirement for the work you'd like to do.
▶ Putting off decisions until you lose your job or you burn out.
▶ Keeping your feelings of dissatisfaction to yourself, or dumping them only on your family.
▶ Expecting your work to bring you complete personal fulfillment or believing it's unrealistic to expect work-related gratification.
▶ Staying where you are because you're afraid of failing in the next endeavor.
▶ Believing you owe a lifetime commitment to your current employer or partners, your next job, or even your legal career.

Understanding Today's Workplace

"America has entered the age of the contingent or temporary worker, of the consultant and subcontractor, of the just-in-time work force—fluid, flexible, disposable. This is the future. Its message is this: You are on your own."

—Lance Morrow, essayist and journalist

■ ■ ■

Well-known workplace futurists like William Bridges, Peter Drucker and Charles Handy believe we're now witnessing the death of the job. While other labor experts are more conservative, all admit that the relationship between employer and employee is no longer what it was and isn't likely to return to its former state. Before starting the hard work of defining your preferences and building your career, you need to be aware of the rapid metamorphosis of today's work environment, and what these changes mean for you, the legal profession and the future of work itself.

> The relationship between employer and employee is no longer what it was.

First, let's get some perspective here. The job as we know it has been a short-lived aberration in the history of work. As recently as a century ago, 90 percent of all Americans were self-employed. Jobs—narrowly defined roles within a larger organization—evolved as part of the Industrial Revolution. Even though the Industrial Revolution started in the United States in the mid-19th Century, farmers were still the largest single group of workers in every developed country in the world until World War I; domestic servants were second.

It was only after World War II that the Industrial Revolution had truly altered the composition of the workforce. By then, blue collar workers had become 40 percent of the workforce and replaced farmers as the largest work group. Their new dominance led to innovations that we have come to take for granted: the 40-hour work week, health insurance benefits, retirement programs, and other mandated protections. Those givens of employment, however, are now declining as we've stepped on the fast-track into the Information Age.

Think about it. We've moved from an agrarian- to an industrial- to an information-based economy in little more than a century. Just as the Industrial Revolution shifted power from landowners to manufacturers, the Information Age has transferred influence from those who create goods to those who remain flexible in the world of ideas and data. Examples of this power shift are found in the wealth of Microsoft's Bill Gates, investor Warren Buffet and entertainment mogul Michael Eisner—all gurus in the information economy.

Today, blue collar workers are only about a fifth of the workforce and shrinking (farmers have decreased to only five percent of the workforce; servants as a class have pretty much disappeared). So-called "knowledge workers," those who manipulate and apply ideas and data rather than work directly with products, or who work in an administrative capacity, have become the largest class of employees. They were 39 percent of the workforce as recently as 1995; the Bureau of Labor Statistics predicts that they will increase to 43 percent by 2005.

In 1993, author and futurist Peter Drucker predicted that the next ten years would see a "restructuring of businesses more radical than at any time since the modern corporate form emerged in the 1920's." So far, we've witnessed a restructuring that reflects flexibility and efficiency as its core values. William Bridges, author of *JobShift,* defines the core of the emerging workplace as "the project, and an organization built around a changing mix of projects," supported by a small cadre of full-time professional, technical and managerial workers, as well as a contingent labor force when needed. Says Bridges, work that is not central to the mission of the organization is outsourced to other organizations.

The Impact on the Legal Profession

Changes in corporate America in the last 20 years have directly affected the way law is practiced.

Before 1980, individuals were the main consumers of legal services; solo and small firm practitioners could easily meet their needs. In the 1970's, nearly all law school graduates were absorbed into the legal profession. Most law firm associates made partner in four to six years. Billing by the hour was the standard, with management expectations tied to total hours spent on legal work, client development, law firm and professional matters.

In 1980, the corporation surpassed the individual as the primary revenue source for large law firms. Since only the full-service law firm could adequately serve the diverse needs of most corporations, law firms took on large classes of associates, merged with other firms to create a national presence, and brought in specialty firms to broaden their expertise. At the same time, advances in automation demanded huge investments in equipment and telecommunications, greatly increasing their costs of doing business. The law firms responded by increasing hourly billing rates and asking associates and partners to bill more hours. As a result, average per partner profits among the largest law firms nationwide increased from $305,000 in 1986 to $433,000 in 1989, and average hours billed by New York City associates grew from 1780 annually in 1982 to 2290 in 1987—the equivalent of three added months per year!

Then, starting in the late 1980's, legal work contracted. Most lawyers blamed competition (or too many lawyers) for the downturn. The weakness of this argument, however, is that the ratio of lawyers to population decreased significantly in the 1970's and 1980's without any shortage of work, because the increase in lawyers was always matched by growth in demand. More Americans got divorced, sued for product liability or made discrimination claims. Increased government regulation created the hot specialty of environmental law. More sophisticated and complex corporate restructurings, takeovers and bankruptcies required more lawyers to complete them. Technological advances produced the burgeoning area of intellectual property law while the global marketplace created demand for international business transaction lawyers.

Problems developed as the consumers of legal services got smarter. Corporations, hit by huge outside legal bills, brought more work in-house, hired non-lawyers or former lawyers to handle conflict resolution internally, and exercised line-by-line oversight of the bills for outside services they did purchase. Using self-help guides written by other lawyers, individuals handled their own divorces and wrote their own wills. Even the court system contributed to shrinking demand by funding free pro se services and requiring mediation of many matters.

As corporations demanded more efficiency and lower cost in their legal services, they shifted their business away from large, all-purpose firms in New York, Chicago, San Francisco and Los Angeles to small and mid-sized specialty firms and law firms in smaller cities. In the early 1990's, some megafirms went bankrupt or broke up into smaller specialty organizations as a result. Once-stable law firms, especially those that grew rapidly in the 1980's through mergers and acquisitions, laid off associates and asked less productive partners to withdraw. Fewer associates were offered partnership after waiting ten years or more. Many new admittees, facing a legal job market unable to absorb all of them, resorted to solo practice, or even employment outside the profession, to repay student loans of up to $100,000.

Now, in the late-1990's, the market is again expanding. But increasing costs of doing business—frequent equipment upgrades, higher malpractice insurance premiums, expenditures on marketing and client development—require careful attention to the bottom line. Since clients increasingly question the way they're billed, lawyers cannot simply raise their rates or increase their billable hours to maintain their income.

As a result, understaffed law firms are hiring again, but with some new twists. They may hire new graduates only on an hourly or project basis. They may test candidates and their need for another associate by hiring experienced lawyers on a temporary basis, or calling them non-partnership track associates. Many have dispensed with training budgets so that when they do hire permanent associates, they limit themselves to lawyers with experience they've gained elsewhere. Lawyers with "books of business" may associate with firms as "of counsel" rather than as partners to give both sides a chance to try out the arrangement. The overall law practice environment has become much more tentative and flexible.

The Employable Knowledge Worker

With changes of this magnitude comes a new definition of career both in and outside of the law. Harvard Business School's Rosabeth Moss Kanter and nationally-known management guru Tom Peters join William Bridges in saying that the career of

The Seven Rules of the New Workplace

▶ Take responsibility for your own career development.
▶ Follow your interests.
▶ Be adaptable and flexible.
▶ Make it your goal to build a career portfolio rather than to climb a career ladder.
▶ Invest in life-long learning.
▶ Expect frequent periods of unemployment, under-employment and "job" changes.
▶ Look at technological savvy as a requirement, not an option.

the future will be defined by projects rather than jobs, with success based on reputation rather than job titles. Bridges, in his must-read book *JobShift,* says that "security resides in the person rather than the position, and to a cluster of qualities that have nothing to do with the organization's policies or practices." He says that every worker's occupational security depends upon three characteristics: employability based on the right abilities and attitudes, vendor-mindedness rather than loyalty, and resiliency.

"The new compact between company and worker dismisses paternalism and embraces self-reliance," says *Business Week.* "In companies that are flattening hierarchies and, bit by bit, decentralizing decision-making, workers are gaining greater control over what they do. Self-direction has superseded the doctrine that workers do only what they're told."

In other words, employment security now lasts only as long the project you're working on. Only the naïve professional believes he or she can succeed simply by responding to assignments handed out from above. You can no longer be a passive participant along for the ride. If you can't hustle another assignment, you may lose your employment to someone who can.

So how can you develop a secure and satisfying career in a transforming workplace? You must take control by changing the way you view your work. Looking at your career only as a mechanism to pay for the leisure activities you really enjoy will severely limit your employability. The best way to create long-term employment security is to tap into your well of personal interests, and to find a way to align those interests and activities with your work.

Your assignment is to take steps to understand what motivates and stimulates you, to analyze your talents and knowledge base, to make connections with others who share your interests and goals, and to seek work that is a natural extension of who you are. In addition, you must continue to learn and upgrade your skills, become skilled in several different applications and stay connected with colleagues in and outside of your work environment. You'll find it much easier to make up the rules as you go along if you're at ease in a work environment you've chosen.

Expecting change and being willing to change will also help. One veteran practitioner (now a trial court judge) suggests that you not think about your career as a 35-year commitment. Instead, ask what you want to do for the next five to ten years. "We need to reorient our thinking about our careers," says Judge Faith Enyeart Ireland of King County Superior Court in Seattle, Washington, "so that we go with the flow of whatever seems to be right at the time, use it as a building experience, and then move on."

Is This Plan Realistic for You?

"Advice is what we ask for when we already know the answer but wish we didn't."
—*Erica Jong, author*

■ ■ ■

The message in these first three chapters is that now, as never before, it's up to you to build a career that feeds you, your family and your soul. It's also your responsibility to select a career that truly interests you, not that offers the kind of money you hope to earn or better chances of employment than other fields. And your selection must be made consciously, not through the old random access method.

> It's up to you to build a career that feeds you, your family and your soul.

But is the approach to career development outlined in this book realistic for everyone? Are there special groups who are better off ignoring the realities of the new marketplace? In this chapter, I respond to questions from those who believe they might be the exception to the general rule.

▶ *What about the large number of lawyers who are at the low ebb of success, who never developed a solid track record? How can we possibly expect to choose our next career?*

Advice to choose a direction based on your preferences may seem hollow when you're struggling with a beaten-down sense of self. But it's even more important for you than for someone with a long history of wins.

You already know why you've been unsuccessful in law so far: You don't fit in. Stated more positively, your unique profile of interests, skills, personal values and workplace preferences is more suited to another field. There's no shame in that. Ever since law school, though, you've been told—directly or subtly—that you're a failure because you weren't born with the proclivities that make a satisfied lawyer. Now, after many years of trying unsuccessfully to turn yourself into something you're not, you've come to believe it.

The process outlined in this book will help you overcome this unfair self-characterization. Better yet, once you've done your homework, you'll have an advantage over other lawyers. Since the general public regards lawyers as so many peas in a pod, hiring personnel will assume you are well-educated, capable, intelligent, hard-working, responsible, and persistent. And you can turn your admission that you "never fit into" the legal profession into proof that you don't deserve the negative stereotypes.

▶ *All that advice about following your bliss is great for a kid of 25 with no kids to support. I'm close to 40, bored to tears at work and have three kids to get through college. How can I get more career satisfaction with those restrictions?*

Yes, you have obligations and limits on your time. Yes, you've come to identify yourself with being a lawyer. Yes, it's unlikely that you can make a significant career change and immediately earn the kind of money you need to pay for your children's college education. But you can't know what your options are until you're willing to invest in self-assessment and research.

It's possible that your boredom will disappear if you simply approach your work differently. It's also possible that there is well-paid work "out there" you'd enjoy more than what you're doing now. You can't know if either possibility is real, though, until you take the time to find out.

"When you are young and you have a lifetime ahead of you," says former practicing lawyer Rick Rogovy, "you are more willing to trade your limited life units for cash. The older you get, the more valuable those remaining units become." So don't delay too long. The only way to overcome your good reasons to maintain the status quo is to develop a vision of something better. (See Chapter 9.) The good news is that there's no risk in exploration, and you may find great rewards.

▶ *I'm 55 years old and was just asked to leave the partnership I joined as a first-year associate 30 years ago. I don't know who will have me now that I'm gray-haired and fired. Isn't it unrealistic to think that I can move into a new career at my age and station in life?*

During the lowest point of the Depression, the national unemployment rate was 25 percent. That means that 75 percent of those who sought employment found it.

A   Successful Career Development

Of course, times are different now, with many more women in the workplace and fewer positions for generalists. But look at it this way: Even if the unemployment rate jumped to 50 percent, half of the working population would still be employed.

No matter how many years you have behind you, the question to ask is, "What kind of person is likely to be selected to fill one of the new or existing positions that open up every week?" In up markets and down, the people who get hired are the ones who know themselves, their skills and their values well enough to convey persuasively that they're the right person for the position, who are willing to persist toward their vision despite repeated rejections, and who continue to make the contacts that lead to at least 80 percent of all job-hunting success stories.

The best strategy, then, is to focus on a target by first looking inward, especially at those dreams you've been repressing for years. Once you have clarity of vision, get out there and meet other people in the most natural way possible. Join organizations in your area of interest. Make friends. Do volunteer work. The more engaged you become in the new alternative, the more likely you are to uncover unadvertised openings and develop the kind of reputation that will get you employed.

And yes, certainly you'll encounter age discrimination, but much of it will give you an edge rather than limiting your options. Employers have come to appreciate the loyalty and commitment that come with maturity (see Chapter 25 at page 185); your age may be just the ticket you need to gain access to a new career.

> ▶ *I'm the kind of person who only knows whether I like something after I try it*
> *out. How can I know if I'm right for any job until I've actually worked in it?*

Claiming you don't know what you like to do until you've tried it is an intellectual laziness that can lead to future problems. You've accumulated a pool of experiences—through summer jobs, clerkships, volunteer work, hobbies, travels, political advocacy and school projects—from which to define your preferences and strengths.

It's not always easy to see the connection between your past employment and your future career, but there's always a connection if you take the time to analyze it. Consider the common experience of working as a camp counselor. In this role, you guide and mentor those who are experiencing the loss and excitement of a major change in their lives. Fights may erupt among the campers; you use your empathy, wisdom, enthusiasm and leadership to help them resolve their differences. You work a structured day and develop camaraderie with other counselors. Defined in this way, the work of a camp counselor compares to that of a prosecuting attorney or public defender, mediator or matrimonial lawyer in a small law firm.

Even though you have had adequate experiences to sketch a picture of an appropriate direction, you needn't be absolutely certain about your ideal career focus when you start your career. Just select an area that intrigues and seems to suit you now, let your career develop and stay conscious of its movement.

▶ *I'm a recent law school graduate. Everyone tells me that I'll be wasting my education if I don't at least try out the practice of law. They say it will be good experience for anything else I do. Should I listen to their advice?*

Don't make the mistake of trying out the practice of law because you think it will give you the opportunity to develop skills that might be important in the future, especially if the skills are ones you don't now have. You might believe that experience as a trial lawyer will provide public speaking and extemporaneous thinking skills you've never had before. More likely, though, if you lack those aptitudes you'll bumble around, destroying your self-esteem and self-confidence in the process. Then, you won't have the recommendations you need to move into a more appropriate field down the road.

You may also become trapped by your professional identity. Today's practice environment pretty much dictates that you specialize. A narrow, technical expertise coupled with job security and a healthy income can make it very difficult to change focus later.

Ultimately, though, the answer to your question depends upon you and your goals. Consider the following examples:

▶ If you want to be a legal journalist, practicing law or working in the courthouse would be a valuable background.
▶ If you want to be a corporate department manager, presenting yourself as a former practicing lawyer might hinder that change.
▶ If mediation is your ultimate goal, it doesn't really matter one way or the other. There are at least as many paid non-lawyer mediators as lawyer mediators, and having the educational background is often enough to distinguish you from your competitors.

On the other hand, if you've already tried out the practice of law in your summer clerkships and didn't like the experience, you might be better off ignoring the advice you've received. If you take the time to introspect and research, you'll know whether the choice you're considering is a good one for you, or just for all those people who are giving you their advice.

> ▶ *I recently moved to a new city for both a career and lifestyle change. I know that I'm interested in a variety of careers and jobs, but I have a hard time focusing my search or setting goals. At this point, I'm planning to take this state's bar exam to keep my options open. What do you think of my plan?*

By taking the bar examination, you might be taking an expensive and time-consuming detour. You might rationalize your decision by telling yourself that you're keeping your options open, but you only need an active license to practice in any particular state if you plan to practice law in state courts. If you want to find law-related work, or employment within the legal profession that does not involve state court practice, you'd be better off investing the same time, money and energy in self-assessment and research.

Should you decide to look for work outside the legal profession, you may cut off more options than you create by taking the bar exam. Non-legal employers will wonder why you bothered to invest in state bar membership if you really wanted to enter their field. No matter how you explain it, those employers will probably believe that you're applying for a non-law position only because you couldn't find work as a practicing lawyer, and that you'll be out the door as soon as you do.

What you ought to do is confront your real problem: your lack of focus and commitment to a goal. You must choose among your interests and skills in order to create a clear career path. That ability to choose only develops through comprehensive and honest introspection.

COMING TO TERMS WITH CHANGE

The Roots of Dissatisfaction

"In order that people may be happy in their work, these three things are needed: They must be fit for it; they must not do too much of it; and they must have a sense of success in it—not a doubtful sense, such as needs some testimony of others for its confirmation, but a sure sense, or rather knowledge, that so much work has been done well, and fruitfully done, whatever the world may say or think about it."

—*W. H. Auden, poet*

∎ ∎ ∎

A career in trouble is like a beef stew that just doesn't taste right. The stew can contain many fine ingredients: fresh carrots, lean meat, red wine, spices and tomatoes. But throw in some old potatoes or too much salt and your stew is ruined.

The success of your career—as with the stew—has everything to do with its ingredients and proportions. You may be engaged in the wrong kind of work or be working with the wrong people. On the other hand, your work and work environment may suit you, but you may lack a balance among work, family and time for self. The only way to better your situation is to carefully analyze your life and pinpoint the trouble spots.

No matter what your situation, you can begin your analysis by examining the six factors that contribute most to work dissatisfaction among lawyers:

> The only way to better your situation is to carefully analyze your life and pinpoint the trouble spots.

- ▶ Holding onto unreasonable expectations;
- ▶ Reaching an uncomfortable phase of career development;

▶ Living life out of balance;

▶ Failing to set appropriate limits with clients and colleagues;

▶ Toiling away in an unpleasant work environment; and

▶ Lacking work that calls upon your talents and preferences.

Holding Onto Unreasonable Expectations

Dissatisfaction results when expectations collide with reality. Vague or ill-conceived reasons for deciding to go to law school, or into private practice, can lead to disappointment in later years.

You might have headed to law school with the expectation that your education would be a magic ticket to a dream destination. "I went to law school and thought it was interesting, but did I know anything about what lawyers did before I entered?" said one former practitioner. "Did I ever know a lawyer? Had I ever been inside a law firm? No, but that didn't daunt me. I figured that after all those years in school, I'd be a professional, have flexibility in my life and work a nice schedule."

After graduation, you might—like this woman—have accepted your first job with no real appreciation of the nature of the work or the work environment:

> I was a first-year law student when I heard you speak at my law school. At that time, I could not imagine anyone wanting to give up a career in the law for an endeavor in another field. In fact, I thought your presentation was close to blasphemy. I have now been practicing law for almost two years, not including the summers and semesters of internships. I am a city prosecutor and am in court every day—just the way I always dreamed. I hate it.

Once in practice, you might have thought that the profession would afford you continuing opportunities for advancement and challenge, or that your practice would be steady and predictable. This is not the reality of law practice. One Chicago practitioner describes it like this:

> To do it right is a hard job. You cannot try cases without very long hours. Your life is not your own. Judges and others control your schedule. You have only yourself and your wits and experience. You have no "investment" or equity in a company. You are only as good as what you did today.

If you entered the practice of law thinking otherwise, you're probably dissatisfied

Expectation	Reality
Intellectual Challenge	▸ New admittees who enter large law firms may find their work limited to low-level functions such as document review and organization.
	▸ The complex state of the law and the threat of malpractice actions encourages increasing specialization, which leads to repetitive work and diminishing intellectual challenge.
	▸ High billing rates and client expectations of the lowest possible fee prohibit the pursuit of more stimulating lawsuits that might change, challenge or clarify the law.
	▸ Competition for clients may limit the quality of the legal work you obtain.
Helping Others	▸ Involvement in the legal process often inflicts on clients more trauma than benefit.
	▸ A successful lawsuit generally translates into money for the client, which neither heals trauma nor solves underlying social problems.
	▸ Corporate lawyers may feel too remote to appreciate the results of their work.
	▸ New associates have little client contact.
	▸ Criminal lawyers invest substantial time and effort in making a difference for society and their clients, but see the same people churning through the system over and over again.
Change the World	▸ Opportunities to work in the public interest are few and poorly paid.
	▸ The wheels of justice turn very slowly.
	▸ Impact litigation seems merely to move money from one needy group to another, without increasing society's overall commitment to the poor.
	▸ Many law firms restrict associates and partners from pursuing impact litigation and other pro bono matters, until they have fulfilled burdensome billable hour quotas.
	▸ The high cost of litigation substantially limits clients' willingness to fund lawsuits that change, challenge or clarify the law.
High Income	▸ The practice of law has become less profitable for most lawyers since 1980.
	▸ Only a small percentage of law school graduates earn the high incomes reported in the national media.
	▸ Due to minuscule raises, associates with two to seven years experience often earn little more than entry-level lawyers.
	▸ Some lawyers earn less than the legal secretaries who work for them.

Expectation	Reality
Security	▸ Law firms laid off large numbers of associates in the early 90s. Now they're making no promises to new associates.
	▸ Fewer associates are now expected to become equity partners.
	▸ Equity partners may be voted out of their firms if their profitability declines.
	▸ Law firm stability has eroded as a result of mergers and acquisitions, or of equity partners' willingness to take their practices to more profitable firms.
	▸ Clients shop for the best deals.
High Status/ Respect	▸ Lawyers are rated near the bottom of all professions in popularity.
	▸ A 1993 ABA poll found that 34 percent of the public expressed negative feelings toward lawyers.
	▸ In a 1993 *National Law Journal* poll, 31 percent of the respondents felt lawyers were less honest than most people, up from 17 percent in 1986.
Recognition	▸ Positive feedback from coworkers and clients is rare.
	▸ Associates complain that they always hear about their mistakes, but seldom are complimented for their achievements.
	▸ Lawyers are in the unusual position of facing someone on the other side whose one job it is to tell them they are wrong.
	▸ A lawyer's work often makes someone else unhappy.
	▸ Lawyers are so busy meeting client needs that they fail to notice what their colleagues are doing.
Autonomy	▸ The representative role requires some lawyers to advocate positions that run counter to their own moral codes.
	▸ Increased bar association oversight interferes with lawyers' ability to work autonomously.
	▸ Court attempts to speed up the litigation process interfere with the practitioner's ability to control scheduling.
	▸ Associates tend to deal with only portions of cases.
Versatility	▸ Law schools actually teach a specialized course of study.
	▸ Non-legal employers may negatively stereotype lawyers.
	▸ In the 80s, business school replaced law school as the preferred training for corporate managers. Now, law school graduates may be interviewed by corporate executives who were hired with those credentials and expectations.

The Good Things about Practicing Law

Money
Intellectual challenge
Status
Prestige
Autonomy
Variety
Camaraderie
Winning
Flexibility
Professional longevity
Relationships with clients
Access to organizations
   and events
Being in a project-driven
   business
Intellectual engagement
   and stimulation
Ability to facilitate change
Ability to help others in need
Accumulated knowledge
Focus on problem solving
Networking opportunities
Power to influence others
   and society
Professional identity
The thrill of trying cases
Having a socially acceptable
   outlet for aggressive behavior

The Downsides of Practicing Law

Not enough money
The billable hour
Working with, against or around difficult people
Limits to your ability to help
Guilt about not being able to fix everything
Being on a financial treadmill
Repetition
The poor public image of lawyers
The lessening need for lawyers
Being vulnerable to public opinion
Having no control over time
Performance anxiety
Too little time for contemplation
Client demands and expectations
Being responsible for serious consequences
Guilt from knowing the client will pay for
   your mistakes
Increasing overhead
Exposure to malpractice claims and the
   high cost of premiums
Long hours
Constant deadlines and time pressures
The way it takes over your life
The interminable nature of the problems and process
Having to keep emotional distance from your clients
Unpredictability
Office and legal system politics
Law office administration
Competition
Current turmoil in the profession
High expectations of clients, colleagues,
   court system, society
Isolation
The adversarial system
Having to keep too many balls in the air
Having to live with wrong or unfair outcomes
Knowing that legal services are expensive

Rising Dissatisfaction Among Lawyers

In 1990, an ABA survey showed that a fifth of all lawyers were dissatisfied with their current jobs, up 25 percent from 1984. Another 43 percent evaluated themselves as only "somewhat satisfied." As noted by *California Lawyer,* "If this were a survey asking respondents how they felt about their last sexual encounter, 'somewhat satisfied' would be an indictment."

A more recent study by the Rand Corporation concluded that California lawyers were "profoundly pessimistic" about their careers; only half would again choose to become lawyers. Seventy percent of those responding to an informal *California Lawyer* fax poll said they would change careers if the opportunity arose.

Among the private practitioners polled by the ABA in 1990, women were disproportionately dissatisfied. More than half of all female solo practitioners, and 42 percent of female partners, defined themselves as dissatisfied. Among male private practitioners, the highest rate of dissatisfaction was found among those who practiced alone. The highest overall level of dissatisfaction—almost double the 1984 rate—was reported by one of the smallest segments of the population: in-house corporate counsel. The lowest rate of dissatisfaction was expressed by those employed in government.

The ABA concluded from these results that dissatisfaction increased from 1984 to 1990 because of the rise in negative work factors such as "the pressures and [time] demands of law firms and clients, the element of speed created by the advent of fax machines and computers, and the increasing lack of courtesy between lawyers."

Structural changes in the business of law have been accompanied by what some would call a deterioration in the quality of practice. Lawyers across the country provided this list of the changes they've noticed in the last ten years:

▶ A substantial decrease in civility and honesty among practitioners;
▶ More stressful economics of practice;
▶ Lack of predictability in law firm organizational structure;
▶ The increased speed of practice caused by computers, fax machines, cell phones, and efforts to trim court backlogs; and
▶ Less training and mentoring of young lawyers.

The ABA survey was administered prior to the economic retrenchment of the early 90s when entire classes of associates and law firm departments were laid off, adding insecurity to the list of negative work factors. In addition, it now takes between ten and 12 years to make partner in New York City and eight or more years in other cities. "For many lawyers today, work means logging many more stressful hours without the promise of financial advancement," said *U.S. News and World Report* on April 1, 1996. The next few years could see a continued rise in the levels of discomfort and dissatisfaction among practitioners.

You'll find books and articles about lawyers and the legal profession referenced at the beginning of Appendix 1.

now. So what were you expecting when you enrolled in law school, or when you first entered the practice of law? Do any of the frequently expressed expectations about law practice listed on pages 25 and 26 sound familiar to you? Are you now experiencing the disappointing reality?

If your legal career has not met your expectations, whatever they are, and you fail to accept that reality, you will be dissatisfied. Says author Stephen Levine, "Suffering is wishing things were different from the way they are." There are only two cures for career dissatisfaction caused by unrealized or unrealistic expectations: If you don't like it, change it. If you can't change it, don't worry about it. Either take steps to remedy the situation, or accept it as it is.

Reaching an Uncomfortable Phase of Career Development

Every career moves along a predictable arc, progressing through five distinct phases of development.

Orientation: You figure out the rules of the game.
Challenge: You prove your competence.
Establishment: You climb the ladder.
Cruising: You operate on a comfortable plateau.
Disengagement: You begin to let go.

Every phase repeats a pattern of growth as you develop new skills, stabilization as you perform those skills in a productive way, and transition between the demands of this phase and those of the next. In general, times of growth are marked by excitement and challenge, times of stabilization by competence, and times of transition by reassessment and anxiety.

Coming to Terms
with Change

Some people cycle through all five phases several times in one career as they move from job to job, or as they receive promotions or handle a variety of projects for the same employer. Others pass through the phases in one slow process from law school graduation to retirement. At any stage, difficulties can create the urge to change just to escape the discomfort.

Take a few moments to consider where you are in the life of your career.

In the first phase, **orientation**, you learn the rules of the game while engaging in a variety of tasks for the very first time. The orientation experience varies with the environment you've chosen. If you choose to practice law, you'll first have to familiarize yourself with its procedures and peculiarities. Marla McGeorge, a lawyer-turned-veterinarian, remembers the difference between "actually learning the craft" and floundering every time she walked into court, "trying to figure out which seat to sit in and what side of the courtroom table to choose." I'll never forget my own anxiety in determining when I had to say, "May it please the court" and when I didn't. (I'd moved on to the next phase of development when I realized it didn't make any difference at all!) You'll also absorb more esoteric lessons, like the unwritten codes of professional courtesy and the flexible meaning of deadlines.

The orientation phase demands that you act without always knowing what you're doing—an uncomfortable feeling if you're accustomed to being competent and in control. In the past, experienced lawyers helped new lawyers through these trying times by providing on-the-job training. Today's extremely competitive and client-driven law practice environment has lessened the amount of mentoring that occurs. Dissatisfaction may arise if you're trying everything for the first time without enough input and guidance from your superiors.

Simply living through the discomfort of feeling foolishly incompetent—getting to the point of doing something the second or the third time—will sometimes cure your career ills. To reduce your discomfort in the meantime, identify lawyers, paralegals or even legal secretaries who are more experienced than you and to whom you can turn for help. Ask discreetly for help from one of these office colleagues whenever you're faced with an unfamiliar task. If you're working alone or have difficulty getting support from others in your office, join a relevant bar association. This contact will provide a network of friendly experts. You can repay their kindness by assisting them with research or by making simple court appearances for them at no charge.

After orientation comes the **challenge** phase, a time of working hard to prove your competence. During these years, you operate along a stimulating learning curve, becoming more and more skilled as a fourth motion is followed by a fifth and a first trial is followed by a second. The risk during this phase is that you'll have to handle cases or matters before you've developed the necessary expertise, or that you'll take on more work than you can competently handle. To avoid these pitfalls, develop working associations with more experienced practitioners.

The challenge phase is particularly stimulating and engaging. As a result, few choose to make career changes during this period. Some of you, though, may be forced to look for other work due to financial pressures, employer instability, downsizing, or getting fired. Being forced to make a change can be demoralizing and may cause you to reconsider, or even abandon, your commitment to the legal profession. But it's unwise to base career changes on hurt and disappointment.

In the third phase, **establishment**, the goal is to climb the ladder of success. Everyone defines the word "success" differently. For some, the end is purely financial— a bigger salary. Others seek increased responsibility, flexibility, respect, security, influence or recognition. Sometimes a long-range target—becoming a judge, or securing a high-level management position with a former client—is the definition of success.

There are three risks in the establishment phase. The first is that you will allow your desire for a good income and a good reputation to control your actions to the point where you neglect personal relationships, especially marriages. The second is that you will drive so hard without thinking about where you're going that you become trapped by "golden handcuffs" or, as anthropologist Joseph Campbell put it, you reach the top of the ladder of success, only to discover you've placed the ladder against the wrong wall.

The establishment phase may present another problem as well: There aren't enough spots at the top for everyone. As you compete with more people for fewer opportunities, you might find your ladder is shorter than expected. For example, after eight years of apprenticeship in a large law firm, you might be told you're no longer on partnership track. Or, as an associate counsel in a corporate legal department, you might have to accept that the current general counsel is healthy, committed and young, and blocking your upward mobility.

The phenomenon is referred to as "plateauing" and may have more to do with arithmetic than ability or productivity. Only a tiny fraction of the workforce makes it to the top. That leaves the majority stuck somewhere below, with one of three options: move to new work, accept the situation or redefine success.

The **cruising** phase begins when you've mastered the practice of law and reached a comfortable plateau: a place where you know your job, can easily meet its challenges, and feel both personally and financially secure. Some lawyers will cruise happily until retirement. Many others will feel restless or bored, especially those who thrive on the excitement and tension fueled by having to learn. This is the point at which you may hear yourself saying, "I've done everything I want to do in law."

Boredom sets in when you stop taking calculated risks, the quality that creates success in the first place. Risk avoidance can also result in job insecurity. Studies have shown that as professionals gain seniority, they lose the very quality that created their success in the first place—their willingness to risk. This immediately lowers their self-esteem, and leads to lower productivity and work quality. When law firm policies or financial reversals call for layoffs, they'll be targeted for termination.

You can improve your longevity while also reinvigorating your career by adding an element of risk to your work day. As a subject matter specialist, you might experiment with new projects, branch into another area of practice, or strike out on your own. Long-time litigators might take a case or two to trial rather than pushing for settlement or letting a younger associate get the experience. Experiment with esoteric ventures to stretch your mental muscles. For example, several lawyers at a San Francisco firm designed a CD-ROM full of advice on preparing clients for depositions. A group in Seattle put together a video for their clients to help them get ready for their initial estate planning meeting; it's now being sold nationally.

If you've saved a lot of money or have no immediate concerns about being let go, you might accept the level of accomplishment you've already attained, relax into a less grueling pace, and look outside work for new personal challenges. Or you might regard yourself as a part-time practitioner while marketing such personal services as teaching, designing seminars or law office software, or writing how-to manuals.

Senior associates and partners in larger firms may be able to get others to recognize the value of the roles you do find rewarding—teaching, training, mentoring, research, efficiency—without having to continue to grind away at more tedious duties. One lawyer turned down two offers to join other law firms after his firm finally recognized his leadership ability and asked him to chair the litigation department. Other lawyers have accomplished this goal by creating new roles within their firms—for example, client services manager, recruiting administrator and director of professional development.

If you believe you are in the cruising phase of your career, you may in fact have already entered the **disengagement** phase, a period of gradually letting go. Disengagement can lead to retirement or a new career, or it can lead to procrastination, loss of interest, or depression. In the words of one human resources manager, you can become a person who has "retired but forgotten to announce it."

Our nation has operated for decades with the expectation that everyone first gets educated, then works and raises a family, then retires at age 65, at which time the "leisure" years begin. Keep in mind, though, that this attitude developed when life for most American males ended before age 65. Ken Dychtwald, Ph.D., pointed out in his book, *Age Wave,* that with life expectancies moving into the 80s and 90s, it's unrealistic to expect to have only one career in a lifetime. Any activity will become less stimulating and enjoyable after 20 or 30 years of repetition. It's also unrealistic, especially in these times of rapidly developing technology, to believe that you can stop educating yourself in your 20s. And how can anyone delay having fun until age 65 and actually live that long!

To avoid the pitfalls of the disengagement period, it's important to take action: Negotiate a retirement package; train others to handle those aspects of practice for which you have lost interest; switch to a mentoring role; get involved in community activities. Do something that makes you feel a little bit afraid and a whole lot exhilarated. That something may just lead you to a new career, where the five-stage cycle will begin anew.

Living Life Out of Balance

Fulfilling work does not, by itself, create a fulfilling life. For that, you need a balance among pleasurable commitments to work, relationships with others and with yourself, leisure activities, and challenge. Some would add spiritual development as a fifth dimension. If any of these areas is not fulfilling, finding better work will never fill the gap.

Many lawyers make the mistake of blaming their work environment for inadequacies in other parts of their lives. You focus your attention on work because it has been the arena in which you have felt the most control and experienced the greatest success. It seems easier to try to make your work environment "perfect" than to find the "perfect" relationship, or to develop a fulfilling personal life.

Even if you find your work interesting and your work environment pleasant, you might complain that it has become routine. Decreased challenge often goes hand in hand with increased specialization and experience. When the stimulation you depend upon from your work disappears, you might feel the urge to change your work to recharge your life.

A greater challenge might be to reach new levels of connection in your personal life: developing emotional closeness with a teenage son or daughter, taking steps to revive a failing marriage, or nourishing a long-term romantic relationship. Indeed, "studies . . . have demonstrated repeatedly that more than anything else, the quality of life depends on two factors: how we experience work, and our relations with other people," says Mihaly Csikszentmihalyi in *Flow: The Psychology of Optimal Experience.* Author David Myers agrees. Studies reported in his book, *The Pursuit of Happiness,* show that "supportive, intimate connections with other people seem tremendously important" to feelings of happiness or well-being.

Challenge can also be generated in other ways, and in other parts of your life. As counsel for the Seattle City Council, Dace—introduced at the beginning of Chapter 1—felt stuck in her job and personal life. To compensate, she accepted a friend's challenge to try scuba diving. She loved it, and soon began diving in much of her spare time. Her passion led her to the Grand Cayman Islands for a vacation. In speaking with a local Caymanian, Dace discovered that the government was looking for someone with unusual qualifications: a lawyer and skilled diver who could examine firsthand the coastal waters and then write and enforce regulations to protect their pristine quality. Dace grabbed the job. Marriage soon followed.

"Leisure time—not money—is becoming the status symbol of the 1990s," says John F. Robinson, director of the Americans' Use of Time Project at the University of Maryland. Yet leisure time can be a scarce commodity for lawyers. If this is true for you, take on the formidable challenge of scheduling free time every other day. It'll do wonders for your health: A study at the State University of New York at Stony Brook found that engaging in pleasurable activities every 48 hours counteracts the repression of immune function caused by daily stresses at work. As an added benefit, you might rediscover forgotten or ignored passions that could be applied in your work.

Consider Jim, for example. His high school fantasy had been to fly for a commercial airline after a tour of duty with the Air Force. That dream ended when he lost out on the competition for Air Force ROTC. At age 35, he decided that his mistake had been to choose law school by default; he wondered if it was too late to become a commercial pilot. In the course of his investigation, he was told by a lawyer-turned-commercial pilot that he probably still could get into the field at his age, as long as he logged the necessary flight time. Just one small problem: Jim had never flown a plane. At that point, he signed up for lessons. A year later, Jim was spending his free time flying his own small plane, while enjoying his tax practice and time with his family. Simply scratching an old itch had enabled Jim to abandon his thoughts of leaving the legal profession.

At this point, take a moment to think about your leisure activities. Did you regularly engage in competitive activities like squash, tennis, chess or marathons? It may be that your motivation for participating in those so-called leisure activities stems from the same competitive drive that led you into the practice of law. If so, they're more appropriately characterized as work. Then again—and you're the judge here—those activities may be supplying the stimulation that is otherwise missing from your life.

True leisure activity is purely fun and frequently calls upon talents not required in your work—unfettered creativity, movement, rhythm, or teamwork. Some lawyers act in community theater, write novels or lyrics, or enjoy white-water rafting. Others join Toastmasters to improve their public speaking, or take singing and dancing lessons for sheer pleasure. Accepting the challenge of creating more time for self-expression, interpersonal connection and leisure can give you a genuine sense of satisfaction without a change of work environment.

Honestly review your life and ask yourself whether you are currently receiving fulfillment in work, relationships, leisure and challenge, or whether you are falling short somewhere. If you are, first concentrate your attention on activities and commitments in that area. Progress could have a snowball effect. You may find that if you work on relationships or develop engaging leisure activities, the work you thought was not satisfying suddenly seems fulfilling enough.

The process can work in reverse as well. Sometimes in changing your work, you open yourself up to fulfillment in other areas of your life. When you let go of your identity as a lawyer or as a member of a particular firm or economic stratum, you may relate to others in a new way, becoming aware for the first time of the barriers you erected between yourself and others by wearing your lawyer persona.

Through my work as a national seminar facilitator and career consultant, I've noticed that excessive time demands can lead to diminished *job satisfaction.* Many lawyers, however, point to their *career choice* as the culprit because the problem seems epidemic within the profession. With increased competition and overhead, and decreased profit, many of you find your lives increasingly out of balance; you simply have no time for other interests, family and friends, not to mention your own needs. These pressures could be the only cause of your diminished satisfaction; leaving the profession to escape only them could be a big mistake.

Failing to Set Appropriate Limits with Clients and Colleagues

Directors of attorney assistance programs across the country have observed a pattern in lawyers common to other well-educated professionals: defining responsibility in terms of their obligations to other people, without considering how that sense of responsibility might hurt themselves. If this sounds like you, you preface every choice with a single question—"What are the expectations of those who depend on me?"—and never get around to asking another important question—"What can I do for myself?"—because you fear if you do you'll never be able to meet the needs of everybody else. Talk about a dilemma!

Your unwillingness to disappoint others could very well be the only cause of the imbalance between your personal and professional lives. Your solution could be as simple as saying no more often and limiting the amount of time you spend at work. But when you think about saying no, you have to worry about losing the client, disappointing or angering partners or superiors, never getting another case, not being able to keep the kids in private school or put them through college, or defaulting on the mortgage. Heightened competition—not only between firms but among lawyers within the same firm—has added a real threat to your ability to turn down work.

If these concerns are part of your life, your first step is to identify what specifically is preventing you from saying no to others. Is it a fear of:

- ▶ Not meeting the expectations of your superiors?
- ▶ Angering or disappointing your clients?
- ▶ Angering or disappointing the person who referred the matter to you?
- ▶ Never getting another case if you turn this one down?
- ▶ Not making a good impression?
- ▶ Compromising your income or future opportunity for advancement?

Now, evaluate how realistic your fear really is, considering the experience of others you know. For example, are there any other associates or partners in your firm who seem to be able to turn work away without losing respect or income? How can you model yourself after them?

Fear of repercussions is usually much worse than the repercussions themselves. Saying no to a client may keep the client from spending money needlessly and could actually lead to gratitude instead of resentment; saying no to a superior may demonstrate your sense of responsibility to other commitments or your common sense in handling your legal work; saying no to new clients may lead to the perception that you are so good and so busy that only the special few clients get to come in your door.

Toiling Away in an Unpleasant Work Environment

According to a study conducted by *Newsweek* during the summer of 1996,

87 percent of those polled considered their workplace "a pleasant environment." Do you feel the same way? If it's the environment that's not working for you—that is, the people with whom you work, or the office atmosphere itself—you'll enjoy your work more if you avoid those people or move to a more compatible location.

But how can you know if those environmental factors are the most significant roots of your dissatisfaction? One young lawyer tells of her mistake in diagnosis. The only woman in a firm of ten lawyers, Cheryl decided that life would be better in a firm with more women. About that time, a headhunter called; she was looking for a real estate associate for a large firm. "I decided it was destiny calling," she recalls. "I'm thinking about going to a large firm, a headhunter calls me, and it's a match made in heaven." She stayed two years, all the while hoping she'd feel more comfortable as she gained more experience and when she was more senior. "It took me a long time to wake up and say, 'Hey, Cheryl. It's not going to get better.'"

There may be nothing wrong with making one job change as a step toward understanding what's wrong. A boss from hell can make your life so miserable that, until you get away from him or her, you truly can't know whether you'd still be unhappy if he or she disappeared. But Danny Hoffman, a Stanford Law School graduate who works as a legal headhunter, sees many lawyers needlessly changing jobs to escape these environmental concerns. The first move occurs when the thrill of getting a job out of law school wears off and you wake up to the discomfort of living in a particular city or undertaking a lengthy commute. In the second stage, Hoffman says the firm itself is the defined problem. Whether working for an unpleasant partner or hating the workaholic atmosphere of the firm, the unhappy associate searches for a more congenial environment. After the next move, the young lawyer unhappily concludes, as one disillusioned associate put it, that "I've had the same terrible job in two different buildings." At that point, it becomes apparent that it's the work itself that's the problem.

Though it's painful to face the prospect of continuing to work in an uncomfortable environment, even for a few more months, you should resist the temptation to run from your current job (or the profession) as a solution. It may be that your boss is difficult, the office too stuffy or you want more flexible work hours. But if you move to another job that satisfies only that concern, you may soon discover that you dislike the work as well. By then, though, you may not have the emotional or physical energy, or the money, to make another disruptive career move.

The bottom line is that you have to look at whether the work of a lawyer suits you before you can determine whether your environment is the most significant factor in your dissatisfaction. The best thing you can do for yourself is to examine—even for just a few hours—how well matched you are to your current work.

Lacking Work that Calls Upon Your Talents and Preferences

Every person is born with, and develops in life, a unique personality profile—a combination of interests, skills, values, and people and environmental preferences. Being employed in an area that doesn't suit your profile is like trying to write your name with the hand you don't ordinarily use. Sure, you can do it; sometimes you can even write legibly that way. Yet the process always feels awkward and uncomfortable. If forced to use your non-dominant hand whenever you sign your name, you'll try to avoid situations that require your signature. In terms of job or career dissatisfaction, the equivalent tendency is to avoid certain projects and tasks—or even getting out of bed on mornings you have to face them.

The work of a lawyer involves an extraordinarily wide range of skills. You might procrastinate when facing some tasks but feel great energy to accomplish others. For example, you might love meeting and communicating with clients but hate having to research a brief. So you'll gladly take interruptive phone calls and schedule emergency conferences with clients, but never seem to find the time to draft a summary judgment motion or detail-heavy probate inventory.

Many lawyers find their skills misapplied in this way. Young lawyers with good people skills apprentice by spending solitary years in the library; lawyers who loved the legal analysis, research and writing they did in their early years are expected to switch to a rainmaking (or client development) role as they mature.

Lawyers who dislike what they do as lawyers, as opposed to *how much time* they spend or *with whom* they spend it, often complain about the contentiousness, competitiveness and lack of cooperation in today's professional environment. Or, they dislike paper-intensive, time-sensitive, rule-driven work and wish to enter a field that permits more flexibility, creativity and variety.

Occasional clashes in values tend to be manifested in personality conflicts with opposing counsel, judges, or clients or coworkers. On the other hand, clashes with the essential values of the legal profession—competition, structure, power and conformity among others—will trigger persistent and escalating feelings of conflict or anxiety.

To help you determine whether your work is compatible with your skills and values, pay attention to your emotional responses. When you're in the right line of work:

- ► You approach your work with enthusiasm and high energy, not anger, boredom or lethargy.
- ► You tend to initiate work rather than avoid it.
- ► You want to lead or join in activities rather than complain about them or withdraw from them.
- ► When faced with a new project, you feel stimulated to learn rather than tempted to procrastinate.
- ► When you've finished a task, you feel proud of the accomplishment rather than relieved that you're done.

Review the list of character traits shared by contented lawyers and the Personality Preference Quiz that follow. If you find yourself out of sync, invest time in completing the exercises in the self-assessment chapter before making any other changes.

A Dozen Traits Shared by Contented Lawyers

1. Display a love of learning
2. Pay attention to details
3. Respect the rules
4. Possess strong analytical abilities
5. Achievement-oriented
6. Competitive
7. Steady and stable ✗
8. Patient and persistent
✗9. More realistic than idealistic
10. More conventional than innovative
✗11. More dispassionate than emotional
✗12. Thick-skinned

Personality Preference Quiz*

1. Do you like to get emotionally involved with your work?
2. Do you dislike or attempt to avoid conflict? ⅄
3. In resolving conflict, do you prefer deciding what's fair based on the circumstances of each situation? ⅄
4. Do you like to create or start projects and let others finish or maintain them?
5. Do you dislike paying attention to details?
6. Do you prefer short-term projects?
7. Do you value efficiency? ⅄
8. Do you like to do things your own way, on your own schedule, and in order of your own priorities?
9. Do you get more satisfaction being part of a team than being a solo act?
10. Do you want to change the world?

A "yes" answer to any of these questions ought to raise serious reservations about the wisdom of using your law degree to practice law. There may be some appropriate options for you in the legal profession, but you should take time for self-assessment and more thorough research of alternative career directions.

*Excerpted from *Running from the Law.*

Distinguishing Burnout from Dissatisfaction with Your Work

"Success can eliminate as many options as failure."

—*Tom Robbins, novelist*

■ ■ ■

In the last six months, have you noticed that:

▶ You used to love your work but now it exhausts you emotionally or physically?

▶ You feel you're accomplishing much less compared with your past performance?

▶ You're dedicated to your clients and colleagues but no one seems to appreciate your efforts?

▶ You feel increasingly cynical about your work, your employer, or your clients?

▶ You believe only you can do the work you do as well as you do it, and that your clients and colleagues would be irreparably harmed if you decided to quit?

▶ You're no longer interested in the hobbies or pastimes you used to enjoy?

▶ You feel tired rather than energetic?

▶ People wonder why you look tired or "not so good"?

▶ Nothing much matters to you?

▶ You're increasingly forgetful about appointments, or find yourself misplacing possessions or overlooking deadlines?

▶ You don't have as many friends as you once had?

> Burnout is an unacknowledged state of exhaustion that occurs when you consistently make choices for the benefit of others at the expense of your own needs.

▶ You need more time alone than you used to?

▶ You're more irritable now when driving in traffic or waiting in lines?

▶ You're getting unexplained headaches or stomachaches or backaches?

▶ You find yourself frequently feeling angry and striking out at others?

If you answer "yes" to any of these questions, you're exhibiting at least one symptom of burnout. Although you can burn out from devoting yourself to work you don't enjoy, burnout is not the same as dissatisfaction with your job or career. This chapter helps you determine whether it's your work or your attitude toward your work that's the problem.

What Is Burnout?

Burnout is more than simply fatigue. Much more. It's an unacknowledged state of exhaustion that occurs when you consistently make choices for the benefit of others at the expense of your own needs.

When you've completed a long trial or brief, or you've concluded a complicated business deal, and you've been working night and day for weeks to do so, you might describe your state of exhaustion as burnout. But it's just as likely to be the temporary effect of overwork. To distinguish between the two conditions, consider your reaction to the suggestion that you take some time off. If you take it, you're not burned out. You probably are burned out if your response is anything like these:

I can't take time off. What would my clients (or boss) say?
I have so much work to do; there's no way I can leave.
They need me here. I'm the only one who can do this work.

According to Dr. Herbert J. Freudenberger, author of *Burn Out,* victims of burnout are "dynamic, charismatic, goal-oriented people" or "determined idealists." Burnout, he says, "usually has its roots in the area of your life that seems to hold the most promise." For lawyers, that area is work.

Lawyers tend to exhibit two signs of chronic burnout: an I-just-don't-care-any-more attitude—often accompanied by heavy drinking or overeating—or increasingly compulsive activity. "The manic defense against depression," says James Hillman, co-author of *We've Had a Hundred Years of Psychotherapy and the World's Getting Worse,* "is to keep extremely busy—and to be very irritated when interrupted. Your schedule is one of your biggest defenses."

The Roots of Burnout

Burnout among lawyers can result from consistently working too much to meet the demands of your superiors, from being expected to perform in a way that goes against your sense of right and wrong, from being pulled between bosses clamoring for your time and attention, or from never getting any praise from your superiors no matter how impressive your work.

More commonly, though, burnout is caused by a work style that's almost required by the legal profession. Compare the attitudes that contribute to burnout (as identified by Dr. Freudenberger) with the demands of the practice of law:

▶ *Feeling under pressure to succeed all the time.* You don't imagine this pressure; it's inherent in your role as an attorney. Your clients brings you problems. It's your job to take on their burdens so they feel better and you feel responsible.

▶ *Needing to generate continuous excitement to keep from feeling bored.* Trial lawyers and mergers and acquisitions specialists are especially prone to this affliction. As one former practitioner put it, "I think I was a law addict." There may also be an institutional fear of, or scorn for, relaxation. That attitude alone can lead to burnout.

▶ *Making one area of your life disproportionately important.* Clients demand that you meet their needs before you think about anything else. Firms expect you to put your work first. Lawyers are often competitive about how hard they work. Think about it. Do you know of a law firm that rewards the lawyer who regularly gets home in time to eat dinner with the kids as generously as the one who bills 2,500 hours a year? In an office standard of overwork, a macho attitude of "you're not committed to the firm unless you share our work habits" prevails.

▶ *Being inflexible once you've taken a stand on something.* In agreeing to represent a client, you've agreed to promote that client's best interests. You can't suddenly decide the other side's position is the better one; you must stick to your guns.

▶ *Feeling a lack of intimacy with the people around you.* You're a lawyer; you're expected to separate yourself from the problem and remain rational at all times. You often submerge your own beliefs and values when you advocate a client's position. You can generate inner confusion when you advocate a position for one client one moment and the opposite for another client the next. How can other people get close to you if they can't see through your camouflage?

▶ *Being unable to relax.* Who can relax when six deadlines are converging or everyone around you is questioning your decisions? Computers and fax machines have accelerated the process to the point where a crisis mentality is the norm. How many times have you received something by overnight delivery or fax and, without regard for its contents, assumed that it was more important and required a quicker response than if you had received it through the U.S. mail? The court system has aggravated the problem by creating programs to speed trials and discovery, and to schedule motions and trials with shorter notice periods. And the lack of civility among lawyers results in more surprise motions with little notice. Then, of course, clients often delay seeking out help for their problems until the very last minute.

▶ *Being unclear about your priorities, characterized by shifting back and forth between long-range and immediate goals.* You don't control your schedule; it's in the hands of other lawyers, the whims of clients and the court system. Who can focus on long range goals when urgent short-term matters continually interrupt?

▶ *Always being worried about preserving your image.* You aren't imagining the pressure to look and act a certain way. The rules of ethics require that you uphold a high standard and noble image as an agent of justice and the court system.

▶ *Taking yourself too seriously.* If you don't take yourself seriously, who else will? Your entire mission is to be taken seriously by your clients, opposing counsel and their clients, and the court system.

▶ *Identifying so closely with your activities that if they fail, you fall apart.* Your clients hire you to win for them. When you lose a trial, you've failed them and that means you've failed as a lawyer. It's even worse if you get caught in an act of legal malpractice; you have a fiduciary obligation to act in your client's best interests. It's a rare lawyer who can get through either of those events without feeling personally destroyed.

B Coming to Terms with Change

A participant at a Los Angeles seminar once asked me, "How do you address the fundamental psychological barrier of turning to a non-professional career—that is, not a doctor or lawyer—and not feel you are stepping down into a job that anyone with less smarts and skills could do?" That lawyer, by so over-identifying with the title and role of lawyer, was a clear candidate for burnout.

How to Distinguish Burnout from Dissatisfaction with Your Work

Burnout can occur for reasons other than job or career dissatisfaction, or as a direct result. For example, your current work may suit your preferences; all your expectations of practice may be fully realized. Yet, if you consistently put your work first and yourself second, you'll eventually burn out. On the other hand, you can also burn out when you remain in work that does not suit you, and subordinate your own needs to its demands.

In the final analysis, the two conditions only differ in the mindset that produces them. Burnout stems from a basic denial that some important commitments in your life are, or have been, made only to meet the expectations of others. Dissatisfaction with your work develops as you slowly realize you've made some bad choices.

Whether you're burned out or dissatisfied with your work, the solutions are the same: serious introspection, and the development of supportive relationships.

Don't expect instant results. As you begin to explore your relationship with your work, you may feel even more confused. Insight develops gradually; recovery occurs in spiraling circles. But they will happen.

The importance of outside support, especially by peers, cannot be overemphasized. Isolation is one symptom of burnout. The deeper you sink into your dissatisfaction, the less willing you are to admit it and to discuss your malaise with others.

One successful practitioner developed, and finally acknowledged, an alcohol problem. With the support of Alcoholics Anonymous, he admitted his vulnerability, and then confided his turmoil about his professional direction to some of his more successful colleagues. He was surprised to find they, too, were unhappy despite the self-satisfied images they radiated. Suddenly, he realized that for years he had compared his "insides" to his peers' "outsides," assuming that they relished their work while he alone struggled. That fateful connection with other lawyers caused him to rethink, and successfully redirect, his career.

Increasing your contact with others *can* provide you the insight and courage that leads to change. But you must take the first step. You'll find additional resources to help you confront and deal with burnout in Appendix 2 and 3.

Accepting Your Natural Resistance to Change

"It's not so much that we're afraid of change, or so in love with the old ways, but it's that place in between we fear. It's like being between trapezes. There's nothing to hold onto."

—*Marilyn Ferguson, author*

. . .

The first time I questioned my choice of law as a career was in 1979. "I don't want to be a lawyer anymore," I told a colleague over dinner. We both felt as if I'd confessed to treason. My friend was shocked. He told me I was perfectly suited to the profession and it would be a terrible mistake to think about another career. Thoroughly chastened, I slapped the handcuffs back on for another six years.

> Resistance to change is real and justified.

During that time, I adapted. I began adjusting my practice to emphasize what I enjoyed doing and minimize what I didn't. I turned down clients I knew would be trouble—either personality-wise or financially—and cases that didn't interest me enough to want to learn the law. Eventually, I narrowed my practice to matters involving families or residential real estate, the two subject matters that continued to engage me, allowed a high level of client contact, and in which the law itself was not too complex. I bought a network computer system so that I could draft my own work, avoid hiring a full-time secretary, cut down on overhead, and reduce the hours I had to bill. At that point, having withdrawn from a small partnership to practice on my own, I added fiction writing into my work week. All the while, I diligently put money into savings to fund an unknown future that smelled like freedom.

By January 1985, I was frustrated enough with my life and career to flee to Tahiti. I was also hopelessly tied to my professional identity and an irrational belief that I was such a sensitive and conscientious lawyer that my clients would be irreparably dam-aged if I quit. One day at my health club, an exercise buddy suggested I take a long sabbatical. A sabbatical? Was she insane? Too many clients depended upon me. I would be throwing away a lucrative and stable practice. I'd develop a reputation for irresponsibility and a lack of dependability. Half an hour later, my brain awash in endorphins, I decided it was possible. I hurried back to the office, projected cash flow and expenses, determined which files I could transfer to other lawyers and which ones I felt morally committed to completing, and scheduled my sabbatical to begin six months from that day.

By the time I closed my office doors, I was almost certain that I would not find career satisfaction as a practicing lawyer or judge. Even so, I suffered a deep reactive depression. If I wasn't a lawyer, then who was I? If I wasn't billing for my time, then what value did I have as a person? It was only by reaching out to others who had made similar choices in researching and writing my first book, *Running from the Law,* and then establishing a local support group for lawyers in job or career transition, that I was able to climb out of my depression and move on to the next phase of my journey.

A writer for *California Lawyer* criticized the resistance experienced by me and the other lawyers I profiled in *Running from the Law.* To her mind, lawyers who want to switch careers should, in the words of the Nike billboards, "Just do it." Oh, if only it were that easy. Resistance to change is real and justified. It's a lot easier to advise someone else to make a change than to take that step yourself.

Indeed, there are always many good reasons to stay where you are. How many of these justifications sound familiar?

> ► *Overall, it's really not all that bad where I am.*
> ► *I like my corner office.*
> ► *Some days are better than others, but even the bad days I survive.*
> ► *I like the predictability of this work: I know that over the course of a week or a month, I'll be facing the same good things and the same bad things.*
> ► *My work offers intellectual challenge, financial security and other positive qualities that I might not find in other employment. Who knows how much worse it will be if I move on?*

▶ *I can't let my partners and clients down. How will they function without me?*

▶ *A career transition might trigger problems with my spouse or kids. I have others' needs to consider first.*

▶ *The job market now is pretty scary! I've seen other people quit their jobs and end up unemployed for months.*

▶ *I really don't have time to think about this now.*

It's natural to experience some resistance when you're thinking about change. The resistance is only a problem when it goes on too long. "One of the big lessons they tried to get across to us in the Air Force was when to bail out," said former practicing lawyer Rick Rogovy, now owner of New Hope Software. "Too often, pilots ride their planes into the ground because it seems more comfortable and familiar inside the cockpit of their crippled airplane than hanging outside from a parachute that might not open."

Similarly, scientific studies have shown that if frogs are dropped into boiling water, they hop right out to save their lives. But if they're placed in cold water that is slowly brought to the boiling point, they remain in the pot to their death.

The main reason we resist change is that with every change comes the risk that we'll lose something important: our sense of security, relationships, routine, certainty, self-esteem. We all have different tolerances for risk. But lawyers, trained to find precedents for every choice, naturally avoid risk. "Lawyers want to know for sure that career planning is going to work," says consultant Ava Butler. "They want facts and evidence. That's their training. But there are so many unknowns in any career change, and it's that fear of the unknown that keeps many lawyers unhappy and stuck."

Without taking the risk of letting something end, there can be no beginning of something better. You have to let go of your commitment or attachment to the old before you can develop something new. That ending and those feelings of loss are the starting point for the change. In fact, you know you've initiated an ending when you find yourself feeling unhappy or anxious for no apparent reason.

Unfortunately, between the ending of the old and the beginning of the new is a middle, an uncomfortable place full of confusion, doubt, tension and frustration. This time of inertia, according to Oakland, California, career consultant Lesah Beckhusen, may even serve to buffer you "from making another wrong decision or from realizing your worst fears, that there might not be anything better out there."

Some lawyers attempt to avoid the messy change process and all its discomfort and uncertainty. Instead, they remain stuck in their dissatisfaction until some external event galvanizes them into action—getting fired or laid off, or developing a precarious medical condition. Some lawyers keep working until they burn out, then quit in a self-righteous huff with nowhere else to go. At a time when you most need energy and confidence, avoiding change can leave you exhausted and with badly damaged self-esteem.

Let's face it. When you initiate change, you enter an awkward, uncomfortable, even depressing period of time, a time when you no longer want to wear your current

Some Little-Known Facts about Change

▶ The average American changes jobs every three years and careers every ten.

▶ Contrary to general perception, positive feelings motivate most change.

▶ A sudden insight or unpredictable event, rather than a carefully-developed plan, usually triggers action.

▶ You are more likely to change on your own volition than at the urging of colleagues, relatives or self-help groups, or doctors, therapists or other professional advisors.

▶ In order to change, you have to step out of your "comfort zone" and face your fears of humiliation, failure, discomfort or pain.

▶ In order to change, you have to think about old situations in new ways.

▶ Outward change happens to us. Inner change occurs only with intention.

▶ Change does not occur in a straight line.

▶ There is no timeline for change. Everyone changes at his or her own pace.

▶ Change is always stressful.

▶ Confusion and dissatisfaction are the two most obvious signals that something needs to change. They are symptoms that something is wrong in your life and that you're going to end up exactly where you don't want to be if you don't change directions.

▶ Stress and frustration may be the first signs that you are changing.

▶ You have less to give to others when you are changing.

▶ Change always triggers loss and the emotional reactions that accompany it: shock, denial or resistance, bargaining, grief and acceptance.

▶ Planning for change provides a measure of security, but it is impossible to plan for the range of emotions that accompany it.

identity but you haven't found a new one to put on. Those uncomfortable feelings persist even after you've chosen a new career if you haven't progressed far enough to create the same kind of firm-footed sense of belonging you had before. The discomfort eventually recedes as you become more a part of your new career and less identified with what you've left behind. But it's important to recognize that you cannot—let me repeat, cannot—move from the old to the new without passing through that uncomfortable place in between.

The good news is that every lawyer who truly wants to make a change will do so. The first step in doing so is to attach a name to the barriers that are impeding your progress. The next chapter helps you do just that.

Reasons to Maintain the Status Quo

"We prefer the security of a known misery, to the misery of an unfamiliar insecurity."
—Stan McCleary, lawyer-turned-psychologist

■ ■ ■

The first step in moving past your resistance to change is to define what's good about where you are now. Even though you may dislike your work, or your unemployment, or your lack of a secure future, you have plenty of reasons to maintain the status quo. Those reasons create resistance that mere dissatisfaction cannot budge. That's why you've been "bitching and moaning" to your friends, or why you always resolve your criticism of your current situation by telling yourself, "Oh well, at least I'm employed."

> "Often what holds us back is an undefined fear."

You can also look at your resistance to change in the opposite way: What's so bad about where you're going? Peter C. Jenkins, a lawyer and consultant from Gaithersburg, Maryland, suggests making a detailed list of what it is you fear most. "Often what holds us back," he says, "is an undefined fear."

To identify your fears, answer the following questions:

▶ What am I afraid I'll lose?
▶ What is the worst ending I can imagine?
▶ What do I hope to gain?
▶ What would an ideal ending look like?
▶ Who will have to let go of what when the change occurs?

Now, synthesize your answers to the preceding questions into one or more specific barriers to change. I've identified barriers commonly mentioned by other lawyers in the lists that follow.

When you make a list of the fears that are holding you back, your reasons to maintain the status quo can appear insurmountable. And they will be, until you initiate the process explained in the next chapter.

The Unknown	Lack of Time or Timing
▶ Not knowing what else to do	▶ Having no time to look for something else
▶ Not knowing about other options	▶ Having no time to think about doing something else
▶ Not knowing where to start	▶ Thinking you'll have more time after a certain case ends
▶ Not being able to imagine having work you love	▶ Having a hard time concentrating on transition when the demands of your caseload keep interfering
▶ Not believing you could ever earn enough money doing what you really love	▶ Needing to give the profession more of a chance
▶ Not having the right background to do what you really want to do	▶ Worrying that you're giving up too soon
▶ Having to make a decision about which direction to take	▶ Hoping it will be better when you're a partner
▶ Only knowing how to practice law	▶ Hoping the situation will improve (e.g., the partner you hate might die, leave or miraculously change)
▶ Fear of not finding anything else	▶ Waiting for things to get bad enough
▶ Fear of being under-employed	▶ Believing it will look bad on your résumé to change employment after only a year
▶ Fear of getting into a profession with even fewer women or minorities	▶ Feeling that your investment hasn't paid off enough to justify leaving
▶ Fear of getting into something that's no better—and could be even worse	▶ Thinking you're too old to change
▶ Fear of having regrets	
▶ Fear of losing or wasting your investment in time or education	
▶ Losing the comfort of knowing what's expected of you	
▶ Knowing you will have to make a big investment in any new venture	
▶ Wondering if you could just make an adjustment where you are	

B Coming to Terms with Change

Money Concerns	**The Reaction of Others**
▶ Thinking it's smarter to wait until you get fired or laid off so you can collect unemployment	▶ Not wanting to let your [partners, clients, parents, spouse, kids, relatives] down
▶ Knowing your children will be going to college soon, and that you have to pay for their schooling	▶ Knowing your [clients, partners, boss] need you
▶ Realizing that you're deeply in debt	▶ Feeling that your family expects you to continue to support them in the style to which you have all become accustomed
▶ Refusing to accept the prospect of earning less money	▶ Reneging on your commitment to put your kids through private school or college
▶ Not knowing how you'll pay your student loans	▶ Knowing your family expects you to be a "professional"
▶ Being attached to the lifestyle your high income provides	▶ Fear of losing the respect of your colleagues
▶ Hating your work, but loving the security	▶ Fear of invoking the wrath of your parents or spouse
▶ Having a spouse and 2.3 kids to support	▶ Fear of setting a bad example for other women or minorities
▶ Having to pay the kids' private school tuition	▶ Feeling that a certain project or client needs you to handle it right
▶ Needing $100,000 per year just to survive	▶ Fearing failure to live up to your potential
▶ Worrying that you'll end up a bag lady or homeless	▶ Fearing being seen as a failure
▶ Worrying that the bank will take back your house	▶ Not wanting to lose the relationships you've built
▶ Worrying that you'll never have financial security or a respectable income again	▶ Fearing you'll be rejected by your social network
▶ Missing the good life from law firm parties	▶ Fearing your friends will turn on you
▶ Being reluctant to give up staying in nice hotels on someone else's dime	▶ Fearing your colleagues will shun you
▶ Giving up benefits like health insurance, paid vacation, pension plan	
▶ Missing perks like a secretarial staff, copy room, library, free lunches	

Self-Esteem and Identity Issues

▶ Not believing in yourself

▶ Feeling lucky that you have so much and guilty that you would give it all up

▶ Hating to give up the prestige, automatic respect and ego boost that come from being identified as a lawyer

▶ Liking the professionalism of the business

▶ Wanting to keep the credibility and recognition you've earned

▶ Not wanting to feel like a quitter

▶ Appreciating the power, control or autonomy you now have

▶ Liking your freedom and flexibility

▶ Not wanting to give up the intellectual validation and challenge of your work

▶ Hating to start again at the bottom

▶ Worrying that you won't be taken seriously in the next endeavor

Overcoming Resistance to Change

"The significant problems we have cannot be solved at the same level of thinking with which we created them."

—*Albert Einstein, scientist*

■ ■ ■

Now that you have a pretty good idea of the barriers that are keeping you where you don't want to be, it's time to think about dismantling them. The key to breaking down your barriers, no matter what they are, is the same. This chapter explores the formula.

Oakland, California, career counselor Lesah Beckhusen identified four factors that distinguish lawyers who make significant changes in their work from those who don't:

> Your resistance to change will always equal or exceed your dissatisfaction.

▶ They know it's possible to make change happen in their lives because they have done it before, although not necessarily in their legal careers;

▶ They are so unhappy that the unknown becomes more appealing than the known;

▶ They have a clear objective that really interests them, and they have the time and resources to act upon the idea; and

▶ They have accepted the costs and losses involved in making the change.

Organizational systems experts have devised a simple formula for Beckhusen's observations: Your resistance to change will always equal or exceed your dissatisfaction. But once your dissatisfaction takes on a vision of something better, and you identify a first step toward achieving that vision, you'll always overcome your resistance. At that point you begin to move forward.

What the formula confirms is that no matter how unhappy you are with the status quo, all your good reasons to stay put will keep you there if you're simply trying to escape from them. It's only when your motivation to change stems from your attraction to a new goal that your barriers—financial or otherwise—will gradually (and sometimes magically) erode. When you can associate enough pleasure with the idea of achieving your new goal, you'll be motivated to attack the "barriers" that, until now, have held you back.

Some of you had a vision of wanting something better when you opened this book, met with a career counselor or attended a career seminar. Although it may not feel like it, you've already begun to move past your resistance to change by taking a small step. Now you need to continue to take more small steps to crystallize and achieve your vision.

The motivation to put resistance behind you develops in five fairly typical stages, according to researchers at the University of Rhode Island. The first is pre-contemplation—casually thinking about the change, but remaining unconvinced. This is the "bitch-and-moan" stage I mentioned at the beginning of Chapter 8; it can last for many years without developing any apparent momentum.

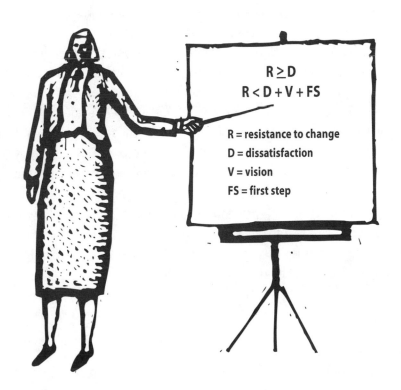

$$R \geq D$$
$$R < D + V + FS$$

R = resistance to change
D = dissatisfaction
V = vision
FS = first step

The process then progresses to contemplation: "I'm going to do this in the next six months." Smart lawyers invest in self-assessment and reflection during this time. The next stage brings a starting date. The fourth stage starts full-blown preparation, which leads to the fifth stage, actual initiation of the change.

You can keep yourself in motion by asking yourself simple questions like these:

▶ Do I want to work these hours?
▶ Do I want to work in these clothes?
▶ Do I want to work with these people?
▶ What would be one step better than where I am now?

Sometimes, making minor alterations to your current situation will solve the problem, at least temporarily. "There are people who are unable to move to something new in one jump," says Chicago career counselor Sheila Nielsen, "but they can shift the rudder a little bit and get a sense of real relief."

To continue moving past your barriers, turn to the self-assessment chapters in the next section of this book and work diligently through the exercises. Follow that introspection with research, as outlined in the succeeding section. By the time you finish, you'll have turned your ambiguous notion of something better into a concrete description of the work that would best suit you. At that point, we'll return to your barriers to change to see how they can be lowered, or dismantled completely.

Those of you who have burned out or become demoralized by your professional experiences may have to find time for renewed enthusiasm before you can move on. You may find value in reading the books on change identified in Appendix 3. If your barriers to change are so severe that you can't face the thought of looking at what you want right now, I suggest you seek out professional help. One lawyer put it this way:

> Don't be afraid to go to a pro and say, "I've got a problem." How do you think you get your clients? People have troubles; they come to a lawyer. Lawyers have troubles; they go to a psychologist or career counselor and say, "I want to get out of this but I don't know how to do it."

SELF-ASSESSMENT

Why Self-Assessment Is Essential

"The resistance to a new idea increases by the square of its importance."
—*Bertrand Russell, philosopher and mathematician*

■ ■ ■

Lawyers make a living turning the ambiguous grays of life into black and white. Unfortunately, most lawyers tend to look at their career problems with the same certainty, quickly deciding what's wrong without pausing for reflection and introspection.

> Lawyers make a living turning the ambiguous grays of life into black and white.

For some of you, the decision to enter law school itself was the result of such a process. Do any of these declarations sound like you?

- ▶ I didn't have the right background for an MBA or MD.
- ▶ I didn't know what else to do with my life.
- ▶ I didn't like the sight of blood.
- ▶ I hated all my science classes.
- ▶ I figured other people would think I was trained to do or be anything.
- ▶ I thought accounting would be boring.
- ▶ I thought a JD would be more versatile than an MBA.
- ▶ I thought the education would assure me a good job upon graduation.
- ▶ I wanted a profession with prestige, respect and status.
- ▶ I wanted intellectual challenge in my work.
- ▶ I wanted to avoid the draft.
- ▶ I wanted to change the world.
- ▶ I wanted to earn a lot of money.

▶ I wanted to get a job in the real world.

▶ I wanted to help others.

▶ I wanted to learn how to think.

▶ I wanted to postpone decision-making about my future.

▶ I wanted to right societal wrongs.

▶ It seemed like something I could do.

▶ It was shorter and less costly than medical school.

Going into the practice of law right after graduation or a judicial clerkship might have been another such decision. Did your justifications for choosing law practice resemble any of these?

▶ I didn't want to waste my education.

▶ I figured that maybe I'd like it once I tried it.

▶ I got good grades.

▶ I had student loans to pay off.

▶ I thought I should at least try it out.

▶ I was offered a job.

▶ It seemed like the practical thing to do.

▶ It was the easiest thing to do.

▶ That's what I was trained to do.

▶ That's where everyone else in law school was going.

▶ The money was good.

If you identify with any of these statements, it's time to break your pattern. This applies if you are a law student who panics at the thought of practicing law, a dissatisfied associate, an experienced practitioner stuck in a specialty you didn't choose, or an unemployed lawyer. Your challenge now is to take a closer look at who you are, and how that profile matches up with the work that appeals to you.

Many lawyers and law students bristle at the thought of slowing down for self-assessment. Sometimes, this avoidance is fueled by a kind of "magical thinking"—believing that the perfect work will materialize if you just wait for it to come along. Similarly, you may be stopped by a mistaken belief that the usual rules of job-finding don't apply to you—your credentials are so superior that employers and headhunters should be clamoring for your services.

At the beginning of your career, you might claim that you can't know what you'd like to do until you've actually tried it. Other times, avoidance stems from simple impatience: a real or imagined sense of financial emergency, or fear that the competition is hot on your heels and you'd better "run awful fast just to stand still."

You might also be holding onto the belief that you can only operate within a narrow, self-defined territory.

- ▶ I can only go this far.
- ▶ I can only make this much money.
- ▶ I can only initiate this much of a change.
- ▶ I'm a lawyer; I can't really be an artist.
- ▶ I'm a parent; I can't jeopardize my family's security.
- ▶ I'm a woman in law; I have to stay here to represent my gender.

Sometimes the fear has more disturbing origins: not wanting to discover how far you are from work you would find truly meaningful. The perfect work for you might lie immediately beyond the boundaries you've established. But how will you know until you stretch your limits and begin thinking outside the box?

The resistance of some may stem from the indoctrination you received as bright, competent children. Your educational system graded you on a curve, measuring your performance against a standard and rewarding you for scoring in the upper part of the scale. The system did not encourage your unconventionality or your desire to seek your own path.

Law school reinforced that message. By accepting precedent as the primary rule of law, you came to respect tradition, wanting to forge new ground only if it connected logically with the old. By focusing on words as the basis of human communication—rather than actions, body language and feelings—you were taught to ignore your instincts and make only logical decisions. "Law school, and all the steps one takes afterwards are a process of conformity," says one former practicing lawyer. "It is extremely difficult for graduates to break away from their professional training and not practice law—especially to do something that is completely creative and has no rules or boundaries—coming as they do from that background."

The problem with what you learned in law school is that successful careers are built on passion rather than logic, and redirecting your career requires risks that often cannot be justified. I can't tell you how many letters I've received from lawyers who mustered the courage to move on even though "from the outside looking in, people didn't understand what my problem was." The steps that lead to successful careers are frequently illogical and without precedent. They make sense only in hindsight to those who initiate them.

Although introspection adds an extra step, it's always worth the investment. Here are three reasons why:

It's the foundation of credibility.

Most of you believe you'll be hired because of your credentials. You're convinced that your achievements matter most. It's true that credentials—those past achievements that prove your competence—are critical to job-finding success, but most employers are looking for something more.

Authors James Kouzes and Barry Posner, experts on the subject of leadership, researched the subject of credibility and wrote a book of the same title. They discovered that it's far more important to be honest with others about yourself and your motivations, to have a vision for the future and be able to articulate your honesty and vision in a way that inspires others, than to have exactly the right credentials. In other words, credibility is based more on the subjective qualities of honesty, vision and enthusiasm than on competence.

Bill Gates, founder of Microsoft, agrees:

> My approach in an interview is to find a business-related topic the candidate says he or she cares passionately about, and then try to gauge whether the person has gone out of his or her way to learn about it and think of it in new ways. Talking about a subject a person cares a great deal about allows me to really explore the lengths to which he or she might go on a project we assign.

As David Maister, a Boston-area management consultant and former professor at Harvard Business School, puts it: "People don't care how much you know until they know how much you care. Enthusiasm and the hard work it inspires count for more than an extra piece of ability." Stop for a moment and reread that quotation. It's critical for your future.

All of you have competencies and credentials. You couldn't have entered law school, passed the bar exam or practiced law without them. In short, you already can claim one of the foundations of credibility. But you undermine your chances of getting hired when you place too much emphasis on your credentials while ignoring your occupational passions. Bernard Haldane, the father of modern career counseling, has found that job seekers secure jobs in half the time if they focus on their dependable strengths rather than their weaknesses.

It's the foundation of job-hunting success.

Steve Gustaveson enrolled in a career evaluation workshop in 1988 to find out why he wasn't feeling fulfilled as a litigator in the Attorney General's office. The answer he discovered—that he preferred an activist advisory role and needed more opportunity to teach—led him to embark upon a well-planned research process. Six months later, a new position was created in the A.G.'s office with a job description that seemed to have been written just for him: program advisor to the Division of Children and Family Services, involving consultations with managers on legal and policy issues, legislative work and training. The self-awareness he gained by exploring his preferences and strengths paid off. His new boss told him that he was chosen over more experienced candidates because he was able clearly to articulate what it was about the job that appealed to him, and precisely why he was qualified to handle it.

As a lawyer, you tend to be goal-oriented, intent on achieving results and closure. The result is a search for work that focuses on one question: "Who else will hire me?" With that single-mindedness steering you, you may suppress or ignore your own preferences, try to make yourself fit into the obvious choices, and end up competing with those whose preferences naturally lead them to that type of work. The result is failure, partly because you can't muster the passion and enthusiasm that impresses employers, and partly because you lack the commitment that motivates you to hammer away at potential leads until they turn into opportunities.

Repeated failure in looking for work can lead to job-hunting phobia. When you send out feelers by way of a mass mailing and receive no responses, or advertise your services in a newspaper and your only calls are from others thinking about doing the same thing, you get discouraged and suspend your efforts. To paraphrase David Maister, there's nothing more depressing than to be rejected for a job you didn't want in the first place.

Without a clearly defined goal, it's difficult to remain motivated through the disappointments, rejections and reversals that mark any career transition. Take law school as an example. If you knew then how much discomfort you'd experience to earn your degree, many of you might never have enrolled. Once you were there, though, the belief that the effort was worth the goal of securing better work than you could get with only an undergraduate education kept you motivated enough to read the casebooks, go to class, cram for exams and face the posted grade lists. Without a sense of the value of the education, you might never have graduated.

The same process occurs when you change your work. When you create an appealing vision based on your strengths and preferences, you have the motivation to persist until you bring that vision to life.

It's the foundation of career satisfaction and success.

Self-assessment helps you avoid a career move that, as one psychologist and former practicing lawyer puts it, "merely changes state rooms on the Titanic." Through introspection, you figure out what you would like to be doing with your time, not what you think you could get paid to do.

That passion will create your success. Think about the most successful entrepreneurs and entertainers in America: Bill Gates, Oprah Winfrey, Michael Jordan, Arnold Schwarzenegger. They all love their work. In the words of the late billionaire Malcolm Forbes, "The only career advice that is of any value is to do what turns you on."

What Is Self-Assessment?

"The most successful people are those who do all year long what they would otherwise do on their summer vacation."

—Mark Twain, author

• • •

Self-assessment boils down to answering three questions:

> ► Who am I?
> ► What do I want?
> ► What am I willing to give up to get what I want?

These three questions *must* be explored in the sequence described, even though our inclination is to start with the third question, phrased something like this:

> ► How can I find a job that will pay enough to cover my student loans?
> ► What career will allow me to continue to support my spouse and children in the style to which all of us have become accustomed?
> ► What kind of work will let me make a change without disappointing any of the people who rely upon me?

When you begin by asking what you are willing to give up, the answer is usually "nothing"—especially when you focus on obligations to your family, or the frightening level of debt you've incurred to get where you are today. Your answer ends the inquiry. If, on the other hand, you start by asking, "Who am I?"—if you look objectively at your skills and preferences, then mix in the motivation that comes from your dreams and desires—you progress. You can connect your preferences to a meaningful career direction, and then research whether the quality that is important to you is at risk in the new field. If it is, you can find out how much of what's important to you will be sacrificed in the move and whether the new goal is worth the loss. You can also explore how you might get some of that quality in other ways or parts of your life. When both your preferences and your desires remain in question, however, fear of the unknown will keep you unhappy and stuck.

Who Am I?

The question, "Who am I?," is not meant to be an existential, spiritual examination of the ultimate meaning of your life. Instead, it asks you to make practical, bite-sized inquiries into your unique preferences and strengths in five areas:

- ▶ interests;
- ▶ skills;
- ▶ values;
- ▶ people contact; and
- ▶ work environment.

Interests are subjects to which you are drawn, topics about which you read and inquire, areas that intrigue you. Some people are generalists with broad interests that frequently change. Others are specialists who focus on one subject or field. Subject matters that many lawyers find appealing include international affairs, human behavior, social policy, constitutional law and high technology. Other interests are listed on page 103.

Skills are your natural abilities and those you have developed through experience. (See the lists of skills common to lawyers on pages 90-92 and 105.) Analyzing the skills you've developed, as well as the skills you most enjoying using, is the foundation of transferable skills analysis and a key to making any kind of an unconventional change in employment.

Research by the Johnson O'Connor Foundation confirms that you enjoy work that calls upon your natural aptitudes—those skills that come most readily to you— and dislike work that asks you to rely on skills you don't have. Likewise, many studies have shown that the tasks that come easily to you are the ones you do best. The closer you can get to work that draws upon your natural aptitudes, the more you'll reduce your risk of layoff, and increase both career satisfaction and your chance of reaching your greatest potential.

The problem with this notion—the "do what you love, the money will follow" theory—is that you may feel guilty about engaging in tasks that come too easily to you. You may believe that struggle—not ease—equates with real accomplishment and if it's not hard, it's not valuable. But if you study those who've reached the top of their fields, you'll find they typically describe their work as play, as something they'd do whether or not they were compensated for it. They've enhanced their natural talent and interest in the field with hard work.

At the other extreme, you might avoid certain tasks or frequently put them off. You'll be happier and more productive if you find work that doesn't use those skills. A small-firm practitioner for 15 years, John spent most of his time meeting and talking with others. He loved to empathize with his clients and brainstorm solutions to their problems. In the meantime, files stacked up on his desk, begging for completion, especially when the matter involved a lot of details, rules or complex documentation. When John realized that his procrastination was not a personal failing, but an indication of his preference to work with others in a fast-paced environment, he closed his law practice. He now sells law firm software for a company large enough to provide substantial support and follow-up.

Most people possess a narrow but compatible range of natural aptitudes, which are easily found in one type of employment. Some claim a broad range of talents, or a few widely diverse skills; it's harder for them to find a single occupation that is sufficiently challenging and engaging. If you are one of these people, devote yourself to a cause, involve yourself in leisure activities that make use of the unused aptitudes, or split your time between two careers to avert dissatisfaction.

Values are the intangible guiding principles and goals that bring meaning to your work and motivate your involvement and commitment. Some values shift as you mature and grow, but most guide your choices throughout a lifetime. Common values preferences among law school graduates include recognition, autonomy, variety, intellectual challenge and helping others. Page 108 in Chapter 14 lists other values preferred by lawyers.

If your work clashes with your values, you may produce easily enough, but you won't feel good about it. You'll experience a gut conflict, an unsettling doubt that you're doing the right thing. If your work is consistent with your values, however, you'll feel motivated to do more, even if the work itself is difficult. You'll want to accomplish your goals in order to express that value.

Your preferences in the **"people contact"** area are the ways you like to interact with others, both coworkers and clients. Here you need to define the ages, personality traits and cultural backgrounds of the people you prefer as colleagues and clients: children or adults; bright, accomplished people or those with learning problems; troubled individuals or those with everything under control. Consider also whether you prefer to work alone, with one or two others, or with larger groups. At least one lawyer in any group of ten prefers an isolated environment, akin to being a cloistered monk, for introspective, analytical work. Others prefer a team approach, working together with a compatible group toward a common goal. There are also those who prefer to have one-on-one interactions make up their work day. See page 109 for people preferences expressed by lawyers.

Environmental preferences involve the physical and intangible aspects of the workplace itself: the office atmosphere, your work schedule, the aesthetics of the physical setting, the degree of freedom and flexibility in office management. Some of you feel uncomfortable the moment you put on your coat and tie in the morning; you'd much rather throw on blue jeans and a sweatshirt. Others hate "dress down" Fridays. You might feel cooped up in an air-conditioned office without windows that open, while your colleague next door loves his corner office in a high-rise building.

It's important to explore and define all five areas, and prepare a complete view of your preferences, if you want to make a meaningful change. Former career consultant Larry Richard of Philadelphia explains why:

> When a psychological need is met, it recedes, and you don't think about it. You may decide to leave one job because you can't stand the high pressure and demanding work hours. But the new job, with set hours, doesn't provide the variety and intellectual challenge you did like—but didn't realize you liked—in the last job.

The most reliable way to identify your preferences is to analyze your good and bad past experiences and define the qualities that tie them together. This type of analysis will often be more accurate than what you've learned about yourself from family and friends, or from experiences in past employment. For example, you may think of yourself as liking to write, but when you study your most enjoyable experiences, you discover that you were actually doing more talking than writing during the best times. The only reason you're now focusing on writing is because you've had more opportunity recently to write and you find it more enjoyable than the legal research and document organization that have been an even greater part of your responsibilities.

When you complete the blank Ideal Job Grid in Chapter 14 on page 99 as completely as the samples that follow it, you will have developed at least a preliminary answer to the question of who you are. If you have trouble filling in your grid, or if you sense that the resulting picture is not accurate or whole, complete the self-assessment exercises contained in the next two chapters and try again.

But don't skip this task, assuring yourself that you already know "pretty much" what your preferences are. Write them all down in the appropriate boxes to make your analysis tangible. It's too easy to overlook what's important to you if you don't have it down in black and white.

What Do I Want?

Every self-assessment process must combine the practical and measurable with the fantastic and illogical. The next question, "What do I want?," switches to the subjective, examining your dreams for the future and the motivations that tie you to a career, an employer, a task, a goal. Combining answers to both questions creates forward movement.

The "What do I want?" inquiry delves into the irrational and illogical, an approach that those of us who have been trained as lawyers often resist. "If I had to come up with the major issue that makes working with attorneys a real challenge," says Lesah Beckhusen, "it is their almost exclusively left-brained thinking about how the world works." Lawyers are trained to rely upon rational, linear, organized thought. But, says Beckhusen, human beings are motivated by what they want, not by what is logical or practical. Beckhusen advises lawyers to use their intuition and feelings to create a vision of what they want. Then, they can use their left-brain skills to get them there.

Acknowledging your occupational dreams can be unnerving if you have spent your life concentrating on the expectations and needs of others. Who says it's possible to get what you want? But meeting your own needs by pursuing what you want creates an important paradox: It motivates you to achieve career success, thereby also allowing you to meet the needs of those who depend upon you.

Some career consultants suggest exploring the question of what you want in terms of the impact you'd like to have on the world. Richard Bolles, author of *What Color Is Your Parachute?*, calls this motivation the "integrating factor," and defines it as that which you think most needs fixing in the world. Similarly, former practicing lawyer Arnold Patent, author of *You Can Have It All*, suggests that as part of your goal-setting you describe a perfect world as you see it, remembering that "a perfect world is a fun place to be."

Others talk in terms of personal fantasy. In *Wishcraft,* Barbara Sher prescribes goal-setting with a twist.

> When you say "This is what I want," you're not fooling. If I could wave a magic wand and POOF! you'd have that goal right now, you honestly think you'd be delighted. The acid test for any goal [is to] try living it in the imagination. How does it feel? Love it? Great. Hate it? Change the target.

The question can also be posed in terms of motivation: What challenges you to get and stay involved? That motivation can be found in the outcome—building something, completing a project, winning—or in the circumstances—a competition, a deadline, a need to be met, a disaster to avoid. Dennis T. Jaffe, Ph.D., and Cynthia D. Scott, Ph.D., MPH, authors of *Take This Job and Love It,* find three basic motivations:

▶ External reward (e.g., salary, advancement, bonus, job titles or special perks, and even termination or reproval);
▶ Peer respect or a feeling of importance or connection to a group; and
▶ Internal validation or meaning, usually as a result of using your creative capacity and growing in your work, learning, meeting challenges or participating in decision-making.

Similarly, MIT Sloan Fellows Professor Edgar H. Schein defines eight "career anchors":

▶ Technical/functional competence;
▶ General managerial competence;
▶ Autonomy/independence;
▶ Security/stability;
▶ Entrepreneurial creativity;
▶ Service/dedication to a cause;
▶ Pure challenge; and
▶ Lifestyle.

The answer to the question, "What do I want?," may also be discovered by studying the way you spend your time. Nancy Ashley, a veteran practitioner who moved from private practice to human services consulting, described her transition:

Everyone laughs at me now because it was staring me in the face all the time. I had done volunteer work for years in human services—child advocacy issues, food banks, starting a domestic violence shelter. Had I only looked at how I used my time when it was my own choice, I probably could have saved years of agony trying to figure out a new direction. It just took me a while to recognize the signals that everyone else could see.

Ultimately, the answer to the question, "What do I want?," is your own personal definition of success. And it may not be motivated by noble urges. In the words of David Maister, former associate professor at Harvard Business School:

> The keys to what you really want are the things you don't like to admit. "I don't like to admit it, but I need to be the center of attention." Okay, find a job that will let you show off. "I don't like to admit it, but I really want to be rich." Fine, go out and make lots of money. Play to your evil secrets; don't suppress them.

Barbara Boivin—who had tried general practice, and both criminal prosecution and defense, in her eight-year legal career—listened to David Maister's quotation at three consecutive career planning seminars. At first she resisted the concept, because her "evil secret" was that she wasn't interested in a career at all. She preferred to work in well-defined, short-term projects in a variety of fields. Eventually, she was able to flip her shameful secret into a positive attribute: an ability to orient herself quickly to new areas and environments, especially when the tasks involved research and mediation. Once she accepted this truth about herself, she generated a series of temporary, diverse and well-paid assignments: completing a research project for a mediation practitioner, designing a plan for coordinating solid waste and recycling contracts, reviewing municipal codes for statutory and constitutional inconsistencies, and filling in for a hearing examiner on maternity leave.

Like Barbara, you'll progress in developing a satisfying career when you get to the point where your secret is no longer "evil" but a quality you can verbalize proudly to others.

What Am I Willing to Give Up to Get What I Want?

Visualize a child with an armful of toys who sees one more appealing toy. When she reaches for the new toy, she drops at least one she's already holding. When she tries to retrieve that first toy, she drops the new one. Before long, the child discovers that the only way she can grab the new toy is to let go of at least one other. There's a clear parallel between her experience and the career transition process.

You always have to give up something to get what you want. One law school graduate who moved into foundation administration for a law-related organization faces this reality yearly. At every annual meeting of the organization's board, at least one judge or lawyer tells her that she's wasting herself in her current position. Someone as bright as her really ought to be a practicing lawyer, they insist. She doesn't agree; she's sure that practicing law would be the wrong choice for her. But she has to admit that she's given up a certain amount of respect and approval by making the choice she has.

As discussed in Chapter 7, every change—no matter how desired and fortunate—involves a loss of some kind. Choosing what to give up completely, set aside temporarily, or accept less of is difficult when they all seem essential to your well-being. Answering the first two questions, "Who am I?" and "What do I want?," and creating a picture of the type of work and work environment you want, makes it much easier to answer the last question. Once you're in touch with your preferences and dreams, you'll be able to evaluate more realistically how to attain your new goal and still meet your other obligations.

Letting Go of Your Identity as a Lawyer

As I said before, you're always going to have to give up something to get what you want. Those who consider yourselves "successful lawyers" may lose the external rewards associated with your position: from the prestige of your financial resources and professional status to the respect accorded a quality work product. When you discard your title, you may also lose the self-esteem it fostered.

Leaving the profession is also traumatic for lawyers who have not found success in law. You might have felt like a failure from the time you entered law school until you handled your last court case. Even though a part of you recognizes that your talents must be more suited to other careers, your self-esteem has been so battered by your experience in law that the mere thought of making a change is equated with more failure and frustration. Your professional identity—the ability to introduce yourself as a lawyer or a law school graduate—may be your greatest sense of pride. If you renounce even this accomplishment, what do you have left to offer?

In a study done by two Minnesota career services offices, lawyers with nontraditional career paths cited their belief that others perceived their position as having less prestige than law as one of the common drawbacks they experienced. On the other hand, the benefits they cited most often were improved quality of life including more independence and flexibility, more time for family, less stress and more fun. Would you trade some money and prestige for those benefits?

The Conflict Between Money and Meaning

"Above the poverty level, the relationship between income and happiness is remarkably small," says social commentator Jonathan Freedman. According to the *Utne Reader* magazine, 62 percent of Americans say that "a lot of money" is important to a good life. Yet only six percent of those earning more than $50,000 annually say that they have achieved the American Dream, as compared with about five percent of Americans earning less than $15,000 per year. And only a quarter of all people winning a million dollars or more in the lottery quit their jobs.

Despite the overwhelming evidence that money does not buy happiness, the conflict between money and meaning is one of the most difficult for lawyers to resolve. Those of you who are experienced practitioners might now be earning good money (and appreciating its advantages) but you're no longer satisfied with your work. To find fulfillment, you must trade the assurance of a comfortable, or even regular, income for the risk and invigoration of a meaningful change.

Others of you—especially solo practitioners, small towns lawyers, or public interest lawyers—might be earning too little money. It could be that you place a higher priority on the meaning you derive from your work—whether contribution to society or to your individual clients—or on your lack of pretentiousness, than on the money you earn. You fear that if you shift into better paying work, you'll sacrifice your integrity.

You might also envy those in lucrative practices or those receiving regular salaries in private industry or government, but you can't overcome what you believe is your inadequacy to find that type of work. You may be placing a higher priority on autonomy, self-direction, and control than on the income you generate.

Whether the problem is too much money or too little, the solution is clarity developed through introspection.

The Conflict Between Work and Family

Some of you may love your work but wish you could spend more time with family and friends. Those of you who are parents might like to quit working, or reduce your workload to a part-time schedule, but fear you will never regain career momentum.

Still others never find the time to explore personal interests or simply relax. You may all believe that your families are your highest priorities.

But think a moment about these situations. If you work long, hard hours for a good income but seldom see your families, you might be placing a higher priority on the needs of your clients or coworkers, or on supporting your family's lifestyle, than on actually spending time with your family. Likewise, those of you who don't want to "get off the partnership track" are placing a higher priority on that goal. If you don't have time for yourself, you may be acting quite consistently with your priority of spending time with your family, or you might be placing an even higher priority on your work, with time for self coming last. None of these choices are wrong per se, but refusing to acknowledge that all your priorities cannot be weighted equally can cause frustration and guilt.

Sometimes the conflict between work and family lives more vividly in the mind than in reality. Gordon, with nearly 20 years of law practice behind him, hated his work but confided in a group workshop that something was preventing him from leaving the law. He had promised to put his sons through college, and the only way he could meet that commitment was to keep practicing law. When someone in the workshop asked whether he'd shared his dilemma with his sons, Gordon looked shocked. "I can't do that," he said. After all, he'd given his word, and that was that.

He arrived at the next meeting looking ten years younger and 100 times happier. He had told his eldest son about his career conflict and was astonished by his response. His son urged him to quit. He said he admired his father for putting himself through college and wanted the same opportunity to prove himself. More importantly, he missed the supportive, fun-loving father he had before Gordon's depression set in.

Two years later, I ran into Gordon at a CLE seminar. He was wearing a brown city bus driver's uniform and a big smile. He'd left his partnership about six months after the workshop ended. Now, he supports his family—and his interest in fiction writing—by driving a city bus, teaching in a paralegal program and handling a little bit of legal work out of his house.

Resolving the Conflicts

None of these conflicts require all-or-nothing solutions. You don't have to give up money to find meaning in your work. You don't have to drive a bus just to spend quality time with your family. You don't have to go bankrupt to achieve career satisfaction. You simply need to clarify your values, then make the compromises that bring your priorities and the realities of your life into closer alignment.

Until you identify a next step and engage in some interpersonal research, though, you can't know how much you're going to have to give up or whether the sacrifice will be worthwhile. The point is to begin your introspection and analysis and deal with this last issue when required. You won't have to make decisions about household expenses and outside obligations until you choose a direction and confirm the sacrifices it will require. By then, you'll know whether the loss will be worth the reward.

Another way of looking at the situation is found in Stephen Covey's book, *The Seven Habits of Highly Effective People.* He calls attention to four categories of priorities. The first, those that are both important to us and urgent, get done. Those that are unimportant and urgent command our attention and also get completed. To relax after spending the day focusing on all of life's emergencies, we make time for activities like watching television that are neither important nor urgent. The priorities we neglect are those that are important to us but not urgent, precisely the category of most meaningful changes in employment.

Maintaining the status quo is making a choice to perpetuate your current priorities. If you don't feel comfortable with those, the only healthy choice is to begin to explore others. The process is sure to trigger doubt and anxiety; but knowing your priorities, knowing what you are giving up and why, makes the choices and process much easier.

The next three chapters take you through the process of examining yourself and synthesizing your discoveries into a statement of your essential workplace preferences.

Self-Assessment
Exercises

"Listen to your stomach, not to your head. Your head will rationalize you right into a job you shouldn't have."

—Ray Bradbury, author

. . .

This chapter contains a series of exercises that will reveal to you your employment preferences. You'll get the best results if you work through all of the exercises, and take at least 20 hours to do it. You might want to schedule a weekend retreat to complete the process; or you can break up your self-assessment into mini-explorations, say an hour or so every other day for five or six weeks. If you're in a hurry, concentrate on just the "Quick and Easy Self-Assessment Exercises," "Your History of Achievement" and "Figuring Out Your Passions," devoting at least five hours to the process. *Do not under any circumstances skip this process entirely.*

> You'll find you discover new aspects of yourself, and clarify your overall preferences.

Keep your responses together and accessible in a self-assessment diary or notebook. Frequently review what you've recorded to find patterns and themes. Self-discovery is like peeling an onion. You'll find you discover new aspects of yourself, and clarify your overall preferences, as you complete each new exercise.

There's no one right way to do this process. But, if you're like most people, you'll find you get more done when you work within a framework and have deadlines. This book provides the framework. To get the deadlines, sign up for a class or a series of career counseling sessions, or find a friend to work with you. Input from other people—especially those who have nothing to gain or lose from your choices—will add to your self knowledge.

But don't expect one book or one course to tell you everything you need to know. That's why I've included a list of other self-assessment books and testing instruments in Appendix 3. If you apply only a fraction of the time and effort to self-assessment that you devoted to obtaining your law license, you'll greatly improve your chances of enjoying—and doing well in—your next line of work.

Quick and Easy Self-Assessment Exercises

▶ For an entire month, note on your desk calendar what you most and least enjoyed doing every day. At the end of the month, summarize and categorize the preferences you have recorded.

▶ Close your eyes for 30 seconds once a day for a week and visualize your ideal work place. What does the office look like? Are others around? Who are they and what are they like? What are you wearing? Write down what you see.

▶ Close your eyes for 30 seconds once a day for a week and visualize your ideal day. Write down what you see, even if it has nothing to do with going to work!

✓ ▶ Spend ten minutes with a pad of paper and pencil, or at your computer keyboard, writing down all the things you would do if you knew today that you would be dead in six months.

✓▶ Think about people you envy. Write down what they possess that you wish you had.

✓▶ Write a list, very quickly, entitled "Things my mother and father told me about money, careers and work."

▶ How, specifically, would you change your daily life if you won a $200,000 annuity in a lottery.

✓ ▶ Finish these sentences, with as many things as apply:
I don't like to admit it, but I really need. . . .
I feel happiest when I'm. . . .
If money and background were not considerations and I could have any kind of work I wanted, five years from now I would be. . . .
When I was a child, I always want to grow up to be a. . . .
One thing I've always done well is. . . .
I tend to procrastinate when facing. . . .
Time passes most quickly for me when I'm. . . .

➤ Look back at your life, from your earliest memories of childhood on, and write down all of the daydreams you remember about work.

➤ A genie has granted you three wishes. What are they?

▶ Read the Sunday paper. After you've finished, review the entire newspaper and record the headline of every article you read the first time through. Then, put the titles into categories such as real estate, business, fashion, food or people.

▶ In ten minutes of continuous writing, without removing your pen from the paper or fingers from the keyboard, answer this question: What do I like to do when I'm not working?

▶ Write a description of yourself. Touch upon your interests and define your personal style, including the way you like to dress, live, and interact with others. Be certain to list those skills at which you excel and those you enjoy using, whether or not they have anything to do with employment. Use active verbs and vivid nouns and adjectives. Do not compare yourself to others.

▶ When do you procrastinate? Be specific about what you're doing and what else is going on around you. Then evaluate for each situation whether you've had a prior bad experience with this type of task; whether the subject matter or the task is unfamiliar and you're not interested in learning about it; or whether the timing isn't right (i.e., you were tired and needed a break, or it was premature to act at that time).

▶ Prepare a one-page description of your long-range career goals (as far into the future as you can see). As part of your description, state in one sentence what kind of contribution you would like your work to make to yourself, your family, your community or the world.

When you have completed the exercises, evaluate the results in several different ways. First, look for the themes that tie them together. Then find the contradictions.

Next, break down statements into component parts. For example, if you say you'd like to work in international affairs, ask yourself why. Do you want to travel? Are you interested in cultural diversity? Does communication among differing people draw you? Do you like the challenge of learning new things? Are you seeking the variety that international contact might bring?

Finally, extrapolate from your fantasies to real life situations that contain the same or similar ingredients.

Your History of Achievement

List the achievements of your life—from school, recreation, church and work. Include any activity in which you took a leadership role, in which you helped to create a product or in which you wrote, spoke, taught, researched, coordinated or constructed, no matter how insignificant your contribution might seem now. List any activity that stands out in your memory as an accomplishment. For each, describe in writing the pertinent details about your involvement, including both the nature of the project and the results you achieved. These achievements need not have been acknowledged by others.

To come up with the list, first scan your memory. Then review calendars, diaries, scrapbooks, and files for records of your involvement in work, school, community and other activities. Go back at least five years, or to the beginning of your legal career, whichever is longer. Finally, ask friends, relatives and business acquaintances for their recollections of your achievements. Do not discount their feedback; record every suggestion made.

When you have finished gathering the information, organize your list chronologically to serve as a data bank for future résumé writing. Then review the list, marking those achievements about which you still feel proud and that you'd enjoy repeating.

Figuring Out Your Passions

Jot down 50 of the most enjoyable experiences of your life. Focus on events you remember as absorbing, fun, rewarding or fulfilling; when time passed by without notice because you were so thoroughly engaged. Choose events you enjoyed as they were unfolding, not ones that look good only in retrospect because of the result you attained, or because you received positive feedback or reinforcement. Include at least ten experiences from your childhood—finger-painting, your favorite games, your first camping trip, whatever!

An event may be something as simple as a memorable sunset, or as unusual as a trek in the Andes. When choosing a more complex event, you might want to isolate the high points and consider each one a separate experience. The point is to get in touch with experiences that lifted your spirits, that were easy and fun, and that you would gladly repeat.

Then write a list of ten awful experiences—when time dragged or was filled with frustration, dread or fear. Again, consider only the process and not the result.

When both lists are complete, spend at least an hour answering the following questions as they apply to the group of experiences you have recorded:

► How often were you alone and how often with others? What were you doing when you were alone? How did those activities differ from your activities with others?

► How many others were with you? What was the nature of your interaction with them? Were you conversing or participating with them, or quietly working alongside them? Were you engaged in group activity? What kind?

► What were the personality characteristics of the people around you? Up-beat? Analytical? Responsible? Daring? Supportive? Competitive? Challenging? Smart? Artistic? Athletic?

► What were you doing? Was it physical, mental or both? Were you passive or active, moving around or staying in one place; conveying or receiving information?

► What was the purpose of your participation in each event? Personal growth, building something, enjoyment, making change, helping others, competition?

► In what environments did you find yourself? Indoors or outside, sunny, rainy, dark, bright, crowded, spacious, formal, informal?

► Were you relating emotionally, intellectually, physically or spiritually to your surroundings?

► Were your activities internalized—that is, thoughtful or meditative— or external to yourself—for example, teaching, advising, coaching, viewing entertainment?

► What was the tempo of each event? Fast-paced, relaxed, both?

Note that the answers to these questions may be contradictory. You may enjoy being alone and being with others, or engaging in high energy activities and sitting peacefully outside in the sunshine. Include these observations in your answers to the questions.

Show and Tell

Go through your files and mementos to create what one career consultant calls a "brag" or "show and tell" file. Look through records of your accomplishments and involvement in any kind of activity. Set aside the course outline, seminar brochure or publicity for any program you helped to coordinate. Hunt for anything with your name on it, such as letterhead, business cards, newspaper clippings and examples of your work product. This material will help the process of updating or targeting your résumé, and can sometimes be used for illustrative purposes during an interview. At this point, though, look at what you've pulled out and find the themes tying everything together.

Things I Really Love to Do

Draw a line down the middle of a piece of paper. On the right side, write a list of activities that you really enjoy in any part of your life. Spend at least half an hour reviewing the last year to come up with as many activities as possible. If you have a hard time thinking of enjoyable activities in your recent past, think of a time in your life when you were generally content, and record the enjoyable events of that period.

When you have completed your list, study each activity you identified to determine what skill(s) you were employing when you engaged in that activity. Record the skill(s) on the left side of the paper opposite each activity. For assistance in coming up with names of skills, refer to the "Sample Ideal Job Grid Entries" on page 105 as well as the skills lists starting at page 90.

Newsmagazine Review

Read quickly through a national news weekly like *Time, Newsweek* or *U.S. News & World Report.* Select the six articles that you found the most intriguing and read from beginning to end. The articles can be of any length. A feature page dealing with a common topic such as "People" or "Week in Review" may be considered one article, or you may break it down into several selections. If you can't find six articles you really enjoyed, read other magazines until you come up with a full half-dozen.

Tear out the six articles and study them as a group. Write down any themes you see repeated in more than one article, as well as the contradictions. Better yet, explain to someone else why you chose the six articles and ask for his or her impressions.

Classified Ads Review

Skim the entire "Help Wanted" section of a Sunday newspaper. For a better selection, you might want to purchase a *New York Times, Washington Post* or *Los Angeles Times* that includes the complete classified ad section, not just nationally-advertised positions.

As you read through the entire section—including those parts devoted to specialties like health care and sales—circle every ad that appeals to you for any reason, even if the salary is too low or you're not qualified for the position. Now, take a closer look at all the ads you've circled, and clip out between a half-dozen and a dozen that most intrigue you, again ignoring the issues of salary and eligibility.

In looking at each ad you've chosen, write down the specific characteristics of the job that appeal to you, and those that don't. Then determine what themes link the ads you've chosen. Again, I encourage you to ask others for their impressions of your collection.

What Makes Work Meaningful to You?*

Read the six qualities listed below and rank them in order of their importance to you, with 1 being most important and 6 being least important. Be certain to answer the way you really feel, and not the way you think you ought to!

THE BEST WORK FOR ME WOULD:	Rank
1. Make use of my special talents	_____
2. Pay me well.	_____
3. Let me be creative and original.	_____
4. Make me well-known and respected.	_____
5. Let me work with people, rather than things.	_____
6. Give me an opportunity to help others.	_____

Add the points for the statements paired below and write the totals in the space provided.

_____Statements 1 and 3 (SE)

_____Statements 5 and 6 (PO)

_____Statements 2 and 4 (ER)

Now, rank the three pairs, with the lowest total ranked number one (your highest value) and the highest, number three (your lowest value).

Explanation of Results

ER refers to "external-reward." If this is your highest value, work that brings

---

*Adapted from *The Book of Tests,* Michael Nathanson, Viking Penguin, Inc., 1985.

wealth, prestige, power, security, status, respect or similar rewards also brings personal fulfillment. If external reward is your highest value, you are well-suited to the law. The first time you introduce yourself as a lawyer, you'll receive some of the reward you seek.

If you value external reward and are just starting your legal career, your best bets are employment in conventional areas of practice with private, corporate, public interest or government legal employers. As you proceed through your career, you might want to run for political office, lobby for a judicial appointment, or network your way into a management position with a former corporate client.

PO means "people-orientation." You need to work with or help other people, rather than concentrating on data, ideas or things. In law, those with a people orientation ought to represent individual clients—not business entities or faceless classes—or have frequent interaction with others. You also will prefer to work with client needs and problems that the legal system can directly remedy such as plaintiffs' personal injury or employment law work, legal services to the poor or disadvantaged, guardianship and probate, family or elder law, and consumer problems. Outside the profession, you might enjoy a retail environment, being a therapist or counselor, or working in education, daycare, placement, or employment counseling.

SE means "self-expression." The ability to be creative and to express yourself in your work is very important to you. Those who value self-expression need to deal in more creative areas of practice, such as fast-paced trial work, deal-making, or emerging or rapidly changing areas of law. Also, the more autonomy you can create for yourself, the more chance for creativity you will find. For that reason, self-employment is often attractive to those with this preference. Legal writing, especially for a newspaper or magazine, could provide a good opportunity for self-expression. Outside the legal profession, journalism, entrepreneurial ventures and the arts can be satisfying options.

Those with a strong preference for self-expression are likely to become dissatisfied with law over time. Early in your career, you'll have much to learn and many opportunities to talk, write and create solutions. Later, you'll probably discover that the rules and repetition of the legal environment, as well as your role representing someone else's interests, stifles your ability to express yourself. To avoid dissatisfaction, you'll have to find outlets for your creativity, whether in your work or free time.

The emphasis you place on certain values can change during the course of a career. Many lawyers start out seeking external reward in the form of the certainty of employment after graduation. Once they become established in the profession and enjoy the financial security and status they sought, a need for self-expression or helping others might take precedence.

What Do You Value?

Read quickly through the following list of values, crossing out those that are not at all important to you. Then review the list again, checking those that are very important to you. When you have finished this second review, allocate an imaginary $1,000 to purchase the values you would most like to have—those qualities essential to your sense of personal fulfillment. Assume you have none of these qualities now. Spend the entire $1,000—no more, no less.

___**Achievement** *(accomplishment, results brought about by persistence)*

___**Adventure/Excitement** *(action, risk and a fast pace)*

___**Beauty/Aesthetic Value** *(appreciation and enjoyment of beauty)*

___**Autonomy** *(independence, personal freedom, making your own choices)*

___**Creativity/Self-Expression** *(innovating new ideas, designs or solutions)*

___**Emotional Well-Being** *(peace of mind, quickly resolving inner conflicts)*

___**Physical Health** *(physically well, sound and strong in body)*

___**Honesty/Authenticity** *(being frank and genuinely yourself with others)*

___**Humor/Wit** *(a sense of humor, holding things in perspective)*

___**Intellectual Challenge** *(learning new things, stimulating the mind)*

___**Justice/Fairness** *(treating others impartially, wanting equity for others)*

___**Knowledge** *(seeking truth, information or principles out of curiosity)*

___**Love/Family** *(affection, intimacy, caring, attachment to a family)*

___**Loyalty** *(maintaining allegiance to a person, group or cause)*

___**Morality/Personal Integrity** *(maintaining ethical standards or honor)*

___**Nature** *(contact with or appreciation of the natural world)*

___**Physical Appearance** *(concern for one's physical attractiveness)*

___**Pleasure/Fun** *(enjoyment, gratification, playfulness)*

___**Power/Influence** *(having authority; power to get things done)*

___**Recognition** *(acknowledged as important or significant, respected)*

___**Religious Conviction** *(communion with or activity on behalf of God)*

___**Safety/Security** *(protection from threat or danger)*

___**Service/Helping Others** *(devotion to others' interests, serving a cause)*

___**Skill/Competence** *(being good at something)*

___**Tangible Results** *(see, touch, hear, smell or taste the results of your effort)*

___**Variety** *(regular contact with a broad number and type of experiences)*
___**Wealth/Possessions** *(owning things, ample money for things you want)*
___**Wisdom** *(mature understanding, insight, good sense, and judgment)*
___**Work Productivity** *(being actively productive)*

When you have spent the entire $1,000, list the six items for which you spent the most money. These are the qualities you value most highly and should emphasize in your work. Make certain these values are included on the "Must Have" side of your Ideal Job Grid in Chapter 14.

Fantasy Job-a-Week Game*

Pick one type of work you think you might like and "wear" it for a week. Start with the first field that comes to mind, no matter how silly you think it is. If you're really stuck and can't come up with fantasy work, go to the classified ads, close your eyes and pick one. Three rules: You can't think about whether the work pays enough money; you can't think about whether you're qualified to do the work; and you can't think about what others will think if you switch to this field.

When you've worn the work profile for a full week, list all the things about it that bring you joy as well as the qualities the work is missing. When you're finished with the first type of work, try on another one. After several weeks of exercising your imagination, study your choices and determine what your choices and responses have in common.

Writing a Classified Ad for Your Ideal Job

Write an ad for a fantasy position. Assume that you have the appropriate education, experience, and physical qualities for the position and that it would pay you $1,000,000 annually (or more, if that doesn't seem like enough to you!) as long as you continue to be engaged in it. The job can be one specific activity or role, or a combination of functions and roles that would not ordinarily be found in just one job—or in any job at all. You may include environmental conditions like work hours, location and vacation if they are crucial. Describe the skills called upon, the kind of interaction you would have with others, the work product and as many other details as you can conjure.

---

*This exercise was suggested by Connie Talmadge of Denver.

Your Lasting Contribution

Imagine that you've been told you have only five years to live. You'll be completely healthy and full of energy until the moment of your death, and a loving benefactor has provided you with unlimited funds to support you and your dreams until you die.

Now, imagine that today is a day in the middle of those five years. You've already traveled around the world, made peace with your friends and relatives, relaxed, and read all the classics. Now you've decided to concentrate on creating a legacy to leave behind, a way to be remembered by future generations. To what do you devote yourself? How are others impacted by your work? What kind of reward do you receive for your work before you die? What do others say about you and your legacy after you die?

Your Fantasy Employment

Describe a typical day in your fantasy employment. If you prefer, you can speak in term of projects, a typical year, or a series of job functions.

- ▶ Where are you? What do you see, hear, smell, taste, feel? What kind of clothing are you wearing?
- ▶ What does your environment look like? Is there any equipment? Do you operate it?
- ▶ Are there other people around? What are they doing? What are you doing in relation to them? If there's no one else around, what are you doing?
- ▶ Are you speaking? What are you saying? Who are you saying it to?
- ▶ Are you reading? What are you reading?
- ▶ Are you writing? What kind of writing?
- ▶ What else is happening? Observe what's going on around you.

Calculating the Real Costs of Change*

Turn to the list of barriers to change you identified in Chapter 8. Imagine each one to be true and write down the very worst consequences you can imagine from making the change despite your reasons not to.

---

*This exercise was suggested by Peter Jenkins of Gaithersburg, Maryland.

Next, think about and write down in detail all the potential benefits you would gain by living your life the way you have imagined it could be. Get a clear, detailed picture of what this positive change would mean for you in terms of opportunities, relationships, and physical and emotional well-being.

Now, determine what you have already lost in terms of opportunity, relationships and physical and emotional well-being by not having made a move to something that is a better fit for you. Take a hard look at what you will continue to lose every day if you don't make a change. Finally, project what it will cost in terms of these qualities one year, five years, ten years and 20 years from now if you continue your present course. Again, provide details and write down everything that comes to mind. The more directly you experience what it will mean if you do not change your situation, the better.

Setting Your Priorities

To determine your current priorities, list a maximum of four positions, career paths or work-time arrangements under consideration. Without identifying the specific position, career path or work-time arrangement in your notations, list all the reasons why you are attracted to each option under "pros" and all the reasons why you do not want to, or feel you can't, make that choice under "cons."

When you have finished, cross out or combine any reasons that duplicate one another. For example, if one of your "pros" is an attraction to making your own hours, don't also list as a "con" that you dislike keeping a regular schedule. And be certain that you've identified the precise preference. For example, distinguish among flexibility (having choice about the hours you work), time demands (the amount of time you're required to spend), and autonomy (having sole authority to determine how much time is required to get the work done).

Next, rewrite each reason so that it reflects a quality or core value, being as specific as possible. (Refer to the list of values at page 108.) For example, if one of your reasons was "income," write down how much income you require. If avoiding private practice comes up because it's "too cutthroat," explore what it is that's actually behind your reason, i.e., whether you prefer a non-competitive environment, want a relaxed work pace or prefer more collegiality and cooperation. When you have finished, you will have listed all the reasons, both positive and negative, that are keeping you in a state of conflict.

Now, review your list of positive and negative reasons and spend $1,000 to buy the five that are most important to you. You must spend the entire $1,000, but you cannot spend the same amount on any two reasons. Then, list those five reasons in descending order with the one you paid the most money for at the top and the one you paid the least money for at the bottom.

Then, compare your life as you are currently living it with the reasons you prioritized. First, record your daily activities for at least one full week. Exclude time spent sleeping, eating (unless your meals are combined with some other activity like a business meeting or family socializing), and dressing. At the end of the week, add up the number of hours or minutes you spent on each of your five most important reasons, as well as other activities that consumed more than an hour of your time during the week. Ascertain whether there are significant differences between what you say is most important to you and how you actually spend your time. Again, record without censorship your thoughts about this analysis.

Congratulations! You just completed a thorough self-assessment process. By now, you've learned a lot about your preferences, but look into the self-assessment resources listed in Appendix 3 if you'd like to learn more. Then work through the next two chapters to refine the picture. Chapter 13 helps you understand and define your transferable skills. By following the instructions in Chapter 14, you'll synthesize all you've learned in this, the next chapter and any other self-assessment you've done, into an overview of the best work for you.

Transferable
Skills Analysis

"Most of us think of what we do as a fixed, non-transportable thing. But if we think of our job as three separate skills . . . the parts can be reassembled elsewhere.
—*Carole Hyatt and Linda Gottlieb, authors*

■ ■ ■

The application of skills from field to field is the essence of transferable skills analysis. For example, here's the *Occupational Outlook Handbook's* description of the qualities of a good computer systems analyst. See how closely it parallels those of a practicing lawyer:

> Someone who can think logically, has good communication skills and likes working with ideas and people. Must be able to handle a number of tasks simultaneously, concentrate deeply and pay close attention to detail. Prefer someone who can work independently, but can also work in teams on large projects. Must have a facility with making technical language and theory understandable to the lay public. Continuous study will be necessary to stay up-to-date with developments in the field.

> The application of skills from field to field is the essence of transferable skills analysis.

"Legal training is broad training," says New York City career counselor Celia Paul. "I teach clients that they will be hired because of their skills and that it's up to them to translate their skills into something marketable." This chapter takes you through the first step of transferable skills analysis: the process of identifying the core skills you have developed as a law student or practicing lawyer, the ones you like to use and the ones you'll want to market to employers.

First let's look at the skills you develop simply by making it through a few classes in law school. (They're outlined in detail below.) By the time you graduate from law school, you've developed great analytical skills and good oral and written communication

Skills Developed in Law School

Reading Casebooks	digest large quantities of material	**Memo Writing**	clarify information
	learn technical jargon		communicate technical concepts
	read a lot		compare for accuracy and content
Classroom Attendance	concentrate		edit
	listen intently and thoughtfully		generate solutions
	deal with difficult people		proofread
	withstand or flourish in a highly competitive environment		research
			solve problems
	withstand pressure		write persuasively
	respond to challenges	**Moot Court**	listen critically and intently
Studying	discipline		speak cogently and persuasively
	exchange information and ideas with others		speak in public
	organize time and materials		think quickly on one's feet
	prioritize		articulate or advocate a position
	work with others	**Clinical Education**	negotiate
Briefing	analyze logically and in linear progression		active listening
	generalize ideas from extensive reading material		interpret for others
			convey complex notions in simple terms
	identify issues		meet deadlines
	interpret technical jargon		counsel or advise
	synthesize information		work in a team
	think critically		assist others with less education and knowledge

Data-Related Skills Developed by Lawyers

CASE MANAGEMENT

accurate memory for details

analyze

anticipate problems or needs

classify expertly

conceptualize

coordinate operations or data

discover similarities or dissimilarities

establish priorities among competing
   requirements

experiment with new approaches

file so as to facilitate retrieval

gather information

handle many tasks and responsibilities
   efficiently

innovate

interview individuals to obtain
   information

keep track of details

manage

memorize rules and procedures

organize

plan

plan on the basis of lessons
   from the past

recognize the need for, and locate,
   outside experts

recognize when more information is
   needed

research

see the big picture

strategize

summarize

synthesize

troubleshoot

OFFICE MANAGEMENT

allocate scarce financial resources

budget

maintain fiscal controls

project costs

OPEN NEW FILES

assimilate new data quickly

learn new things

read quickly and comprehensively

WORK PRODUCT

apply what others have developed to
   new situations

communicate technical information

compose

conceive new interpretations
   and approaches

consolidate

edit

interpret documents

keep others informed

make practical applications of
   theoretical ideas

persuade

persuasive writing

summarize

technical writing

update

People-Related Skills Developed by Lawyers

CASE/OFFICE MANAGEMENT

brainstorm

bring projects in on time and
   within budget

critique

delegate authority

develop projects

lead

make hard decisions

manage

prioritize

supervise

COURT APPEARANCES

act immediately on new information

deal well with the unexpected or
   critical event

decisive in emergencies

easily remember faces

improvise

make presentations

quickly size up situations

speak clearly, articulately and
   engagingly

PRACTICE DEVELOPMENT

collaborate

identify needs and solutions

network

reciprocate

sell

PRACTICE MANAGEMENT

continually seek more responsibility

follow through

organize time expertly

responsibility

self-direction

systematically accomplish tasks in
   order to obtain objectives

work well without supervision

SETTLE CASES

negotiate

persuade

sell a program or course of action
   to decision-makers

WORK WITH CLIENTS

allay fears

clarify values and goals of others

confront others with difficult
   personal matters

counsel

develop rapport and trust

disseminate information accurately

empathize

employ "active listening"

explain complicated theories or
   procedures in simple terms

gain cooperation among
   diverse interests

give professional advice

handle emotional outbursts

hone and use powers of observation

identify problems, needs and solutions

inspire others

intuit

keep confidences and secrets

perceive and assess the potential
   of others

resolve conflicts

train, teach, educate

skills. You also are conscious of time management and computer literacy, and have learned about dispute resolution and negotiation. This may not seem like much to you, coming from an environment where everyone around you shares these skills. But consider the situation of one frustrated employer in 1996. He wanted to pay $12 per hour to workers with just three qualifications: basic literacy, the ability to pass a drug screening test, and the willingness to show up at work five days per week on time. He never found enough candidates.

The practice of law hones the skills you developed in law school, and adds additional talents to your arsenal. A number of the data-related and people-related skills developed in law practice are listed on page 91 and 92.

You don't develop your transferable skills in a vacuum; you develop them through your work, leisure and volunteer experiences. To familiarize yourself with the skills you've developed, break down the tasks, cases and projects you've handled into the skills you used to complete the work. I'll illustrate by analyzing the task of taking the deposition of a medical expert. The main components of accomplishing that task are as follows:

- ▶ review file;
- ▶ consult partner about opposing counsel and the case;
- ▶ review the medical records;
- ▶ read articles about the medical problem;
- ▶ plan deposition questions;
- ▶ analyze questions asked by opposing counsel;
- ▶ make objections.

The core skills used to accomplish each part of the process were as follows:

- ▶ *review file:* assimilate new data quickly, read quickly and comprehensively.
- ▶ *consult partner about opposing counsel and the case:* collaborate; anticipate problems; identify problems, needs and solutions; recognize when more information is needed before making decisions; plan; come up with a strategy.
- ▶ *review the medical records:* learn medical terminology; read and understand medical records; extract and evaluate information; interpret medical terms.
- ▶ *read articles about the medical problem:* recognize the need for and locate outside experts.

▶ *plan deposition questions:* investigate, gather information.
▶ *analyze questions asked by opposing counsel:* apply standards to another's performance; make practical applications of theoretical ideas.
▶ *ask questions:* interview; pose technical questions; respond to unexpected answers.
▶ *make objections:* think quickly; apply standards to facts; explain.

Now it's your turn. Analyze the following tasks common to law practice in the same way, first breaking them down into their component parts and then locating the "generic" name for the skills used to complete each part of the process. (Refer to the preceding skills listings, and those in the next chapter on page 105.) Limit yourself to tasks you've actually performed. If you haven't yet worked as a lawyer or law clerk, analyze tasks from other jobs you've held, or from school or volunteer projects.

▶ Advising a corporate department manager
▶ Answering interrogatories
▶ Arguing an appeal or motion
▶ Attending the deposition of a client
▶ Litigating a jury trial
▶ Mediating a dispute
▶ Meeting with a client for the first time
▶ Negotiating an agreement
▶ Preparing a complaint
▶ Preparing a trial brief
▶ Preparing for trial
▶ Presenting a trial to the court
▶ Writing a contract
▶ Writing a legal research memorandum

Once you have the analytic process down, you'll want to compile a list of the core skills you've developed so far. Review the exercises you completed in Chapter 12, especially "My History of Achievement" and "Things I Really Love to Do." Compare those experiences to the lists of skills in this chapter and on page 105 of Chapter 14 and make a running list of the skills you identify.

Then sort the skills into levels of competency. You can place an asterisk next to those you perform particularly well, and a downward arrow next to those you can

Sample Skills Evaluation

PROFICIENT	COMPETENT	INEPT
reading	calculating	abstract analysis
public speaking	editing	keeping track of details
developing rapport	organizing	administering
coming up with ideas	technical writing	small tool work
explanatory writing	designing	coordinating
motivating	researching	detail work
synthesizing	supervising	planning
leading	implementing	
listening		

only stumble through. The rest will be considered average. Or create a chart like the one above.

The fact that you have a skill does not mean you ought to seek work that uses it. You'll do a better job and enjoy your work more if you focus on those skills you both enjoy using and can do well. The next part of transferable skills analysis is to determine which of the skills you've developed you'd really like to use.

Go back to your list of skills, and circle those you enjoy using. Refer to this list in the next chapter when you create your Ideal Job Grid.

The point of this analysis is to identify the skills you've acquired and the experiences that prove your competence. The next step of transferable skills analysis, described in Chapter 16, will be comparing the skills in your toolbox to those demanded by other types of work.

Creating Your
Ideal Job Grid

"Far and away the best prize that life offers is the chance to work hard at work worth doing."

—*Theodore Roosevelt, 26th president of the United States*

■ ■ ■

The next step of the self-assessment process is to take the results of the exercises you completed in the last two chapters and synthesize them into the components of the best work and work environment you can imagine. "I'll be lucky if I find a good job," you say. "What's the point of figuring out what would be ideal?" There are several good reasons. First, you'll broaden your notion of the fields that suit you and thereby multiply your options. You'll also create a complete picture of the work and work environment in which you thrive. That way, you'll avoid making a career move that avoids one annoyance while supplying others. Most important, you'll be better at articulating to potential employers your match with their needs.

> Your ideal job grid will multiply your options and clarify the best work and work environment for you.

The five-step process of creating your Ideal Job Grid takes several hours to complete. First, review the sample Ideal Job Grids that follow to get an idea of the end-product you want to create. Remember, this grid represents extremes—the very best qualities of the best work you could possibly have. (Some people prefer instead to look at the grid as a synthesis of the qualities they want in an ideal life.)

Then review the results of the exercises in the last two chapters as well as any career testing or prior self-assessment work you've completed. Make a note of words and phrases that appear repeatedly in the exercises, as well as those qualities that otherwise attract you. Then place those words and phrases in the most appropriate category. Please include interests, skills and other preferences even if you cannot imagine how you'd get paid to use them, or you are afraid using them would require you to change careers, go back to school, or take a pay cut.

To review from the last chapter:

- ▶ *Interests* are subject matters to which you are drawn, topics about which you read and inquire.
- ▶ *Skills* are the abilities you've developed.
- ▶ *Values* are the intangible guiding principles and goals that bring meaning to your work and motivate your involvement and commitment.
- ▶ *People* preferences refer to the kind of contact you'd like to have with others, both co-workers and clients, including the nature of the interaction you favor and how many others you prefer to work with at any one time.
- ▶ *Environment* involves both the physical and intangible aspects of the workplace itself: the office atmosphere, your work schedule, the aesthetics of the physical setting, the degree of freedom and flexibility in office management.

The first time through, you will probably have dozens of entries under some categories and none in others. The third step is to eliminate repetition by including any particular term only in one category. For example, creativity could be a talent of yours you list under skills, or a fascination with other people's creativity that you place in the interests box, or a preference to work with creative people that you'd place in the people box, or the kind of love of new ideas and things that makes your entire work meaningful and is therefore included as a "Must Have" value. If you have a hard time deciding in which of the boxes to place a quality, it probably belongs under values.

Avoid putting opposites of the same quality on both sides of the grid. For example, under "Environment," either indicate that you want a light and spacious atmosphere on the "Must Have" side or write on the "Must Avoid" side that you don't want a crowded, dark workplace, but do not include both.

After you have deleted repetitive entries, think about the remaining words and phrases. Delete any to which you respond neutrally, with two exceptions:

> ► Include any descriptors that emerged in a majority of the exercises even if you don't think they're that important to you.
> ► With respect to interests, include subject matters that are appealing but may not rise to the level of a "must." List up to a dozen interests you find appealing or would be happy to learn about.

Make certain that anything you include is a "must have"—an element that if absent would make your work feel unsatisfying or, on the "Must Avoid" side, if consistently there, would make it intolerable. The only exception to this rule, as previously stated, is that your interests do not have to rise to the level of a "must."

Refrain from including by-products such as "enjoying my work," "feeling like I'm contributing to society," "fulfillment," and "work that is meaningful to me." The assumption is that if you found work that contained all ingredients of an ideal position, those responses would naturally occur.

Avoid terms that can have different meanings to different people. For example, "professionalism" could as easily mean that you wish to wear a suit and tie and carry a briefcase as work in a highly ethical environment. Instead, choose the word or phrase that precisely conveys your requirements. (The sample Ideal Job Grid entries that follow might be helpful here.)

Finally, narrow your entries to no more than a dozen per category on the "Must Have" side, while making sure you list at least eight preferred interests, skills and values. Limit yourself to ten entries under each category on the "Must Avoid" side, but there are no minimum requirements on this side of the grid. If no strong preference stands out for a "Must Avoid," leave it blank. Notice that the grid does not include the level of compensation you require for your next position. Assume you would earn as much money as you need to support yourself and your family.

interests, skills, values, people, environment

Ideal Job Grid		
	MUST HAVE	MUST AVOID
Interests		
Skills		
Values		
People		
Environment		

Sample Ideal Job Grid #1		
	MUST HAVE	**MUST AVOID**
Interests	medicine/health human behavior children movies/TV fiction & self-help books fads/trends	physics advanced math military strategy
Skills	idea generation sharing insights advising listening public speaking reading, writing & editing designing or creating identifying root issues	sole responsibility for clerical tasks purely abstract pursuits keeping track of details
Values	autonomy variety innovation tangible goals or products focus on a "cause" influence	"win at all costs" attitude doing it only for the money
People	communicative growing cooperative working independently but with others around	closed-minded adults isolation
Environment	flexibility natural light complex but harmonious mobility	smoky air rigidly competing deadlines

Sample Ideal Job Grid #2		
	MUST HAVE	**MUST AVOID**
Interests	recreation/the outdoors real estate business new things publishing	religion mental health
Skills	problem solving building or repairing creativity business start-up analyzing planning	purely theoretical work repetitive or procedural work people management
Values	variety the unusual challenge competition curiosity	
People	smart humorous upbeat supportive appreciative	emotionally trying situations women superiors incompetence autocratic leaders
Environment	informal flexible hours seasonally Western Washington in the summer	fast-paced totally outdoors

Sample Ideal Job Grid Entries

All samples are suggested for the "must have" column. (If you're like other lawyers, you probably have much less trouble figuring out what you prefer to avoid!) The lists are long, but they're certainly not exhaustive.

A Note on Interest in "Travel"

Many lawyers list "travel" as one of their "interests." Before you place the word in the interest column, explore what it is about travel that appeals to you. Is it the opportunity to learn about *other cultures* (interest: cultural diversity, foreign cultures) or simply to *learn new things* or to *adapt* (both valuable skills)? Do you crave the *mobility* (environment), the *variety* (value or environment), or the *time away from work* (environment)? Or are you interested in the travel industry itself? If it's the latter, then list travel in the interest column. If it's any of the others, or some other reason, place that characteristic in the appropriate category.

TRAVEL
cultural diversity?
learn new things?
mobility? variety?
time away from work?

Interests

accounting	current events	human relations	movies	self-help
acting	design	human rights	music	skiing
animal rights	ecology	indigenous	music therapy	social issues
animals	economics	cultures	musicians	social justice
anthropology	education	information	mysteries	social science
antiques	electronics	inner city	mythology	sociopathic
architecture	entertaining	problems	nature	behavior
art	environment	insurance	nutrition	software
astrophysics	fads & trends	intellectual	organizational	applications
athletics	fantasy	property	psychology	spirituality
bankruptcy	fashion	interior design/	other cultures	sports
bicycling	fiction	decorating	outdoors	swimming
books	finance	international law	parenting	technology
business	fine arts and	inventions	people	television
career choices	artists	investments	philosophy	the decision-
children	fitness	irony	photography	making process
civil rights	food	issues of the	physics	the past
classical ballet	foreign cultures	elderly	physiology	the unusual
community	foreign relations	journalism	poetry	toys
activism	foreign trade	jurisprudence	political satire	travel industry
computers	furniture	labor law	politics	wilderness
constitutional	gardening	language	poverty law	women's issues
law	group dynamics	law	psychology	words
consumer	health	legal theory	public issues	work safety
protection	history	lifestyles	public policy	youth
cooking	history of law	literature	publishing	
crafts	horses	magazines	religion	
criminal law	housing	math	residential real	
criminal	how things work	mechanical	estate	
psychology	human behavior	things	rhetoric	
criminality	human	medicine	science	
culinary arts	motivation	modern jazz	science fiction	
cultures	human potential	morality	securities	

103

A Note about Wanting to Avoid "Selling"

Do you believe that you must avoid sales in an ideal career? If so, think about what "selling" really means.

Selling is the skill of making clear the connection between a product or service and the needs of a potential buyer. In other words, it is the art of persuasion—a skill for which you've been trained and which you probably employ daily.

It's probably not persuasion that you want to avoid. So what is it? Trying to force a product or service upon someone who may not want it? Not believing in the value of the product or service you're hawking? Cold-calling by telephone? Being pushy and abrasive or untrustworthy? There *are* salespeople who sell in all of those ways. The good ones, though, believe in their product, target only consumers who might benefit from it, actually have customers come to them, and build credibility and sales through their low-key style and integrity. Would you object to selling like that?

For others, the aversion to sales is more a fear of rejection, knowing that most sales representatives are told no a lot more than yes. Unfortunately, this aversion can interfere with your effectiveness in making a transition.

You may miss out on some appealing career options by not examining your prejudice against sales. The best example is selling interactive computer software systems, a fast-growing niche in the business market. This type of work is suitable for an analytical, systems-oriented problem-solver, with an ability to understand and explain technical concepts in user-friendly ways. A sale results when you make clear that the product's design and its price will benefit the company—the same approach you use in negotiating a settlement or attracting a new client.

I urge you to analyze your aversion to sales before relegating it to the "must avoid" side of your grid.

SELLING
Must I avoid
selling?

Skills

achieve goals	create solutions	focused	manage people	public speaking
act on gut	creative writing	concentration	manage projects	quick thinking
reactions	creativity	follow rules	mechanical	read
active listening	critical thinking	forecast	tinkering	remember details
adapt to new	critical/precise	fundraising	mediate	repair
situations	writing	gather	memory work	research
adjudicate	curiosity	information	mentor	resolve conflict
administer	decision-making	generate	monitor	resourcefulness
advise	decisiveness	enthusiasm	monitor details	review
agility	dependability	guide	motivate	information
analyze	design	identify issues	musicality	see potential
analyze	detail work	identify problems	negotiate	possibilities
information	develop expertise	imagination	notice details	sell
answer questions	develop intimacy	implement	nurture	share
assist leaders	develop	implement	object	share insights
athletic ability	programs	projects	observation	simplify
attention to	develop rapport	influence others	objectivity	complexity
details	diplomacy	initiate	obtain	size-up accurately
brainstorm	directness	innovate	cooperation	speak
budget	discipline	inspire others	oral advocacy	stage a
build	dispassionate	instruct	oral	production
calculate	analysis	integrate	communication	strategize
calm others	edit	components	organize	summarize
close observation	educate	intellectual	organize groups	supervise
coach	efficiency	tinkering	paint	support
communicate	empathy	interview	perceive	synthesize
compose	empirical	intuit	perform	take inventory
computer work	observation	investigate	persevere	take the initiative
conceptualize	empirical research	lead	persist	teach
conflict resolution	empower others	learn new things	persuade	team build
connect people	entertain	learn quickly	physical strength	theorize
to resources	establish rapport	listen	plan	versatility
consensus	evaluate	logical thinking	plan concrete	visual awareness
building	exercise common	long-range	action	win confidence
contemplation	sense	planning	practicality	work under
coordinate	experiment	make people	pragmatism	pressure
cost-	explain	laugh	prioritize	work with
consciousness	expressiveness	make quick	problem solve	animals
counsel	eye/hand	decisions	process	work with hands
count	coordination	manage	information	write
create	facilitate	manage details	provide expertise	
create documents	film	manage money	provide feedback	

A Dozen Skills Preferred by Lawyers in Transition

I reviewed the Ideal Job Grids of over 200 graduates of my career evaluation workshops to come up with a list of a dozen common "building-block" skills preferred by lawyers. I use the term "building block" deliberately. Problem solving was the most frequently mentioned skill preference, but that skill is actually a compilation of other basic skills: analyzing, researching, organizing and planning, and often speaking, writing, advising, persuading and developing rapport.

The 12 basic skills were, in order of preference:

Analyze (including evaluate, clarify and interpret). Every job listed in this book demands the skill of analysis; indeed, I cannot think of a position—or an activity in life—that does not. This preference, therefore, really reflects more what you like to analyze—abstract, theoretical issues or more concrete and structural problems—and how—using common sense, logic or intuition, or having time to study the problem in depth versus having to size up a situation quickly for an on-the-spot solution.

Organize (including synthesize, conceptualize and simplify). This skill usually refers to the ability to take something that has been randomly arranged and put it into better order. The "something" being organized might be people, data, objects or time. You may enjoy creating a new system, or maintaining an old one. Some prefer to tackle highly complex projects; others like to keep the routine moving along smoothly and predictably.

Write (including read and edit). The writing can be creative, technical, investigative, reportage, or persuasive. The pieces can be of any length, from snippets to tomes. You might enjoy going into depth or remaining superficial. Writing style should also be considered: Do you prefer writing with a deadline, having all the time in the world to express yourself completely and accurately, or taking moments here and there to dash off a quick thought?

Create (including innovate, design, generate ideas and brainstorm). Many lawyers associate creativity only with the arts, such as painting and fiction writing, but problem solving of all types calls upon this skill. Do you prefer coming up with your own ideas or to implement the ideas of others? Do you like to start projects, creating something from nothing, or to deal with specific issues as they arise in a project that someone else initiated? Do you have more fun figuring out how to get something going than keeping it going?

Advise (including counsel, coach, mentor, explain, and pass on knowledge or insight). The advice can be conveyed in writing or aloud, one-on-one or to a group. It can be personal, technical, abstract or specific. The common theme is that you are regarded as someone with enough expertise to be helpful; the receiver of the advice wants the benefit of your wisdom and experience.

Research (including investigate, interview and gather facts or information). This skill stems from your curiosity and love of learning, but the preference often falls into one of two categories: oral versus written and personal versus statistical or factual. You may like to spend hours in the library or on-line gathering data; you may prefer to hear the stories of many people. It's all research.

Plan (including develop a strategy). Anyone who likes to plan enjoys analysis, but analyzers don't always like to plan. Planning requires foresight, the ability to anticipate and prepare for future contingencies. It demands a thoughtful approach to problem solving, weighing the possibilities and balancing resources. Planners have a deliberative rather than a spontaneous approach to life.

Speak (including performance and public speaking). The size of the crowd may vary, but by and large, those who enjoy speaking thrive when they're in the public eye. The topic may be humorous, entertaining, educational, political or religious; the style may be extemporaneous or carefully planned. But the goal is almost always to influence, teach or inspire.

Persuade (including advocate, sell, negotiate, inspire, and motivate). This is the main skill you learn in law school; it's odd that it isn't higher on the list of preferences. You can persuade orally or in writing. Some view the skill as something close to coercion; others see it rather as motivating others to follow the most reasonable path.

Manage (including coordinate details or people, supervise, monitor, administer and pay attention to details). Planners often like to manage, because the two skills require the same foresight. The big difference between the two is the degree to which attention to detail is required. Planners notice the detail in order to come up with the plan; managers must keep track of the detail in order to keep progressing. Some only like to manage people, others only data. Project managers often oversee both.

Develop rapport (including empathize and active listening). This is the preference that shows you're a people person. You prefer to relate to others on a feeling basis, making connections on a gut rather than an intellectual level. You may want to use the skill in a counseling session, to market a product or service, or to generate enthusiasm. The goal is always to build trust.

Observe (including listen, perceive and visual awareness). You must observe to develop rapport, but you can also observe without developing rapport. This talent involves either noticing details in your surroundings or reading body language and other non-verbal communications. Trial lawyers use this skill to read juries and to determine whether their message is getting across. Negotiators and mediators must be good observers to uncover the unspoken positions that are impeding agreement.

Values

achievement	control over	helping others	moderation	safety
action	decisions	high drama	morality	security
adventure	cooperation	high profile	novelty	self-expression
aesthetics	courage	high risk	order	sensuality
alleviate	creativity	holistic view	originality	shared
suffering	diversity	honesty	personal growth	enjoyment
authenticity	effectiveness	hope	playfulness	sharing
autonomy	ethics	improvement	pleasure	simplicity
balanced lifestyle	excellence	independence	power	social relevance
beauty	excitement	individuality	practicality	social utility
cause-orientation	expertise	influence	predictability	solitude
challenge	fairness	innovation	prestige	spontaneity
change	family	integrity	productivity	stability
client-centered	flexibility	intellectual	push personal	structure
closure	focus	challenge	limits	tangible results
comfort	forthrightness	intellectual	relationships	the unusual
competence	freedom	stimulation	religious	usefulness
complexity	gaiety	justice	conviction	variety
concrete goals	hands-on	knowledge	respect	wholesomeness
conformity	harmony	loyalty	responsibility	
connection	health	measurable	risk	
control	helping a cause	results	routine	

Do You Want Independence or Autonomy?

Independence, according to Webster's, is the quality or state of not being dependent as in not subject to control by others, not affiliated with a larger controlling unit, not requiring or relying on something else and not looking to others for guidance in conduct. Autonomy, on the other hand, means the quality or state of being self-governing, i.e., having control or rule over oneself.

Many lawyers initially define their desire for self-governance as independence, but upon further reflection realize they really value autonomy. They want to be able to control their own environment, make decisions in their work based on their own notions of right and wrong, but want to work collaboratively or at least with others around to share ideas and the workload. When you're deciding which value best reflects your preference, remember that independence is a more broad-based desire to be free from the constraints of working with others, either above or below you. Autonomy is more limited: the desire to control your own work environment and decision-making on your own projects, but not necessarily to work alone or to have sole responsibility and power to affect the course of a project or case.

People

adversial roles	dependable	insightful	practical	tactful
appreciative	eccentric	intelligent	reasonable	team work
be in authority	enthusiastic	interactive	relaxed	trustworthy
bohemian	fair	large institution	reserved	undemanding
business-like	flexible	leader	respect	urbane
camaraderie	forthright	liberal	differences	value driven
collaborative	frequent	lively	respectful	well-informed
committed	interaction	loyal	responsible	wholesome
compassionate	friendly	mature	self-aware	women in
competence	gentle	meet new	sense of humor	authority
congenial	genuine	people often	sensitive	work alone
considerate	goal-oriented	mutual respect	shared values	work
cooperative	great minds	one-on-one	small group	collaboratively
creative	honest	open	smart	work
dedicated	humor	people-oriented	sophisticated	independently
democratic	independent	positive	supportive	

Do You Want to Be Part of a Team or Just to Have Other People Around?

Webster's defines teamwork as work done by several associates, each performing a part, but all subordinating their personal prominence to the efficiency of the whole. This type of work arrangement is unusual among lawyers. Lawyers tend to organize themselves in projects where one, usually senior, lawyer is responsible for guiding and controlling the effort and everyone else works in a lesser role. The senior lawyer takes all the credit for a job well done and usually takes the heat for failure. This is not teamwork.

Some lawyers confuse the notion of teamwork with a preference to have competent help in completing tasks, to work with other people around, or to be able to brainstorm and discuss cases. Determine whether you in fact are willing to subordinate your need for recognition or prestige to the success of the group before deciding that teamwork is one of your preferences.

Environment			
a lot going on	frequent travel	predictable	steady work pace
access to the outdoors	friendly competition	private office	stylish
active	full days	private spaces	support staff
aesthetically pleasing	group setting	regular hours	telecommuting
automated	growth encouraged	relaxed	time for exercise
calm	informal	respect for diversity	time for reflection
casual	intense	rural	uncomplicated
changing	light	schedule control	uncrowded
close to nature	long vacations	security	unstructured
competitive	long-term projects	semi-arid	upscale
consistent work flow	mobility	sense of community	urban
constant work flow	natural light	short-term projects	visually stimulating
control over time	okay to be average	smoke free	well-defined duties
commitment	ordered	social	well-equipped office
discrete projects	organized	sophisticated	wide open space
fast-paced	outdoors	spacious	work at home
flexible	peaceful	stable	work at own pace
formal	physical activity	state-of-the-art	

The Work-Hours Question

With demands escalating in the practice of law, many of you yearn for work that gives you more control over your time. You might define it in terms of a part-time schedule or working a steady 40-hour week. Regular hours, regular vacations or taking comp time might be your goals. Again, consider carefully what you want.

Would you mind occasional long hours and intense pressure if you loved the work and believed in the goal? Or do you want a set schedule with no variation in workload, pace, pressure or time commitment? Is it okay to work long hours as long as you get to pick the hours and where you perform the work? Do you like the idea of working on projects that demand a lot of time and attention for three or four months and are followed by a similar period off? Concentrate on the rhythms you prefer rather than merely reacting to the demands of the typical workplace.

RESEARCH

An Overview of Alternative Careers

"There is around and about us a constant beckoning world, one which insinuates itself into our lives, arousing and creating appetite where there was little or none before. We choose a thing because it just happened to be beneath our noses at that moment in time. It is not necessarily what we want, but it is interesting, and the longer we gaze at it, the more compelling it becomes."

—*Clarissa Pinkola Estes, author*

■ ■ ■

What can you do with your law degree and practice experience besides practicing law? Truly, the options are almost unlimited. Over 700 positions are listed in Appendix 4 with job descriptions for some in Appendix 5. None of the positions listed in Appendix 4 are jobs that I believe someone with a law degree or legal background could or should be able to get. Instead, they are all options that actual law school graduates have secured. For inspiration, this chapter highlights some of the more common nontraditional ways lawyers and recent graduates make use of their legal backgrounds inside, outside and around the law.

If you're still trying to figure out what you want to do next based on what's hot or where the opportunities are, consider these sobering facts. *Working Woman* magazine predicted in 1992 that opportunities in bankruptcy and environmental law would carry the legal profession through the end of the century. By August 1996, those two specialties were the only ones declining in a booming legal market according to *The National Law Journal*. At

> The options for what you can do with your law degree besides practicing law are almost unlimited.

the same time, both *The National Law Journal* and *USA Today* touted intellectual property and employment law as the specialties to pursue. Firms were fully staffed in employment law by 1998. I suspect that intellectual property needs will taper off in a few years as well.

A better perspective on "hot" specialties is provided by a 1996 *National Law Journal* study of big-firm practice over a 17-year period. Employment law was hot in 1979 and 1995 but low throughout the middle period. Real estate practice rose steadily from 1979 to 1989 and then fell just as steadily. Litigation was the only practice area that remained stable and large, at almost one-third of all practitioners.

As you read through this chapter, remember that the best career direction for you has to do less with what's booming than what you're capable of doing and impassioned enough to pursue at all cost.

Nontraditional Law Practice Alternatives

The real news in law practice opportunity comes from emerging practice trends like contract (or temporary) lawyering, independent general counsel arrangements, and legal research services.

Contract lawyers perform legal services for other lawyers on an intermittent or impermanent basis. Their prominence in the legal profession coincides with tremendous growth in the entire temporary services industry. Many large and specialty law firms hire contract lawyers, often through placement agencies, as temporary associates, paying them on an hourly basis to work full-time (that is, overtime!) in the law firm for a minimum of three months or until they are no longer needed. Other contract lawyers work on a project, a rush or an as-needed basis with a number of different solo and small firm practitioners, government agencies or in-house legal departments. Neither the contract lawyer nor the hiring lawyer has any guarantee that the relationship will continue beyond the agreed-upon period or project.

Independent general counsel (also known as part-time in-house counsel) are private practitioners who contract with a number of corporations to provide in-house legal services on a less than full-time basis. They usually charge hourly rates significantly lower than those of comparable outside counsel, or a guaranteed monthly retainer, and work on-site at the corporations.

Legal research services contract with law firms to produce memoranda on requested points of law. The research may or may not be generated by lawyers; sometimes a computer-research specialist or law student performs the services.

Working Within the Legal
Profession as a Non-Practitioner

The rapid growth of the profession, technological advances, and changes in client expectations have provided tremendous opportunity to law school graduates who want to work within the profession without practicing law.

In some law firms, former practitioners with business skills have created niches for themselves as managers and office administrators. Those with marketing instincts have taken positions as directors of practice development, client services or marketing. To pursue interests in education, training and human resources, still others now manage in-house professional development programs or associate recruiting.

An entire industry has emerged of service providers to the profession, many founded, operated or staffed by former lawyers. Any edition of *The National Law Journal* or the *ABA Journal* will offer dozens of examples: computer software vendors, contract lawyer placement agencies, and jury, marketing or management consultants, among others.

In 1988, the *New York Times* called legal publishing a "new growth industry." Some former practitioners have taken advantage of this explosion by publishing, writing for, or distributing newsletters and journals catering to legal specialties. Conventional legal publishers and legal research services also hire former practitioners in departments as diverse as sales, management, marketing, training and acquisitions. We've also witnessed dramatic growth in the mediation field. Former (and current) practicing lawyers act as mediators, and participate in the training, marketing and administration of alternative dispute resolution services. At the current time, though, there are more lawyers who want to be mediators than the market will support. See the ADR section of Appendix 4 for more information about the limitations of, and alternatives to, the mediation field.

Providing Legal Information to the General Public

Lawyers have also designed products and services that explain legal issues and procedures to the lay public. Examples include do-it-yourself divorce and estate planning books and software programs, seminars that explain the defamation laws to journalists, and systems designed for intellectual property protection.

Those who wish to teach, or speak more and write less, might move into the burgeoning "preventive law" seminar business. Former practicing lawyers are frequently hired to teach corporate employees to deal with a diverse workforce, avoid sexual harassment and learn to resolve conflicts without involving the legal staff.

Educational Administration

Law schools are feeling the pinch of competition. Students now demand more services for their tuition dollars, hence the growth in law school career services and counseling offices. The schools also must develop better relationships with alumni to encourage their financial contributions. Positions in career services, alumni relations, fundraising, and CLE program planning are plentiful.

General university administration also offers opportunities. Universities want to limit the number of EEO and ADA complaints that end up in court by hiring investigators to look into the complaints and work out "reasonable accommodations" with the professor and the student. Other aspects of risk management, human resources, technology transfer and contract negotiation and administration also provide spots for those with legal backgrounds.

Regulation or Enforcement Specialist Within Business or Government

Similar positions can be found in the corporate and public sectors. As the law has become more complex, the demand has grown for lawyers to act as interpreters for non-lawyers. Some lawyers find positions inside corporations or the government in which their familiarity with the law is used on a daily basis. For example, Tom, a sixth-year associate in a large law firm, secured a position as a training administrator with an aircraft manufacturer in which he ensures that federal and state health, safety and environmental regulations are being met by the company's numerous training departments. In this job, he uses the skills he developed in trial practice: the ability to understand the intent of the regulations, to organize materials for training consortiums, and to mediate discussions among groups of people with vastly different opinions and agendas.

In general, corporations are interested in lawyers with knowledge relevant to compliance and enforcement functions (e.g., EEOC, ADA, affirmative action, environmental or other regulatory matters, employee benefits, internal ethics consultant, labor relations manager). Purchasing agent and contract administration positions are also prevalent in government offices, especially civilian positions with the military. Corporations and federal, state and local governments all want to limit the number of suits filed against them, thereby reducing legal fees and the disruption caused by employee involvement in the matter. Many employ former practicing lawyers in-house to intervene in conflicts before they reach the point of a lawsuit. These entities also hire lawyers for litigation oversight.

Using Your Creativity

Joyce Laher, Director of Career Services at Hamline University School of Law, and Gina Sauer, Assistant Dean for Career Services at William Mitchell College of Law, both in the Minneapolis-St. Paul area, surveyed over 50 lawyers who followed nontraditional career paths. The skills used most frequently in their new positions were:

▶ identification of issues;
▶ presentation skills;
▶ writing;
▶ negotiation or mediation;
▶ persuasion;
▶ fact analysis;
▶ ability to work independently;
▶ ability to distinguish
cases;
▶ teamwork;
▶ counseling; and
▶ awareness of risk or liability.

These 11 skills coincide rather closely with the dozen most preferred by lawyers in transition (listed in Chapter 14 on pages 106-108) with one significant exception: Although the fourth most desired skill among lawyers who wish to change their work situation is creativity, the 50 lawyers in nontraditional fields did not seem to call upon it much in their new endeavors.

Some people associate creativity only with the arts. Others see creativity in problem solving, systems design, case management and project development. If you try to express your creativity through the law, you'll be most content in a practice with frequent jury trials or one that concentrates in a rapidly developing area of law.

New admittees 15 to 20 years ago entered a profession exploding with creative thought. Many visualized an unending future of advances in consumer protection, civil rights and social welfare reform through the legal process. By the 1980's, however, this kind of creative thought seemed more common in the mergers and acquisitions, bankruptcies and workouts of the business world. Now, the best areas for creative work are intellectual property, computer law, and international law.

Lawyers in other specialties are often motivated to look outside the law to express their creativity. You can follow the lead of lawyers who flex their creative muscles by designing educational seminars and tapes, publishing special interest newsletters on legal topics, or writing mystery novels in their spare time. You can also start your own law practice or business—in or outside of law—where creative problem solving in marketing and management can make the difference between success and failure.

Nonprofit Management

The growing number of practicing lawyers, combined with new specialization and mandatory continuing education requirements, have led to increases in bar association size and numbers. Every new bar group or function provides opportunities for practitioners to manage or supervise the operations. Discipline, CLE, attorney assistance, mentoring, public affairs and lobbying functions are frequently handled by lawyers.

Nonprofit organizations outside of the legal profession often hire lawyers as directors or project managers, or as specialists in development or planned giving. Mark spent six years working in a Manhattan insurance defense firm, and one year as a lawyer in city government, then accepted a planned-giving position in the development office of New York University. He now designs testamentary plans which maximize benefits to both the donor and the beneficiary. Although Mark had no experience in estate planning before this job, he impressed his new employers with his ability to learn what was needed, a skill he developed in handling a wide variety of court cases.

Leaving the Law Behind

It's hard to imagine a career that wouldn't use any of the background we develop as lawyers. Those who return to school to become high school teachers make use of the insight, self-discipline, and knowledge they developed as lawyers. Even a couple of Pacific Northwest entrepreneurs who decided to lead mountain treks using llamas called upon their legal experience to navigate the licensing process.

Those lawyers who move the farthest from the profession, though, seem to gravitate toward the following fields and positions:

- ▶ Entrepreneurial ventures, ranging from restaurants like the California Pizza Kitchen chain developed by two lawyers in Southern California, to retail operations like the Sharper Image, founded by former practicing lawyer Richard Thalheimer, to publishing successes like Nolo Press and the Zagat (restaurant rating) guides.
- ▶ Communications in areas as diverse as publishing, editing, writing, and reporting for newspapers, magazines, television, radio and public relations companies, not to speak of well known successes like John Grisham and producer David E. Kelley.
- ▶ Real estate development, property management, construction, remodeling and interior decoration led by well-known developers Jim Rouse and Andrew Cuomo.

▶ Teaching, in both public and private schools and at all levels, from
elementary school through graduate level work.

▶ Counseling, with or without an advanced degree and focusing on
individual psychotherapy, family or career issues.

As I said at the outset, these opportunities are only a starting point. The possibilities are almost limitless if you let your preferences guide you into the marketplace and use your skill and sophistication to get ahead. I recently heard a story about a new admittee who loves working with her hands and creating a tangible finished product as proof of her efforts. She took a position in a picture framing shop to supplement her earnings while building a contract practice. A few months later, she was promoted to manager of the shop and stopped marketing herself as a contract lawyer. Her employer was amazed at how fast she learned, how responsible she was and how well she understood business management. She attributes the development of all of those qualities to her legal education and training.

Working with
Your Ideal Job Grid

"I have frequently seen people become neurotic when they content themselves with inadequate or wrong answers to the questions of life. They seek position, marriage, reputation, outward success or money, and remain unhappy and neurotic even when they have attained what they were seeking. Such people are usually confined within too narrow a spiritual horizon. Their life has not sufficient content, sufficient meaning. If they are enabled to develop into more spacious personalities, the neurosis generally disappears."

—*Carl G. Jung, psychiatrist*

■ ■ ■

If you had a clear notion of the direction you wanted to head before you started the self-assessment process, and your introspection still points that way, you can skip this chapter and move on to the information-gathering process in the next section.

If you haven't a clue what to do with your Ideal Job Grid, give yourself time to acclimate to your new self-image, especially if it diverges from your lawyer or law student persona. Then, make a list of trusted friends and colleagues, show them your Ideal Job Grid, and follow a script like that suggested in "I'd Appreciate Some Input" on the next page. You might also present your Ideal Job Grid to a career or vocational counselor for the same kind of input. Keep a record of all the responses.

> Make sure your Ideal Job Grid depicts what you want and not what you think is realistic.

Part of the purpose of this exercise is to check the accuracy of your grid. If the suggestions are a little off the mark, you've omitted or misstated a few elements. If you feel lukewarm (or downright repelled) by the suggestions made, then your grid depicts not what you want but what you think is realistic, or what you believe you should enjoy, or what you suspect you could be paid well to do. If your grid is either slightly or seriously off-base, revise it until the suggestions it elicits energize and uplift you.

Then, concentrating primarily on the skills, values and interests that constitute an ideal environment for you, review the lists of jobs in Appendix 4 and highlight any that match your requirements or appeal to you. Remember to evaluate the possibilities

I'd Appreciate Some Input

My Background

I've practiced law for five years, mostly in commercial and tax areas. I hated trial work; I also worked in the legal department of a corporation.

During law school I worked at a small consulting firm, doing environmental, education and organizational development work. My job involved a lot of research; it also involved brainstorming, creating fun exercises as educational tools, and creating a product like a report, manual or contract proposal. The job often had tight deadlines and crazy hours, followed by time to goof off. I look on those times more favorably than any I've had since becoming a lawyer.

My Ideal Job

I like a fair amount of independence combined with some real teamwork. I'd like to spend one-third of my time on research (quiet, thinking time); one-third with a small group of creative, constructive, secure people where we would be developing each other's ideas and editing each other's writing; and one-third producing some sort of product—something tangible I can look at and say, "I helped put that together and made it work."

Other Factors

I avoid telephones. I don't like driving and would prefer to walk to work or commute a short distance by public transportation. I may be slow, but I'm also creative. I see humor in most situations.

How You Can Help?

What types of job should I consider? What types of businesses should I contact? Do you know anyone I should contact in the areas you've suggested? May I tell them who referred me? Thanks!

based on your assessment of your strengths, desires and goals, not on expediency or a sense of resignation to the inevitable.

You might also want to review one of the following VGM Career Horizons books if its title corresponds with the spirit of your Ideal Job Grid:

▶ *Careers for Bookworms & Other Literary Types;*
▶ *Careers for Computer Buffs & Other Technological Types;*
▶ *Careers for Culture Lovers & Other Artsy Types;*
▶ *Careers for Environmental Types & Others Who Respect the Earth;*
▶ *Careers for Film Buffs & Other Hollywood Types;*
▶ *Careers for Good Samaritans & Other Humanitarian Types;*
▶ *Careers for Gourmets & Others Who Relish Food;*
▶ *Careers for History Buffs & Others Who Learn from the Past;*
▶ *Careers for High Energy People & Other Go-Getters;*
▶ *Careers for Financial Mavens & Other Money Movers;*
▶ *Careers for Talkative Types & Others with the Gift of Gab;*
▶ *Careers for Cybersurfers & Other Online Types;*
▶ *Careers for Travel Buffs & Other Restless Types;*
▶ *Careers for Writers & Others Who Have a Way with Words.*

You can also refer to *The Dictionary of Occupational Titles,* a U.S. Department of Labor publication found in most public libraries (explained more fully in the side bar on the next page.) It lists some 35,000 jobs in 300 occupational categories. There are also books listed in Appendix 3 that contain descriptions of a broad range of jobs and careers.

As you're investigating the broad possibilities, compile a list of the jobs that might satisfy the requirements of your job grid. Then pick six to eight ideas that most appeal to you and research them according to the instructions in the next chapter.

The DOT

The *Dictionary of Occupational Titles (DOT)* classifies jobs and assigns each a three-digit identification number based on levels of skill required in each of three categories: data, people and things. "Data" refers to the worker's relationship with information. "People" refers to the role the worker holds in relationship to others. "Things" are machines, tools, and other instruments necessary to complete the worker's job tasks. The *DOT* classifies thousands of different jobs in terms of the highest level of functional expertise required for the position.

The three scales are as follows:

DATA	0	**Synthesizing**
	1	Coordinating
	2	Analyzing
	3	Compiling
	4	Computing
	5	Copying
	6	Comparing
PEOPLE	0	**Mentoring**
	1	Negotiating
	2	Instructing
	3	Supervising
	4	Directing
	5	Persuading
	6	Speaking/Signaling
	7	Serving
	8	Taking Instructions/Helping
THINGS	0	**Setting Up**
	1	Precision Working
	2	Operating/Controlling
	3	Driving/Operating
	4	Manipulating
	5	Tending
	6	Feeding/Offbearing
	7	Handling

According to the DOT's classification, most lawyers display high skill levels when dealing with data and people, but operate at a much lower level with things. So "lawyer" is categorized as both 107 and 117. 107 implies that some lawyers coordinate data (1), mentor people (0), and handle things (7). Lawyers categorized as 117 (all except trial lawyers according to the *DOT*), negotiate with, rather than mentor, others.

As you can see from their characterization of the work of lawyers, the *DOT*'s evaluation of job functions is not completely current or accurate. Most lawyers would argue that they synthesize data (0) in order to perform any case analysis. And with computers in many lawyers' offices, their relationship with "things" has probably moved to the level of "operating/controlling."

To use the *DOT*, look up jobs with numerical evaluations similar to those in law, or that reflect the highest skill level in each category you'd prefer to use. Other 107's include director of religious activities, chief psychologist, dean of students, clinical sociologist and foreign student advisor. Examples of other 117's are academic dean, hotel management, athletic director, financial aid officer, trust officer and manager of a Christmas tree farm.

Researching
Your Options

"Knowledge is of two kinds. We know a subject ourselves, or we know where we can find information upon it."

—Samuel Johnson, novelist

■ ■ ■

Now that you have worked through the self-assessment process and generated a list of job options inspired by your Ideal Job Grid, it's time to narrow your focus to the one or two fields that most intrigue you. At this point, though, you might not know enough about the options you've gathered to decide what interests you most—or whether you ought to be interested at all! The next step is to research those options that appeal to you enough to want to learn more about them.

> Over a third of the jobs of the future do not exist today.

As you progress through this step, keep in mind these predictions: In the next ten years, more than half of all existing jobs will change fundamentally, and 30 percent of all current jobs will be eliminated. More important, over a third of the jobs of the future do not exist today; they will reflect changes in technology, or deal with concepts and products that are now being developed or that may only be a glimmer in someone's imagination. An example of such change is the law library. "The law firm library may become a casualty of the information age," said *The National Law Journal* on October 2, 1995. "Indeed, the ease of access to information brought about by networked CD-ROM technology and online services may render the traditional conception of the library obsolete."

You can avoid being left behind by new developments, and ride in with new industries (much like those who entered the computer software field less than two decades ago), by following your interests rather than pursuing what you perceive to be the existing opportunities.

Written Research

The first place to look is the public library or the Internet. You'll find a wealth of information on any field of interest in websites, books, periodicals, anthologies, and sometimes in special files maintained in the business department of your local library. Resources particular to individual fields are identified in Appendix 4. Those that are more general are listed in Appendix 2 and 3.

Pay particular attention to the professional associations in your areas of interest. These groups serve as both clearinghouses of information (newsletters, magazines, journals, employment guides and seminars) and job-search vehicles (by announcements of job vacancies, job banks, and networking opportunities). Reading the association newsletters and reviewing their program announcements may give you a preliminary sense of whether the subject matter and issues facing those working in this field genuinely interest you. Larger associations are topically referenced in Appendix 4. The *Encyclopedia of Associations,* referenced in Appendix 3, is carried by most public libraries and provides thousands of other leads.

To brush up on effective research techniques, refer to the electronic job search books cited in Appendix 3 or to *Researching Your Way to a Good Job: How to Find and Use Information on Industries, Companies, Jobs and Careers* by Karmen Crowther.

Anything published in books or even weekly magazines will be less up-to-date (especially in an era of electronic communication) than discussions with individuals currently working in your targeted field. You can participate or "lurk" in professional discussion groups on the Internet to get an idea of the issues currently facing your field(s) of interest. Attending programs sponsored by local chapters of national organizations will also help you determine whether the industry is as you expected it to be, or whether you have some misconceptions about its scope and function. It is also important, though, to talk directly to those who work in the industry. This step of the research process is known as "informational interviewing."

Informational Interviewing

An informational interview is an opportunity to learn about a field of interest, one specific person's job duties, or a business environment. It is not a veiled plea for employment. It is also not intended to result in a job with that person or firm (although sometimes it does). Your invitation to talk should be based on your genuine need to know more about a career field before determining what you want to do and where you want to work.

Informational interviewing not only helps you determine what direction to head, it also has proved to be one foundation of successful job-hunting. When Richard Bolles and John Crystal studied job hunters in the early 1970's, they discovered that the most successful had interviewed lots of people simply for information before they ever went out on an actual job interview. They screened potential fields, then individual industries and finally organizations to confirm their interest in a particular career direction. Bolles, and other authors and consultants like him, advised others to mimic these successful job hunters by engaging in the person-to-person research process they named "informational interviewing."

Perhaps as a result, job-seekers in the 1980's inundated corporate human resources departments with requests for informational interviews when they were actually fishing for a job. That thinly veiled deceit led some employers to look upon the term with suspicion; many with hiring authority now refuse to respond to those requests. Even human resources employees under orders to avoid informational interviews, however, will talk to a friend of a friend about their job and company. Be certain, then, that your request for an informational interview is just that, and not a ploy to get hired.

Getting Started with Informational Interviewing

Once you start the process of talking to other people it seems easy. But it's often hard to make that first call or write that first letter. The fears keep getting in the way: fear that the people you contact won't like you or won't have time for your questions; fear that your mind will go blank or you'll say something stupid. You may procrastinate and worry rather than take the first step.

You may even develop "phone phobia." As Stephen Feldman, a psychologist and former practitioner, puts it, "When the phone rings for lawyers, it's like a time bomb going off. You can never tell what kind of crisis or attitude is going to come at you through the receiver." After ten years of intermittent unpleasantness with clients, witnesses or opposing counsel on the other end of the line, I know I developed resistance to telephone networking.

To move past the fear, start modestly. Talk to your best friends about the direction you're considering. For practice, interview people about subjects that interest you but in which you don't wish to be employed. One Texas lawyer in transition started by talking to quilters, watercolor painters and folk art collectors—artisans she admired—even though she was planning to find a job in nonprofit fundraising. This experience taught her that most people like to be asked questions about themselves and their interests, and are usually generous with their time and information.

If telephoning someone you don't know is intimidating, write a letter introducing yourself first and indicate when you will be following up with a telephone call. Or bypass the telephone altogether by attending a lecture or class on a relevant subject matter. Then, ask questions of the speaker and talk to at least one other attendee.

If you cannot find anyone who works in a field of interest, turn to the experts you've discovered in your library research. Call or write the author of an article you found interesting, or someone who was profiled in a newspaper or magazine. Go ahead and reach to the top. Don't assume that those people would not be interested in speaking with you. Usually they're flattered that you are seeking advice from them. Sometimes they even remember what it was like to be looking for work!

Be cautious about deciding your career direction after talking to only one person. "Find three people for each career field," says Cindy Chernow, Director of Alumni Career Services at UCLA. "If you find only one person in a field and that person has a poor attitude, it could give you a negative impression about the job and dampen your interest." Of course, the opposite can also occur; one person's great experience may be equally atypical.

Informational Interviewing Etiquette

The best way to arrange an informational interview is to make your request as non-invasive as possible and to communicate your enthusiasm. You might start by introducing yourself and explaining how you got that person's name. For example, "I saw the announcement of your career change in the *Business Journal*," or "My friend, Jane Doe, who I understand you also know, told me about your new job teaching first grade and suggested that I give you a call."

Then state the purpose of your call: "I've been thinking about going into elementary education myself and I thought I ought to talk to another lawyer who has made the change before I enroll in the local certification course. I'd love to know how the change has worked for you."

Don't assume that your contact will be delighted to spend time with you. Inquire directly: "Could I buy you a cup of coffee, or meet you some place, to ask you some questions about your work?"

Suggested Interpersonal Research Questions

▶ Could you describe some of your daily activities in the position you now hold?

▶ What tasks do you typically perform in your work?

▶ What skills do you need for this work?

▶ What is the overall objective of this job (i.e., why do you do what you do)?

▶ What do you like and dislike about your work?

▶ What are the major benefits and drawbacks of this work?

▶ What is the work environment like? If there are different environments in which this work is performed, what are they like?

▶ How did you get into this work? How did you get into your current position?

▶ What qualifications are necessary or desirable to become employed in this area or to succeed in this field?

▶ How can my legal training or skills be of benefit in this field?

▶ What is the best way to obtain a position that will start me on a career in this field?

▶ At what level could I enter this field with my current qualifications?

▶ What is the top job you can have in this career?

▶ Are there other areas of this field to which people may be transferred, and what are they?

▶ What current demand is there for people in this field? Do you expect that level of demand to continue?

▶ What future opportunities or developments do you see in this field?

▶ What is the compensation range for this field/work?

▶ What are the employment prospects in this field?

▶ If I want to change to this type of work, what are the best ways to find out what is available?

▶ Who else should I talk to, and where else should I go for more information? May I use you name as a referral?

If there is any resistance, assure your contact that you are not seeking employment at this time, that you don't expect to be told about any current openings, that you don't care if there are any such openings at his or her company. Instead, explain—but only if it's true —that you are researching your ideal job and want to learn more about a particular job function, or industry, or the background you ought to have for the kind of work you envision.

D Research

Sometimes the referral name will provide an instant entree; other times you'll be turned down. In any event, don't take it personally. The contact may:

▶ have a strained relationship with your friend;
▶ be extremely busy or in a lousy mood;
▶ honestly believe she has nothing to offer you; or
▶ not be a particularly helpful person.

If you're unlucky enough to be turned down by your first contact, be sure to call another contact right away. You're not likely to receive the same treatment twice in a row. Most people really want to help and will be surprisingly generous with their time and knowledge.

Talk to as many people as possible. Nearly every interview produces at least one bit of useful information, and you can't know in advance which ones will be most helpful. Be gracious in receiving the information as well. Never say, "I've already tried that and it didn't work," or "That doesn't interest me." The people you contact are trying to help. If you respond negatively or ungratefully, they probably won't think of you in the future when opportunities do arise.

Don't go into the meeting cold, expecting the interviewee to know what you need to be told. Do as much research as possible at the library or on the Internet before the meeting so you'll know what to ask. Write your questions down and bring them with you. Have enough focus (in terms of questions or requests for information) so that you don't make your contact feel you're both wasting time.

You might wonder whether you should "waste" an informational interview on a networking contact who might actually have a job opening. If your intention in meeting with the contact is to get a jump on the position, don't ask for an informational interview. Be a straight shooter and ask for what you really want—a job interview. Assuming you're still in the clarification process, however, go ahead and schedule a research meeting. You may discover that you don't want to work in that field or in that firm. You may also develop a solid rapport with the person that could lead to future employment. Whatever happens, be sincere.

If an opening arises later, realistically appraise the degree of rapport you developed with that contact. If it was cold, you're not likely to get far on a second call. If it was good, remind the contact of your prior meeting, and let him or her know of your interest in the position. If you really hit it off, your contact will remember you and be happy to help. He or she might even be embarrassed about the oversight in not contacting you first, and be even more eager to provide assistance.

Keeping at It

At first, talk to as many of the people who are suggested as possible and ask each contact for the names of others who might be helpful. As you get farther into your research process and refine your focus, you'll want to be more discriminating in following up. But beware of being too selective. Nearly every interview produces at least one bit of useful information, and you can't know what you will learn, which interviews will be most helpful, or which bit of information could change your life, until after the fact.

If you follow this process of researching the fields that interest you, especially through personal contacts, your job search may take you in unexpected directions— much as a new lawsuit does. As you progress through the discovery process you sometimes realize that you're working with a different cause of action. Similarly, when you begin to research one potential direction, you may realize that you were mistaken about what the work entailed, but you discover another direction that more closely matches your requirements.

The point is to let the research process evolve. Sticking to the process, and keeping an open mind when making contacts, will ultimately help you find a new direction.

BEING REALISTIC
ABOUT TRANSITION

Is This the Right Time for Change?

"I said to my soul be still and wait without hope
for hope would be hope for the wrong thing
And wait without love
for love would be love of the wrong thing
There is yet faith
but the faith and the hope and the love are all in the waiting
And do not think
for you are not ready for thought
So the darkness shall be the light and the stillness the dancing"

—T.S. Eliot, poet

. . .

Now that you've chosen a direction and researched what you might find there, it's time to think about barriers to change. Not just any barriers to change—your barriers.

The underlying consideration in every barrier to action is timing: Is this really the right time for a change? Some of you may feel you have no choice; you've been pushed into action by an external force like lay-off, forced retirement, loss of a big client, illness, or bankruptcy. Even so, you can choose how far to take the change right now and what to delay until a better time.

For some of you, the question may be whether this is the time to head in an entirely new direction or just to find work within the same field. You definitely should postpone a career change if you're still unsure of your direction after all the self-assessment and

> You can choose how far to take the change now and what to delay until a better time.

research you've completed. This is especially true if you've been disenchanted with law for less than three years, and you aren't strongly drawn to any alternative, or if you aren't sure yet what field attracts you and you have a job (or can easily find another) that provides enough flexibility or financial security to let you continue to concentrate on self-assessment and research.

You're ripe for career change if and only if you can honestly say:

▶ You're dissatisfied with the practice of law and you're strongly drawn to an identified new career; or

▶ You feel you've reached the end of your career path in law and are unlikely to grow further in the profession; or

▶ You never had the opportunity to pursue another more appealing career, and you now wish to act upon that long-suppressed desire; or

▶ You've experienced a seismic shift in your life interests, goals or values that has capped your interest or belief in the law, and you wish to move toward your new objectives in another line of work.

Often, timing has more to do with lacking the wherewithal to support yourself or your family for the three to 12 months it can take to locate a better job, or the six months to two years it can take to switch to another field. You may also wish to put off a change because you can't afford the pay cut that will accompany a new line of work. Your concerns may be even more pragmatic—you want to buy a house and need your current income to qualify for a mortgage. These are all legitimate reasons to postpone a change. No matter what your reason, though, you can work around even these barriers by following the steps outlined in the next chapter.

There may be other timing issues as well. Some of you simply have too many demands on your time and energy right now. For example, if you're undergoing a marital separation or divorce, grieving over a recent death, caring for someone in your family who is gravely ill, experiencing a serious health problem or strain from some other personal matter, or preparing for a major trial or transaction closing, this is not the right time for change. Certainly you must resolve the current crisis before you initiate another.

On the other hand, if there are always unusual demands on your time, you need to look at those demands more critically. Let's face it. What difference does it make if you bill the most hours in your department if you're planning to leave in six months?

Who cares if you can't meet all the requests of your most unreasonable clients if they're going to be someone else's clients soon?

Those demands may be getting in the way simply because you haven't made peace with the status quo. Maybe you need to tell your current employer or partners about your dissatisfaction and ask for some accommodations. If money is your only motivation for making a change, consider whether your employer rewards longevity with increased pay or offers training that could make you more valuable when you do move on. It might be prudent to hold off on your transition until you feel comfortable that you've given your current situation a chance to prove itself.

But if you get a sick feeling every time you think about making a substantive change, or if it terrifies you to think about not being a lawyer, read Chapter 20 on easing your way into transition and Chapter 22 on adjusting to the prospect of leaving the law. If you don't have the right background to move into the kind of work that suits you, get some hints from Chapter 21 on ways to fill in the gaps in your credentials.

Improving Your
Financial Situation

"Money is better than poverty, if only for financial reasons."

—*Woody Allen, filmmaker and author*

■ ■ ■

Financial barriers can appear insurmountable at the beginning of a transition:

I come from a family of modest means, the kind of impoverished intelligentsia where it's almost a disgrace if you make too much money using your mind. I carried on that tradition during my 20's. I worked part-time as a secretary so that I could be involved in politics, art and literature. When 30 rolled around, I was not making any money, not married, and hadn't written a best-selling novel. That was when I decided to go to law school.

> Money is always a problem in transition but seldom stops those who are committed to their change.

I was desperately poor the whole time I was in school. By the time I graduated, I really wanted some creature comforts. I wanted all the stuff that the hard work had gotten me and I bought it all, banking on my future high income.

I started having fantasies about leaving the law in my second year of practice. I had the $20,000 fantasy where someone gave me $20,000 and I used it to pay off all my short-term debt and start fresh without having to go through bankruptcy. I had the $50,000 fantasy where someone gave me $50,000 and I paid off short-term debt and lived for a year without working. And the $100,000 fantasy, where I paid off short-term debt, lived for two years without working and remodeled my kitchen.

Ten years later I was still having those fantasies. I was also whining and moaning and wringing my hands about how I didn't have time to be creative and how the practice of law was so soul-deadening. One friend responded by saying, "Well, you ought to sell your house and car and go starve in a garret and be an artist." My friend issued a wake-up call to me by putting it in those terms. I said to myself, "Wait a minute. None of those fantasies are going to happen and I'm not going to starve in a garret so I've got to figure something else out."

My bottom line was that I had to keep my house. I wasn't willing to sell half my possessions or make my cat claustrophobic or get depressed by living in an apartment. I wasn't willing to scale back to the kind of bohemian, on-the-edge existence that wasn't so bad when I was in my 20's.

I'm not married. My only dependent is a cat. I never thought that this was an advantage until I quit my job. People started coming up to me and saying, "Gosh, I wish I could quit my job but, you know, the kids, the spouse, just too many responsibilities." My response was, "That cuts both ways." I didn't have a back-up person as a married person does, even if the spouse isn't working. I didn't have the emotional support network that a family person can have. Everyone thinks they have a problem. Everyone thinks the other guy's situation is better.

Money is always a problem in transition. No matter how much you've saved or you owe, the prospect of doing without income for a while, or facing a large pay cut, or not knowing what the financial repercussions of your decision will be, can be daunting.

Money concerns, though, seldom stop those who are committed to their change. Deborah Guyol, the lawyer who introduced this chapter, noticed that her anxiety about money disappeared when she quit her job, even though her money worries did not. "That's what gave me the blinding insight that money issues are a red herring," she says now. "They're really not the issue. They're just a convenient receptacle for all the anxiety that's generated by being unhappy in your job."

That doesn't mean financial concerns are all in your head. Every job or career transition involves at least some monetary investment: from lost work for interviews, self-assessment and anxiety attacks; a lower salary, travel expense, career counseling. To minimize the negative impact of that investment on your life, consider following these steps:

Look at the Details

In my individual consultations with lawyers who want to make a change, I ask how much less money they can afford to earn. Most have never thought about it in that way. Their answer to my next question about how much they're now spending is the same: They haven't a clue. To break through the financial barrier, you must pay attention to those "details."

Most lawyers don't want to look at the details. Doing so—and this is the real psychological barrier—may confirm you don't have the financial wherewithal to make the change. Even more threatening is the prospect that you do have enough money, thus eliminating a convenient excuse for staying stuck.

Start by creating a balance sheet. List all of your assets (e.g., savings and checking account balances, stocks, bonds, other investments, retirement fund, pension and profit-sharing plans, expected inheritance, accounts receivable, real estate, personal property) and their estimated values. Then deduct all liabilities (e.g., mortgage, automobile loan, revolving credit, student and other personal loans). A loan application form from your local banker can help you organize this information.

The process may be painful, but the balance sheet will tell you whether you have assets that could be available for spending or borrowing against while in transition. One lawyer decided she would tap her IRA if she had to (she never did). Another reallocated to his transition the $25,000 he'd saved for a down payment on a house. Your study will also show you what liabilities to reduce before starting the change process.

Then begin evaluating your spending patterns. Review your checking account records for the last full year. Calculate expenditures for housing, utilities, insurance, food, clothing, transportation, entertainment, travel, unreimbursed work expense, uninsured medical and dental expenses, and any other relevant categories. This is no time for "guesstimates." (Most people substantially underestimate the sums they spend on categories such as entertainment and dining out.)

If any of your expenses turn out higher than you think you're actually spending, or if you spend more than $100 per month in cash, keep track of every dollar you pay out for another month to confirm or adjust the figures. Save receipts for all cash purchases. If you're not offered a receipt, ask for one or make an immediate notation on a slip of paper. Then add those expenditures to the total.

From this historical review, calculate your total expenditures on both an annual and monthly basis to determine the reserves or resources you'd need to maintain your current spending patterns.

Stop Spending Thoughtlessly

The analysis you've just completed will help you pinpoint what may be self-defeating spending patterns. Deborah Guyol spent a frustrating year trying to reduce her credit card debt before taking a closer look at her habits. "What I discovered was that clothing was my luxury item," she said. "I had to buy a lot of really nice clothes to keep from going crazy in my job. Once I decided I was going to leave, it was easy for me to say, 'Okay, no more new clothes.'"

Become more conscious about your spending for big-ticket items as well. I've noticed that many of those contemplating career change have recently, usually subconsciously, made an expensive financial commitment: purchasing a luxury car or a new home with a big mortgage, or taking a vacation that maxed out their credit cards. Those choices could be interpreted as a substitute for the change they really wanted. But their misdirected energy now restricts their freedom to make a real change.

It's wise to limit your spending when the first thoughts of dissatisfaction emerge. Decide where you can trim your expenditures and begin doing so. Watch out for "impulse buying" and, in general, put a lid on purchasing. Stop investing in nonessentials; by now, you should know what yours are. Forego or postpone major purchases, vacations or expensive entertainment. Put your credit cards away and pay off any revolving debt you've already incurred. Create an agreement among your family members to discuss and agree on every purchase above a specified price before making it. Change your attitude toward the money you earn from one of expectation to one of gratitude and scarcity.

Cutting back on your spending needn't be a form of punishment. Acknowledge your need for play and pampering while you accept the fact that the way you meet those needs might have to change. Even though Deborah Guyol stopped buying clothes, she decided it was important to keep the "small treats" in her life. "It's like a diet," she says. "If you try to cut out everything that's fun, you won't be able to stick to your plan." Deborah kept her "little luxury" of a daily cappuccino and brownie.

Recognize your modest lifestyle for the tradeoff it is: Spending less money is an investment in your future well-being and success. "Simple living is not about being deprived in any way," says Janet Luhrs, a former practicing lawyer who now publishes *Simple Living*, a nationally-distributed newsletter. "Simple living is about freedom. Freedom to choose the kind of life you want. Freedom to enjoy what is important to you."

E Being Realistic about Transition

Budget for Transition

When you get close to making the move, calculate a projected job or career change budget. Identify expenses directly caused by your current employment (e.g., commuting, parking, clothing, dry-cleaning, lunches, and entertaining clients). You might find when you quit your current job, burdensome expenses will disappear—for example, if you have time for household chores you now pay others to do for you, or if it's more convenient to go for a bike ride or run than to drive to your expensive health club downtown.

Be sure to include your estimated costs of self-assessment and job-hunting (e.g., career or psychological counseling, courses, testing, workshops, résumé production, workbooks, travel, networking meals). Don't be afraid to allocate liberal sums here. Your investments will be returned in the accelerated results they produce.

Once you've gathered all the necessary data, write a detailed description of your goal without concern for its economic viability. Define the specific work you are seeking (by now you should know), and how long it will take to find it. By industry rule of thumb, a change in employment takes from three to six months, or one month for every $10,000 in salary. If you plan a career change—especially if you expect an income of $50,000 or more—assume it will take one to two years.

Be sure to include time for a sabbatical, travel, additional education, or child-rearing, if that is part of an ideal scenario for you. Remember, at this point you are not concerned about the feasibility of your plan. You are simply exploring a "worst case" scenario.

Then calculate the reserves you'll need to fund the change you contemplate. Multiply the number of months you believe your transition will take by the expenses you believe you will incur. If you are concerned that you're going to be laid off (see Appendix 1), or if you would like to quit your job while you're job-hunting, this nest egg should provide adequate funds for your period of unemployment. Or, decide how much money you are willing to invest in your career reformation. The amount you decide upon is your "nut."

Tackle Your Debt

Those of you who have accumulated more debt than you can carry if you earn a penny less will have to take steps to reduce your load. The most obvious approach is to stop incurring new charges and start making more than the minimum payments each month. That's a tall order if you're habituated to the credit card life. Here are some other suggestions for shrinking the size of your debt.

- Use a cash (or debit) card whenever possible. You get the feel of using a credit card without paying interest; the money comes directly out of your checking account.
- List your credit card accounts and minimum payments in descending order of current balance. Determine how much beyond the minimum payment you can afford to pay each month. You need to stretch here; this number assumes you're cutting back each expense as recommended earlier. Every month, make the minimum payment on all accounts and add the extra amount to the first card listed. When that card has been paid off, apply the extra payment to the next one down. Take a scissors to credit cards with zero balances if you're tempted to use them again.
- If you're facing student loans, negotiate an extended payment schedule with each lender or try to consolidate all of the debt into a new loan with a longer term. That should reduce your monthly obligation. You might also want to pay off the debt by refinancing your home.

Build a War Chest

Your calculations will tell you what to do next. You may already have saved the money to take the steps you envision. At this point, you just need to decide that your future well-being is worth the investment. (One former practitioner renamed her security savings a "freedom fund" in order to reflect this decision.) You may also be able to tap some assets you hadn't previously considered.

- Borrow from a relative, or from your retirement plan or life insurance policy. Draw upon credit card or home equity lines of credit only as a last resort.
- Loot the kids' college accounts. If college is years away, you'll have plenty of time to repay what you withdrew. If college is right around the corner, the drop in your income and assets could help your child qualify for financial aid and government loans.

Sometimes just being willing to use the money is enough. Deborah Guyol's decision to tap her IRA account if she needed to gave her the courage to quit her job. Almost immediately, she started to receive contract legal assignments. She never had to touch those funds.

If you don't currently have the funds but the "nut" seems doable, work toward accumulating the money. Find creative ways to supplement your income.

▶ Take a second job, such as teaching nights at a community college or serving as live-in manager of an apartment building.

▶ Figure out what freelance services you might be able to sell. Some lawyers have solicited editing projects or offered courses through local adult education programs.

▶ Rent extra space in your house or apartment for residence or storage. Take a close look at the possibilities—a spare bedroom, an unused recreation room, your garage or other off-street parking.

▶ Sell items you aren't using or that you are willing to trade for a more fulfilling work life. But don't sell your house if you can avoid it. The cost of replacement housing could exceed what you're paying now. And you'll aggravate the stress of a career transition by imposing another major change upon yourself.

▶ Use (or be certain to be compensated for) all of your accrued vacation and sick leave, and take advantage of a law firm sabbatical policy.

If the "nut" is much too large, redefine your goals until you reach an amount you think you can manage. Then, save this amount of money as a cushion. Or, think about ways to maintain your cash flow while still having time to search for work. Inquire about opportunities for contract legal work, or suggest a part-time or freelance arrangement with your current employer or partners. (See Chapter 20 for more information on alternative work schedule arrangements.) Look for an interim, less pressured position that will bring in money while you're networking. You may even want to take a low-paying "McJob" just to keep the cash flowing. Bob McSweeney worked as a pizza delivery person before finding work as the director of a local non-profit. "I'll never forget the day I drove into the driveway of one of our county district attorneys who knew me on sight," says Bob. "As he was pulling the money out of his wallet to pay for the pizzas, he looked up and said, 'What the hell are you doing?' I told him I was working at my bridge job and having a wonderful time!"

Keep at It

Persist toward your financial goals. Evaluate your progress periodically and adjust your spending habits as you go. If after a few months you see little or no progress toward accumulating your "nut," reevaluate your goal, or ask friends to help you brainstorm new ways to generate money or reduce expenses.

You might also consider postponing your career change, perhaps until you conclude a matter that could generate additional cash, or until your children are in school full time and your daycare expenses are lower. (See Chapter 18 on timing.) In the interim, lay the groundwork for your transition by getting active in appropriate industry or professional organizations, enrolling in educational programs, or polishing the skills you plan to use in your next venture. All the while, remain conscious of your spending and saving.

You'll find additional resources to help you take control of your finances in Appendix 3.

Finding Stepping Stones

"Wherever we are, it is but a stage on the way to somewhere else. And whatever we do, however well we do it, it is only preparation to do something else that is different."

—*Robert Louis Stevenson, author*

∎ ∎ ∎

If the time is right and you can handle the change financially but you still don't feel ready for transition, you may need to break down the process into small steps. "It's like crossing a stream," says former practicing lawyer Rick Rogovy. "You go from rock to rock, not from bank to bank."

Nancy Ashley, a partner in a commercial law firm who moved into human services consulting, prepared this summary of the steps (and time) she took to accomplish her career transition:

▶ Distinguish career dissatisfaction from fatigue
(two years);

▶ See first career counselor (six months);

▶ Put career change on hold to concentrate on getting
married and buying a house (18 months);

▶ Attend small self-assessment workshop with other
lawyers and continue with support meetings
(six months);

▶ See a better career counselor (nine months);

▶ Quit job to conduct about 60 informational
interviews, find contract lawyer work to keep afloat
financially, volunteer in human services field
(six months);

▶ Work in two part-time human services planning jobs (three months);

▶ Receive full-time job offers from both employers.

> Even if the time is right, you may need to break down the process into small steps.

Finding ways to step into transition will help those of you whose jobs sap you of the time and energy needed to work on change. When you can't jump from what you're doing now to a better position without generating too many negative financial and practical consequences, you tend to do nothing. Dividing the process into interim steps breaks through the inertia caused by contemplating too big a change.

The most common stepping stones, listed in order of effectiveness, are:

▶ Changing things where you are;
▶ Taking some time off;
▶ Switching to an alternative work schedule arrangement;
▶ Working as a contract lawyer; and
▶ Taking one or more steps in the wrong direction.

Changing Things Where You Are

According to consultant Lesah Beckhusen, only lawyers who have successfully handled change in the past will be able to move successfully through a major career change. If you feel you have no control over your current work environment, focusing first on making changes where you are now will build confidence for a later change. It may even be that taking this step will be enough; minor adaptations to your work environment often result in major shifts in satisfaction. If the situation does not improve, however, you'll be more willing to pursue other options because you'll know you gave your current job, or the law itself, a fair chance.

To start this process, write down exactly what you do each day in your job for a couple of months. (You can get a historical perspective by reviewing past time slips.) Where appropriate, break down the experiences further into their component skills, values and other preferences. For each task (or skill, value, preference) indicate your feeling for it: liked, disliked, neutral.

Compare the results to your Ideal Job Grid. What tasks that you perform frequently use skills you've listed in the "must avoid" column? How often and in what fashion do you work with other people and how does this compare to what's in the "must have" side of the grid? Is there a gap between the values you want to express and those you are expressing in your work?

Once you've pinpointed the most troubling conflicts, consider what you can do about them. What do you have the power to change? Don't rely only on your appraisal. Get advice from others who also know the players.

E   Being Realistic about Transition

Some kinds of changes are within your power to make: saying no more often to clients, firing your worst clients, hiring someone else to collect money or handle the type of work you dislike, changing your retainer policies, requesting better compensation or more feedback, and taking courses to help you learn to deal with difficult people. Changing the behavior of a dishonest, vindictive or otherwise unpleasant colleague (as opposed to changing your response to that person), or turning down disagreeable assignments when you're a junior associate, are not changes you can make on your own.

Now for the hard part: Muster the courage to make some small changes. If the change you seek is not under your control, ask your employer for what you want. If an obnoxious partner is making your life miserable, ask to be relieved from working with him. If you think you'd be happier working on deals than going to court, request a change in departments, accepting a reduction in pay or seniority if necessary. Discuss the possibility of reduced pay in return for a four-day work week, two months off a year, or some other adjustment to billable hour requirements.

One parent of a two-year old was commuting about three hours daily and becoming increasing dissatisfied with her work environment. When she studied the situation more carefully, she realized that she enjoyed the work but hated the way it consumed her life and felt uncomfortable with the work style and personalities of some of her colleagues. She was expecting a $4,000 raise but proposed to her employers that instead they pay for a small office near her home. She would work there three days per week, and use the time she saved on commuting to develop business contacts and potential new clients in that city. The firm agreed to the proposal.

If the issue is purely financial, confront it head on. If you're not being compensated fairly, figure out exactly how much you want and ask for it. If you want a review, request one. If you want a raise, say so. If you think you should receive a bonus for the business you bring into the firm, then ask for that kind of compensation arrangement. If you are interested in becoming a partner in the firm, start bringing up the subject.

Your employers are busy people who will respond to the demands of their cases and families before they ever think of you, unless you make yourself a priority. If you want their attention, demand it firmly but politely. Don't let the situation get to the point where your resentment might erode what would otherwise be a good working relationship.

If the change *is* under your control, you might want to model your efforts after those of other lawyers:

- ▶ Figure out what kinds of clients you like to work with and solicit only those clients. Turn down clients who you know will end up being thorns in your side.
- ▶ Let go of the clients that drive you crazy. One small firm celebrates with an "Ex-Client of the Month" party.
- ▶ Practice the kind of law that invigorates you, or about which you are passionate. If this is a new area for you, take on only one case at a time, perhaps working pro bono, to build your expertise.
- ▶ Turn down all clients who can't pay, no matter how sorry you feel for them, unless you make a deliberate decision to take the case pro bono. Demand substantial up-front retainers from all paying clients. If a client can't come up with the money, you can't spend the time on the case.
- ▶ Add to the variety of services you offer, mixing bread-and-butter work with more esoteric ventures. Work at a wider range of competency levels.
- ▶ Delegate those aspects of your practice that you feel responsible for but that others could do more efficiently and effectively. The cost should be recovered by your increased productivity in the areas you do enjoy.

Taking Some Time Off

Sometimes you have to create an end to one commitment before you find the energy for something new. Sabbaticals, vacations and leaves of absence can provide just the break you need.

A 1991 law school graduate, Bill started his career by working in a small corporate law firm, first on a contract basis and then as an associate. After nine months, he realized he wasn't in the right place. In May 1992, he quit his job to attend an international law conference in Australia. When he returned a month later, he knew he didn't want to go back to corporate law but didn't know what else he could do. Rather than accepting his former employer's offer to return to his job, he devoted his time to self-assessment.

Within a few months, he'd "cleared away enough goo" in his head to develop a picture of his preferred next step: a job in international affairs or human rights. He told everyone he knew of his desire. By August, he had obtained a position as the Director of Policy and Legislative Affairs for the Foundation for International Cooperation and Development, a nonprofit organization that sponsors conferences and symposiums to address the economic and political issues caused by the break-up of the Soviet Union. His duties included gathering and disseminating information, writing letters and promotional materials, creating educational packages and helping to coordinate the international conferences sponsored by the foundation.

Denver lawyer Connie Talmadge used an open-ended hiatus to redirect her career. Eight years ago, she walked away from a lucrative "big time" litigation practice to spend the next two years "turning forty" and, as she puts it, "trying to find new and comfortable ways to respond when my lawyer friends asked what I was doing, since it looked to them like I was doing nothing." It was a hard question for her to answer because, at least for some time, she *felt* as though she was "doing nothing." In fact, she was trying to decide what was important in her life, whether she was entitled to be joyful, and what type of employment was most likely to add joy to her life.

Connie was shocked to discover how much of her identity and self-esteem was tied to being a lawyer. As a result, it took much time and energy to sort through the "Who am I?" question. In the end, though, she says, "I was able to clean my closet of all the clothes that belonged to the person who used to live in this house and I am now more at home than ever." Connie is now the director of the statewide ADR office for the Colorado Judicial Branch, a job that better suits her skills and values.

You might believe you can't afford to take time off. If so, I recommend *Six Months Off: The Sabbatical Book* by Hope Dlugozima, James Scott and David Sharp. It suggests a variety of ways to make a sabbatical feasible.

Switching to an Alternative Work-Schedule Arrangement

A less drastic method of creating more time for career transition is to negotiate a part-time or other alternative work schedule arrangement with your current employer or partners. One lawyer worked part-time in her law firm for two years to have time to volunteer for a nonprofit organization. The group eventually created a position for her as its first public policy advocate.

Solo practitioners also create part-time practices that lead to change. The first step is to lower your overhead, usually by moving the office into your home, paying for a good answering service, and meeting clients in a conference room rented by the hour from another law firm. The second key to success is to pick a narrow practice area that involves almost no unexpected court appearances. Contested divorces and custody battles, personal injury and criminal work are problematic; estate planning, tax, adoption, bankruptcy and guardianship are not.

Telecommuting will also create time for change. You can equip your home with a telephone, computer, high-speed modem and a fax machine, and carry on your relationships with clients and your law firm as if you were in the office next door. Some telecommute daily; others spend two or three days each week at home; still others leave town for months at a time while taking their office with them. By working from home, you cut down on the hours spent dressing for success and commuting, freeing some time to devote to your transition. The significant reduction in overhead may also make a part-time arrangement financially feasible for the solo practitioner.

There's one more way to buy more time away from the office. Negotiate with your boss (even if that boss is you!) for two more weeks of vacation or a couple three-day weekends each month, rather than an annual raise. Or every week, work at least one full day out of your home. Discover how much more efficient you can be in a day's time when you don't have the constant interruptions that occur in an office environment. During the natural breaks you take during a day, you can head to the library to research careers that interest you, take contacts to lunch, enroll in educational programs that will enhance your credibility or volunteer for the right organizations.

For additional help with creating an alternative work schedule, turn to the resources listed in Appendix 2 and 3.

Working as a Contract Lawyer

The most common alternative work schedule arrangement among lawyers these days is temporary or hourly work, known as contract lawyering. Contract lawyers, many of them former partners or associates of the law firm, provide their services on a freelance or hourly basis. They are often paid for every hour billed to a client. Most lawyers negotiate directly with one or more law firms to work a fixed number of hours per week, or on an irregular, project-by-project basis.

Others receive their assignments through temporary agencies. Most large legal communities nationwide now support several agencies that place lawyers with the appropriate skills in law firms that need short-term, specialized assistance. Some concentrate on corporate placements; others place lawyers in a wide geographic area, even internationally. Placement agencies usually tack a surcharge onto the hourly fee you are paid and are responsible for collecting from the law firm. (Sometimes, if the agency doesn't collect, you don't get paid.) At times, the lawyer is brought in to complete one project, e.g., researching and writing an appellate brief or attending a deposition; other assignments are longer term and cover a number of different projects.

How to Negotiate a Part-Time Schedule with Your Current Employer

Take a look at yourself. Are you good at what you do? Are your skills and experiences in demand? You'll be in a better position to proceed if you know what you have to offer.

Take a look at the employer you want to approach. Is the organization considered innovative or conservative? Find out—if you can—about their part-time personnel employment policies. Some employers discourage the practice, and some encourage it only for certain groups like new parents, pre-retirees and students.

Take a look at the job itself. Does it have some of these special characteristics that might make it easier to do on a part-time basis:

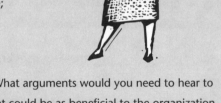

- ▶ Self-contained (in terms of time);
- ▶ Independent projects or cases;
- ▶ Peak workloads;
- ▶ Potential for overlapping coverage;
- ▶ Multiple skills needed; and
- ▶ High stress.

Put yourself in your employer's shoes. What arguments would you need to hear to be convinced that a part-time arrangement could be as beneficial to the organization as to you? Prepare yourself to be an advocate of part-time employment.

Draft a proposal. Include the tasks and responsibilities you would handle working part-time, a suggested schedule, techniques for communication, your ideas on fair handling of salary and benefits, the advantages to the employer and answers to other anticipated employer concerns.

Be positive! Don't apologize for wanting to work less than full-time. You can work part-time and be a high-quality, committed professional.

1994, Linda Marks. Used with permission.

Contract employment provides benefits to both law firm and lawyer. Law firms gain the tangible benefits of handling fluctuations in workload cost-effectively and passing on the contract employee's fee, usually with a surcharge, to the client. They also confirm the value and compatibility of a potential permanent employee before making a long-term commitment.

Advantages to the lawyer in transition include:

► Higher compensation for every hour worked than would be received on a part-time employee basis;
► More control over scheduling and the ability to take off time for research and networking;
► The ability to maintain cash flow while searching for work or changing careers, without making a long-term commitment.

The flexible work schedule of contract legal work may give you time to study, write, network or start a small business. New York City lawyer Peter Zerilli uses contract work to pay the bills while he tries to establish himself as a writer. "It's not a permanent job, which is a very important psychological factor for me," he says. "I can still feel I'm doing something leading toward the goal of supporting myself by writing full time."

Lawyers who want to leave the profession but accept contract assignments to tide them over until they find another job also use contract work to test their decisions. Michael Goldenkranz and Robert Hoon were supporting wives and kids when they decided to shift their career focus. Their freelance relationships were such unpleasant reminders of their reasons for wanting to leave law that they became even more motivated to create what they wanted. Both worked about six months as contract lawyers before securing new permanent positions.

The Complete Guide to Contract Lawyering: What Every Lawyer and Law Firm Needs to Know about Temporary Legal Services, by me and Portland, Oregon, contract lawyer Deborah Guyol, provides a wealth of information and many inspirational stories about developing opportunities to do contract work.

Taking One or More Steps in the Wrong Direction

Sometimes it doesn't even matter what you choose to do; taking any step at all redirects your career.

Nancy Walseth quit her job as an associate in a medical malpractice firm. After two months of readjustment, she decided to become an elementary school teacher and enrolled in a certification program at a local college. Her first course was called Art for Elementary Teachers. "As part of that course, we were required to have colored pens and to doodle if we ever had time," she recalls. "I finished my tree early one day and doodled a cartoon that was a parody of myself. I threw it in my portfolio and forgot about it." Shortly afterward, she decided she couldn't stand the educational psychology courses required for certification and dropped out of the program. But her art teacher tracked her down and told her that she had a gift for cartooning. Soon after, she began penning Doonesbury-like cartoons featuring a sardonic woman lawyer, Ann Ominous, as the central character. Those cartoons were later published in a book.

But Nancy didn't stop there. About three months after she quit her job, she started to get telephone calls from lawyers asking if she could help with their legal work. For three years, she had enough contract assignments to earn as much working five hours a day, five days a week as she had made as a full-time lawyer! Her freelancing period, as she calls it, ended when she stopped feeling as confident as she had in the beginning. "It was harder for me to be sure that I had read every single advance sheet on a subject when someone called," she says.

At that point, she met someone who owned a sailboat brokerage. The company was in a growth phase and needed help with computerization. "I ended up working half-time downtown as a lawyer and half-time out at the boat place helping set up systems," she recalls. After about a year, she finally dropped her malpractice insurance coverage and stopped practicing law. She now co-manages the business. "The uniform is jeans, tennis shoes, sweatshirts," she says. "I sweep the place and kill the spiders. It's like what I wanted to do when I was five years old and used to fantasize about being a grocery store owner, except we're selling boats instead of candy bars."

As you can see from Nancy's story, when you're in transition your compass needle may point in many unexpected directions and still lead you to a place you want to be. Although making the first move may feel like jumping off a cliff, take heart. You're actually just stepping off a curb onto a path that leads to change.

Filling the Gaps

"Your best chance of bridging whatever handicap you have or think you have is careful preparation on your part."

—*Richard Nelson Bolles, author*

. . .

When the work you seek is completely different or too many steps away from the paid or volunteer work you're now doing, you'll probably need to strengthen some weak spots and fill in your résumé with the kind of credentials and life credits that will get you work.

As a highly educated person, you're conditioned to look at formal education as the best way to expand your knowledge base and establish your qualification for the next field. The problem here is that education will only provide a knowledge base; when you've earned the degree, you still have to get experience.

Getting more education isn't automatically a bad idea. But it is an expensive and time-consuming tactic, and may not advance your career any faster than the other techniques outlined in this chapter. I've seen many lawyers head back to school, but only two groups of them actually needed their new degrees to do what they wanted to do: those who decided to teach in public school, and those who wanted to be licensed therapists. In most other situations, advanced degrees were superfluous and a waste of money. In my experience, LLMs, except perhaps in tax, are rarely useful.

> A law degree provides enough education to qualify you for employment in almost any field.

The good news is that a law degree provides enough education to qualify you for employment in almost any field, even teaching and counseling. It's true that the conventional jobs in those fields—public school instructor or clinical psychologist—have rigid educational licensing requirements of their own. But you can teach or counsel with no more background than your law degree, legal experience and other "life credits."

In the counseling area, the Oregon State Bar's Attorney Assistance Program (referenced at the beginning of Appendix 2) is staffed solely by former practicing lawyers, rather than licensed therapists, who manage and facilitate its peer counseling programs. In the teaching field, lawyers work as paralegal, CLE and law firm training instructors, and teach law-related courses such as political science, criminal justice, sports management, and business law in colleges across the country. In fact, over 1,000 such teachers have formed the Academy of Legal Studies in Business (referenced in Appendix 4 under "Education").

So before you enroll in the local university, consider whether one of the following techniques will be equally effective in making you an attractive candidate for your chosen field:

▶ Volunteer work;
▶ Internships;
▶ Freelancing;
▶ Consulting;
▶ Experience-building interim jobs;
▶ Building a business; or
▶ Non-degree course work.

Volunteering

Many of you already volunteer for nonprofit organizations. You might be sitting on the board of directors; chairing a committee, a fundraising drive or a program; or leading lobbying efforts. In the course of your involvement, you're developing friendly relationships based on mutual respect. Those relationships can lead to wonderful work opportunities.

Mary was employed as a public defender for several years and grew tired of the one-on-one helper role. After engaging in self-assessment and some research, she targeted waste management as an area with great social utility and less of the futility she felt as a public defender. She volunteered for a citizens' recycling group for another year while continuing to practice criminal defense. That experience gave her the background she needed to land a one-year contract as a recycling coordinator in another state. She now oversees about ten different waste reduction and recycling projects back in her home town.

Working in professional associations is an especially effective way of escaping your current legal specialty. If, for example, you're a civil litigator who would like to move into transactional work or environmental litigation, join the appropriate interest section of the ABA, or your state or local bar association. You'll receive publications that will identify the heavy hitters in that field. You'll educate yourself about emerging issues in that area of law. If you also attend general membership meetings, special events and educational seminars, you'll meet people who may be able to assist you in your transition.

Internships

If it's experience you lack, consider an internship or informal apprenticeship with a nonprofit agency, the government or perhaps one of the contacts you've made. One lawyer in transition who wanted to get into nonprofit management offered to assist an overworked director of an influential arts organization. Through this unpaid work, she was able to attend state and local association meetings and networks. Over the course of a few months, others in the arts community began to see her as a peer, rather than a "wannabe." She also developed some actual work product in the field, which gave her credibility in interviews.

Freelancing

In certain fields, getting practical experience on your own is almost a requirement. Pamela Brownstein, executive editor of the *New Jersey Law Journal,* sees a number of résumés from lawyers who seek editing and reporting jobs. "The résumés that impress me the most generally are those that are accompanied by a [non-brief] writing sample because I can get a feel for the candidate's skill, potential and initiative." If you are interested in making the transition into journalism, you need clips. Suggest topics to local, regional or national publications and let them know you are available for additional assignments.

"There's a truism: writers write," says lawyer/journalist Monica Bay. "It's that simple. Start writing, even if it's just letters to the editor. Most papers welcome commentaries and opinions, and if you become a regular contributor you will get to know the staff."

Consulting

Bob McSweeney had acted as counsel for several nonprofit organizations and had noticed how the people at the top, like so many small business owners, didn't know much about running a business. He met another former practicing lawyer who had founded a Center for Management of Nonprofit Organizations. Bob took several classes at the center and started to consult with nonprofits about their business management. He ended up organizing twelve nonprofits over a period of two years, and became "fairly familiar" with what you have to do to make a nonprofit work. "But I was doing this for other people," he says, "And it was like passing out the dinners but not getting to eat yourself." He finally got to the table when one of his consulting clients hired him as its new executive director.

It can be difficult to convert volunteer work into paid consulting, but this is one of the most common ways to build a new career. Jane Lynch decided that nonprofit work was more appealing than family law practice. Her first step was to get involved with half a dozen organizations in her community, all of them concerned with family violence education. One group needed an executive director. She negotiated a stipend to handle the work until a search could be completed. That experience opened her eyes to the opportunity for project work with others. Jane is now developing a consulting business she hopes will eventually replace her law practice income.

Experience-Building Interim Jobs

It's often difficult to tell when a replacement job is a bridge to better work or an end in itself. For example, one woman wanted to move away from practicing law and into nonprofit management. She accepted what she thought would be a short-term position as head of a bar association pro bono program to get nonprofit experience she could transfer outside the law. Eight years later, she's still happily running the program—and still practicing law, but only in a supervisory capacity.

The job that's supposed to be "the" job may also turn into an interim job in hindsight. In 1988, Gail Hunter realized that civil litigation, and probably the practice of law itself, was not for her. She enrolled in a self-assessment program and discovered that her interests, skills, values and workplace preferences translated into a job in sports management. Gail was a good athlete and had worked with amateur sports organizations as both player and manager. Even so, it took a year of research and national networking to land a relatively low-level management position 2,000 miles from her home supervising the awards program for the NCAA Championships Department. That job, however, led to a more challenging position with Major League Baseball Properties in New York City.

Building a Business

Earl and Kate, marriage and law partners, spent over a year developing their home-based business in ceramic Christmas tree ornaments while operating their bankruptcy law practice. First, they researched the market for a product they thought would be salable. Then they experimented with making the products until they had something store owners wanted to carry. They did all this while maintaining a full-time law practice. "I cut out every ounce of dead weight in my practice," says Earl. "Every minute at the office was productive so I had big blocks of time to devote to the ornaments. It got to the point where I was working at the law office only as long as the parking meter would last—120 minutes at a time. I went in and moved through my work as fast I could." As soon as it appeared they could make enough money selling Christmas tree ornaments, they closed the office.

Non-Degree Course Work

If there's anything you really do need to learn, don't hesitate to enroll in a university extension or other continuing education course. Eduardo Munoz learned through a self-assessment workshop that he loved technical analysis, working with computers and a team environment. When he researched his options, he realized that he needed more technical knowledge before he would be employable as a software designer or engineer. He enrolled in a local university's nine-month certification program in software engineering; soon after completing it, he joined a small design team working on cutting-edge products for a fast-growing computer company.

At this point, let's return to the question of additional formal educational credentials. Sometimes, another degree is essential to your career plan. But before you enroll, make sure you are not falling into the trap of postponing your career decision, rather than pursuing it.

First, you need to know what field you want to enter, not what degree will make it easier for you to get work. You probably earned your law degree to make yourself more marketable and look where it got you! "The legal job market is littered with disappointed attorneys who paid $40,000 to $60,000 for advanced degrees without first performing a 'due diligence' on whether the effort would pay off in enhanced career opportunities," says District of Columbia career counselor Linda Sutherland.

E Being Realistic about Transition

The next issue to explore is what practical advantages you think the educational investment will yield. To find out, research answers to these questions:

▶ How much will it cost?

▶ How long will it take?

▶ How much more money or opportunity will it yield?

▶ What positions could you obtain without earning another degree or certificate?

▶ How long will it take you to work your way from an entry-level position to the type of position you hope the extra credential will qualify you for?

Ask these questions of career services representatives in your schools of choice, prospective employers and related professional or trade associations. Ask schools about the track record of their graduates. Those with degrees that enhance marketability will provide you with their statistics; others will not.

You may want to return to school even if a cost-benefit analysis does not justify the additional financial investment. It may be that conventional employment suits you better. Or your subjective motivations—a yearning for the student lifestyle, a love of learning, a need for a break from wage earning—may outweigh any financial considerations.

It's also possible that the education you receive will make you appreciate your legal work all the more. A personal injury lawyer wanted to help others more than she could as a lawyer. She earned a masters in psychology with the intent of becoming a therapist. Rather than leave the profession, however, she changed her practice focus. She now specializes in lawsuits brought by abused women against their abusers, and uses her new education to help clients cope with both their original trauma and the stress of the lawsuit itself.

Adjusting to the Prospect of Leaving the Law

"I don't want to leave Hell. I know the names of all the streets."

—*Anonymous*

■ ■ ■

I wore a tie for eight years, every week day and sometimes seven days a week while I was practicing law. One of the adjustments I had to make—a friend dubbed it "tie therapy"—was to learn that I didn't have to have a tie on to have my brain work. It may sound funny now, but it was a major adjustment. I truly thought you had to choke the blood supply off to get your brain working. It took me about six months to get to the point where I could go to work and feel good about myself without the tie. It sounds silly now, but those are the type of hurdles that I think you have to overcome when you leave the law.

> No question about it. Leaving the legal profession is a difficult choice.

No question about it. Leaving the profession is a difficult choice. Many practitioners admit that one of the main reasons they attended law school was for the external rewards associated with being a lawyer: money, prestige, respect, security. When they surrendered the title, they let go of what had become an identity as much as a career. For many, the forfeiture was as disorienting as losing a spouse or a limb.

The reactions of others can make the process even more difficult. "There is still a stigma to changing careers after practicing law," says former practicing lawyer Wendy Leibowitz of American Lawyer Media. "Almost any career is perceived to pay less than the law. It is more socially acceptable to change firms many times, or hang out your own shingle, than to leave the practice of law."

Being Realistic
about Transition

"One of the most self-defeating things that I did to myself was thinking that there was something wrong with me for not liking my work," says one former practicing lawyer. "I had this perception that everybody else in my firm was doing really quite well. I used to look at them and think, 'How come you like it?' I was trying to figure out what was wrong with me that I didn't like it. I kept thinking if I just fixed whatever was in myself, then I could be like them and like it too."

You may fear that if you announce that you're thinking of leaving the law, you'll invite an onslaught of negative comments. Maybe your family and colleagues will think you've gone crazy; certainly they'll see you as a failure. According to a survey of Minnesota law school graduates working in nontraditional environments, the most common personal obstacle encountered in making their transition was opposition from friends, family and the legal profession. This barrier was bigger than their own anxiety and feelings of shame or failure, and worries about financial sacrifice and loss of prestige.

Michael Whithers, now executive director of Metropolitan Family Services in Portland, Oregon, remembers early on in his transition bumping into some of his lawyer friends and telling them that he had left the law and was working on a new career. "Before I could even get to telling them what I was doing, their eyes would cast down to the sidewalk," he recalls. "They were embarrassed for me. I used to be a partner in an A-rated law firm. What happened to me?"

Doug Stam, who left law and ended up managing the sports marketing department at Nike, remembers the feelings his decision to leave law practice triggered in himself and others:

> About the first 30 days after I announced I was leaving, the lawyers who met me on the street would say, "Well you can't do that." I'd say, "Why can't I?" And they'd say, "Well you don't have anything to do, and you've got a great practice." And I said, "Yeah, but I don't like it." And then their eyes went down to my shoes, and they walked on. I felt some of the same feelings that these folks did. I felt guilty or that I wasn't good enough when I was around my lawyer friends .
>
> After I got on at Nike, I'd get these phone calls: "Say, you know, I'm really kind of dissatisfied with private practice myself. And I can't quite pull the plug like you did, but could I come out and talk to you?"

No matter what your professional status, your choice to trade your lawyer identity for a different model will trigger a period of emotional ups and downs. It's an awkward, uncomfortable, even depressing time when you no longer want to say, "I'm a lawyer," but you haven't progressed far in your new direction. Consider this man's experience:

> I practiced general civil law for nearly 15 years, the last ten of which I operated as a solo practitioner. I maintained a diverse clientele and rendered services in nearly every discipline of law. Despite the variety of my career experiences, I had no passion for my work.
>
> About a year ago, I burned out and quit my practice without any career plans. My business telephone line and stationery are my only remaining ties to the legal profession. The past year has been filled with near-equal doses of doubt, anxiety, frustration and self-discovery. Reading about others who have dropped out of law has been a newfound source of reassurance and inspiration and, in that regard, has provided much needed relief to my understanding wife. Only recently have I begun my search in earnest for a new career.

Breaking ties to the profession leaves you without a sense of belonging. And that's a terribly uncomfortable state. But look at the trade-off this way: If you're now living with the pain of being somewhere you'd rather not be, you'll only trade one uncomfortable feeling for another. The good news is that once you start the process of moving closer to satisfaction, you'll eventually feel much better. On the other hand, if your fear of the future keeps you stuck, you'll be doomed to the doldrums for a lot longer.

"Before you make a break from the law," says one former practicing lawyer, "you have to overcome your own ego. My ego was right there in front of me all the time. It said, 'I'm a lawyer' on a big plaque and I kept running into it."

How can you break through this daunting barrier? The most important ingredient is support, reaching out to others who have made the change before you or who are struggling through the same process. I'll illustrate with my own experience.

Most of my self-esteem was tied up with my success in law—as a student, in practice and as a bar association leader. My confidence sank like a stone when I realized that my one-year sabbatical was really my first step out of the profession. I felt like the person I had been as a teenager—horridly insecure and afraid. I didn't want to set foot in any law offices because I felt like such a failure.

E Being Realistic about Transition

Nearly a year later, I understood myself well enough to know that I would never return to the practice of law. But other than a vague notion of being a writer, I still hadn't identified any concrete options to pursue. I gradually fell into a low-grade but persistent depression and avoided locations and social events that might attract other lawyers.

My malaise didn't ease until I started to research my first book, *Running from the Law,* and was able to connect with other lawyers who had made the same decision. I could look at them, see what remarkable people they were and how much they enjoyed their lives, and slowly recognize that I had the same potential.

The more involved I became with the issue of career change for lawyers, the better I felt about my decision, although I wasn't free of insecurity. It was hard to admit that my early income as the founder of a support group for transitioning lawyers was so much less than what I used to earn.

Eventually, I replaced my lawyer persona with others: "human being," "author and public speaker," "wife," "friend" and "former practicing lawyer." Now, more than 11 years from the day I closed my office doors, I'm proud of my flexible and creative lifestyle and can say, quite honestly, that I have absolutely no regrets about my choice to leave the practice of law. But I would never have completed my transition if I hadn't reached out to others.

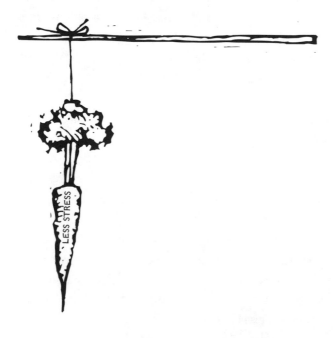

PART F

IMPLEMENTATION

Three Keys to a Successful Job Hunt

"People are always blaming their circumstances for what they are. I don't believe in circumstances. The people who get on in this world are the people who get up and look for the circumstances they want, and if they can't find them—make them."
—*George Bernard Shaw, playwright*

. . .

How would you describe today's employment market? Competitive, depressing and frustrating—or interesting, challenging and provocative? Is it puzzling, disorganized, amorphous and confusing? Or would you say that it is simply normal: the way it always has been and will always be.

The truth is that in spite of the competition, frustration and disorganization, today's market is full of opportunities for those who employ a highly personalized and focused search. The random access, "I'll take anything" search, in contrast, will be depressingly unproductive. Applying en masse to every employer you hear of, and responding to every remotely relevant classified ad, will add up to nothing. You will not enhance your job-finding luck by flooding the market with your résumé. Like playing the lottery, the odds of hitting the jackpot with an appropriate position will be long indeed.

> Successful job hunts are based on initiative, and take time and effort.

We all know that successful job hunts are based on initiative; they take time and effort. No one will come looking for you. What is less understood is that today you must find the opportunities yourself, and put yourself in what—to some law school graduates—is the uncomfortable position of being the pursuer rather than the pursued. "Lawyers end up buying into society's view of the profession," says New

F Implementation

York City career counselor Celia Paul, "that they merit prestige, respect, big money, and that anything less is beneath them. I call it an 'entitlement mentality.' It's something I really have to work with."

At times, getting through a thorough self-assessment and research process will be enough to secure work. Just doing that painstaking homework may generate enough opportunities to avoid a more orthodox search. But don't feel bad if you now need to move on to the last step of transition. To handle your search for work in the most effective fashion, follow these three rules:

▶ Focus on the employer's needs at all times. In other words, to paraphrase John F. Kennedy, ask not what the employer can do for you, ask what you can do for the employer. Chapters 24 and 25 explore this strategy in more detail.

▶ Concentrate your marketing efforts on active, personal contact with others. Only if you have impeccable, directly relevant credentials should you gamble on passive methods like classified ads, résumés or cover letters. Fortunately, there are many interactive, warm and active ways to look for work outlined in Chapters 26 and 27.

▶ Be persistent in pursuing a flexible plan. The opportunities you seek may be elusive; the ones you do encounter may not, at first glance, appear to meet your needs. Keep an open mind and follow through anyway. The suggestions in Chapters 28 and 29 will help you strike a balance between persistence and flexibility.

Focusing on the Employer's Needs

"Success will continue to reward people who see opportunity where others see only problems."

—Anonymous

■ ■ ■

Melanie Rowland wanted to get out of government and into environmental activism, but was having a hard time finding work. Then she got a brainstorm. She researched the regional office of the Wilderness Society in her area to see if she could find a place for herself. In doing so, she learned that they lacked someone to handle the legal challenges presented by the spotted owl controversy. She studied the organization's budget, and also investigated the grants available to them so she could convince the agency's director that he could afford to hire someone to oversee that issue. She also wrote a job description for the position (including lobbying, media and public relations, fundraising, grant writing, training and evaluating emerging litigation) that perfectly reflected the sum of her work and volunteer experience. Yes, she got the job that she created.

> Employers hire new people for three reasons: they have a need, they accept the cost, and they recognize the fit.

Melanie's story illustrates how and why people get hired—whether for jobs, project work, legal representation or consulting. Employers hire new people for three reasons:

- ▶ They have a need; they want to or must get something done that they can't or don't want to do with current staffing.

▶ They accept the cost; they believe they can afford to pay someone else to do the work.

▶ They recognize the fit; they become convinced that one particular person (you) will do a better job of performing the work than anyone else under consideration.

Your task as a job-hunter is to try to match the employer in all three areas. Let's examine each in detail.

Need

Work opportunities develop for two reasons—maintenance and growth. An employer is either replacing a current employee or adding staff to handle new demands. When filling a "maintenance" slot, the employer has already resolved the issues of need and cost and can concentrate solely on fit. When deciding whether to "grow" the work force, the employer must first focus on need.

In a steadily expanding, information-based economy like we have today, many work opportunities for professionals develop in the growth category. In fact, a Harvard Business School study found that nearly half of those employed in professional, technical or managerial work had positions created for them, rather than moving into existing slots.

When a company is expanding, those with the power to hire are very busy. As a

Special Advice for the Small Business Market

Did you know that:

▶ Small businesses add virtually all of the net new jobs to the economy?
▶ Small businesses employ over half of the country's private labor force?
▶ Small firms hire more employees who are younger workers, older workers, women and part-timers?
▶ The small business sector comprises nearly 95 percent of privately-held firms?
▶ Small businesses account for 39 percent of America's gross national product?
▶ Small companies produce two and a half times as many innovations per employee as large firms?

For all these reasons and more, if you're moving from the practice of law to a nontraditional alternative, look for opportunities in the small business sector. When approaching a small business, keep these points in mind:

▶ Small businesses tend to want applicants with a demonstrated willingness to assume responsibility; commitment to hard work and doing the job; a high energy level; a team spirit; and good oral communication and interpersonal skills.

▶ Most jobs with small businesses are filled only as the need arises and begin immediately, unlike larger companies with long-term personnel forecasting and predetermined job categories.

▶ A small business probably will not have a personnel department, standard hiring procedures or fixed job duties, salaries and benefits.

▶ The top two hiring methods used by small businesses are non-employee referrals and employee referrals.

▶ In most cases, you will interview with the company founder, who probably is not a trained recruiter and who is taking valuable time from other concerns to talk with you. Interviewing with a company founder is a lot like talking to a parent about his or her child. The company represents a substantial personal and financial investment for the owner. The owner is looking for employees who will share that passion for the company and its future.

▶ Since everyone in the organization may want to get in on the hiring decision, you may have to talk to many people before you are hired.

▶ Small companies do not have the time or budget for extensive training. You must convince the interviewer that you know (or can quickly learn) about the business and can work without direct supervision.

▶ In a small company, you will probably be called upon to perform many roles. Emphasize your flexibility and willingness to perform whatever is necessary. You will likely be involved in decision-making and planning, so also emphasize your leadership and teamwork skills.

▶ Do not express fear of risk or uncertainty. (But research the stability of the company before you sign on.)

▶ You probably will have to negotiate your salary. Consider salary components that tie your compensation to your or the company's performance. (See discussion in Chapter 29 at page 241.)

result, they're more likely to need extra staff but less likely to have time to invest in an open hiring process. To minimize competition and maximize your chances of finding work, don't wait until they've found the time. Jump in before the employer recognizes the need, or while the employer is still assessing the problem, by finding out what an employer isn't getting done (that ought to be).

With 15 years of legal experience, the last eight as senior law department manager and assistant general counsel for a health insurance company, Michael Goldenkranz wanted "to be more in the happiness business." Through a careful self-assessment process, he mapped out four major professional interests: hospital service providers, in-house legal, community service and education. Then he began to make contacts.

In the course of his networking, he heard that a local hospital was in danger of losing its not-for-profit status because of a failure to contribute to the community. First, he studied the hospital's operations. Then he began a dialogue with the senior staff about what they saw to be the hospital's needs. Within a few months, he'd successfully proposed a new position for himself as assistant to the president. His job description, which he wrote, included counseling the hospital staff on risk management; advising on governmental, legislative and regulatory issues; serving as employee ombudsman and advocate; and maintaining the hospital's not-for-profit status by assessing community needs and recommending community service projects.

How do you find out what a particular employer needs? Gather intelligence. Read the newspapers, especially the business section of the daily paper and any specialized business journals in your area. Watch the court dockets: Is one company appearing often as a defendant? It may need preventive law help or litigation oversight. Talk to employees about what they see as the company's challenges. Talk to competitors to get the same information.

"Perhaps the most efficient way to [find out about a company] today is by studying the company's site on the Internet's World Wide Web," says Bill Gates of Microsoft. "On a website you can learn not only about employment opportunities but also about the needs and challenges the company faces. In fact you can often learn more about a company on the Web than you would by actually spending a day at the company."

Cost

Figure out how you can save or make the employer money, or how your presence will make life easier for the employer without being too costly. One of the best places to begin is your own client list. One former practicing lawyer believes there's real opportunity for people to convince business clients that they need you. "If it's a client you've known for years, you probably know a lot about their business," says Doug Stam. "Tell them what it will cost them a year for you to come on their payroll and what you can provide: contract writing and review, outside counsel supervision, discovery work, personnel problem intervention or workers' comp claim review and resolution."

A lawyer with private practice litigation experience read that a local corporation without in-house counsel was involved in extensive litigation. With some accuracy, he calculated the company's legal costs, arranged to meet the company president and showed how much money would be saved by hiring him to oversee the litigation and handle routine discovery work in-house. By focusing on the realities of today's cost-conscious professional environment, he overcame the president's reluctance to add another full-time salary to operating expense by demonstrating a clear financial benefit to the company.

The same tactic of focusing on cost may lead to temporary or project assignments (referred to as contract work among lawyers) that eventually turn into long-term employment. (See Cindy Vranizan's story at page 229.) If you want to sell yourself into something temporary that's likely to become something permanent, follow these tips:

First, target the right employers. Start your search with small to mid-sized companies. Many now hire temporary workers to help with what seems to be a temporary increase in workload. When that spike begins to look permanent, the contract employee suddenly becomes the most attractive candidate for the new position.

Lawyers with experience in civil litigation or transactional work may discover good contract opportunities with corporate legal departments. Small but growing companies with only one in-house lawyer may need temporary assistance with product chronologies, due diligence, routine filings or discovery work that may evolve into a permanent position as the company grows.

Whenever you talk with potential employers, communicate your flexibility. Make clear that you are willing to prove your suitability for a permanent position by starting out with a temporary assignment. But don't offer to take on a project without compensation when you already have experience in the area. That signals more desperation than talent.

Do your best work. When an employer is dissatisfied with the work of a temporary worker, there are no second chances. For that reason, accept only assignments within your competency and experience. Get clear instructions up front and repeat what you've been told to confirm you heard it correctly. If you'll be creating a written product, ask for samples so you can meet the employer's expectations of style and format. Then check in regularly as you progress to make sure you're still on track, and offer the very best product you can on a timely basis.

Most of all, make yourself indispensable. The employer wants you there to meet an urgent need at the right cost. Produce cost-effective results on that project while remaining alert to—and suggesting—other ways you can help out. Your temporary role will become permanent when you assimilate yourself into the company's operations and your presence is taken for granted.

Fit

Your task as a job-hunter is to demonstrate to the employer that you'll be a better worker than anyone else under consideration. The only way you can achieve this goal is to know both your strengths and the needs of your targeted audience. "My general advice to job applicants," says Microsoft's Bill Gates, "is to find out as much as possible about a company in advance. A demonstration of deep corporate knowledge on the part of a job applicant impresses me—and almost any other prospective employer."

Once you understand the employer's needs, you must articulate your value in terms the employer can understand. This is the second half of transferable skills analysis and is an essential part of job-finding success.

Failure to think in terms of transferable skills can be a significant barrier for lawyers. You get so comfortable using technical terms—taking depositions, writing briefs, filing motions—that you may not see the relationship between your legal experience and the demands of other fields.

Being able to articulate the transferability of your skills is just as essential for those applying for jobs in different areas of law, or in another state, as for those looking outside the profession. The meaning of technical terms used in law may differ from jurisdiction to jurisdiction or practice to practice. For example, "taking a deposition" means the same thing as "writing an affidavit" in some areas; in others, it refers only to a recorded question-and-answer session with both sides present. An instruction to "write a memorandum" in a transactional practice usually refers to a request for legal research on an issue of law. In a trial practice, it could refer to the same thing, or to a "memorandum of points and authorities" filed with a motion.

If you prepare a résumé or speak using legal jargon, whether you're taking a nontraditional step in law or looking for work outside the profession, you'll probably be misunderstood. Describing yourself as a civil litigator, or listing a job function of "motion practice" will be meaningless to many hiring personnel; they may have absolutely no idea what tasks you accomplished and what skills were demanded by your work.

At this point, you might seek to locate employers who know enough about lawyers to see the relationship between your background and the work for which you've applied. In fact, the most frequent request I receive from both lawyers and law students is to identify employers that hire lawyers in non-legal positions, and headhunters who market lawyers into alternative careers. My response is always the same: There are no such employers or headhunters.

It's totally up to you to correct the general public's very strange perception of what it is you learn in law school and in practice. One former practicing lawyer characterized it this way:

> How many of you have had the experience of having somebody walk up to you and say something like, "If I took my gold collection and put it in a living trust, and had my grandchildren as beneficiaries, and meanwhile could drop income, would I get an income tax benefit?" You look at them and say, "I don't know. I don't know anything about estate planning." And people look at you like, "Boy are you stupid. You're a lawyer. You don't know that?" What they think we learn in law school is a whole bunch of rules about everything. And that's not so.

When looking for work, it's your responsibility to translate what you've actually learned into easy-to-understand terms. For example, you could say you've learned to think, analyze, and find information, to persuade, to listen well and to persist no matter how difficult the process. You could also explain that you've had to adapt yourself to a wide variety of people and situations and as a result can operate very smoothly in most environments. Of course, whatever skills you emphasize must be necessary to success in the area you've targeted.

The good news is that once you finish the self-assessment process—especially answering the question, "Who am I?"—it's easier to articulate your strengths and qualifications in terms both legal and non-legal employers will understand. When you add the research you've done for each employer, you're fortified to handle an effective search.

F Implementation

The point is, your pitch should be tailored to each potential employer, highlighting those aspects of your background and experience that align with their needs. Consider former columnist Anna Quindlen's experience. After a good interview for a highly competitive position, she sent the hiring editor a ragged piece of a grocery bag with letters cut out of a newspaper forming the message, "Hire Anna Quindlen or you sleep with the fishes." She was instantly hired. Had she applied to a large law firm, it's unlikely her creativity would have been met with the same enthusiasm.

In the same way, marketing yourself as an established lawyer when you're trying to create a new career will be ineffective. One lawyer wanted to move into an equity management position with a sports manufacturer. To begin his search, he sent out several dozen cover letters, enclosing a conventional, chronologically-organized résumé in which he emphasized his impressive legal background, and asked to be considered for any "appropriate" positions. Not surprisingly, he received no callbacks. Later, he revised his résumé to emphasize his experience in financial management and the sports industry, and wrote individually-tailored cover letters that told of his interest in acquiring both a management and a financial interest in a start-up sports manufacturer. By speaking directly to the recipient's needs, he was able to uncover some intriguing opportunities.

Overcoming Objections to Your Background and Experience

"I am having a hard time getting prospective employers to take me seriously in my areas of interest, magazine editing and public relations. More to the point, they take me too seriously because I am a lawyer. I do not have a problem with starting at the bottom; but I am finding it extremely difficult to get anyone else to believe that I want to. I need to find an employer who is able to appreciate my experience as a lawyer, or at least overlook it and not allow it to be a hindrance to hiring me.

—*East Coast lawyer in transition*

■ ■ ■

Almost half of those surveyed in a Minnesota study of law school graduates who chose nontraditional careers said they faced employer resistance. For some, the objection stemmed from a prejudice against lawyers; for others it was simply the employer's inability to recognize the transferability of their skills and background. As a result, the grads understood it was up to them to market their degree and legal experience. They couldn't expect an employer to make the connection for them.

> All you have to do is be prepared to answer the stereotype questions.

Stereotypes about lawyers are an "easy roadblock for an interviewer to throw in the way of an applicant," says Ken, a lawyer stockbroker. When Ken wanted to change from law to institutional equity sales, he formulated answers to many legal stereotypes. "It really doesn't matter what you say as long as it is somewhat plausible," he says. "All you have to do is be prepared to answer the stereotype questions."

The first step in countering any objection is intensive self-study and preparation. Why are you moving into this field? What are your strengths and what "life credits" and experiences demonstrate them? You're going to have a hard time overcoming objections to your background and experience if your only reason for applying for another position is that you aren't making enough money in your current one.

The next step is research: Ask contacts in the new job or field what stereotypes or objections they anticipate someone with your background will face. (This information-gathering process is described in Chapter 17.) Then honestly evaluate whether those objections apply to you. If they do, figure out why the objectionable qualities might be an advantage to the employer. If the objections are not true for you, be prepared with examples from your past that prove they aren't.

Before you approach employers, prepare at least one story for every objection you anticipate. Then you can weave into your conversation examples of things you have done that show you do not fit their stereotype. For instance, if you anticipate they believe you are not a team player, respond to a question like "What do you enjoy most about your job?" with something like this: "The best part of practicing law for me has been working as part of a team to get a large commercial transaction closed."

Don't try to conceal the truth, hoping the employer won't care. You may have learned how to hide your feelings in court, but it's harder to remain impassive in a job interview. Your anxiety triggered by a half-truth may show in your body language or voice quality and be perceived as deception or dishonesty.

Don't wait for the employer to bring up the subject. Instead, raise the objection yourself as soon as you feel you've developed some rapport. You needn't linger on it though. Simply point out the situation, acknowledge that the employer may be concerned about it, and explain why it will not interfere with your ability to meet the demands of this job.

Then turn your apparent vulnerability into a strength. Someone who's been fired can always explain how he grew from the experience. A new graduate can point out that she's ready to be groomed into the type of lawyer the employer needs—and that she's willing to accept a lower salary to get the experience. The experienced lawyer can tout his ability to be profitable from the very first hour, pointing to the wisdom and maturity that come with age.

Now let's take a look at the objections lawyers and law students can expect to encounter, and what must be done to overcome them.

You have no directly relevant experience.

This is where transferable skills analysis will play a very big role in your success. If there's nothing on your résumé or in the background you've articulated so far that leads the employer to believe you can do the job, you need to explain how your background has prepared you for the work.

"When I was looking to change from law to institutional equity sales," says one former lawyer, "I formulated answers to many legal stereotypes. For example, when someone mentioned that law school trained lawyers for litigation, not sales, I mentioned that presenting a case in court really was a matter of presenting your facts or arguments in the most attractive, concise and forceful manner, exactly what a good salesperson should do."

Sharon Gerber used a similar argument when applying for a management position with a Los Angeles temporary placement agency after several years as a family law lawyer in Texas and a subsequent stint as a professional liability claims specialist in Southern California. She pointed out that to be effective in her work, she had to develop strong people skills, manage outside counsel and deal effectively with many very stressed lawyer insureds. "There is not a tougher group to manage than lawyers," she said. "I think I'll do just fine with staffing specialists."

The strongest point most lawyers can make is their ability to learn quickly. For example:

> In the practice of law, I've worked under pressure to solve a wide variety
> of problems in many different industries and fields, and for diverse clientele.
> One of the reasons I've been able to perform this work is my ability to get up
> to speed rapidly in new areas. I'm certain that ability compensates for what-
> ever I lack in actual experience.

Sometimes, though, simply acknowledging the validity of the employer's criticism can get you the job. Deborah Moore applied for a position as a human rights advocate when she was a year out of law school and had been helping her parents' business with their employment law matters since graduation. When the interviewing panel asked about her lack of experience, she was honest. "No, I don't have a background in human rights," she said. "But the work I've done representing individual rights in the workforce, and doing employment law work, has taught me how to advocate for people without power." One of the interviewers later told Deborah that the hiring committee admired her honesty. When she was hired, she was simply told to "brush up" on the city human rights statute before her first day of work.

We don't want a lawyer in this job.

According to a story in the *New York Times*, "Lawyers trying to switch careers say they are often typecast as narrow-minded, confrontational and unimaginative." Career consultants agree that your best strategy is to deal with those stereotypes head-on. One tactic is to take the high ground by explaining that you just didn't have "the killer instinct." That bit of humor answers the anti-lawyer objection before the interviewer has a chance to say, "We don't want to hire a lawyer because they're too argumentative and competitive."

Being perceived as a "glory-seeker" will be another impediment to work in the corporate world. Corporations want team players, not superstars. But lawyers are rewarded primarily for being high profile. Think about it. How do lawyers get new clients or partnership slots? By being recognized for being exceptional in some way: winning the most cases, bringing in the most business, billing the most hours. In contrast, accomplishments are owned by the department or division in a corporation, not any one individual. Put doubts about your capacity to be a team player to rest by describing your accomplishments with phrases like "contributed to," or "participated in" or "worked as part of a group." In short, play up your team spirit.

You can also be more direct in confronting these objections. If you think the interviewer holds but isn't voicing some prejudices against lawyers, bring them up yourself and explain why they don't apply to you. One non-threatening way to bring up the subject is to acknowledge your awareness of lawyer stereotypes and tell the interviewer that you've done a lot of thinking about how you would present yourself to fellow employees or potential clients to overcome their prejudices.

For example:

▶ Some might believe that with my law background I'm not a team player. My experience shows that not to be true. In my position as volunteer coordinator of the hospital fundraising project, I managed a team of 20 volunteers. All but one of them worked with me on the project from start to finish, and we raised 20 percent more money than in any previous year.

▶ One of my frustrations practicing law was the tendency of my peers to find fault with ideas and then reject them before researching and developing them further. That's one of the main reasons I'd prefer to get into an idea business like public relations. I consider myself a creative problem-solver. I want to generate and implement new possibilities, not strike them down before we've had a chance to explore them.

▶ I know that some employers regard lawyers in sales environments as

deal-breakers rather than deal-makers. One thing I prided myself in when
I was practicing law was my ability to get people who seemed pretty far
apart to agree on something reasonable for all of them. As an example,
I was able to settle a real estate lawsuit that had been pending for seven
years and involved 15 parties.

In the process of separating yourself from negative associations with lawyers,
don't make the mistake of dismissing your legal background. You want to demonstrate how your legal background makes you a bonus employee (or as San Francisco
career consultant Hindi Greenberg puts it, a "two-in-one" employee). You'll be able
to understand lawyers and the legal system, interpret legalities for the rest of the organization, and use your non-legal people and team skills to get the job done. In other
words, your legal knowledge will add another valuable dimension to your work.

On the other hand, if any of these stereotypes *do* apply to you, don't argue that
they don't. (If you're accused of being contentious and confrontational, you'll only
prove the point!) Instead, show how that characteristic strengthens your credentials.
For example, "Sometimes being confrontational is an advantage in a management
position. You need to have the courage to deal with difficult people, to confront
them and get the issues resolved. My legal training has taught me not to fear conflict
and to hit problems head on."

Why would a lawyer want a job outside the profession?
You must be a loser lawyer.

No matter how well you craft your cover letters and résumés, no matter how
sincere your enthusiasm and commitment to a new endeavor, as a law school
graduate or practicing lawyer you will inevitably be asked: "Why do you want to
leave the profession?"

First, be flattered. It suggests the interviewer holds you in high regard. It's possible the interviewer wanted to be a lawyer and cannot understand why anyone in
your position would be dissatisfied. Many members of the general public regard law
as a glamorous field they might have pursued if only they had the talent and persistence. To some, anyone who would leave the profession is suspect.

If you can't find a job practicing law, or if you haven't come to terms with
leaving the legal profession, the question—"Why do you want to leave?"—will hit
you like a brick wall. In fact, you might be asking yourself the same question and
wondering "Am I a failure?"

Such feelings may cause you to behave as though you have failed. One former lawyer was complimented by an interviewer for having a "very, very great" background. The lawyer's response was, "I do?" The interviewer replied, "Yes, but you still think there's something wrong with not wanting to practice law anymore." She hadn't mentioned her feelings, but her body language somehow signaled "failure" to him. People want to hire successes. Present yourself as somebody who has made a conscious, well-considered decision to do what you're doing.

It's easier to explain your new direction when you've taken the time for self-assessment. It's nearly impossible when you haven't. The point is to come up with your own heartfelt explanation for wanting to move toward the position under discussion, rather than away from your current one.

For example, one successful candidate for a position as assistant director of a law school career services office explained her motivation as follows:

> I've been working with families in crisis as a matrimonial lawyer for three years; client contact has been the most enjoyable part of my work. Career services work appeals to me because I want to remain involved in a field where I'm in close contact with people in the midst of change but I'd prefer to work in a cooperative, rather than adversarial, environment.

You can't afford to take this job.

The subtext here may be the same as the objection we just covered: "Why would someone as well-educated as you consider taking a job that pays so little money? Something must be wrong." It could also be that the employer is worried you'll quit as soon as you find a job in law that pays better; that subtext is handled at the end of this chapter. Usually though, this objection is raised when the employer assumes your salary demands will be excessive. Alison Cooper anticipated that objection when she lobbied for a position as director of career services at a Texas law school.

At the time Alison began her job search in university administration, she was earning $75,000 annually as a third-year associate in a large Dallas law firm. In preparation for what she knew would be a huge cut in pay, she had paid off her credit card debt and rented an inexpensive apartment in a less desirable part of town. When she heard about the opening as director of career services, paying $25,000 per year, she immediately applied. The review committee, however, assumed she wasn't aware of the salary and discarded her résumé. Undaunted, Alison obtained an interview by contacting several employees of the law school and describing to them the steps she had already taken, thereby assuring them of her willingness to accept a substantial pay cut. She was hired. Within two years, she was promoted to assistant dean for alumni relations, and her salary doubled.

You're too young.

Generation Xers must keep in mind the stereotypes they'll face, and be prepared to counter them with concrete examples. Many employers today have been burned by younger workers without enough commitment and courtesy to keep regular work hours, give adequate notice of quitting, or follow rules of professional etiquette in dress and communication. Your personal demeanor in an interview will speak volumes. At the same time, be prepared with stories of projects you saw through to the end, commendations you received for good attendance, or other examples of how you've met the expectations of prior employers.

You can also point out the advantages of your youth:

▶ Being as young as I am, I have the energy to devote to my work. I have no ties keeping me in the city and I'm willing to relocate and travel regularly.

▶ I'm aware that I don't have a lot of experience and as a result I'm willing to take a somewhat lower salary than you're offering (or than I deserve) for the privilege of learning from you. With me, you'll be getting more than your money's worth.

▶ I'm not likely to make the mistake of thinking that I know something I don't.

You're overqualified.

Second-career lawyers, especially those who reached a high level of responsibility before enrolling in law school, must defer to those who will be your teachers, even if they have fewer "life credits" than you. Susan Gainen, Career Services Director at the University of Minnesota School of Law, says that you need to express your interest in and willingness to be a junior member of a team. Younger employers may expect someone with your experience to disrupt the balance of power. It's your job to make them comfortable that you won't.

You're too old.

This objection actually suggests a number of questions: Will you work well with younger managers? Will your salary expectations be too high? How long will you stay

185

with the organization before you retire? Do you have any illness or disability that will interfere with your performance of the work?

The American Association of Retired Persons suggests that you emphasize the positive attributes of your age, including your accumulated experience, maturity, judgment, perspective, increasing responsibility, and consistent achievement. You can also point to your stability.

The Bureau of Labor Statistics estimates that only three percent of workers in their 50s change occupations in any given year while 12 percent of those age 25 to 34 take the plunge, and the annual career change rate for all ages is around ten percent. As a result, according to the national outplacement firm Challenger, Gray & Christmas, corporations believe that younger workers will stay an average of three to five years, while those in their early 50s are likely to remain until at least age 65. Since low turnover generally translates into increased efficiency, the older worker recoups for the employer any losses resulting from a higher salary or a shorter period of employment before drawing retirement benefits.

You might also try some of these arguments:

- ▶ Because of my age and status, I don't have the "family v. work" conflicts of so many other applicants. I can stay at work as long as it takes to get the job done.
- ▶ I have enough life experience to know that no job is perfect 100 percent of the time; I've learned to appreciate the positive factors of each assignment.
- ▶ I'm a seasoned veteran. I won't require training or orientation; I can dive right in without supervision and make a contribution immediately (as opposed to a younger job seeker's untested potential). Therefore, I'm worth a somewhat higher salary.

Above all, know that you're in good company in facing these prejudices. Because there are many older workers, and even more to come, books and pamphlets written just to your concerns have been entering the market. All of them—referenced in Appendix 3—show you how to highlight and underline your strengths, package a presentation, and present being an older worker as an advantage.

You were fired from your last job.

Joyce Lain Kennedy, who writes a syndicated newspaper column about job-seeking, suggests you tell the truth about losing your job, but take the opportunity to demonstrate how you've grown from the experience. In an interview, honestly but briefly recount the reasons for your termination, taking responsibility for everything including a difficult boss. Explain why you will not repeat the same pattern in this job. For example, you now believe in deferring to your boss's expertise, or your personal problems have ended, or you've learned to ask for help when you don't have the experience or knowledge to handle something.

Don't try to hide the truth, hoping that you won't be found out. Many employers want to know about your last employment, even if you don't list a reference for that position. It's best to provide the name of a contact who will speak fairly of your work. Be aware, though, that sometimes the hiring personnel will sidestep your recommendation and contact an acquaintance of theirs to confirm your explanation. Anticipate the worst of what your former employer might say, accept responsibility for that evaluation, and explain what you learned from the experience.

Your résumé has a noticeable time gap.

If you've been unemployed for a long time, determine why and how it relates to this job application. Have you now broadened your job search after evaluating the transferability of your skills? Were you trying to move into a different field but now realize you're more suited to this area?

Kennedy suggests that if you've had an illness and are now completely recovered, "stress that your illness is not likely to recur and briefly speak of your doctor's encouragement to get back to work. If your health outlook isn't that rosy, bone up on Americans with Disabilities Act provisions."

If, instead, you took a long, unpaid "sabbatical" to travel, raise children, or just recover from burnout, seek employers who understand and appreciate adventure, balance, or personal growth. Before applying, review the lessons you learned during your break. Then present that unconventional detour in its most positive light, turning it into a strong selling point. As an example, one young lawyer spent a small inheritance skiing in Europe and generally fooling around during a two-year sabbatical from private practice. He later obtained a position in-house with a sports manufacturer by explaining how pleased he was that he'd taken time out when he was young enough to enjoy it, and how eager he now was to get back to work.

You're a woman.

You'd think by now that gender would be less of an issue in hiring than it is. But statistics prove that women are still being penalized for not being men. Women earn only about 70 percent of the salaries of men who do exactly the same work. In the legal profession, ABA studies indicate that, after ten years in private practice, only one in five women have made partner, compared to three out of five men.

Female applicants face one primary prejudice: You'll be more committed to your personal life than to your family (as evidenced by the probability that you'll want some time off to give birth and raise your children). One black female partner of an overwhelmingly white, male megafirm attributes her success with the firm in part to her fierce loyalty. She believes that this characteristic, fostered in men from an early age, is one which male partners and clients expect without qualification from their colleagues. She also has remained unmarried and childless throughout her 20-year career; the quality she calls loyalty could also be defined as undivided attention to the firm.

To overcome this subtle and always unexpressed attitude, let the interviewer know that you're accustomed to juggling multiple responsibilities. Were you a parent in law school or when you were studying for the bar examination? Have you taken on a demanding volunteer project while handling a heavy caseload? Did you nurse someone close to you back to health while holding down a full-time job? The more examples you cite of times when you've successfully balanced conflicting demands, the better.

You're a member of a minority group.

"Your objective isn't to turn someone who's against you, or who believes in negative stereotypes, into an avid supporter," say Michael Kastre, Nydia Rodriguez Kastre and Alfred Edwards in *The Minority Career Guide.* "Rather, your goal is to reduce that person's negativity enough so that it doesn't hinder your career."

Most of the prejudice you'll encounter will relate directly to the question of whether you'll be compatible with the organization. Demonstrate your conformity through your actions and past history. If you cannot show a fit, ask yourself how much you want to join a club that doesn't want you as a member.

In other words, expect prejudice and choose potential employers based on your tolerance for bigotry. Either seek employers with reputations for open-mindedness, or set out to be a paradigm shifter or trailblazer. No matter what choice you make, you must show the employer not only that you can do the job, but that you will fit in.

One law student with stellar credentials sought a position with one of the major large firms in town. Her goal would have been completely reasonable, except that she was a transsexual who dressed in tight dresses and spike heels, and wore thick make-up. Her look and style excluded her from consideration by any conservative law firm; she also let every interviewer know she was in the midst of a change in sexual identity. Certainly she deserves credit for being courageous. Still, she only reinforced the stereotypes and prejudices she tried to overcome.

You have a disability.

Don't hide your disability. The fact that you've gotten as far as you have speaks well for you. As opportunistic as this may sound, your disability may give you an edge when applying to large private and public employers who wish to demonstrate their commitment to a diverse workforce.

Your attempts to cover up your disability may also backfire. A deaf lawyer with excellent law school credentials wanted to keep her hearing difficulties secret, fearing employers would see her impairment as interfering with her ability to do a good job. In several interviews, she did not hear the questions posed and responded inappropriately. By failing to reveal her hearing loss, she conveyed exactly what she feared she would: The employers thought she was inattentive or unintelligent.

The best approach is to be straightforward about your disability without asking for sympathy. Show through your accomplishments (and a couple of glowing recommendations) how capably you've met the challenges of your disability in other environments.

You'll quit as soon as you find a job in the law.

If it's true, play fair. Admit that you'll continue your search for legal employment and point out what you'll be able to contribute to their operation in the meantime. Also assure them that you'll provide whatever length of notice they require. But don't expect this argument to sell very well, except for temporary or project assignments.

That raises one last point: Showing employers that their objections are unfounded does not mean you'll overcome those objections, or that you'll get the job. The employer's prejudice may be intractable and, of course, you're often competing with others who are more qualified than you. But you'll never get anywhere if you can't at least address the employer's concerns.

Repeatedly running into the same objections may mean that you need to get some educational, volunteer or internship credits behind you. It may also mean that you ought to target different employers. A small entrepreneurial venture may appreciate a jack-of-all-trades more than a large company where functions are sharply defined and separate. A history of providing good results but remaining in jobs for only a short time will make you an appealing candidate in temporary, project-driven, consulting or contract work situations.

Marketing Techniques

"When everyone thinks alike, no one thinks much."

—*Walter Lippman, journalist*

. . .

One of the big debates today among career counselors concerns the relative success of marketing techniques. What percentage of job-hunters get their jobs through networking? 85 percent? 75 percent? Fewer? Are many people hired through the Internet? How many employers rely upon classified ads, mail campaigns or headhunters? You won't find anything close to a consensus.

The percentages don't matter much, though, because all the experts do agree that a job search emphasizing active, personal contact with others is much more effective than one that doesn't. It's okay to use conventional job search techniques like mailing out résumés and responding to classified advertisements. But if you want to wage a cost-effective and time-efficient campaign, spend most of your time on techniques that are interactive rather than solo, warm rather than cold, and active rather than passive. Getting together for coffee with a colleague of your Aunt Lucy is the classic effective marketing technique. By the

> A job search emphasizing active, personal contact with others is much more effective.

same token, mailing your résumé to everyone Martindale-Hubbell lists in your area of interest is one of the least effective ways to find work. Let me explain.

"Interactive" self-marketing involves more than face-to-face contact. Ear-to-ear (not ear to voicemail), keyboard to keyboard, and sometimes e-mail to e-mail contact also works. Attending a seminar or meeting only counts as interactive if you actually talk to the people around you!

A technique is "warm" when you have some connection to the person you're contacting. Either you've been referred by someone who has given you permission to use his name in introduction, or you graduated from the same school, you attended the same church or belong to the same interest group, or you've read an article the person wrote or heard her speak at a program. It's the opposite of cold-calling, which is contacting someone you know nothing about and who knows nothing about you.

An "active" technique is one you initiate yourself. You don't wait for someone to notice what a fine worker you are, and offer you a fantastic job at an astounding salary. You don't wait for someone to read your résumé and pick up the telephone to call you. You follow up your letter with a telephone call a few days later.

Lawyers tend to resist the interactive, warm and active job-finding techniques. "Lawyers like to feel special, that their career issues are different from the average Joe," says consultant Ava Butler. "They feel that because they have paid their dues in law, that they're paid up forever." But lawyers aren't different and they're not entitled to special treatment in the job hunt. They have to go through the same hoops as everybody else, making contacts and building an image.

The Marketing Grid on page 192 lists just about all the ways you can find work. I've organized the techniques into four categories: (A) on your own, (B) in a group, (C) one-on-one, and (D) as a leader. For over a year, I asked the lawyers and law students in my national seminars to select the method that led to their last job. At least three-quarters of every group identified a technique from Category C: one-on-one.

Since none of the techniques in category A is interactive and few are warm or active, only those with impressive, directly relevant credentials should rely on those options. That's not to say you shouldn't pursue any of them; just don't let them limit your other efforts.

Category B techniques are good ways to warm up your contacts, but must be combined with Category C techniques to be effective. More experienced lawyers, those who want to be entrepreneurs or consultants, and those hoping to enter a new field at a high level, should supplement their Category C work with liberal amounts of Category D techniques.

The rest of this chapter explores each category of job-finding techniques in more detail, and gives you tips for making your efforts as effective as possible.

A/On Your Own

Responding to Classified Advertisements

In 1996, you might have scanned the classified section of your local newspaper or bar association publication and remarked on how slim the job market was. A few weeks later, you may have heard about three colleagues who secured exciting new jobs you never saw advertised. Lately, you've probably noticed a ten-fold

The Marketing Grid

A/On Your Own

Respond to a classified advertisement

Mass mail letters/résumés

Mail résumés to targeted employers
    without follow up

Post announcements in law libraries

Place a "position wanted" ad

Respond to a government job posting

Work with a legal search consultant

Post a home page on the Internet

Mail letters/résumés to colleagues

Write author of relevant article or book

B/In a Group

Attend a job fair

Attend a law school recruiting interview

Attend alumni association meetings

Attend religious gatherings

Attend seminars/lectures

Attend social functions

Attend sports events

Perform nonprofit volunteer work

Seek out a campaign volunteer position

Take on committee work

C/One-on-One

Ask friends and family for leads

Talk to colleagues about openings

Ask neighbors & acquaintances for leads

Call on individual employers

Converse with other lawyers
    on the Internet

Do cold-calling

Follow up letters/résumés by telephone

Contact those to whom you've
    been referred

Go door-to-door

Initiate conversations at any function

Initiate conversations in the law library

Take a contact to lunch

D/As a Leader

Write a column for a newsletter/journal

Accept or solicit speaking engagements

Write and publish articles

Chair a fundraising campaign

Chair a volunteer project

Chair a bar association committee

Direct a political campaign

Edit a bar association publication

Found an information-and-support group

Involve yourself as a community activist

Lead reform or investigation efforts

Run for a professional association office

increase in the number of ads. Yet you still know of people who can't find work.

Many job-hunters operate with the mistaken belief that all jobs are published or posted somewhere. Some even believe it's a legal requirement for employers to do so. You might also be under the common misconception that jobs are advertised solely to communicate news of an opening. In point of fact, advertisements are placed for many other reasons as well:

- ► To satisfy EEO requirements;
- ► To comply with regulations requiring the posting of open government positions;
- ► To justify the hiring of a non-resident alien;
- ► When there's no one in-house who wants the position;
- ► When the position pays a below-market salary;
- ► When the employer seeks applicants unfamiliar with its poor reputation;
- ► When the employer needs to combat high turnover;
- ► When the employer plans to hire from within or has already identified another outside candidate, but wants to confirm there's no better applicant available.

Even when an advertisement has been placed for the sole purpose of attracting applicants, the person chosen for the position is often someone who found out about the opening through a Category C method. A non job-hunter sees the advertisement, thinks of a job-hunting friend and passes the word on. Then, the job hunter telephones a contact at the company, rather than mailing in a résumé, and gets an interview without sending a cover letter and résumé.

David, a lawyer and CPA, read a classified advertisement for a position as a controller. He casually mentioned the opening to his next door neighbor and discovered that his neighbor knew the president of the company. He suggested that David telephone the president, using his name as a reference. David followed the lead, was interviewed and hired. His first day on the job, he found about 200 never-reviewed résumés and cover letters stacked on his desk for his reply. His own was in the middle of the pile.

Generally, those who *do* succeed in obtaining employment by mailing in a cover letter and résumé in response to a classified advertisement are currently employed and have a background that precisely fits the job requirements. They probably also have impressive credentials such as graduation from a top ten school or employment with a well-known law firm or company. But the vast majority of job-finders will *not* find their next position by simply responding in writing to a classified ad.

Placing your own classified ad will yield even more disappointing results. This passive job search tactic conveys more arrogance or desperation than initiative.

F Implementation

"Headhunters"

Executive or legal search consultants, otherwise known as "headhunters," are hired by law firms, government agencies, universities and corporations to find the ideal person to fill a high-level position. Some headhunters work on retainer from the employer, usually to fill a key position in a large corporation or public agency. Others are compensated only if they successfully place an applicant. In either event, they are paid a substantial fee (as much as 40 percent of an annual salary) to locate candidates whose experience closely matches the job profile provided to them.

Since most legal search consultants are paid a contingent fee, law firms may ask several to compete against each other to fill an open position. The headhunters usually target associates from large law firms who have two to five years of experience and who either graduated from prestigious law schools or have outstanding academic records, or (more commonly in a shrinking market) are associates or partners with esoteric or "hot" specialties or an existing client base.

In the non-legal market, executive search consultants are interested primarily in currently employed, seasoned managers working at the highest levels of private industry or government. Like headhunters in the legal profession, they seek candidates from good schools and good companies who are involved in professional organizations, have published articles and are known for their public speaking skill. Rarely are headhunters interested in the inexperienced job-hunter or even the most experienced mid-level manager.

Due to the economics of their business, neither legal nor executive search consultants try to find a job that particularly suits you. In addition, they generally won't work with you to create your selling points or help you redirect your career. Instead, they're commodity brokers. They market your experience and credentials only as they directly and obviously satisfy the employer's specifications.

As a result, *there are no legitimate headhunters anywhere in the nation who try to place lawyers in non-legal positions.* Be wary of any firm that advertises such a service, especially if it requires an up-front fee.

Even if a headhunter might be interested in you, working with one cannot be categorized as an effective job-search method. You're developing a relationship with an intermediary, not with potential employers, and you're waiting for the opportunities to come to you, as passive a stance as you can take. Only if you are looking for a different job within the legal profession (especially if you wish to move from a law firm to a corporation, or to a new geographic area), and fit the general profile, should you even contact a headhunter.

The best way to get a headhunter's attention, according to *New York Times* business columnist Mary Rowland, is to make the contact while you're still employed. Prepare a straightforward, one-page cover letter and chronological résumé on conservative stationery. State your current situation, what you'd like to do next, what parts of the country you would consider, and your salary expectations. Then follow up with a telephone call to determine the recruiter's interest in you as a potential placement.

Mail Campaigns

It shouldn't surprise you, but employers today receive more unsolicited résumés than they can possibly read. Consequently, the mass mailing of cover letters and résumés yields disappointing results. Done right, however, selective mailings can be an effective way to mine for openings.

To distinguish your letter from the rest, personalize your correspondence. Before you send the letter, try to learn more about each recipient. Better yet, locate someone who actually knows the employer and will let you use his or her name in introduction. Then, open your letter with a reference to that person, or by mentioning the recipient's practice area, affiliation or latest high-profile case.

Follow up every letter with a telephone call a few days later. Don't expect your contacts to telephone you; this happens rarely. And don't mail so many letters at once that it would take weeks to reach everyone. Networking expert Cynthia Chin-Lee, author of *It's Who You Know,* says that you don't want to wait so long that the person could have read your letter and forgotten about it. Equally important, don't wait so long that *you've* lost interest or convinced yourself that if the recipients were interested they would have called *you* by now.

Take advantage of any phone calls that lead to friendly voices, even if the contacts make it clear they are not hiring. Turn those strangers into colleagues—and potential referral sources—by inviting them to coffee or lunch.

Most important, persist. If you proceed with the notion that your mail campaign will require at least as much time and effort—and as much strategic planning—as a difficult lawsuit, you'll find employment.

B/In a Group

Volunteering and Affiliating

Volunteer work is a good way to develop the contacts you need, especially if you are reluctant to telephone people you don't know. A leadership role will get you the farthest the fastest; even support roles like registering attendees at seminars or editing the newsletter will introduce you to the players in the field.

A 1994 University of Connecticut Law School graduate got her first "job" at the end of 1995 by volunteering for a community organization. One member of the board alerted her to a city government opening as a discrimination investigator; other board members lobbied hard for her to get selected out of 75 applicants.

The more involved you get in the organization, the better. Doris successfully led the local humane society's effort to legislate antivivisection laws. With this high profile involvement, she became well-known and respected by the society. A year later, the society director resigned and a search began for a replacement. Even though Doris's employment background was strictly limited to public service law practice in a non-supervisory role, she sold her leadership abilities to the society's board of directors by pointing to her efforts on the anti-vivisection campaign. She was hired because they knew her, liked her and respected her.

Joining—and participating in—professional associations related to the area you'd like to enter is another great way to develop contacts, build credibility and get the inside track on job openings. Some associations even operate job hotlines for their active members.

Peter was drawn to alternative dispute resolution while practicing in a small litigation firm, and decided to learn everything he could about that area. He joined and then chaired the ABA's ADR committee, spending his own money to attend functions across the country. When his job situation soured, he spread the word among his ADR contacts that he was looking for new employment. At the same time, he continued his commitment to ADR by volunteering to assist with a lawyer-sponsored nonprofit mediation program in his area. Another volunteer for the program was so impressed by Peter's experience, enthusiasm and commitment to ADR that he immediately hired him when a position opened up in his corporate law department.

When you get a chance to work with someone you respect, whether you're volunteering, or being paid for your services, do your best. As in Peter's situation, your enthusiasm and the quality of your work will be the keys to your future networking success.

To make your affiliations and volunteer work really count, join an organization with a goal or mission you endorse, or a subject focus you find truly fascinating. Don't be so calculated as to choose a group based on the number of potential employers as members. The point is to connect with people with whom you have an innate bond.

What if you're shy and terribly uncomfortable around strangers? (One *Wall Street Journal* columnist estimates that 40 percent of the population falls into this category.) Prepare a few "small talk" questions to serve as conversation openers. Make them open-ended so that the other person does most of the talking at first! Questions like "How did you find out about this group?" or "What do you know about the speaker?" or "How long have you been involved with this group?" or "What drew you to this topic?" will break the ice in a non-threatening manner.

Practicing can make it easier. Give a friend a list of questions and rehearse your answers. Keep at it until your words flow smoothly. Ask questions as well, and listen carefully to the answers. Sometimes you can get so nervous that you forget to hear the response; that makes it a lot more difficult to come up with the next question or comment.

Make a point of talking to someone at the first meeting you attend. To find a likely companion, scan the room for someone who looks as lost as you may feel. Or ask permission to take a seat next to a group of people who seem to know each other well and let them know this is your first encounter with the organization. Prepare yourself for this initial contact by telephoning group headquarters before you arrive to find out as much as you can about the agenda and the group.

Whether or not you have trouble talking to strangers, make sure that you convey a clear impression of who you are and where you're going. Be honest and straightforward about your employment situation. The people you meet through your participation won't know how to help you if you don't let them know what you need.

To make sure your self-disclosure flows well, rehearse a short description of yourself before you attend the first meeting. Make it one that connects your interest in this organization with your talents and career goals. If you can't come up with that kind of introduction, you're getting involved with the wrong group!

Keep a supply of your business cards easily accessible—in a coat pocket rather than your wallet or purse—and exchange cards with everyone you meet. Write a note about each person on the back of the card to remind you of your conversation. When you return to your office, follow up by telephone or mail with the people you've met and liked.

It's okay to attend one meeting as an observer just to get comfortable. By your second, though, you'll need to take some initiative. Raise your hand when volunteers for a new committee or task force are requested. Offer to write or edit articles for the newsletter. If you're shy or reserved, lend a hand with behind-the-scenes organization for a social or educational event. You'll then be able to attend as one of the in-crowd.

C/One-on-One

Lesah Beckhusen worked with a group of unemployed 1995 law school graduates to assist them in proactive marketing. The group had "incredible resistance to networking as a way to uncover positions," says Beckhusen. It took numerous discussions to break through their cynicism and resistance. But those who tested the ideas while still in class came back feeling empowered.

"The real job market is word-of-mouth," says Jeffrey J. Mayer, author of *Find the Job You've Always Wanted in Half the Time with Half the Effort.* In fact, conventional wisdom in the career counseling and job-search industries is that four out of five job hunters find new employment in this "hidden" job market. Lee Hecht Harrison, a national outplacement firm, defines the "hidden job market" as those "unadvertised,

Networking Success Story #1

At the beginning of her third year at Chicago-Kent College of Law, Cynthia Tackett decided she didn't want a traditional law firm job with long hours and constant conflict. The career services director at her law school, Lisa Abrams, suggested that she read this book and begin informational interviewing with women in law-related fields.

One of her first interviews was with a woman who worked as a claims attorney at an insurance company. Cynthia's father knew the woman, and thought she could provide some guidance for his daughter. Eight months later, the claims attorney called Cynthia with the news that her company had an opening for a first-year attorney in a newly created division that focused on Cynthia's area of interest, managed healthcare.

During the series of interviews that followed, Cynthia retold the story of how she found out about the opening. She explained to this lawyer that she didn't want to be the great trial lawyer she had always thought she wanted to be. He responded with the admission that, after five years at a big Chicago law firm, he felt the same way. "He then held up a copy of this book," says Cynthia, "and suggested I read it. I told him that I had not only read it, but had attended a seminar with the author a few months before." That interviewer is now her immediate supervisor! "Needless to say," says Cynthia, "the book helped facilitate a great interview and helped me get the job of my dreams, at a higher salary than I requested!"

often even unidentified, positions that someone gets because they talked to the right person at the right time."

According to *The Fordyce Letter,* an employment industry newsletter, only one percent of the employers they studied had ever hired an applicant because of a mailed-in résumé. On the other hand, 99 percent hired those who contacted them directly. The U. S. Department of Labor and the *Harvard Business Review* confirm this result. According to studies conducted by both, approximately 75 percent of all jobs are found through personal and professional contacts. This process of making contacts is commonly known as networking.

How Employers Use Networking

"I learned a long and bitter lesson about the importance of building a network and the futility of my sit-home-and-wait strategy," said one anonymous lawyer writing to a bar association newsletter. "I had a quality résumé, and yet my career was in ruins. My eventual employment was a textbook example of how networking works: The open position was desirable enough to attract hundreds of applicants. Yet the job was never advertised. In fact, I was the only candidate interviewed."

Employers want to find the best person for the job—but expend the least possible effort and expense. Placing an advertisement in a local newspaper doesn't cost much; following up on all the applications does. One reason employers hire through contacts is that they prefer to hire people they know. It's also less time-consuming to talk to a few people sent in by associates than to review hundreds of applications and interview dozens of qualified candidates.

At times, simply advertising the position results in networking contacts that lead to the perfect candidate, enabling the employer to ignore the many who respond by mail to the advertisement. (Read about David's experience on page 193.) Employers also network among themselves to find new employees. Those people who have made contacts and developed rapport will be remembered and referred. In these times of downsizing, the network method of finding new hires has become even more widespread. More and more employers (including some law firms) are encouraging current employees to find the right candidate for an open position by offering to pay a bonus for their successful efforts.

Jim Rupp was a sixth-year associate when he started his hunt for an in-house corporate position. About nine months into his search, he noticed a position advertised by ABC Corporation for a lawyer with two to three years experience. He mailed in his cover letter and résumé and waited for a reply. A week later, he was told by letter that he was overqualified for the position, but that his résumé would be "kept on file" for future reference. At the same, Jim continued to make contacts. The general counsel for XYZ Corporation wanted to hire him, but couldn't get authorization for another salary. In the meantime, ABC Corporation realized that it needed a more experienced lawyer for its open position. Rather than advertising again or looking through résumés like Jim's that had supposedly been retained, ABC's general counsel telephoned XYZ's general counsel for referral to a qualified candidate. Jim's name was passed along, and he was hired.

At a seminar on job finding, Jim first explained his employment as a stroke of luck. Upon reconsideration, he realized it was more a matter of hard work. If he hadn't made personal contacts with dozens of potential employers, his name wouldn't have gotten to the right people. He then quoted the late entrepreneur Armand Hammer: "Luck seems to come to you when you work 17 hours a day!"

How Networking Really Works

Some of you might consider networking awkwardly calculating. You see yourself picking up the telephone to talk to a complete stranger about something you know and care nothing about. You worry that you'll find yourself begging for a job, or manipulating the listener to do something he or she does not want to do. That is definitely not networking.

Networking is community building. It is "the ability to create and maintain an effective, widely-based system of resources that works to the mutual benefit of yourself and others."

Most of us network in some form every day. You network when you ask a fellow lawyer for input on case strategy. You network when you investigate a client's case by telephoning potential witnesses. You network when you contact experts and acquaintances for leads and information about purchasing a new house or car. So what's so off-putting about networking for job leads? It's the same investigational process.

To start, flip through your address book and your memory to make a working list of everyone you know—from your best friend to your pharmacist. ("Who Are Your Contacts?" on the next page may assist your memory in coming up with networking possibilities.) At this point, don't even think about whether they might have any information about your area of interest, or whether they might know anyone who does.

Once you've created a thorough list, identify which of your acquaintances are most likely to have contacts—or to know others who do—in your fields of interest. Ask friends, relatives, acquaintances, and business associates for names of individuals

Who Are Your Contacts?

- Family
- Prior coworkers
- Current coworkers
- Judges
- Law school professors
- Law school students
- Law school staff
- College acquaintances
- Sorority or fraternity members
- Alumni association
- Professional associations
- Volunteer affiliations

- Children
- Neighbors
- Customers or clients
- Armed Forces
- Doctors
- Dentists
- Accountants
- Bankers
- Insurance agents
- Sports team members
- Athletic club members
- Counselors

who might be able to provide job leads or information. You can also use your list to locate someone who is acquainted with the person responsible for hiring a specific position, and use that person's name to obtain an in-person interview. In a job search, no connection is too remote.

Friends, colleagues and acquaintances are some of your best sources. According to Jack Erdlen, CEO of an outplacement and human resources consulting firm, people tend to give preferential treatment to those people they or their friends know. And don't underestimate the contacts family members can provide, says former practicing lawyer and now career consultant Joan Bibelhausen of Minneapolis. One of Joan's clients discussed his career goals with his future mother-in-law at a holiday dinner party. As it turned out, his future in-law had a friend who was well-placed in an organization he had been pursuing. The friend in the company clued him into a temporary position; he was hired within a week. That experience gave him the credibility he needed to secure another permanent position later.

Be sensitive to how you approach people. "If you call someone up and ask them to help you to do something that they cannot do effectively, you engender guilt," says Chicago career counselor and former practicing lawyer Sheila Nielsen. "Your friends feel uncomfortable because they do not know of a job for you. That is why they cut short their conversation." Sheila suggests that you ask your contacts to assume a role they can handle effectively, such as advising you on the marketplace or counseling you on job search techniques.

It's natural not to feel entirely comfortable calling people you don't know, no matter what the subject. If that's true for you, call people you *do* know, write letters, or seek out information through a computer network. The community-building process has all sorts of channels. For tips about the etiquette of networking, reread the discussion about informational interviewing in Chapter 17 at page 130.

Whenever you meet or talk to someone new, ask that person for names of at least three others who might be able to help you, and request permission to use your contact's name in making your introductions. Never use a contact's name without prior approval.

Networking Success Story #2

At the end of 1990, Rob Hoon, then a fifth-year associate at a mid-sized insurance defense firm, was given an ultimatum: commit to the firm or leave. His gut told him to leave, but he worried that leaving the firm might mean leaving the law. He was "reined in," as he puts it, after a timely meeting with a career counselor. The counselor suggested that since he'd only practiced in one type of legal environment, he ought first to spend time evaluating his preferences and then research the legal profession to see where else he might apply his talents.

Rob took the advice by enrolling in a self-assessment workshop for lawyers. Through that process, he got in touch with his love of troubleshooting, i.e., anticipating potential problems in complex organizations and brainstorming solutions to those minor problems before they could blow up into crises. Remembering peak experiences from his college days, Rob targeted higher education as the right environment for him. Then, by talking to other practitioners, he discovered that the work of lawyers in the Higher Education Division of the Attorney General's office closely matched his profile of an ideal job.

Like many other lawyers in transition, Rob accepted a temporary contract position with a litigation firm to cover family expenses while he was working toward his goal. This experience only confirmed what he had learned through the workshop process: He did not want to practice law in a civil litigation environment.

Despite his persistence, it took Rob much longer than he'd anticipated to secure the position he really wanted. He became discouraged and was tempted to accept a less appealing alternative. Again, he listened to some good advice, this time from a lawyer already employed in the Attorney General's office. "Don't give up on the slow hiring process," he'd said. "Remain flexible enough to jump when the right offer comes along."

After being warned that higher education slots were so coveted that positions were always filled from inside, Rob received an offer in March 1991 to work in the Attorney General's office at Washington State University in Pullman, Washington. This occurred almost simultaneously with the decision he and his wife made to move to a small town so they could afford to live on one paycheck. (They were expecting the arrival of their second child at the time.)

Rob's new position turned out to be 90 percent advisory and problem-solving, involving conversations and group meetings rather than memos and the library. Through introspection, patience, persistence, and networking, Rob, in his own words, "put [him]self in the position to get a little lucky." He thrived so well in the university environment that he was soon promoted out of the Attorney General's Office and into a position in general administration as executive assistant for business affairs.

When you contact a lead, be specific:

- ► Who should I contact at your company to find out about job openings in my field?
- ► Do you know anyone who might be aware of current openings?
- ► I'd really appreciate some advice about my job-hunting tactics.
- ► Could you review my résumé to see if it adequately addresses the needs of my market?
- ► Would you be willing to drop off a copy of my résumé with the head of a particular department?
- ► Could you arrange an interview for me with the hiring authority?
- ► Could you put in a good word for me with the hiring director?

If you know someone who is hiring for a job, call that person, explain that you are looking for work and, if you feel comfortable, indicate that you are aware of the opening. If your contact does not associate you with the position or encourage you to apply, either she's looking for different qualities than you possess or she has already picked someone for the position.

Meeting with Your Contact

Ask your contacts and their referrals for short, face-to-face meetings rather than conducting your questioning over the telephone. This way your contact will be able to attach a face and personality to your name. You might also develop a rapport that will assist you in the future.

Sometimes it helps to request a very short period of time—15 minutes to half an hour. If you are granted an interview based on that representation, be prepared to leave when the agreed-upon period has elapsed. The contact may wish to extend your meeting, but leave the choice to him or her. Offer to pick up the tab for both of you if you meet over coffee or a meal.

Walk in with an agenda: to gather information about the job or employer, to identify the background they expect when filling positions, or to obtain direct leads and specific help in getting an interview.

Following Up

Send a personalized note of thanks to every person who helps you. Tailor each note to the recipient, letting the person know how you plan to use the information you received. Have you contacted one of their referrals? Did you read the magazine article they cited? At their suggestion, are you now exploring a different market than before? You might also enclose some information you believe your contact would find useful.

Stay in touch with your contacts over the course of your job search by telephoning or sending a short note every couple months. While your job search is primary in your mind, it's probably not their major concern. If they fail to hear from you, they may forget about you, assume you've found a new position, or conclude you are no longer interested in working with them.

Have others network for you. Telephone past employers and coworkers who respect you and your work to ask for their help. See if they'll make the appointment for you.

Using the Internet or Other On-Line Resources

Even though *USA Today* claims that "companies love the Internet as a cheap and efficient way to fill jobs," it's difficult to write about the relative value of online networking in any but the most anecdotal fashion. The technology hasn't been around long enough to have been thoroughly studied, and the services are changing so rapidly that what is here today may literally be gone tomorrow. Still, the Internet cannot be ignored.

Networking Success Story #3

Jim Latting was an associate at a prestigious but very demanding law firm when he decided to look for a workplace that would encourage a balance between his personal and professional lives. Based on his impression of the legal job market, he targeted in-house corporate counsel as a position that would permit the lifestyle he sought. He arranged to meet with a former associate of his firm, now employed by a corporation, to explore this possibility. This lawyer disabused him of the notion that an in-house legal department would encourage a balanced life, suggested that a small-firm environment might be more to Jim's taste, and referred him to another former associate of their law firm. Even though he had ruled out small firm practice, Jim kept an open mind and followed her lead. The second associate referred him to a partner in a small business-oriented law partnership for more information. That firm, which emphasized life outside the office and required lower billable hours as a result, just happened to be quietly looking for another compatible associate. Jim was hired and soon after became a contented partner.

I know that online and e-mail interaction can be effective in obtaining work because I've had success with the method myself. A lawyer e-mailed a question to me in response to an online discussion I moderated on alternative careers. I answered her questions, then asked if she knew of any sponsors I should contact in her area about presenting my alternative careers seminar. By coincidence, she co-chaired a bar association committee dealing with career issues. That connection led to a confirmed booking.

As with all effective marketing techniques, online activity will yield good results only when your participation is active and friendly. That means you can't lurk; you must reveal your presence in any discussion, e-mail those who make comments you find intriguing, and take advantage of opportunities to make a connection.

D/As a Leader

You might be able to get away with solo and cold marketing techniques if you make yourself visible in a leadership role. This type of activity tends to attract consulting contracts, political appointments, calls from headhunters and inquiries from other employers in your specialty area.

Although many of the examples listed in Category D are solo and cold, none of them are passive. Becoming a leader demands that you expend substantial unpaid hours in the public eye.

A lawyer with ten years of experience in civil litigation invested years in the choice movement, working for a variety of nonprofit groups. She finally consolidated her efforts into one very high profile campaign for the largest nonprofit organization in the area. Her contribution included researching and drafting public policy statements on such controversial issues as fetal tissue research and late-term abortion, and speaking before legislative hearings and community information meetings. The organization's management was so impressed with her ability to articulate the group's mission in a way that professional and lay listeners alike could understand that it created a new policy advocate position for her.

The point is to be visible. Your reputation will eventually attract new opportunities if you let others know that you're interested in considering them.

Picking the Right Methods for You

From the methods listed in the Marketing Grid on page 192, select three interactive, warm and active techniques you haven't yet used that you're willing to try. Then commit to using all three in your job search in the next week. You earn a gold star if you try just one, a solid lead if you try two and you'll probably end up with work you enjoy if you make regular use of all three.

Résumés and Cover Letters

"The résumé should not be the card you pull first off your job-search deck. View the résumé as the modest, imperfect document that it is, and pay attention to other, more crucial aspects of an effective job search."

—Howard Figler, author

. . .

At the risk of being repetitious, let me say again that employers don't hire résumés and cover letters. They hire people. Even so, your marketing materials are an essential part of your job-search campaign. Their presentational quality reflects directly on you. When they are well executed, they enhance your credibility and make the employer want to know more about you. Even more important, the process of preparing them primes you for interviews.

Many career advisors and job-hunters focus on how résumés look. They fuss over choice of paper, type fonts, and style. Admittedly, you'll convey a negative impression if you send résumés on cheap, ripped or dirty paper scattered with typographical errors, misspellings or penned-in corrections or updates. But form is less important than substance when it comes to delivering a positive message. It's the content of your materials that will make an employer think twice about you. This chapter focuses on the best way to present that information.

> Form is less important than substance in delivering a positive message.

Writing a Résumé

An effective résumé presents a dynamic view not only of what you want to do, but of why you are qualified to do it. It clearly answers the question asked by every potential employer, "What are you going to do for me that should make me want to talk to you?" The way to achieve this result is to focus more on the employer's needs than on your credentials or goals.

If résumé writing is difficult for you, you aren't clear enough yet about the connection between you and the particular work for which you are applying. Either head back to self-assessment and develop more clarity about what you want to do, or find out more about the work that interests you.

To prepare for writing a résumé, ask yourself these questions:

▶ What skills are required to perform this job?
▶ What other skills and personal qualities will the employer find attractive?
▶ Which of my work, volunteer or educational experiences prove I possess those skills and qualities?
▶ What results did I achieve in those experiences?
▶ Who among my references will confirm those achievements?

Résumé Writing Guidelines

▶ Write your own résumé.
▶ Rewrite your résumé for each job opening.
▶ Write your résumé as you would a short, persuasive brief.
▶ Organize your résumé to give immediate visibility to your strongest selling points.
▶ Show results, not just titles.
▶ Be descriptive.
▶ Be selective about what you include in your résumé.
▶ Sell your relevant volunteer experience.
▶ Highlight only impressive educational credentials, or those that directly contribute to your qualification for the position.
▶ Include irrelevant honors and awards only if they are prestigious and well-known.
▶ Exclude irrelevant and potentially prejudicial information.
▶ Ask someone else to proofread your résumé for typos and misspellings.
▶ Make certain you can be reached at the telephone number you provide.

To answer the first two questions, find out as much as you can about the position. If you're drafting a résumé for a type of position rather than a particular opening, make certain that you've talked to people in the field to confirm your understanding of the skills and characteristics demanded by the work. Your failure to do so can result in many wasted hours. One woman initiated a job-hunt for project management work, believing that her general legal background in handling cases and clients would suit that employment splendidly. She later learned that project managers must possess technical expertise in the area being managed; management skills are secondary.

It's a little easier to get the information when you are applying for an actual job opening. Some employers, especially government, universities and other large institutions, will provide a lengthy job description upon request. With smaller organizations or positions under development, you'll have to be more resourceful. Talk to the hiring person or others in the department. Ask what problems led to the creation of this vacancy or new position. Find out as much as you can about the business atmosphere.

To respond to the next two questions, refer to the exercises you completed in the self-assessment section, especially Your History of Achievements and Figuring Out Your Passions (page 79), and the chapter on transferable skills analysis starting on page 89. Identify which achievements demonstrate that you can meet the needs of your targeted employers. Don't limit your selections to work experiences. Consider also volunteer, community, personal, church and school projects. Focus on the skills you used and the specific results you achieved (for example, the money you generated or saved, or the numbers of people you led). Then, extract information from that list that will reinforce your qualifications.

The answer to the last question doesn't need to be included on your résumé; many experts claim that references are superfluous because employers assume you have them and will request the information if they're interested in you. But the question is still important now. You need to prepare for an interview at the same time you prepare your résumé; as stated earlier, that's one of the main values of writing a résumé.

It must be obvious by now that you should write your own résumé rather than hiring a résumé preparation service. Although those services appear attractive, in the long run they are not worth the price. Professional résumé writers tend to use the same format, terms and paper for all the résumés they produce. As a result, employers are likely to recognize canned résumés, and wonder whether they want to hire applicants without the will or ability to communicate for themselves. Further, résumé writers may emphasize the skills and experience that they believe will create a strong impression. Those skills and experiences might not attract the employers you want to impress.

Keep in mind another disadvantage. If you invest a lot of money in a résumé, it's only natural to want to make the most of your investment by providing the same résumé to every employer rather than tailoring it for each recipient. This approach will diminish the effectiveness of your job search efforts. For example, government agencies and some large corporations assign low-level clerical employees the task of reading through résumés and comparing them to job descriptions. Only résumés that use the specific language included in the job description will be passed to the decision makers. (See Special Rules for Government Applications at the end of this chapter.) If you use a "one-size-fits-all" résumé, you probably won't even make the first cut.

Most significant, having someone else prepare your résumé deprives you of the opportunity to practice articulating your background and talents in a way that will impress potential employers. If you can't convey your suitability in person as persuasively as your résumé does in writing, you won't get hired, no matter how strong your résumé.

Once you've gathered the necessary information, you need to put together a document that will catch the reader's attention. Workplace rules have changed (see Chapter 3) and employers are no longer looking for someone with the right title; they're looking for someone with the right skills, knowledge base, motivation and results. That means you cannot write an effective résumé in "shorthand," listing titles, dates of employment, salaries, and employers, without any narrative. As *Business Week* says, forget titles and illustrate your résumé with specific examples of the skills, experience and credentials that raise your "employability quotient."

Compare these two descriptions:

Partner, Smith & Jones, Attorneys at Law
January 1991 through June 1998
Civil litigation practice

Partner, Smith & Jones, Attorneys at Law
From 1991 to 1998, handled civil litigation matters primarily relating to personal and real property. 90 percent of jury and bench trials resulted in verdicts better than offers of settlement, taking into consideration expenses of trial. Averaged 2,000 billable hours annually.

A powerful résumé reads like a persuasive brief. Underlying its content is the premise that you are well qualified to perform a specific job. The content itself has only one purpose: to prove that premise.

The first step in drafting your résumé, then, is to define what it is you want to prove. Some résumés contain a job objective at the very beginning; it is, in essence,

Special Rules for the "Scannable" Résumé

Some big businesses and recruiting services save time by electronically reviewing the résumés they receive. Headhunters, company recruiters and other employers with technological savvy may also seek applicants by searching résumé posting services online. Résumés are scanned for key words, phrases, experience, education and skills. As a result, the rules for writing scannable résumés differ in two material ways:

Don't do anything fancy with the appearance of your résumé. Put your name on the first line and place your address and telephone numbers on different lines. Use sans serif fonts like Arial or Helvetica or other popular fonts like Times Roman and Courier. Keep your font size in the range of 10 to 14 points. Limit the use of boldface and avoid italics, script, underlining, graphics, shading, lines. Use a traditional résumé structure, preferably chronological, and choose light-colored letter paper printed on one side only.

Job computers hunt for "titles," not "accomplishments"; they look for the "whats" not the "hows." An employer looking for a lawyer to head its human resources department might enter key words like "lawyer" and "employment law" and "manager" to find the right résumés. Be sure to describe your skills, experience, education, achievements, affiliations and languages spoken with industry jargon and abbreviations, keywords and nouns rather than verbs. You can also include descriptions that would otherwise be considered self-serving like "dependable," "high energy" or "motivated."

For more information on electronic résumés, look for books like *Electronic Résumés: A Complete Guide to Putting Your Résumé On-Line* by James C. and Wayne M. Gonyea or *CareerXRoads: The 1998 Directory to Jobs, Résumés and Career Management on the World Wide Web* by Gerry Crispin and Mark Mehler. (See additional references on job-hunting using the Internet in Appendix 3.)

the résumé's thesis. It's not necessary—some would say it's not even desirable—to include that statement on your résumé. But I recommend that you place it at the top of the page while drafting to keep reminding yourself what you want to prove.

Once you've defined your thesis, organize your qualifications around the requirements of the work. Imagine you are creating a magazine advertisement. How can you get the reader to absorb the essence of your résumé in a single glance? One strategy is to summarize your background in impressive terms right at the beginning. For example, you could present your strongest qualifications in capsule form:

▶ Proven Leader
▶ Experienced Trial Lawyer
▶ Attorney Licensed in New York and California

You might also use such headlines as "Management Experience" or "Legal Background" to emphasize your areas of expertise (see sample résumé at page 215), or highlight your accomplishments with an opening category of "Representative Achievements" (see sample résumé at page 216).

Choosing the correct format—chronological, functional or targeted—will also strengthen your résumé. To illustrate the differences among these types of résumés, the same person's credentials are presented in all three formats starting at page 214.

A **chronological** résumé displays your employment background, education and other relevant experience in order of date, with the most recent occurrences listed first. (See the sample at page 214.) This is the type of résumé most commonly seen in the legal profession. Its purpose is to demonstrate your qualification for a position similar to what you have now, preferably a next step up the ladder of responsibility. It is also the expected form of résumé for traditional employers like law firms, universities, government agencies and large corporations, where the fact that you worked for a specific employer or earned a particular title may be of paramount importance.

A chronological résumé is effective only if you have made steady progress in one field and are seeking a position that is a step up the same ladder. Do not use this format if you are transferring outside the profession altogether, or if you have changed employers frequently, have been absent from the job market for a while, or have a short work history in two or more fields.

A **functional** résumé works well if you have a strong background in two areas—for example, law and management, or trial work and sales—applicable to the position you seek. It is also useful if you want to emphasize capabilities not used in your

212

most recent work or if you have had a variety of different, seemingly unconnected work experiences, such as in temporary, freelance or consulting jobs.

A functional résumé organizes your background by category, rather than in chronological order, to support your thesis. (See the sample functional résumé at page 215.) For example, a lawyer who wishes to combine his law and volunteer fundraising experience in a new career as a planned giving specialist with a nonprofit organization might mix educational, volunteer, and work experience under the two categories of "legal" and "fundraising."

A **targeted** résumé focuses on skills and achievements that establish your qualification for a specific position. (See the sample targeted résumé at page 216.) It is similar to a functional résumé in that it downplays the chronology of your background and emphasizes its substance. Use a targeted résumé when you are very clear about your job goals, when you have several potential directions to go in and want a different résumé for each, or when you want to emphasize capabilities for which you have never been paid. For example, a lawyer without management experience who wants a job as the executive director of a nonprofit organization might begin with a list of results that establish his credibility as a leader, and then follow with specific job and volunteer experience and educational credentials.

Once you have defined your thesis and chosen the best format, you need to prove that you're worth interviewing. You do this by showing, not telling, your qualifications. That means describing actual accomplishments rather than listing job titles and dates.

Go back to the list of accomplishments that demonstrate your suitability for the work you've targeted. Select the strongest examples and describe the incidents in an anecdotal manner. Use dynamic nouns and verbs and pare down the prose to make every word count. Don't use self-serving superlatives like "excellent" communicator or "outstanding" negotiator. Let the results of your efforts speak for themselves (e.g., resolved without trial a real estate lawsuit pending 14 years involving over 700 claimants).

Tell what you accomplished in terms of dollars, numbers and other results. Cite the money you saved or generated in terms of dollars or percents, or the number of people, papers or projects you handled. If your results are hard to measure objectively, describe the scope of your responsibility and the impact of the project on its intended marketplace.

Describe your volunteer activities in the legal profession, or religious or other community organizations, if they demonstrate your ability to meet the needs of the employers you're approaching. Have you served on the board of a nonprofit, taught Sunday

Sample Chronological Résumé

Note: The objective of this résumé is to demonstrate the applicant's suitability as managing partner of the commercial law department of a national law firm.

Jane Doe, Esq.

123 Main Street
Chicago, IL 60601
(312) 555-1212

Chronological Employment History

Partner, Doe & Smith, Chicago, IL   *1992- present*
In nine years, built a start-up, two-partner commercial law firm into an enterprise with average annual receipts exceeding $1,000,000. Limited overhead to 40 percent of gross revenues through efficiency study and implementation. Hired and trained both clerical and professional staff, accomplished all financial forecasting and planning, and introduced computer technology into the office.

Personal law practice emphasized commercial law (transactions and litigation), real estate (leases, financing and sales) and franchise law. Representative practice accomplishments include forming or terminating over 100 closely-held corporations and partnerships, and resolving a real estate lawsuit that involved over 700 claimants and had lasted 14 years before I took over.

Instructor, University of Illinois Extension, Chicago, IL   *1993 - present*
Teach general corporate and commercial law to those currently working in business management.

Partner & Associate Attorney, Rich, Richer & Doe, Lansing, MI   *1985 - 1992*
Engaged in general practice of law including domestic relations, landlord/tenant, business and estate planning and municipal law. Arranged a comprehensive right-of-way agreement between a telecommunications utility and municipality. Served as administrative partner for the firm with responsibility for budget, management reports, and personnel.

Financial Specialist, Federal Highway Administration, Lansing, Michigan   *1979-1983*
Conducted compliance reviews. Assisted in management, fiscal and personnel activities.

Community Contribution

Vice President, North Chicago Youth Services   *1996 to present*
Coordinated the start-up of a project to strengthen child care and health services for homeless children. Developed a system for linking programs, and negotiated and drafted interagency agreements.

Chairperson, Livingston Area Council Against Spouse Abuse   *1989 to 1990*
Initiated a spouse abuse treatment and prevention program. Took the lead role in budget preparation, staffing, fundraising and community involvement.

Professional Credentials

Juris Doctor (Ranked 1st out of 113), 1985
Thomas M. Cooley Law School, Lansing, Michigan
Courses toward MBA, 1980-1981, Michigan State University
Bachelor of Arts, 1979, summa cum laude, Central Michigan University
Admitted to practice law in Michigan and Illinois

Sample Functional Résumé

Note: The objective of this résumé is to combine law practice and human services volunteer experience into a position as a human services program analyst, coordinator or planner.

Jane Doe, Esq.

123 Main Street
Chicago, IL
(312) 555-1212

Human Services Experience

Vice President, North Chicago Youth Services   *1996 to present*
   Coordinated the start-up of a project to strengthen child care and health services for homeless children. Developed a system for linking programs, and negotiated and drafted interagency agreements.

Chairperson, Livingston Area Council Against Spouse Abuse, Inc.   *1989-90*
   Initiated a spouse abuse treatment and prevention program. Took the lead role in budget preparation, staffing, fundraising and community involvement.

Child Advocate, Kings and Livingston County Juvenile Courts   *1988 to 1997*
   Served as an advocate for abused and neglected children for over eight years.

Legal Experience

Partner, Doe & Smith, Chicago, IL   *1992 - present*
   Successfully represented a disabled father against two sons who had stolen and mismanaged his assets. Resolved a real estate lawsuit pending 14 years involving over 700 claimants. Structured the formation or termination of over 100 closely-held corporations and partnerships, accommodating the needs of all parties.

Partner & Associate Attorney, Rich, Richer & Doe, Lansing, MI   *1985 - 1992*
   Engaged in the general practice of law including domestic relations, landlord/ tenant, business and estate planning, and municipal law. Analyzed issues and prepared a persuasive paper on representing the best interests of mentally disabled parents in child abuse and neglect cases. Served as administrative partner for the firm with responsibility for budget, management reports, and personnel.

Professional Credentials

Juris Doctor (Ranked 1st of 113), 1985
Thomas M. Cooley Law School, Lansing, Michigan
Bachelor of Arts, summa cum laude, Central Michigan University, 1979
Admitted to practice law in Michigan and Illinois

Sample Targeted Résumé

Note: The objective of this résumé is to obtain a planning, policy or analyst position in the human, health or public service fields.

Jane Doe, Esq.

123 Main Street
Chicago, IL
(312) 555-1212

Qualifications

Ten years of human services volunteer and progressive legal experience, with special expertise to:

- Research original issues
- Synthesize data
- Clarify and communicate fundamental points
- Coordinate case management
- Negotiate among various constituencies
- Comprehend and apply laws and regulations

Representative Achievements

Initiated a spouse abuse treatment and prevention program. Took the lead role in needs assessment, budget preparation, staffing, fundraising and community involvement.

Coordinated the start-up of a project to strengthen child care and health services for homeless children. Developed a system for linking programs, and negotiated and drafted interagency agreements.

Resolved a real estate lawsuit pending 14 years involving over 700 claimants.

Arranged a comprehensive right-of-way agreement between a telecommunications utility and a municipality.

Advocated successfully on behalf of a disabled father against two sons who had stolen and mismanaged his assets.

Analyzed issues and researched and wrote a persuasive paper on representing the best interests of mentally disabled parents in child abuse and neglect cases.

Structured the formation or termination of over 100 closely-held corporations and partnerships, accommodating the needs of all parties.

Served as an advocate for abused and neglected children for over eight years.

Chronological Employment History

Partner, Doe & Smith, Chicago, IL	1992 - present
Instructor, University of Illinois Extension, Chicago, IL	1993 - present
Partner & Associate Attorney, Rich, Richer & Doe, Lansing, MI	1985 - 1992
Law Clerk, J. David Rich, Lansing, MI	1983 - 1985
Financial Specialist, Federal Highway Administration, Lansing, MI	1979 - 1983

Professional Credentials

Juris Doctor (Ranked 1st of 113), 1985
Thomas M. Cooley Law School, Lansing, Michigan
Bachelor of Arts, summa cum laude, 1979
Central Michigan University, Mt. Pleasant, Michigan
Admitted to practice law in Michigan and Illinois

school, organized fundraising drives or programs, or provided hands-on assistance to those in need? Those experiences may reinforce your value to the right employers.

Look at the résumé on page 216. That lawyer successfully marketed her extensive volunteer experience, combined with the skills she developed as a lawyer, and was hired for a human services consulting position. If your volunteer experience does not seem relevant to the jobs you are targeting, rethink your career direction. Should you be looking in another field?

Most of your résumé should focus on accomplishments that prove your suitability for a specific type of work. But throwing in a few unrelated but impressive credentials won't hurt; it always helps to show depth of character and a history of high achievement. Mention honors such as Rhodes Scholarships, Phi Beta Kappa and high class standing but omit obscure awards, especially if they occurred prior to law school or were earned more than five years ago. Knowledge of foreign languages is appropriately included if it relates to your job objective.

It may not feel like it right now, but your law degree falls into the category of an "impressive credential." That means you ought to include it on your résumé, but its placement will depend upon the thesis you're trying to prove.

Most experts in the legal profession recommend that you place information about your legal education at the top of your résumé if you've just earned it and are applying for a position that will use it. You also want to place your legal education at the beginning of the page if you earned your degree within the last five years from a prestigious law school or graduated at the top of your class and are applying for legal positions. On the other hand, if you earned your degree more than five years ago, no matter how impressive your school or honors, put it at the bottom of the résumé. Solid post-graduate accomplishments are necessary to impress potential employers now.

If you're applying for a position that makes no obvious use of your legal background, your résumé should be organized to de-emphasize your legal background and clearly explain your commitment to and interest in your new field. Reference special courses, seminars or workshops that do relate to your job objective in a prominent location, and place your law degree in an unobtrusive location. You want the employer to see you first as someone qualified for the position under consideration and then be surprised to learn that you've also been educated as a lawyer.

Your résumé should be organized to show that you can focus on the big picture. That means leaving out detail. To pare down your résumé, ask the following about every bit of information:

- ▶ Does the information clearly support your qualification for the position sought? What specifically does it add to the total picture?
- ▶ Do the facts translate into benefits for the employer, or do they merely recite history?
- ▶ Does the information raise more questions about your suitability for the position than it answers? If so, is it worth the risk, or important enough to you that you must include it?

Disclosing political or religious affiliations may trigger negative responses. Decide whether that affiliation, or your involvement with it, is relevant to your qualification for the position under consideration. If not, exclude any reference to it. For example, if you are applying for a position with the Democratic National Headquarters, list your affiliation with party organizations in your area. If you're applying for a position as a litigation associate with a conservative law firm, you'd be better off omitting it, unless you can show that your affiliation is a potential source of business. Of course, if the firm's acceptance of your affiliation is a condition to your interest in a position, keep that information in your résumé.

References to height, weight, sex, marital status, health and hobbies are not relevant and should be excluded. Employers don't even want to look at most of that information because of its potential for exposing them to liability for employment discrimination. One thing you want to avoid is making potential employers uncomfortable with you and your application before they even meet you.

Your goal is to create a condensed but persuasive document. Employers spend much less than a minute (some sources estimate only ten seconds) perusing each résumé. A short résumé forces you to be clear and concise while leaving enough mystery to pique the reader's curiosity. As a general rule, limit your résumé to one page for every ten years' combined educational and employment background, up to a maximum of two pages. Those with more than 20 years' experience may shorten their résumé by focusing on accomplishments during the last ten years.

One final note: Be sure to tell how you can be reached. Some lawyers are afraid of being found out so they list their home telephone number. Employers facing a flood of applicants may not try again if they can't reach you the first time. Get a reliable answering machine, sign up for residential voice messaging and tape a professional sounding greeting, or use a telephone number where someone else is generally around to answer in an appropriate manner, take messages and promptly convey them to you.

Special Rules for Government Applications

The hiring process for most merit-protected positions in government involves specific, often burdensome application requirements. You cannot just mail in a résumé and cover letter and expect to get anywhere. "The first place to start," says Brian C. Conelley in his pamphlet, *Federal Attorney Employment Guide,* "is to recognize that finding a job as an attorney in government is a job itself. To find that job you will need *more* than your professional qualifications."

Because of the complex and strict requirements for each agency, it's better to narrow your search to specific agencies that interest you. If possible, request a copy of each agency's application procedure, and prepare the necessary documentation before you hear of any particular opening.

If you do come across an interesting opening, but the job title does not clearly indicate whether the position is law-related, request a copy of the complete job announcement and description. This form will list all qualification requirements, application procedures and deadlines.

Often, you're asked to complete a statement of experience and training (E & T). This is where the government hiring process diverges from the norm. In this statement, you must outline your job experience and educational background by *using the exact words* contained in the job description, the more frequently the better. The reason for using the exact words is simple: Your application will likely be screened initially by a clerk with little or no knowledge of the demands of the position. These clerks are trained to assign points to applications based on specific, literal satisfaction of posted job requirements. They score your E & T mechanically, without extrapolation or interpretation. For example, if the application asks you to list your supervisory experience, and you indicate that you were a partner in a small law firm, the clerk will not presume that you supervised a secretary, a legal assistant and several associates in that position. You must spell it out specifically, using the word "supervise" over and over again.

Another hint: If the E & T asks you to provide detailed information about a particular kind of work experience, mention that background more than once on your completed submission. "Disconnect your natural intelligence and creativity and break up your education and employment history into a large number of tedious, redundant paragraphs," suggests one successful lawyer applicant. "Restrain the impulse to shout, 'To heck with this! I'm just going to send them my résumé; all the information they want is there.'"

Writing Effective Cover Letters

How many times have you received a letter with first-class postage from a stranger and, after opening it, realized it was a form letter sent to all lawyers in your area but totally irrelevant to you and your concerns? Don't make the same mistake. A letter sent to an unknown recipient is not much better than something addressed "Dear Occupant."

Before you draft any letter, make sure you have a "warm" connection to the addressee. If you have no specific information about the person you want to write, wait to send the letter until you do!

Personalize your correspondence with an introduction that relates you specifically to the recipient. Refer to the name of any mutual acquaintance since it immediately links you with the recipient. (See Letters 1 and 2.) If you can find a point of mutual interest (like an article written by the target), use it to open your letter. (See Letters 2 and 4.) If you have achievements the recipient would find compelling, use them. (See letters 1 and 3.)

The rest of your letter should motivate the recipient to interview you or help you with other referrals. To accomplish that purpose, answer these two questions engagingly:

- ▶ Why have you contacted me?
- ▶ Why should I be interested in meeting or helping you?

You can answer those questions best by concentrating on the first rule of effective job-hunting: Focus on the employer's needs. Emphasize your value to the recipient, not the features of your background or education. A marketing expert with the law firm of Davis Wright Tremaine suggests you respond to the unspoken question, "What's in it for me?," in the first few lines. Don't waste the reader's time with too much detail. Present one or two pieces of information from your résumé that best answer this question.

Although the sample cover letters that follow use different techniques, they all highlight representative accomplishments, relate them to the needs of the employer or industry, and refer to future action. They also all avoid writing flaws common to lawyers: writing in a cold and impersonal tone, using the passive voice and using overly complex words and sentences.

Letters that invite the reader to respond are not written like a business transmittal letter. Starting a letter with stilted language like "Enclosed please find my résumé" conveys distance and impersonality. An opening sentence like, "I'm writing to intro-duce myself to you," is equally professional but more friendly. "Generally speaking," says Richard Andersen, author of *Powerful Writing Skills,* "the more natural the tone of your writing, the more appealing your message will be."

The passive voice also creates an awkward impression. Compare this sentence written in the passive voice—"It was suggested to me by John Doe that I contact you"— with this—"John Doe suggested that I contact you." The active voice moves the eyes along while the passive voice slows them down.

The passive voice is also, according to Richard Andersen, the "language of irre-sponsibility; its purpose is to mislead, distort or disguise." Some would argue that lawyers write in the passive voice for exactly that purpose! Write your letter in the active voice to convey the message that you're trustworthy and straightforward.

You not only want to be considered approachable and honest, you also want your letter to be easily understood. Convoluted sentences can kill good ideas. Notice how the complexity of this sentence—taken from an actual cover letter—weakens the writer's presentation:

> I believe that the breadth of my legal experience at the Bank, as detailed in my résumé, would qualify me for an in-house position with a company/ corporation which may need a generalist who is comfortable with and profi-cient in various legal subject areas which may affect its business operations.

Simplicity is the key. Say what you want to say in an unadorned, straightforward manner. Don't write complex sentences or pick fancy words to make you sound edu-cated and important. They'll make you sound "obscure and affected" instead, says Andersen. See how much stronger the sample sentence above becomes when it's rewritten to follow all these rules:

> As you can see from my résumé, I've been working as a generalist in banking. With this breadth of experience, I will be able to tackle most of the legal issues you encounter in your business.

Respond to anticipated questions about why you left, or want to leave, your cur-rent position or the law in a simple paragraph, without using chatty language such as "You might be wondering why." Here are two examples of straightforward but unapologetic explanations:

In the last year, I have been devoting less time to the practice of law and more to volunteer activities in my three main areas of interest: children, human behavior and adult education. I was attracted to your advertisement [for a new director of a small children's nonprofit organization] because it is hard to imagine an effective program to benefit children that would not also strive to educate adults and foster an understanding of human behavior.

I have decided to move from the practice of law to a position as a pre-law counselor for two reasons. First, I want to continue to assist adults who are in the midst of personal change—the most gratifying aspect of my work as a family law practitioner. At the same time, I would prefer to operate in an environment that relies on education and collaboration, rather than adversarial action.

The last suggestion is to use an active closing. Request a meeting and tell the recipient when you'll call to follow up. If you're writing a thank-you letter, let the recipient know what you intend to do as a next step.

Letter 1: Introductory without Résumé*

Mr. John Smith
Literary Representation, Inc.
15 Park Avenue
New York, NY 10012

Dear Mr. Smith:

Our mutual client, John Doe, suggested that I contact you.

I am an experienced intellectual property lawyer and negotiator, but I would like to increase my contact with authors and publishers by becoming a literary agent. My relevant accomplishments include:

- ▶ Negotiating a publishing contract for a celebrated author that was one-third more generous than his last contract;
- ▶ Obtaining a $25,000 advance for an unknown author;
- ▶ Publishing articles on intellectual property law and negotiations in The Writer's Market and attracting three new clients as a result;
- ▶ Helping six students sell their manuscripts by teaching a seminar at New York University on how to negotiate with publishers.

As you can see from these accomplishments, I have polished my negotiation, persuasion, analysis and editing skills in my legal career. I am eager to perfect my innate marketing ability, and combine it with my existing skills, in a new career as a literary agent.

I look forward to discussing in greater detail how my background can match your firm's needs. I will call you next week to set up a meeting at your convenience.

Sincerely,

---

*Adapted from Career Transitions by Celia Paul Associates.

Letter 2: Introductory with Résumé*

Mr. John Smith, Chairman
Health Research Consortium
1000 Second Avenue, Suite 100
Seattle, Washington 98100

Dear Mr. Smith:

I understand that Bob Roe told you about me and that you are expecting my letter and résumé.

As Bob told you, I want to move from the private practice of law to an administrative position in the public or nonprofit sector. Bob and I had already arranged a meeting to talk about employment possibilities with healthcare organizations when I saw an article in the *New York Times* about your appointment as chairman of the Health Research Consortium. Bob then suggested that I introduce myself to you.

While my proposed career change seems dramatic on the surface, I've actually been involved with public interest organizations as a volunteer for years. I've learned through this activity to design and implement organizational change, resolve conflicts at the individual and institutional levels, write and speak publicly. Although I use these skills in the practice of law, I'm ready to apply them to a purpose I find more fulfilling than corporate finance.

I would like to meet with you to discuss job opportunities at the Consortium, or anywhere else you might refer me. I will be out of town from December 21 through December 28, but will call your secretary on January 4 to arrange a convenient time and place.

Sincerely,

*Adapted from *Career Transitions* by Celia Paul Associates.

Letter 3: Cover in Response to Advertised Position*

Mr. John Doe, Chairman
New York City Bank
1000 42nd Street
New York City, N.Y. 10012

Dear Mr. Smith:

In response to your advertisement in the *Wall Street Journal,* I have highlighted my qualifications that parallel your stated requirements:

You Require a Background in:	I Offer these Accomplishments:
Calling on major accounts	Attracted new clients to my law firm, which resulted in a 30 percent increase in banking business for the firm.
	Developed additional legal work from existing clients, resulting in a $200,000 increase in legal fees.
Securing loans	Secured loans of up to $250 million for numerous legal clients.
General business development	Negotiated business deals, analyzed agreements and organized transactions as both in-house counsel and law firm partner specializing in banking.
5 years commercial lending	5 years as in-house attorney for major New York City commercial bank.
In-depth knowledge of credit	Completed bank credit training program.

I will be happy to discuss how I can meet your needs in a personal meeting. I look forward to your response.

Sincerely,

---

*Adapted from Career Transitions by Celia Paul Associates.

Letter 4: Thank-You*

Mr. John Smith
National Investment Strategies
1541 Market St.
Philadelphia PA 19103

Dear Mr. Smith:

Thank you for meeting with me last week. I enjoyed our conversation very much, particularly our discussion about the demand for commercial jet aircraft and the impact it has had on the Boeing Company. I read in today's *Wall Street Journal* that Boeing's latest long-term forecast predicts a 25 percent greater demand for aircraft through 2005 than Boeing foresaw last year. If that is correct, the future certainly looks bright for the company.

During our conversation, you asked me why I was interested in becoming a securities analyst, and I want to repeat my answer. I most enjoy the financial and strategic aspects of my work in mergers and acquisitions and public offerings, and see securities analysis—more than law—as a logical extension of my love of those kinds of challenges.

I have studied the strengths of many companies through my legal work. At General Motors, I learned how major corporate decisions are made. On my own time, I have invested profitably in the stock market. An evening course gave me a solid grounding in credit analysis. I can use my practical experience and well-honed analytical skills to help your company evaluate businesses and their strategies.

I recognize, nonetheless, that I need more training in quantitative analysis to be an effective securities analyst. I know your company would be an excellent place to acquire the training, and I believe my background will enable me to absorb the education and quickly become an effective member of your team.

Thank you for your time and your interest.

Sincerely,

---

*Adapted from *Career Transitions* by Celia Paul Associates. Used with permission.

Pursuing Your Goal

"The only guarantee in life is that things will change."

—Anonymous

■ ■ ■

Employment transition is not a simple linear process. "Most people feel that they are rounding one big circle over and over again as they pass through periods of excitement and depression," says one career consultant. "As a result, they stop the process after finishing a circle or two. What they are actually doing, though, is traveling in spiraling circles, getting a little closer to satisfying re-employment each round. If they only persist, and accept a certain amount of confusion as part of the process, they find the answers they want over time."

> Perseverance and flexibility will usually lead you to your goal.

In other words, persistence and flexibility will usually lead you to your goal. We'll explore both qualities in this chapter.

Persistence

Perseverance and an unwavering commitment to your goal are keys to completing your job or career transition. Fortunately, having survived law school and the bar examination (and probably an endless lawsuit or two), you have amply demonstrated the ability to persist.

Sometimes, though, the mere thought of all the effort it will take to reach your goals seems daunting. You might make a few half-hearted employment inquiries or send out a new batch of résumés when your work seems intolerable or especially insecure. If those efforts fail and your job pressures ease, you put your career plans back on the shelf. A few months later, work grows unbearable again and the oppressive cycle begins anew. To be effective, your search for new work must continue through good times as well as bad, and requires stamina and commitment equal to that of a part-time job.

Persistence is especially important when dealing with an employer that is creating a new position or starting a new project. The employer's bottom line will look better if the project gets postponed. It's your job to emphasize the value to be gained rather than the dollars lost by hiring you now.

Persistence also means discipline in following up. Check within a few days of mailing to assure that your application or résumé was received. For a status report about your job application with a government agency or large corporation, wait up to a month after the closing period to inquire. A wait of less than a week is appropriate for a small organization. Send a follow-up letter after every interview, letting the interviewer know that you are still interested in the position (if indeed you are) and supplying any additional information about yourself you think might be helpful.

Having a system will assure you actually make the calls and write the letters. You might try one of these:

▶ Maintain a 3" x 5" card file, loose leaf notebook, or computerized record of all your contacts, noting a date and description for every move.

▶ Keep copies of every version of your résumé, noting on the reverse which employers received each one. When you get a response, or make a follow-up phone call, note the date and result on your copy of the cover letter.

▶ Use a "tickler" system to remind you of the follow-up calls and letters you need to send. Tuck notes into your calendar or scheduling software, or create a card file of reminders organized by day and month.

Assume that your search will take more effort and time than you think, and then be pleasantly surprised if the opposite occurs. Despite your best efforts, there will be times when every inquiry is met with a "Sorry, we're not hiring," and each lead you follow is a dead-end. During those times, you'll feel as if you're heading backwards. Some of you will even decide to give up the search. But "try, try, try to be positive," says one former litigator who marketed herself into an in-house transactional position with a bank. "This means you must fight the tendency to be negative, to draw negative conclusions from rejections or what you assume to be your failure to get the right job."

Flexibility

Be persistent in working toward your goal, but allow some latitude in the form that both the job and your search will take. In other words, remain flexible. Picture a battery-operated toy making its way across a room. Before long, it hits a wall. Without a course correction, it continues to bump against the wall until it runs out of juice. Many lawyers resemble these toys in their job searches. They hit the wall and figure that if they beat against it hard enough, they'll eventually break through. "If only I send out 500 more résumés, if only I call 300 more people, if only I wait six more months," they convince themselves, "something eventually will happen." And it does. They, too, run out of juice.

Cindy Vranizan fell into this trap. Eighteen months after graduation from law school, Cindy was still unemployed. Beginning in her third year of law school, she had doggedly responded to advertisements, and sought out friends and relatives, hoping to find a full-time, permanent job practicing law. She kept bumping into her own wall until she faced a second Christmas without funds to buy gifts. Then she tried a different approach. She again contacted a family friend with a real estate practice, told him she needed to generate a gift-buying budget and asked if she could help him organize something on a project basis. When she had contacted him previously, he had been reluctant to take on the financial burden of an associate; this time he acknowledged he could use some help. He also referred her to another overloaded solo practitioner. One project for each lawyer led to others, and by March she was working almost full time for both lawyers. At that point, she renegotiated an arrangement with the real estate practitioner to work in tandem with him on all of his litigation. Six years later, Cindy is earning a comfortable living as a practicing lawyer.

You're much better off if you remain flexible and openminded. Say "yes" initially to every lead, instead of finding reasons why it is unlikely to take you where you want to go. When one job-search method doesn't work, try another. If your efforts to get into one targeted market seem futile, brainstorm other options.

As a corollary, question all of your assumptions. Don't sabotage your chances by assuming that they're not hiring, or you wouldn't qualify, or they don't pay enough, or you wouldn't enjoy that kind of job, until you have made enough inquiries to confirm your suspicions.

For example, Robin targeted human resources as a field in which she could work with other people to set and achieve team goals. During her networking, she heard that an employee benefits consulting firm was looking for someone with her qualifications to work in the "gain-sharing" area. Initially, Robin rejected the suggestion because it involved employee benefits work, something she associated only with numbers. The next day, some inner voice urged her to make the appointment anyway. She discovered that "gain sharing" groups assist employee teams in setting and achieving continuous improvement goals. If she had turned down the opportunity to find out more about the position, she would never have discovered this exciting new area.

For every person who has traveled a straight path from law school to senior partner, you'll find many others who have converted a conventional legal background into a novel career by remaining open to new possibilities. Here are a few more instructive examples:

- ▶ Rees Morrison was a bankruptcy associate who commuted by train each day with a laptop computer. One day he struck up a conversation with another passenger who was using a laptop and just happened to own a law office software company. Soon after, Rees accepted an equity position with the company, and later became a law firm management consultant with Price Waterhouse and Arthur Andersen.

- ▶ Joe Harburg had only a few years of legal experience when he decided he wanted to open high-end shopping malls in Europe. He tried to persuade Sharper Image owner Richard Thalheimer to let him pursue that vision, but ended up accepting a low-paid position in that company's U.S. site-selection department. That experience enabled him to start his own company, which assists national specialty boutique chains in selecting and negotiating the best malls nationwide for their businesses.

- ▶ Michael Anderson was a transactional lawyer who wanted to move in-house but was repeatedly told by companies that they could not afford to hire him. Rather than letting their responses stop his search, he proposed that he work for several companies on a part-time basis. He turned his rejections into a full-time living, and later secured a full-time in-house position with another corporation.

As a "pick-me-up" during those times when you seem to be spiraling away from your goal, try one of more of these course corrections:

▶ Get a sense of accomplishment from tasks you can do in a day instead of believing that getting a job is the only measure of success. Consider your day successful if you nail down an appointment, research an employer or industry, make three telephone calls, write a thank-you letter the same day as an appointment, or put in a full job-search day.

▶ Review your self-assessment materials and reconfirm your commitment to your goals. Are you looking for work you think you can get instead of aiming for what you'd really like to do?

▶ Reevaluate the way you're pursuing your ultimate goal. Are you trying to make too big a leap to your chosen career? Should you be looking at a "stepping stone" instead?

▶ Examine your assumptions—e.g., targeting companies within a one-hour radius of your home, looking at only one industry, or staying within a tight salary range—and remain open to new approaches.

▶ Search for project or consulting work instead of a job. Those temporary assignments often turn into permanent arrangements. Even if they don't, you gain experience and make what could turn out to be valuable contacts.

▶ Ask yourself if you are defeating your job search efforts by pursuing too many different geographical areas or fields at the same time.

▶ Be courageous. Ask friends and professional acquaintances if they know why you haven't been successful in your job search. You could be doing something ineffective that is apparent to others, but not to you.

▶ Be certain that you are tailoring your cover letters to the specific requirements of the position for which you are applying, and that your résumé is directed to the actual person or persons who will hire you.

▶ Consider whether you are being negative, vague, evasive, indirect or dishonest about your credentials or past employment.

▶ Determine whether your stated salary requirements are out of line with the marketplace—either too high or too low.

▶ Spend more time developing contacts who can give you direct introductions to the decision-makers within a company.

The Long-Distance Job Hunt

Many who decide to change jobs or careers, also choose to change geographic locations. Job hunting from a distance creates some additional complications.

If you're lucky enough to have a profile that is unique and in high demand, you can pretty much write your ticket to any city in the country. Headhunters will be happy to assist you, and employers will gladly pay the expenses of interviewing, house-hunting and transporting your goods to the new location.

If you're seeking a move into the same or a similar line of work in a location that's not very popular—places like New York City or Los Angeles, or smaller towns throughout most of the country—you may be able to find work before you leave home. You also may be flown out for interviews and receive a subsidy for your moving expenses.

Those who want to move to a popular area like Boston, Denver, San Francisco or Seattle, or who offer skills that can easily be found locally, will first have to prove their commitment to the new location by moving there, sitting for (and, of course, passing) the bar exam in the new state, or at a minimum, investing in several networking trips.

No matter where you're planning to move, be sure to subscribe to the local newspapers and commercial publications to obtain information about trends, potential employers and job openings in that area. Some of these periodicals publish special directories of law firms and businesses, or profile local law firms, lawyers and business owners. Contact any relevant bar associations, other professional societies, law schools or universities with courses of study in your area of interest to get their publications. Monthly journals and newsletters often contain announcements of job openings. Your knowledge of local issues, lingo and neighborhoods will make you seem less of an outsider.

The resources listed in Appendix 2 offer more assistance in pursuing legal work from a distance.

► Bring your résumé to a career counselor, placement director, or legal search consultant for a critique. You may not be aware of the impression it conveys.

► Seek out professional assistance, whether with a career counselor, a reputable employment service, an image consultant, therapist, personal effectiveness training course, or other career-related seminar or workshop.

► Contact more small to medium-sized businesses and organizations, where most of today's employment growth occurs.

► If you're making five contacts per day, make ten instead. Devote more time to your marketing efforts.

► Ask for feedback from those who have interviewed you for job openings.

► Polish your interviewing skills by role-playing with a friend. Better yet, record the mock interview on a camcorder and review your performance with your friend.

► Join a job-hunters' support group. Look into 40-Plus (see Appendix 3 for further information about this group), or contact your local college or university career center for leads. If you can't find an appropriate group, create your own. Reserve space in a central location like a public library or the bar association and announce a meeting in your local bar association publication. (It will probably be printed at no charge.)

Act now. As one executive search consultant has observed, good things may come to those who wait, but they will be the opportunities passed over by people who didn't wait.

Reaching Your Goal

"We are not won by arguments that we can analyze, but by tone and temper; by the manner which is the man himself."

—*Samuel Butler, author*

- - -

You've written strong résumés and cover letters, contacted individuals in the field you've targeted and have flexibly persisted to the point of getting an interview for an appealing opportunity. How do you best handle this step? What happens if an offer is extended? This chapter looks at the ins and outs of interviewing and negotiating compensation.

Interviewing

Every employer wants two questions answered in an interview:

▶ Will you do a good job?
▶ Will you fit in?

To answer these questions convincingly, you must develop rapport while articulating how your strengths will mesh with the company's mission and environment. Your genuine interest in the work and field makes the crucial difference. Anything suggesting that you don't care enough about the company or the work will sharply reduce your chances of getting hired.

Your legal training should help as well. If you know how to do anything, you know how to persuade others to take your side when there's an arguable reason not to. You do it by knowing the opposition's position as well as your own, and by showing logically and passionately why your position is the better one.

The most important preparation for any particular interview, then, is to research

> Your genuine interest in the work and field makes the crucial difference in getting hired.

the company's conflicts, growth patterns, and needs. Refer to Chapter 17 if you need help in this research. Look for recent items in the news about the company as well as information that could affect the company or your job, such as:

▶ potential new markets, products or services;

▶ potential for growth in the industry;

▶ the relative size of the firm in the industry;

▶ percent of annual sales growth over the last five years;

▶ their product lines or services;

▶ price points in the product or service line;

▶ the competition;

▶ organizational structure including number of branch offices, stores, plants or outlets;

▶ training programs and policies for employees;

▶ average time commitments for those in this position;

▶ typical career path in your field;

▶ the corporate culture.

Once you've finished your research, review the self-assessment exercises you completed in Chapters 12 and 13 to find examples of your experience that prove you have the requisite skills, motivation and enthusiasm to perform the work. Then, draft a one-paragraph summary of yourself that establishes your credibility—one that conveys your honesty, vision, enthusiasm and competence. What do you have to offer this employer? What kind of employee will you make? Where are you heading in your career and how does this opportunity fit into your plans?

Once you get your thesis down, identify stories you can tell about your accomplishments that convey the same message. More than anything, story-telling will illustrate your ability and personal style much more vividly and convincingly than any conclusions you draw about yourself. If you were the employer, which candidate—A or B—would you remember more favorably?

A: I think fast under pressure and get along well with others. People often turn to me as a leader.

B: I've been volunteering at the Red Cross for three years. About a year ago, there was an explosion at an apartment building in my neighborhood. I received a call from the office asking if I could help. I got permission from my boss to take the rest of the day off and drove out to the site. Six volunteers were standing around waiting for the official site supervisor to arrive. It seemed odd to me that he wasn't there. I telephoned his office; they said he'd left 30 minutes ago. I asked the police if they could check the radio to see if there was any obvious reason for his delay. Sure enough, a freeway accident had tied up access. I suggested that we get going in his absence by identifying who needed what kind of relocation assistance. From then on, the other volunteers came to me for instruction and the police and medical personnel kept checking in with me. I was promoted to volunteer emergency supervisor after that event.

Can you see how much better a strong narrative conveys the message than the conclusions, and how it tells more than what was intended? Besides being a leader who thinks fast and gets along well with others, we see a person who cares about the community, is responsible enough to ask permission before dashing out to help, doesn't jump to conclusions, understands protocol and respects the system. We remember the story while the self-description is almost instantly forgettable.

The next step is to practice articulating your presentation. Describe yourself to your closest friends and most trusted colleagues and ask for their honest feedback about the impact, accuracy and effectiveness of your presentation. You'll also want to

Ten Selling Points in an Interview

- ▶ You know what the company does.
- ▶ You're aware of the most recent developments in the industry.
- ▶ You know what the challenges are for this industry and company and you relish the opportunity to tackle them.
- ▶ You clearly want to work for this company.
- ▶ You display no ambivalence about your desires.
- ▶ You don't appear to be desperate.
- ▶ You can point out tangible ways you have benefited previous employers.
- ▶ You're clear about what you do and don't know.
- ▶ You are computer literate in ways relevant to the industry.
- ▶ You accept and embrace change.

role play an interview with a career counselor or savvy colleague, using these common interview questions:

- ▶ What can you tell me about yourself?
- ▶ What are your weaknesses?
- ▶ What are your strengths?
- ▶ Why should I hire you?
- ▶ Where do you see yourself in five years?
- ▶ Why did you decide to leave your last job (or the legal profession)?
- ▶ What kind of salary are you looking for?
- ▶ What is your work style?
- ▶ What were your responsibilities in your last job?
- ▶ What do you think of your last boss?
- ▶ How would your previous supervisor describe you as a worker?
- ▶ What do you know about our company?
- ▶ Why are you interested in our company?
- ▶ Are you willing to work overtime?
- ▶ Aren't you over- or under-qualified for this position?
- ▶ When are you available to begin work?
- ▶ Have you applied with other companies?
- ▶ How do you define success, and how do you measure up to your own definition?
- ▶ What would you do if you won a $10 million lottery?
- ▶ Why should I hire you when I could promote someone from within?
- ▶ Tell me something negative you've heard about our company.

previous boss

Your goal in responding to questions is to hammer home the message that you'll be able to meet the employer's needs in a way that's compatible with the company style. Be certain to support any general statements (e.g., "I have substantial experience in negotiation") with a specific achievement (e.g., "Last year I settled 15 out of 16 cases scheduled for trial") or an illustrative story. Again, the proof is in the details; the right stories will convey your message much more convincingly than any assurances of your ability and commitment.

Whenever you're confronted with a question that raises a negative, offer the most neutral answer you can, even if it's not the entire truth. For example, if you left

Dressing for an Interview

The day before the interview, try on the clothes you plan to wear, checking for spots, tears and fit. (One man, who met with me immediately after a job interview, arrived with a long split in the seam of his trousers; another had a series of pen leaks across his belly.) Male or female, you can't go wrong by purchasing and keeping clean one conservative navy blue, gray or taupe gabardine suit, a neutral-colored shirt or blouse, and polished leather shoes, and wearing the same outfit to every initial meeting. That way, you'll only have to worry about your selection when you get called back for a second round—but by then you'll have a better sense of the employer's dress code.

If you're going to be interviewed by video conference, avoid white, plaids and any busy print that may seem psychedelic on the television screen. Look straight into the camera; that's the equivalent of good eye contact. Avoid broad gestures or abrupt motions.

Don't worry *too* much about your attire though. A survey reported in the *Los Angeles Times* found that inappropriate attire was at the bottom of the list of ways to undermine an interview. (Arrogance was first.)

your last job because you weren't willing to commute an hour each way to work for the Boss from Hell, state that you wanted work closer to home—if this job is indeed an easier commute. Avoid badmouthing your prior employer, no matter how unfairly you were treated.

Your questions will be as important as your answers. Employers can learn a lot about you through the questions you ask. How seriously have you been thinking about the job? How well do you understand the demands of the work? What are your expectations about the job and how mature are you? (That's why it's so important to avoid asking whether you'll have to work overtime, or how much vacation you'll earn, until an offer is actually extended. This type of inquiry demonstrates more commitment to your free time than to your work!)

Be prepared with astute questions. Avoid asking about anything that can be easily answered by reviewing the company's annual report, brochure or web page. Feel free, though, to ask for clarification of information contained in any of those sources, or in a magazine or newspaper article about the company. But don't bring up embarrassing information like lawsuits or labor problems unless they are directly relevant to the position for which you have applied.

Here are some questions you might ask:

► How are employees evaluated and promoted? Is it company policy to promote from within?
► What are your expectations for new hires?
► What characterizes a successful person at your company?
► How would you describe your company's personality and management style? How is work assigned to employees?
► What are the company's growth plans?
► How are you responding to a particular industry trend?

"During the interview, you must let the prospective employer know that you have decided—without regret or hesitation—to focus on this job, with this company, in this industry," says Brandon Toropox, author of *Last Minute Interview Tips*. "You must show you have a clear idea of exactly what you want to accomplish, and that you are itching to start. Most employers can sense this passion. It is an extremely attractive trait, one that interviewers respond to in a positive way."

But don't be too hasty about getting started. Any prospective employer will notice how you plan to treat your current employer. A seemingly innocent question like, "When can you start?," may be posed as much to expose your sense of responsibility and loyalty as to find out how available you are. Two weeks is the absolute minimum unless your current employer wants you gone sooner and the new employer is aware of it. A month is not unreasonable if you have cases to reassign or a practice to close.

Requesting time off before you start is another matter. There's nothing wrong with asking for a break if you know of no reason why your presence is needed more urgently. But if you're being hired to handle a huge backlog or you get the impression they want you there as soon as possible, don't even ask. Just make sure that they understand you haven't had a break for a while and would like to qualify for vacation before a full year has elapsed.

In summary, your goal in any interview is not only to impress the interviewer with your ability to do what the job requires but to convince him or her that you'll be easy to work with, that you have integrity and that your enthusiasm for the job will place you in the "bonus employee" category.

Compensation Negotiations

The rule of thumb about talking money is to defer the issue until you've had a chance to convince those with the authority to hire that you'll be a great resource. In interviews before a formal offer is extended, keep the question in abeyance with a comment like, "I think we can work that issue out." If it looks like an offer will be extended, prepare for the negotiation by following these steps.

First, research your value in the marketplace. Go to the library to read compensation surveys, salary updates by the Bureau of Labor Statistics, and the *Occupational Outlook Handbook.* Business and legal periodicals often feature salary surveys; for example, *The National Law Journal* frequently reports on salaries in the legal profession. "What Lawyers Earn," an annual survey of salaries for lawyers employed in corporate, law firm, public interest, law school and judicial environments throughout the United States, is usually published in the Spring. The newspaper also reprints other studies—for example, an Altman Weil Pensa 1996 survey of in-house attorney salaries nationwide and the Association of Legal Administrators annual survey of principal law firm administrators, controllers, personnel, office and recruitment managers.

Reviewing classified advertisements and talking to executive recruiters and career counselors about comparable salaries will help. Ask your colleagues and networking contacts about salary ranges in their firms or companies. Check as well with relevant professional associations to see if they've conducted any recent surveys. The American Compensation Association (http://www.acaonline.org; 14040 N. Northsight Blvd., Scottsdale, AZ 85260, (602) 922-2020) is another resource. It surveys all phases of employee compensation in business and government.

You can also dial into the Bureau of Labor Statistics online salary information at http://stats.bls.gov, or the JobSmart Internet page at http://jobsmart.org/tools/salary /sal-surv.htm, which offers links to over 200 salary surveys on the Web.

Do the same kind of research if you're being hired on a temporary, project or consulting basis. Talk to others with similar relationships. Check with organizations like the National Association of Temporary Staffing Services (see Appendix 4 under the heading of "Corporate, Business & Banking"), or read *The Consultant's Calling* (see Appendix 4 under the heading of "Consulting") or *The Complete Guide to Contract Lawyering,* to make sure your salary demands fall within the expected range.

Be sure you compare apples with apples. Don't study large or mid-sized law firm salaries when you're about to be hired by a solo practitioner. Don't expect a start-up company to compensate you as well as a member of the Fortune 500.

You must also make certain that you know the requirements of the job. Obtain a complete description of your duties and responsibilities. If there's nothing in writing, ask specific questions and confirm the answers in a letter of agreement. If you're going to be hired for a position that requires something more or less than the standard, adjust your salary expectations accordingly.

Then study the benefits package and take into consideration the added value of perquisites like these:

- ▶ Medical/dental plans;
- ▶ Life/disability insurance;
- ▶ CLE/licensing reimbursement;
- ▶ Vacation;
- ▶ Parking;
- ▶ Health or country club dues;
- ▶ Profit-sharing;
- ▶ Company car, or gas or bus allowance;
- ▶ Child-care/family leave policy;
- ▶ Van pools or public transportation subsidy;
- ▶ Stock options;
- ▶ Pension plans;
- ▶ Legal assistance/counseling;
- ▶ Reimbursement for moving expenses;
- ▶ Training and educational expenses;
- ▶ Seminars;
- ▶ Bonuses.

Be prepared to trade perquisites for salary, especially if your compensation will exceed that of your peers. Consider incentive compensation like stock options, or a percentage of the work you bring in, or fees collected above a base monthly or annual amount. Your willingness to share the risk with the employer may make you a more attractive candidate.

Know your salary history. Make a list of the highest salary you earned at each preceding job. Explain salaries that are artificially low because of unusual perquisites. If you've been temping or consulting for a while, disclose the project or hourly rate you received from sample employers. It's not necessary to provide tax returns to prove your claims.

Law Firm Partnership Negotiations

Two consultants in Brookline, Massachusetts, Deborah Heller and Linda Cunningham, studied professional organizations and discovered these three key elements to partnership success:

▶ The partners must respect each other's professional competence.

▶ The partners must clearly set forth the parameters of their business relationship.

▶ The partners must respect each other's personality differences, although they don't have to be compatible as individuals.

David Coleman, Ph.D., of Transition Management Services in Takoma Park, Maryland, believes that the first two requirements are more important than the third. Personality differences, he claims, can be managed effectively by timely professional intervention.

It is always wise to investigate the reputations of your future partners. Ask lawyers in your community, and judges if they have trial practices, about the quality of their work.

Next, discuss specific partnership terms. Don't be afraid to bring up uncomfortable topics like how much money they're now generating, what they're spending on overhead, their debt load, and what happens if one of them dies. (Of course, you should be prepared to divulge similar details about your own practice.) Their discomfort with the topics, or reluctance to disclose what's really going on in their firm, could be warning signals.

Hammer out the terms of your agreement. Include descriptions of your business goals, degree of autonomy, compensation, decision-making methods, overhead, entrance and dissolution procedures, equity ownership, and management methods and responsibilities. A 1995 ABA publication, *Compensation Plans for Law Firms,* describes ways of distributing profits to partners. *Getting Started: Basics for a Successful Law Firm,* released in 1996, covers successful practice arrangements, ownership options, and partnership agreements, and includes a model partnership agreement on an accompanying diskette.

You might also consider a one-year "of counsel" or space-sharing arrangement to get to know your prospective partners and their operation better. Use this time to discuss fully the terms of any future agreement. The ABA publishes another book that might be helpful here, *The Of Counsel Agreement: A Guide for Law Firm & Practitioner.*

Allow enough time for both sides to consider offers. You may be eager to begin or desperate about your cash flow, but don't let those feelings control you. This is a big decision for both you and the employer; demonstrate your maturity by taking the time to study their proposal and giving them the time to study yours.

Whether you're being hired as a permanent or temporary employee, providing consulting services or joining as a partner or owner, get everything in writing. If you haven't been given a contract or letter to sign, send your own letter confirming what you understand to be the terms of your engagement. You'll quickly receive a response in writing if it's incorrect!

As lawyers, you've learned to advocate for others, not for yourself. As an American, you've been taught that the subject of money is almost taboo. To land the job you want on terms that will make you feel valued, you must set aside these lessons. If you apply the same skill and forthrightness to your own interests that you use in representing your clients, you'll successfully conclude this career move, and prepare yourself well for the (almost inevitable) next.

Steps to Take If You Leave the Profession

"Change begets change."

—Charles Dickens, novelist

. . .

Withdrawing from the legal profession can be as complicated and time intensive as entering it. Here are some steps that will allow you to make a transition that won't come back to haunt you.

Closing an Active Practice

Ethically, you must be certain that every client in your office with an active case knows that you are leaving the practice and has an opportunity to find replacement counsel. You can let them know your recommendation for substitute counsel, but you must obtain their express permission before transferring their case to another lawyer.

When you do transfer a file, send it to the new attorney with a cover letter copied to the client. For pending court cases, file a "Notice of Withdrawal and Substitution of Attorneys" and make certain opposing counsel receives a copy.

> Withdrawing from the legal profession can be as complicated and time intensive as entering it.

Those clients who wish to postpone hiring another lawyer, or who cannot decide on a replacement, can take their files. But before they leave, have them sign a receipt for the file which acknowledges your withdrawal from the case and advice that they promptly find other representation. Then file the "Notice of Withdrawal" with the court and opposing counsel.

Clients with wills or other ongoing but inactive matters should also be notified of your status. Send them a letter which recommends substitute counsel should they need legal services in the future and lets them know where their file is maintained. Also, try to return—by certified mail or personal delivery—any original documents you've been holding for safekeeping.

Cases that Won't Go Away

There may be matters from which the court will not permit you to withdraw, usually ones with a trial or other significant hearing scheduled for the near future and a client who doesn't want to pay a new attorney to become familiar with the case. If this occurs, you only have three good options:

▶ Postpone your departure until every case is concluded.
▶ Close your office, but make arrangements with another firm to accept pleadings and provide occasional conference room space, or set up a temporary home office until you complete the matter.
▶ Associate another lawyer (with your client's permission), and assume the cost of getting that lawyer familiar with the case.

There *is* another option, but I don't recommend it: You can withdraw anyway and face the consequences. One lawyer who did so explained his actions this way, "What are they going to do? Disbar me? I quit!"

Selling Your Practice

Historically, most state ethics codes prohibited the sale of a law practice as a going business. Lawyers attempted to circumvent these proscriptions by:

▶ Inflating the value of the law practice's physical assets and agreeing to refer clients to the purchaser, or
▶ Creating a "quickie" partnership from which one partner would soon retire and receive compensation, leaving the remaining partner with the client base.

Such sales contracts, however, were invariably ruled unenforceable as violations of public policy.

The ABA's Model Rule of Professional Conduct 1.17 outlines the following terms under which a lawyer may sell a practice, including goodwill:

► The seller must cease to engage in the private practice of law in the jurisdiction or geographic area in which the practice was conducted.

► The practice must be sold in its entirety.

► Actual written notice must be given to each client regarding, among other information, the client's right to retain other counsel or to take possession of the file.

At this time, Rule 1.17 is being slowly adopted by selected states. Even if not endorsed in your state, the existence of this Model Rule could argue against the voiding of a sales contract.

In any event, you would be wise to review the provisions of Model Rule 1.17, and to read "Purchase or Sale of a Solo Practice: What Should Be Your Concerns?," by Demetrious Dimitriou in the November-December 1993 *Law Practice Management* magazine.

Transferring Files with Potential Malpractice Claims

Seven years after I closed my practice, the mailman left at my door a notice of an attempt to deliver a certified letter. I couldn't sleep that night, wondering which "time bomb" in my long-closed files had just detonated! To my relief, it turned out to be airline tickets, not a threatening letter. That experience reminded me all too acutely of the haunting stress of practicing law.

It's a rare (and probably deluded) lawyer who hasn't made a mistake. As a result, almost every lawyer has a case or two that raises fears of malpractice claims. This common experience among your peers will probably result in some pretty sympathetic ears when it comes time to transfer those troublesome files to other lawyers.

In order to assure a supportive ear, scan your memory for the lawyers you most trust and respect, and who practice in the appropriate areas of law. Look especially for those with accepting, non-adversarial natures and approach them one at a time. Be straightforward about your anxiety, and come prepared with specific examples of cases you think you've handled badly. The lawyers you consult will probably know how to get the cases back on track.

If you have made errors or oversights that will require your clients to invest in additional legal work, offer right up front to pay the cost. That investment will likely avert any subsequent malpractice claims.

In some cases, your actions will have caused irreparable injury to your client. If you're covered by a "claims-made" policy, notify your carrier of any potential claims before you terminate the policy. Better yet, purchase "tail" coverage (see below) to insure you against claims that are raised after you quit practicing law. One consolation: You won't have to worry that your mistakes will increase your malpractice premiums because you won't be practicing law anymore!

Malpractice Insurance Coverage

Most current policies are "claims made." In other words, you are covered in every annual policy period only for those claims that are actually filed (or sometimes, for those you notified the insurance company might arise in the future). If you have been self-employed or part of a partnership, purchase a "tail" policy (known as an "extended reporting form endorsement"). This policy will protect you against all errors and omissions that occurred before you quit practicing but weren't filed until after you closed your doors. The coverage may last until your death, or for only a limited period, depending upon what you buy. "Tail" policies can cost up to three times the last annual premium, but the investment is essential for peace of mind.

On the other hand, if you were a law firm or agency employee, your actions will probably be covered by the continuing policy of your employer—unless they have also dissolved. In that case, make certain that they have purchased the appropriate "tail" coverage. Remember, though, that if you continue to do a "little bit" of law practicing on the side, you will be personally liable for any claims which arise after policy termination.

Health Insurance

If you will be unemployed or self-employed after you quit, or if the health plan at your new company legally excludes coverage for pre-existing conditions, be certain to investigate the requirements for continuation coverage under any prior group plan. Before you leave your current job, make certain that your employer sends you the legally required notice of the right to continue coverage. (See discussion of COBRA benefits in Appendix 1.) Then, request continuation coverage in writing, following the company's procedures exactly.

Bar Association Membership

It took me eight years to convert my Washington State bar membership to inactive status; I only took the step when I learned I could go inactive for three years without retaking the bar examination. By the end of that period, I knew with absolute certainty that I would never practice law again and chose to remain inactive.

My reluctance to give up an active license to practice law is not at all unusual among former practicing attorneys. Most continue to maintain an active license in at least one jurisdiction. Some remain active in one state and convert to inactive membership elsewhere. Others choose to switch to an inactive membership (especially in states like California where annual dues are so high and you can reactivate without retaking the bar examination). If you do choose inactive status, make certain that you know what is required to become active again should you ever want or need to use your license.

Keeping in Touch

Don't slam the heavy door of the law behind you as you leave. You may be thinking "good riddance" now, but you'll come to appreciate the people you knew and the support you received when you've developed some emotional distance. Your legal education and experience served you well enough to get you where you are now. It will continue to serve you in the future if you respect the commitment of all your former colleagues and keep in touch with those you knew best. Who knows? There may come a day when you need their advice—or they need yours!

Afterword

"If you bring forth what is within you, what you bring forth will save you. If you do not bring forth what is within you, what you do not bring forth will destroy you.

—attributed to Jesus of Nazareth

■ ■ ■

The parents of Ed Zwick, director of *Courage Under Fire, Glory* and TV's *Thirtysomething,* wanted him to attend Harvard Law School. Shortly after he was admitted, the late legal scholar Paul Freund took him to tea. Freund had seen and been impressed by several plays staged by Zwick and also knew of his admission to law school. In their conversation, Freund acknowledged that law school was certainly an option for Zwick, but wondered why he was considering it. Why not continue to do the thing that he did best? To his parents' dismay, Zwick turned down Harvard, accepted a Rockefeller Fellowship to study experimental theater in Europe, and started down his own path toward an exceptionally creative and successful career.

> You can do what is safe or you can take a risk to move toward what thrills you.

By telling you about Ed Zwick, I'm not suggesting that you should never have gone to law school. I tell the story instead to point out that many people will give you advice. Some will urge you to do what's safe; others will encourage you to take the risk to move toward what thrills you instead. Neither choice is inherently right or wrong. But one choice is right for you.

As you make your decision, keep in mind these thoughts of Seattle lawyer Lindsay Thompson:

> At the end of the day, what counts is that people enjoy what they do for a living. We, each of us, know what that will be far better than all the advice-givers and second-guessers around us put together. We just have to listen carefully to ourselves to find out what our answer is.

In a Buddhist fable, a man falls off a steep ledge. To slow his descent, he grabs a sturdy branch growing out of the side of the cliff. As he clings to it, he looks around frantically and spots a small, grassy plateau across the chasm. He sees that it could cushion his fall, but believes it is totally out of reach. Suddenly, he hears a voice. "Let go of the branch and jump," the voice says. "You can make it!"

The man is paralyzed. What should he do? He wants to trust the voice, but he's afraid he'll miss the grassy plateau and die in the attempt. On the other hand, dangling from a branch for the rest of his life holds no appeal. Over and over again, he debates his options, all the while hanging in limbo.

What will it take for him to trust the voice?

A simple leap of faith.

COULD THERE BE

A LAY-OFF IN

YOUR FUTURE?

Perhaps this scenario will ring a bell: You've heard rumors around town that your employer is having financial difficulties. None of the partners will tell you anything directly, but they have come down hard on everyone to watch expenses and increase billable hours. Since associate salaries are one of their largest expenses, you're worried that you're going to be laid off.

The possibility of forced job change has become an unpleasant reality in the legal profession. Law firms followed other businesses in the early 1990's by becoming more budget conscious. Many reduced their workforce (or "downsized"), expecting more work from fewer employees in an effort to keep per partner profits as close as possible to the heights reached in the 1980's. Corporate legal departments also consolidated, closing down branch offices and centralizing litigation. Only a small number of lawyers were let go because of inadequate work; most were the victims of economic retrenchment. The general consensus among economic forecasters is that this recessionary pulling in will continue to be a hallmark of the information economy.

How does this impact you? No job should be considered secure over the long term. Your area of practice—like real estate in the 1980's and bankruptcy in the 1990's—may be hot one year and out the next. A "rainmaker" in your firm may decide to initiate a career change, taking the firm's biggest clients—but not you—along. The firm's largest client may shift its work to another law firm or bring most of its work in-house.

Since predictability is no longer a part of a lawyer's professional environment, you'd be wise to employ these strategies:

Honestly evaluate your vulnerability to layoff. Jeanne Svikhart, of White Svikhart & Associates, a Washington, DC, consulting company on recruitment and training issues, has identified seven categories of lawyers who are most vulnerable to layoff:

▶ Service partners who do not control significant client portfolios;

▶ Partners who practice in an area that has dwindled or dried up because of changes in the marketplace;

▶ Senior associates and partners whose work was tied to a rainmaker who left the firm;

▶ Laterally-transferred senior associates, of counsels, and contract partners who promised more new business than they could deliver;

▶ Senior associates hired laterally who don't perform as expected;

▶ Associates and partners hired through a merger with another firm who don't control business or don't mesh with the new firm culture;

▶ Partners with substantial management responsibilities whose non-billable work is no longer valued.

Confront what's really happening. Those who have been laid off often admit that they had an intuition, or received subtle warnings, that their jobs were in jeopardy long before the actual termination was announced. For example, one laid-off associate of a Wall Street law firm ignored her failure to receive case assignments that would develop her potential.

Rather than disregarding the signals that others probably see, assess your situation by making an objective investigation. First, contact the partners for whom you do the most work. Ask them how you're doing, and what skills they think you'll need to develop over the next several years. Non-responsiveness, waffling, putting you off, or unexpected criticism could be signs that your job is in jeopardy. Then, reconsider your past performance reviews. If the consensus has been lukewarm to negative, or if you've been told that you need to develop new skills or clients and you haven't, you'd better start exploring other options. You also have reason to worry about your future if the firm is losing clients in your area of specialty and you're not bringing in a few profitable ones yourself. On the other hand, if past and present feedback confirm that you're an essential contributor to the firm's future, keep up the good work—

while continuing to keep your eyes and ears open for changes in the wind.

Take the initiative. Unfortunately, some law firms in recent years have been trying to save their own reputations by sacrificing some of their partners and associates, blaming individual performance rather than admitting their layoffs are economically motivated. For example, one firm laid off 15 employees in the same month, citing decreased productivity, poor quality work or lack of commitment to the firm as reasons for their terminations. None of the 15 employees had received any prior negative comments about their performances. At the same time, there were rumors in the financial community that the law firm was behind in its rent.

You'll be a stronger candidate for re-employment if you initiate your job search without the cloud of "termination" over you. You might also circumvent the feelings of worthlessness that will arise even if the firm makes it clear that you were not let go because of poor performance.

Improve your financial picture. On the financial front, cut back on your expenses and build up an emergency fund of six to nine months of salary. You might also want to increase the liquidity of any investment portfolio, and set up a home equity credit line. (See Chapter 19 for specific ways to save money and generate more income.) At the same time, invest time in self-assessment, considering your options in the broadest possible terms. As business columnist Mary Rowland wrote in *The New York Times,* "This is not the time to undergo tunnel vision."

Take care of yourself physically, spiritually and emotionally. This is one of those pieces of advice that's a lot easier to give than to take; but a consciousness about it will help. An impending job loss brings all your coping mechanisms—positive and negative—to the surface. Overeating, renewing a smoking habit, turning to drugs, alcohol or compulsive exercise, and working even harder in the hope of averting the inevitable are common among lawyers. Rather than moving into self-destructive behavior, get regular but reasonable exercise to ease the tension and spend more time with friends. You'll need physical strength and the support of others to make it through this stressful period.

If All Else Fails . . .

Consider these steps if you are laid off:

Educate yourself about termination benefits. All companies with more than 20 employees must comply with the Consolidated Omnibus Budget Reconciliation Act (COBRA). Under this act, continuing group health insurance coverage must be offered to all employees who either leave the company or are terminated, who voluntarily or involuntarily cut back to part-time work or retire before becoming eligible for Medicare, or who become disabled. Your spouse and children will also qualify for coverage.

The employer must notify you of your rights under COBRA within 45 days of your termination date. You then have 60 days to elect coverage and 45 days from the date of election to make your first premium payment. If you comply with the notification requirements, you are entitled to maintain your group health insurance coverage for 18 months after you leave, as long as you pay the cost of coverage plus a two percent administrative fee.

The COBRA rules are very specific and many employers will cut you off if you don't comply to the letter, which means you'd better make each premium payment on time.

If your employer is too small to fall under the COBRA rules, your options are more limited. You could ask your employer to consider you on a leave of absence and let you pay for continuing coverage under the group plan. At the same time, you could apply for an individual policy, perhaps for major medical coverage only.

Negotiate a good severance package. One month to one year's salary (depending upon your tenure with the firm), continued health and insurance coverage, and outplacement assistance are not unreasonable. Don't worry about defining your exit from the firm as a layoff, termination or resignation. Focusing on the reason for your termination diverts attention from your settlement package. And remember the age old wisdom: A lawyer who represents himself has a fool for a client. Consult another lawyer to help you negotiate a better deal. You might want to read "All This and Fired Too: A Journey into the Land of Termination Agreements," Patrick Capuano, *ABA Journal*, March 1993, to learn the wrong approach!

Take income tax ramifications into consideration in your negotiations. Severance pay is equivalent to additional months of salary and is therefore fully taxable. Outplacement assistance can be an exempt fringe benefit when it satisfies one consideration: The employer must receive a business benefit, for example, improving worker morale or deflecting wrongful discharge suits, beyond what it would get by giving the employee a larger severance payment.

When the outplacement assistance is offered in lieu of higher cash severance pay, it *is* taxable. But you may deduct it to the extent that it and other miscellaneous items exceed the applicable percentage of your adjusted gross income.

Leave on good terms. It's hard to feel warmly toward those who made the decision to let you go. But these are the people who will provide references for your next position. If you sit down with the partners before you leave, be positive and try to express your understanding and acceptance of the financial pressures that triggered the layoff.

Stay calm. Don't reach out frantically for the first job you can find. Instead, take a "vacation" to clear your head and work through your anger and depression. Visit friends in another city, hang around town but spend your days doing all the things you didn't have time for when you were working, or invest some money in foreign travel. You'll be operating from a much more clear-headed and strong perspective when you return.

Postpone contacting colleagues and other business acquaintances until you're ready to act. Calling them all immediately may send out off-putting signals of desperation.

Don't limit your search. The more broadly you define your skills, and the more adaptable you make them, the greater your options. Says one expert, "You get desperate when you don't have a well-thought-out plan." You might even consider moving to another geographic location, changing careers, acting as a consultant, accepting a part-time position, creating a job-share arrangement, or taking a pay cut.

Don't pretend you weren't fired. (See Chapter 25.)

Write down your thoughts and feelings. In one study, psychologists asked unemployed, middle-aged professionals to write about the trauma of their job loss or any other topic for 20 minutes on five consecutive days. Interestingly, after eight months more than half those who had written about their job loss had found jobs, while 25 percent of those who had written on other topics and only 14 percent of those who had not written at all were re-employed. Researchers theorized that those who wrote about the loss rid themselves of some of the bitterness that could have sabotaged job interviews. It's clear this exercise in reflection helped those job-seekers let go of their demoralizing past and move on.

Maintain a daily routine. Consider yourself "otherwise" employed by keeping business hours. Set the alarm so that you're ready to answer the telephone articulately by 8:00 o'clock in the morning. Better yet, shower and dress before that time. Then schedule daily informational interviews and trips to the library to research employers.

Stay involved in other activities. Schedule at least one enjoyable activity every day—meeting a friend for lunch or a walk, going to a movie, reading a good piece of fiction. Force yourself to get exercise and to get outdoors every day, even if only for a few minutes. Just before or after you've had your fun, accomplish one job-hunting task—putting in a telephone call to a networking contact, redrafting your résumé, engaging in a mock interview with a friend. Consider also volunteer work and community networking. They provide psychic rewards in a difficult time as well as terrific opportunities for networking.

Be careful getting into the next job. Consider all aspects of the position. Make certain it's a good fit for you, or that you at least know what you're getting into. Do your homework. Talk to others in the company or those with similar positions else-where. Ask questions. And trust your intuition. If you ignore your feelings, you might soon repeat the pattern. Let your gut tell you whether to accept a job or to come on board on a "look-see," project basis only. If you do accept a permanent position, negotiate a severance package or enter into an employment contract before you start.

RESOURCES

TARGETED TO LAWYERS

& LAW STUDENTS

NONPROFIT CAREER
PROGRAMS FOR LAWYERS

Career Services for Attorneys, Alumnae
Resources, www.ar.org; 120 Montgomery St.,
Suite 600, San Francisco, CA 94104; (415)
274-4700. Offers inexpensive workshops in
the Bay Area. Website offers a helpful self-
assessment questionnaire.

Lawyers' Assistance Program Career Services,
Washington State Bar Association, 2101
Fourth Avenue, 4th Floor, Seattle, WA 98121;
(206) 727-8268. Weekly job hunters support
group and individual counseling.

Lawyers in Transition, The Association of the
Bar of the City of New York,
www.abcny.org/joblisth.stm; 42 W. 44th St.,
New York, NY 10036; (212) 382-6657.

Lawyers in Transition, Oregon Attorney
Assistance Program, 722 SW 2nd Ave., Suite
210, Portland, OR 97204; (503) 226-7150 or
(Oregon only) (800) 321-OAAP. Regular
career evaluation workshops, seminars and
individual counseling.

Lawyers' Transition Program, Colorado
Lawyers' Health Program (affiliated with the
Colorado Bar Association), 1900 Grant Street,
Denver, CO 80203; (303) 832-2233.

Check with young lawyers, quality of life or
attorney assistance committees of state and
local bar associations. They may sponsor
periodic career-related programs.

THE CHANGING LEGAL PROFESSION

*Law v. Life: What Lawyers Are Afraid to Say about
the Legal Profession,* Walt Bachman. A slim
personal commentary on the legal profession,
written by a 25-year Minneapolis practitioner.
Hardback; Four Directions Press, 1995.

*Moral Vision and Professional Decisions: The Changing
Values of Women and Men Lawyers,* Rand and
Dana Crowley Jack. A 1990 study of the
dilemmas facing attorneys in everyday practice.
Hardback; Cambridge University Press, 1989.

*Running from the Law: Why Good Lawyers Are
Getting Out of the Legal Profession,* Deborah L.
Arron. The book that broke through the code
of silence about lawyer dissatisfaction. Uses
compelling, first-person case histories to
describe what some successful lawyers did to
find career satisfaction outside of the
profession. Paperback, Ten Speed Press,
1991. Out of print but available in libraries,
career services offices and through the
National Association for Law Placement.

*The Betrayed Profession: Lawyering at the End of
the Twentieth Century,* Sol M. Linowitz. Paperback; Johns Hopkins University Press, 1994.

The Lawyer Who Blew Up His Desk, Joseph
Matthews. Witty, dramatic and often absurd
stories from the memoir of a former public
defender. Paperback; Ten Speed Press, 1998.

*The Lost Lawyer: Failing Ideals of the Legal
Profession,* Anthony T. Kronman. Another
book on the spiritual crisis affecting the legal
profession. Paperback; Harvard University
Press, 1993

*The Lure of the Law: Why People Become Lawyers
and What the Profession Does to Them,*
Richard Moll. A law office management
consultant interviewed practicing lawyers
who see law as a path to money, power,
social change and personal fulfillment.
Paperback, Viking/Penguin, 1990.

Women Lawyers: Rewriting the Rules, Mona
Harrington. Tells what life was like for women
lawyers in the early 1990's and how their
dilemmas reflected social issues of the time.
Paperback; Plume, 1993.

BOOKS ON STRESS AND BURNOUT

1998 Directory of Lawyers Assistance Programs.
See listing at page 308.

*Life, Law and the Pursuit of Balance: A Lawyer's
Guide to Quality of Life,* edited by Jeffrey R.
Simmons. A compilation of articles written by
ABA members. Examines the factors
contributing to career dissatisfaction for

MORE ON LAWYER STRESS & BURNOUT

Stephen Feldman practiced law for five years in the 1960's, and then taught law for another 11 while he earned a Ph.D. in psychology. Since 1982, he's practiced as a clinical psychologist, working with many lawyers and their families. Here he shares his unique perspective on the stresses peculiar to practicing lawyers.

Feldman's Statement: Law was a tough thing to get up in the morning to do. I used to wake up and think, "Maybe it's World War III and I won't have to go to the office. Maybe everything will be called off today."

For me, the anxiety started as far back as law school. I remember once sitting in a class, saying to myself, "I am paying attention, I have read the material, and I don't know what they are talking about. This is frightening." The only thing I could hold onto, I thought, was that I was fourth in the class and there were only three other guys who might be understanding it. If I was at the bottom of the class, I think I would have walked out.

I continued through law school like a little pigeon. I kept pecking, they kept rewarding me, and I continued to be a good student. I remember how tense law school was and how massive the workload seemed to be. The horrible news is that things are probably still that way for most lawyers, but they have just gotten used to it.

Stress is not just a matter of staying late at the office or becoming irritable at home. It is a serious business that can affect the quality and indeed the length of life. And there are stresses peculiar to a lawyer's work.

First, practicing law is the only profession in which there is an equal and opposite professional whose job it is to prove that you are wrong. A doctor does not ordinarily face a second doctor objecting to what he or she does. No opposing preacher is there to argue for the devil. The adversary system means there is little margin for error, as opposing counsel forever lurks, waiting to pounce on any mistake. Additionally, any error is forever part of the record, able to come back to haunt you long after you have retired to Hawaii and quit paying for malpractice insurance.

Besides opposing counsel, the work is often subject to criticism or praise by a third person, namely a judge or a jury. In law, someone wins and somebody loses. Judgments of your work are made virtually every day.

And lawyers continually deal with the heavy responsibility of someone else's money, property, quality of life, family or even life and death. A lawyers faces these issues, and usually several client's problems, all in one day.

One lawyer described the essence of his practice as absorbing the client's energy. The client relieves himself of his stress by passing it on to you. You accept it from the client so the client can leave your office saying, "I feel better." That way, the client will be back.

The pressure never ends. One night, I was lying in bed reading a detective novel. I got to this steamy part that read, "Slowly, he ran his hand along Babs' thigh," and I suddenly found myself wondering whether I'd remembered to file for an extension in the Babs Smith case? Then it hit me. I couldn't even read a dirty book without the law intruding.

Lawyers also continually deal with deadlines. Law is the business of deadlines, and woe to you if you miss that 10 days to file a notice of appeal (or is it 30?), the 20 days to answer a complaint, the statutes of limitations, the interrogatories, and so on and so on. There isn't an event that happens in a lawyer's professional life that doesn't have a time frame and a penalty attached to it.

Along with winning and losing comes conflict. The lawyer's professional life is filled with dispute, confrontation, and occasionally actual hatred. It is rare that a case will be pleasant; even adoptions can have snags. That unhappiness and conflict is reflected in the public's generally low opinion of lawyers as compared to other professionals. This also adds to the stress.

And you are the person expected to have the knowledge and expertise to give answers. Clients don't understand that you usually can't say either "yes" or "no," "black" or "white."

Being both a psychologist and a lawyer, I can speak to the difference in client attitudes. As a psychologist, when I call a client to make an appointment to come in, the response is usually pleasure in some form. It might be relief or gratitude. Almost always there is compliance. As an attorney doing the same task, there is usually hostility or suspicion. At the very least, there is apprehension, fear, tension, distance or coolness.

Similarly, when the phone rings for lawyers, it's like a time bomb going off. You can never tell what kind of crisis or attitude is going to come at you through the receiver.

None of the phone calls may be actual Big Events. But just one may be, and it may be the next call.

I believe it's quite true that as people go forward in the practice of law they learn more and more about less and less. The legal profession is very narrowing to the soul. That's why lawyers need to get away and do something else; to discover there's a whole world out there that doesn't know there are two court systems. They need to remind themselves that the universe that has become so important to them is just a footnote in most other people's lives.

I once said to a nurse I was working with that I had found the secret to happiness in life.

She said, "Great, what's that?"

"What you have to do," I said, "is first figure out what you like to do and then figure out how to make money at it."

She thought for a minute, and then said, "I think that's prostitution!"

It was a great answer, but I still think I had the right idea. It's the whole reason I went into psychology. I like to talk to people; I like to listen to people. Hell, if I like to do that, why not do it and make money too?

Most lawyers don't see their work that way.

---

lawyers and offers suggestions on how to remove or minimize those factors. Paperback; American Bar Association, 1998.

Living with the Law: Strategies to Avoid Burnout and Create Balance, edited by Julie M. Tamminen. Professionals who work with lawyers tell you how to handle stress and avoid alcoholism and burnout. Paperback; American Bar Association, 1996.

Stress Management for Lawyers: How to Increase Personal & Professional Satisfaction in the Law, Amiram Elwork, Ph.D. By far the best of the books on managing stress within the practice

of law. Explores the causes and costs of lawyer stress. Offers practical suggestions to decrease stress in your environment, identify and eliminate harmful thinking patterns and deal with emotions more effectively. Paperback; The Vorkell Group (800-759-1222), 2nd ed. 1997.

The Soul of the Law: Understanding Lawyers and the Law, Benjamin Sells. A psychotherapist and former practicing lawyer examines attitudes that affect lawyers like workaholism, materialism, stress, fear of failure and ethical dilemmas. Paperback; Element Books, 1995.

A2 Resources Targeted to Lawyers & Law Students

ALTERNATIVE WORK-SCHEDULE RESOURCES

A Survival Guide for Road Warriors: Essentials for the Mobile Lawyer. A guide to using technology in an office, on the road, in the courtroom or at home. Practical tips from choosing a notebook computer and peripherals to buying a cell phone. Paperback; American Bar Association, 1996.

Breaking Traditions: Work Alternatives for Lawyers. Essays by lawyers about the problems of defining and creating a new law firm culture, and that outline alternatives to law firm organization and the traditional practice of law. Paperback; American Bar Association, 1993.

Telecommuting for Lawyers, Nicole Belson Goluboff. Advice for law firm policy makers and lawyers who want to telecommute. Paperback; American Bar Association, 1998.

The Complete Guide to Contract Lawyering: What Every Lawyer and Law Firm Need to Know about Temporary Legal Services, Deborah Arron and Deborah Guyol. The first comprehensive guide on temporary work for lawyers. Includes rate setting, marketing, ethical, malpractice and insurance considerations, and how to work with agencies. Paperback; Niche Press, 2nd ed. 1999.

CHANGING LOCATIONS

Attorney's Guide to State Bar Admission Requirements. Examines admission-without-examination options, modified examinations for previously admitted attorneys, transferability of MBE, MPRE and MEE scores, fees and legal specialty certification in 55 jurisdictions. Paperback; Federal Reports, Inc., 2nd ed.

BarPlus, www.barplus.com/statesmain.htm. Comprehensive information about bar exam requirements in all 50 states, accessed by clicking on the state.

"Main St. U.S.A.: An Inside Look at Small Town Law," Steven Keeva, *ABA Journal,* October 1992.

"Small-Town Practice Proves Attractive for Rising Number of Lawyers," Ronald Smothers, "The Great Escape: The Joys and Woes of Resort Town Practice," Joel Kaplan, *ABA Journal,* August 1993.

"Welcome to Paradise. Now Get Out," B.J. Palermo, *California Lawyer,* February 1993. An article about the pros and cons of practicing law in a small town.

MAKING PART-TIME PRACTICE WORK

Robin entered the legal profession in the late 1970's determined to succeed on her own terms. After a few years with a small law firm, she hung out her own shingle to practice with a style and focus that was totally her own. In 1982, after the birth of her first child, she reduced her practice by half. Now, divorced and sharing custody of her two children, Robin has learned what works, and what doesn't, in running a part-time practice.

Robin's Statement: With many years of experience practicing law part time, I know exactly what's necessary to do it.

- First, you have to cut your overhead.
- Second, you have to narrow your scope.
- Third, you have to swallow your pride.

I was prepared for my income to drop 30 percent when I switched to half time, but actually I make as much money now as I did when I was working full time. The key is keeping my overhead down. I work primarily out of my house. In order to sit down with clients occasionally, I rent a tiny office from a law firm with leftover space. For typing, I use a local entrepreneur who does freelance word processing at a very reasonable price. I keep my eye on the cost of supplies, malpractice insurance and accounting fees.

The next requirement is to narrow your scope. I accomplished that goal at the outset by firing the clients who either didn't pay me, or who forced me to beg for a percentage on the dollar. By the time I moved my business home, I could tell on the telephone which clients were not likely to pay. They usually tipped their hand by making the same sort of remarks as the last ten people who wound up not paying. I got rid of all those cases, and now I regularly turn away new business that looks like trouble. I only take cases that are interesting, with people I like and who are likely to pay me. I've lowered my stress and increased my income. The time I work is time well spent.

I have a lot more control over my income by running a much tighter ship. When I worked full time, I'd have 60, 70, even 80 cases going at a time. I was occasionally out of control and always working too hard. Now I'm down to 20 to 25 cases of different sizes, but mostly fairly small. The smaller my operation gets, the more control I have. I'm not under stress, because I weed out most of the bad cases and I know what I'm doing.

Which leads to another element of narrowing your scope: carving out a specialty. When I started my practice, I would take the case of anyone who walked in my door. No more. General practice is too hard now, period. And if you are going to work part-time, it's ridiculous. Now my practice is limited to guardianship and probate, a specialty that's affected by only one section

of the legislative code. I don't have to worry as much about keeping up with changes in the law.

It's important to pick a specialty that avoids complex matters and high-stress litigation. The only exception I would make is a wrongful death case with no liability issues, like a father of three getting run over in a crosswalk by a well-insured driver. But how many cases like that are you likely to get? In 20 years of practice, I haven't gotten one. If you don't have the support you need, you cannot handle a complicated lawsuit against a big corporation. You have to leave that for the full-time lawyers. The case may look attractive, but if it's stressful and will require costs to be advanced, you're getting yourself right back into what you just finished leaving.

Swallowing your pride—the last requirement—means using voice mail instead of employing a full-time receptionist or paying for an answering service. It means doing without the fancy office and the personal secretary. It means that when someone asks if they can schedule a motion on Thursday afternoon, you have to admit that your preschooler's play takes priority. Fortunately, I find other lawyers to be much more responsive to that kind of scheduling problem than they would be if my conflict involved a very important deposition in "my Union Oil case."

I found full-time law practice relentless. There was never any time to breathe. Even if I was vacationing, I was always worrying about my cases. On a part-time basis, things are not as relentless. I work about 25 hours per week. My kids are finally in school, and I have some free time. There's only one problem with this whole arrangement. If you develop a good part-time schedule, it's difficult to imagine going back to work full time.

JOB-HUNT RESOURCES

Alternative Careers for Lawyers, Hillary Mantis. Information and advice about nontraditional careers for lawyers. Paperback; The Princeton Review, 1997.

Beyond L.A. Law: Break the Traditional "Lawyer" Mold, edited by Janet Smith. Profiles of 47 law school graduates who developed careers in and outside of the legal profession. Paperback; Harcourt Brace, 1998.

Changing Jobs: A Handbook for Lawyers, edited by Heidi L. McNeil. Articles on career planning, the job search process, and employment opportunities for experienced lawyers. The alternative careers chapter is excerpted from this book. Paperback; American Bar Association, 2nd ed. 1995 (3rd ed. expected 1999).

Find Satisfaction in the Law, www.findlaw.com/ satisfaction. A website updated by Boston-based Center for Professional Development in the Law. Contains articles on career satisfaction for lawyers.

Guerrilla Tactics for Getting the Legal Job of Your Dreams, Kimm Alayne Walton. A lively and engaging job search guide for law students and entry-level lawyers. Paperback; Harcourt Brace, 1996.

Jobs for Lawyers: Effective Techniques for Getting Hired in Today's Legal Marketplace, Hillary Jane Mantis & Kathleen Brady. Comprehensive yet concise career development assistance for law school graduates. Paperback; Impact Publications, 1996.

JD Preferred! Legal Career Alternatives. A brief overview of the alternative career search for lawyers followed by lists of alternative careers, and in-depth coverage of academic administration, alternative dispute resolution, ethics, insurance and risk management, international trade & investment, media and technology transfer. Loose-leaf compilation; Federal Reports, Inc., 1996.

Judgment Reversed: Alternative Careers for Lawyers, Jeffrey Strausser. Repetitive but solid advice on how to use your legal skills successfully in advertising, marketing, public relations, business management, property management, corporate training, management consulting, educational consulting and publishing. Paperback; Barron's, 1997.

Reasonable Lawyer's Career Guide. A pamphlet prepared by the Michigan-based temporary legal staffing company, Contract Counsel (formerly Americlerk). Contains solid information and advice about the legal job search. Also available online at www.contractcounsel.com.

The Lawyers Guide to JobSurfing On the Internet, Career Education Institute. Lists of websites helpful to law students and lawyers looking for work. Frequently updated. Available for $10 plus $2 for shipping from Career Education Institute, PO Box 11171, Winston-Salem, NC 27116; (336) 768-2999.

The Legal Job Interview, Clifford Ennico. Written by a lawyer, this book tells you what to do before, during and following an interview, primarily for an entry-level position with a large law firm. Paperback; Biennix Corporation, 1994.

The Road Not Taken: A Practical Guide to Exploring Non-Legal Career Options, Kathy Grant and Wendy Werner. A straightforward plan for exploring nontraditional careers written in two parts, one for law school career counselors and the other for students. Photocopied; National Association for Law Placement, 1991.

JOB ANNOUNCEMENT RESOURCES

Attorneys@Work, www.attorneys@work.com. Legal recruitment online. Free and totally confidential for practicing lawyers. Employers are charged for matches. Started as an MBA project.

Cal Law, www.callaw.com/classifieds/index. shtml. Job listings for lawyers in California, sponsored by American Lawyer Media.

CompLaw, the Computer Law Resource, www.complaw.com/joblist.html. Lists announcements for openings mostly in the Southeastern U.S.

Emplawyernet, www.emplawyernet.com. A nationwide online job listing service for lawyers. You can scan the list yourself or have selected listings automatically e-mailed to you. Free to list openings; monthly fee for job-seekers.

Hieros Gamos Legal Employment Classifieds, www.hg.org/employment.html or contract lawyer openings listed at www.hg.org/temp-serv.html.

Law Journal Extra!—Law Employment Center, www.lawjobs.com. Reproductions of classified advertisements from the *National Law Journal* and its local affiliates.

LawJobs WWW, http://lawlib.wuacc.edu/ postlaw/postlaw/htm. You'll find career services overview, bar preparation, employment opportunities and links to other career planning centers for lawyers and law students at this site.

Lawjobs-L. An e-mail discussion group for job hunters in the legal profession. Job announcements sent directly to your e-mail box. To subscribe, send an e-mail message to listserv@lawlib.wuacc.edu. In the body of the message write: subscribe lawjobs-L, followed by your name. Cancel your membership by sending an e-mail message to the same address with the message unsubscribe lawjobs-L.

LawMatch, www.lawmatch.com. Searchable résumé bank with over 400 registered employers participating. No charge to jobhunters for a public/basic renewable one-month listing. You can also place your listing by telephone by calling (800) LAWMATCH.

Lawyers Weekly Classifieds, www.lweekly.com/class.htm.

Legal Employment Search Site, www.legalemploy.com. Links to dozens of legal job listing sites and law school career services offices.

National & Federal Legal Employment Report. A monthly listing of available attorney, court, and law-related professional positions organized by openings within the federal government in Washington, DC, and the rest of the country and other positions in and outside of Washington, DC. Available through Federal Reports, Inc., www.attorneyjobs.com.

Position Reports. One devoted to private sector openings in law firms and corporations; the other entitled "government sector" but also includes law firm openings. Each week's edition lists over 500 attorney job openings compiled from advertisements published in other legal newsletters and journals. To subscribe, (800) 962-4947.

Seamless Legal Job Center, www.seamless.com/jobs/. You can post your résumé here, peruse employer listings and discuss the market with others.

Law school career services/placement offices. Websites usually offer job hunt suggestions and sometimes post job announcements. May also distribute employment announcements by mail.

Contact local, state and regional bar associations. May publish books, newsletters, newspapers and journals which explain the employment conditions in the area or contain classified employment advertisements. Some associations also post job listings in their offices.

Local, state, regional and specialty bar association events. There's no better source of current information about who's busy, who needs help and who is looking for new employees.

GENERAL LEGAL CAREER RESOURCES

ABA Journal. The monthly magazine of the American Bar Association. Contains articles of interest to a broad range of lawyers and law firm managers as well as some classified advertisements for law firm, corporate and law school positions.

Directory of Legal Employers. Lists over 1,000 private, government and nonprofit legal employers gathered together and released annually by the National Association for Law Placement. Paperback; Harcourt Brace, 1998.

Law and Legal Information Directory. Descriptions and contact information for over 30,000 law-related institutions, services and facilities including bar associations, court systems, law schools, legal periodicals, lawyer referral services, legal aid offices, public defender offices and more. Hardback; Gale Research, 9th ed. 1996.

Law Guru.com, www.lawguru.com/classifieds/ jobresources.html. Links to legal job sites and employment resources.

Law Info, www.lawinfo.com/employment. Online source for locating lawyers and legal resources. Includes a lawyers and law firm index and professional development resources.

Legal Researcher's Desk Reference, edited by Arlene L. Eis. This helpful book lists federal and state elected and appointed officials, attorney general offices, law library suppliers, law-related associations, law schools, legal periodicals and more. Paperback; Infosources Publishing, www.infosourcespub.com, 1996.

National Association for Law Placement, www.nalp.org. An organization of the career services offices of accredited law schools, as well as over 1,000 legal employers actively engaged in the recruitment and placement of lawyers. See full listing at page 314.

National Law Journal. A weekly newspaper that regularly covers trends in the legal profession, law firm mergers, dissolutions and other changes. Classified advertising section, mostly for positions being filled by headhunters and corporations.

OTHER

JOB-SEARCH

RESOURCES

UNDERSTANDING CHANGE

Care of the Soul: A Guide for Cultivating Depth and Sacredness in Everyday Life, Thomas Moore. A long-time bestseller that helps you find meaning in your feelings of depression, disillusionment and emptiness. Paperback; Harperperennial, 1994.

Feel the Fear and Do It Anyway, Susan Jeffers, Ph.D. A how-to book for those experiencing resistance to change. Paperback; Fawcett Columbine, 1992.

Necessary Losses: The Loves, Illusions, Dependencies and Impossible Expectations That All of Us Have to Give Up in Order to Grow, Judith Viorst. A well-written and engrossing look at the life process—from birth to death. Redefines loss and change of every kind as essential and valuable. Paperback; Fireside, 1986, 1998.

The Career Chase: Taking Creative Control in a Chaotic Age, Helen L. Harkness. Insight for adults investigating forced or voluntary career change. Looks at internal issues like unrealistic expectations and shock, as well as 12 myths about modern careers. Paperback; Consulting Psychologists Press, 1997.

The Middle Passage: From Misery to Meaning in Midlife, James Hollis. A well-written look at the changes that occur in midlife, with clear advice for making the second half of life immeasurably richer. Paperback; Inner City Books, 1993.

The Road Less Traveled: A New Psychology of Love, Traditional Values & Spiritual Growth, M. Scott Peck, MD. Over five million copies of the first edition in print. An intriguing book that explores the difficulties of confronting and embracing change. Opening section provides some solid philosophical and practical suggestions for problem-solving. Paperback; A Touchstone Book, 2nd ed. 1998.

The Seven Habits of Highly Effective People: Powerful Lessons in Personal Change, Stephen R. Covey. A guide to implementing meaningful changes in your life. Paperback; Fireside, 1990.

The Three Boxes of Life (And How To Get Out of Them), Richard Bolles. Who says you have to go to school until age 25, be a lawyer until age 65, and then have fun? Not author Richard Bolles. A wonderful perspective on the career-and-life-planning process. Paperback; Ten Speed Press, 1978.

Transitions: Making Sense of Life's Changes, William Bridges. Highly recommended. Helps identify transitional phases, and explores ways to welcome and get through them successfully. A comforting and widely-read resource for people in any kind of personal transition. Paperback; Addison-Wesley, 1980.

When Smart People Fail: Rebuilding Yourself for Success, Carole Hyatt and Linda Gottlieb. Highly readable, anecdotal; helps you see bad decisions or actions, or unfortunate circumstances, as springboards for positive change and growth. Revised and updated for the 1990's. Paperback; Penguin, 1993.

THE CHANGING WORKPLACE

Blur: The Speed of Change in the Connected Economy, Stan Davis and Christopher Meyer. Explores the technological revolution and its impact on modern business operation. Its focus is primarily on commerce, business strategy and beating the competition, not individual career development. Hardback; Addison Wesley, 1998.

JobShift: How to Prosper in a Workplace Without Jobs, William Bridges. A clearly written and persuasive explanation of the forces that have created the modern workplace, with clear advice on how best to pursue your career in this environment. Written by the author of *Transitions.* Paperback; Addison Wesley, 1995. In *Creating You & Company: Learn to Think Like the CEO of Your Own Career,* Bridges follows up with more concrete advice about thriving in the new work paradigm. Hardback; Addison Wesley, 1997.

JobShock: Four New Principles Transforming Our

Work and Business, Harry S. Dent, Jr. Explains why America is about to enter the greatest economic boom ever and how you'll need to adjust your career to take advantage of it. Hardback; St. Martin's Press, 1995.

The End of Work: The Decline of the Global Labor Force & the Dawn of the Post-Market Era, Jeremy Rifkin. A controversial, well-researched study of the global workplace and its impact on individual workers worldwide. Paperback; Tarcher/Putnam, 1995.

The New Rules: How to Succeed in Today's Post-Corporate World, John P. Kotter. A Harvard Business School professor tracked 115 Harvard MBA's for 20 years. The most successful avoided conventional career paths through large corporations in favor of career paths that were "less linear, more dynamic and more unstable." Hardback; Free Press, 1995.

CONFRONTING BURNOUT

Addiction to Perfection, Marion Woodman. An analysis of how our cultural preference for patriarchal values (productivity, goal orientation, intellectual excellence) has been adopted by professional women at the expense of their creative, interpersonally-oriented feminine sides. The author's allegorical style and her many references to mythology and Jungian analysis make for challenging reading, but her depth of insight is well worth the effort. Paperback; Inner City Books, 1982.

Feeling Good: The New Mood Therapy, David D. Burns, MD. A clearly written explanation and application of cognitive therapy (a drug-free treatment for depression), based on research by the University of Pennsylvania School of Medicine. Helpful in building self-esteem and getting past the negative self-talk that sabotages so many attempts to change career environments. Paperback; Avon, 1992.

Overcoming Job Burnout: How to Renew Enthusiasm for Work, Dr. Beverly Potter & Phil Frank. Paperback; Ronin Publishing, 2nd ed. 1998.

Simple Living Guide: A Sourcebook for Less Stressful, More Joyful Living, Janet Luhrs. A former practicing lawyer gives practical tips and tells inspirational stories about people who have chosen to simplify their lives and spend less money. Topics include time and financial management, families, work and clutter. Paperback; Broadway Books, 1997.

The Addictive Organization: Why We Overwork, Cover Up, Pick Up the Pieces, Please the Boss and Perpetuate Sick Organizations, Anne Wilson Schaef and Diane Fassel. The authors define addiction as "any substance or process that has taken over our lives and over which we are powerless." This provocative book provides insight into the ties that bind lawyers to their careers. Paperback; HarperSanFrancisco, 1990.

The Drama of the Gifted Child: The Search for the True Self, Alice Miller. A study of the way children are forced to repress and bury their spontaneity and expression of emotion and how those early experiences create adults who are unable to enjoy life fully. Frequently recommended to over-achieving clients by mental health professionals. Paperback; Basic Books, 1996.

The Truth About Burnout, Christina Maslach & Michael P. Leiter. Identifies source of problem and offers preventive methods. Based on an extensive study of burnout victims. Hardcover; Jossey Bass, 1997.

FINANCIAL CHANGE

The Tightwad Gazette I, II and III: Promoting Thrift as a Viable Lifestyle, Amy Dacyczyn. Three books that present hundreds of cost-cutting ideas gleaned from Amy's monthly newsletter. Paperback; Villard Books, 1993, 1995, 1997.

Your Money or Your Life: Transforming Your Relationship with Money and Achieving

Financial Independence, Joe Dominguez and Vicki Robin. A national bestseller based on an audiocassette course and workbook sold mostly by word-of-mouth for many years. Offers financial management advice for people who wish to express their values in their daily lives without worrying about how much income their efforts will generate. Paperback; Penguin USA, 1993.

ALTERNATIVE WORK-SCHEDULE RESOURCES

New Ways to Work, www.nww.org; 785 Market Street, Suite 950, San Francisco, CA 94103; (415) 995-9860. A nonprofit, community-based resource and research organization that encourages experimentation with work-time options. Counsels individuals seeking new work options and networks with employers and other related agencies. Publishes a variety of books and pamphlets on the subject.

Working from Home: Everything You Need to Know about Living and Working Under the Same Roof, Paul and Sarah Edwards. In over 400 pages, the authors cover all aspects of operating a home-based business, including presenting a business image, dealing with zoning and setting up an efficient work space. Paperback; J. P. Tarcher, 4th ed. 1994.

SELF-ASSESSMENT BOOKS

Career Satisfaction and Success: A Guide to Job and Personal Freedom, Bernard Haldane. Written by the acknowledged grandfather of modern career counseling, this book helps you determine your "dependable strengths" and apply them in the marketplace. Paperback; JIST Works, 1996.

The Crystal-Barkley Guide to Taking Charge of Your Career, Nella Barkley and Eric Sandburg. The authors, pioneers in the career planning industry, take you through three questions:

Who am I? Where am I going? How do I get there? Paperback; Workman Publishing, 1995.

Do What You Love, The Money Will Follow: Discovering Your Right Livelihood, Marsha Sinetar. An intellectual explanation of the philosophy expressed by her title. Well-written, instructive and inspirational. Paperback; Dell Publishing, 1989.

Flow: The Psychology of Optimal Experience, Mihaly Csikszentmihalyi. The author shares the result of his 20 years' research into the components of peak experiences. Paperback; HarperCollins, 1991.

I Could Do Anything If I Only Knew What It Was: How to Discover What You Really Want & How to Get It, Barbara Sher. Best-selling author of *Wishcraft* helps you overcome barriers to change by examining the real roots of your resistance. Paperback; Dell, 1994.

Targeting the Job You Want, Kate Wendleton. An engagingly laid-out self-assessment workbook for busy career-minded job hunters, career changers, consultants and freelancers. Paperback; Five O'Clock Books, 1997.

What Color Is Your Parachute?: A Practical Manual for Job-Hunters & Career Changers, Richard Bolles. Often called the "bible" of career change. Good for those who can never get enough data before they make a decision. Features an excellent bibliography, divided by subject area. Paperback; Ten Speed Press, annually updated.

Wishcraft: How to Get What You Really Want, Barbara Sher & Annie Gottlieb. A good, practical, thoroughly motivating guide to defining and achieving your goals. Paperback; Ballantine Books, 1986.

Work with Passion, Nancy Anderson. Gets to the heart of the career-change process by exploring how you enjoy spending your time and how you can earn a living doing it. Highly recommended as a self-assessment tool. Paperback; New World Library, 2nd ed. 1995.

Your Signature Path, Geoffrey M. Bellman. Helps you define your calling in work and in life. Hardback; Berrett-Koehler, 1996.

Zen and the Art of Making a Living: A Practical Guide to Creative Career Design, Laurence G. Boldt. A highly-rated and thorough tool. Looks at the meaning of work, as well as the process of finding it, in a workbook format. Paperback; Penguin, 1993.

CAREER COUNSELORS

Career counselors neither select your next career nor find your next job. "They should not represent themselves as the ones with all the answers," says one former career counselor for lawyers. Instead, they provide assistance in defining your strengths, exploring appropriate options, researching the possibilities, preparing résumés and conducting interviews.

Career counseling for lawyers, at least during the initial stages, demands a somewhat different approach than for the public-at-large. Most people facing a job or career change seek a higher level of prestige and compensation. Attorneys, on the other hand, often want to discard, or at least de-emphasize, their professional identity, and may move into a field that offers less money and prestige. Some attorneys have encountered career counselors who spend too much valuable time encouraging them to override their intuition, and to stick with their legal careers. Sessions with these counselors ended up merely postponing what turned out to be an inevitable and otherwise satisfying career switch. Thus, look for counselors who understand the unique issues faced by lawyers, and who display no judgments about your desire to leave your current position or the law itself.

Finding the right career counselor requires the same investigative skills you might recommend others use to locate a good attorney:

Obtain referrals from friends or reputable referral agencies. The placement or career services office of a local law school is a good resource.

Decide whether you want to work along a thera- *peutic or task-oriented track.* A therapeutic counselor uses the same techniques as a psychotherapist. He or she will often focus on the barriers and limitations you are confronting in making a change. A task-oriented counselor will usually give you homework assignments (similar to those contained in this manual) to complete between sessions, and then discuss the results with you. This type of counselor might also role-play an interview, and assist you with résumé writing. The best consultant is one who uses both orientations, applying them as needed to your unique situation.

Avoid counselors who charge a non-refundable flat fee for their services. Instead, work with a counselor who lets you choose the services you desire, and permits you to terminate services at any time, paying only for those already rendered. According to *Career Development Magazine,* you should "be skeptical of services that make promises of more money, better jobs, résumés that get speedy results or an immediate solution to career problems."

Avoid counseling exclusively by telephone or the Internet. You can gather information and obtain feedback about the effectiveness of your cover letters and résumés for the purposes you describe, but remote counseling is about as reliable as evaluating the credibility of a witness you've never met in person. Lawyers often decide what direction they want to take out of resignation or a sense of limited options and, with wonderful oral communication and persuasion skills, can sound truly convinced of the appropriateness of their choices. Non-verbal communication will key a career counselor into this misconception and lead you to more suitable options. Telephone and e-mail counselors cannot detect this very important information and are not worth the price. You're much better off working with a well-regarded career counselor in your area, even if that person does not target lawyers as clients.

Make certain that your counselor has actual experience in the process you're contemplating. For example, if you want to change careers, find a career counselor who previously earned a living as

MORE ENCOURAGEMENT ABOUT SELF-ASSESSMENT

Some attorneys respond to their inner signals with the same conscientiousness and attention to detail they applied to their lawyering. They carefully investigate other career possibilities, sometimes on their own but more often with the assistance of a professional career counselor.

Other practitioners work together to plot a reasoned path out of the profession. As an example, two San Francisco lawyers noticed how much time they spent grousing with coworkers about their work. Once they realized that their negative attitude was not going to create a better work environment, they made a pact with each other to take a moment each day to write down the one thing they most enjoyed doing. Even this short mental break helped each of them to focus on what elements in a job would be most satisfying. Within a year, both of them had moved into equally respectable but more enjoyable non-legal positions.

Those who are methodical about their leave-taking are in the minority. Still, their numbers are growing and, to help them, there are an increasing number of career counselors specializing in law—many of them former practicing lawyers. Many other career planning books designed especially for lawyers have been published in the last few years. And seminars about how lawyers can make the best use of their degrees and backgrounds are attracting lawyers in every major city.

For Robert, law school represented a continuance of his long-time drive toward achievement. After only a few years in the profession, on a day he will long remember, Robert realized that while what he'd attained impressed others, it would never be personally satisfying. Once he was able to

acknowledge that, he turned to a career counselor. With guidance and encouragement, Robert carefully plotted his departure from law practice.

Robert's Statement: After three years of practice, I was working on a month-long project in Washington, DC, when the associate review committee called me from New York to give me my annual critique. They said, "You're doing fine, blah, blah, blah, but you don't have enough initiative."

"There's a good reason for that," I wanted to say. "I hate doing this."

I realized then that I could only continue pretending for so long. I didn't like what I was doing, and it was bound to show one way or another. When I realized that, I began asking myself why a perfectly competent person like me was subjecting myself to criticism.

That very same day, I saw a copy of the *National Law Journal* with a front page article about lawyer dissatisfaction. It was a moment I'll always remember; an epiphany. The article appeared at the right time with the message I needed to hear: that I wasn't unusual, or alone, feeling as I did. That what I was feeling wasn't a flaw in my character. That the law is right for some people and not right for others. And that there were people I could turn to for help.

Right then, I decided I was going to get out of law. I circled in red the names of the two career counselors mentioned in the article and investigated them the minute I returned to New York. My counseling sessions started a few weeks later.

We started out by talking about what I would do if I could do anything I wanted. Although I was suspicious at first, that exercise helped me understand that I like to solve problems, to nurture things and make them bloom into something. I don't like to fight, nor do I share those values held in high esteem by most lawyers—competition, aggressiveness, a fast pace, being considered an expert, or getting a case exactly right down to the last detail. I also came to realize that my creativity is severely restricted in law. My writing style is restricted by its conventions, and I can't be as emotional as I would like.

I enjoy writing, researching and advising—things I do in law—but charging a lot of money to shift dollars around from one person to the next isn't enough to sustain me. What I need to do is work toward a purpose which transcends a corporation's goal of making money. From all that analysis, I've concluded that I want to work for a nonprofit organization, doing what I'm doing now but without the fighting.

With my counselor's help, I've picked out a career that is more in tune with my interests and personality and overall values.

And I've decided to quit my law job to look for other work. I've never taken a risk like that before. Now that I think about it, going to law school was a choice I made to avoid risk. By applying, I didn't have to think about finding a job, didn't have to worry about my student loan payments starting. I pushed off thinking about my life, my future and my interests.

I feel proud of myself because, at last, I've taken the time to figure out what I want to do with my life. I no longer want to be a lawyer by default. I'm prepared for the downsides, especially the financial loss. I make $75,000 a year now, but I'm willing to drop to $35,000.

I can't help but think about something my mother told me when I was in law school. I had said something like "I can't wait until the semester is over," and she asked me, "What are you going to do, wish your life away?" That's exactly what I've been doing here. I can't wait until this brief is done; can't wait until this case settles, or until this trial is over. I'm done wishing my life away.

something other than a counselor. If you want help with the job-search process, find a career counselor who has held a number of different jobs, and networked to secure them. Most important of all, if you are seeking work that feels like play, be sure your counselor has tapped a personal passion in choosing this career. One hint: Ask the prospective counselor about his or her hobbies. If you sense that the counselor would rather be concentrating on those activities than meeting with you, keep looking!

Career Counseling Referral Resources

The Career List. A free state-by-state listing of national certified career counselors, To order the list from your geographic area, contact the National Board for Certified Counselors (NBCC), www.nbcc.org; 3 Terrace Way, Suite D, Greensboro, NC 27403; (336) 547-0607. In order to receive certification by the NBCC, career counselors must hold a master's degree or doctorate in counseling or a closely-related field from a regionally-accredited university; their university course work must have included lifestyle and career development, tests and measurements, and a career counseling practicum or internship; they must also have at least three years professional career counseling experience, at least some of it under supervision; and, they must pass the NBCC general practice and career counseling specialty examination.

Check with Career Services and/or Placement Directors of law schools for referrals to well-regarded career counselors—or other programs for lawyers in transition—in your geographic area. They may also sponsor periodic seminars and workshops for students, recent graduates and other alumnus.

TESTING RESOURCES

I recommend two career-related testing instruments: the Myers-Briggs Type Indicator (MBTI) and the Johnson O'Connor Inventory of Aptitudes and Knowledge. The MBTI evaluates personality preferences and helps those who sense they don't fit into an environment, but don't know why. The Johnson O'Connor test identifies your natural aptitudes or skills. This test can be a real eye-opener for those who feel they have no talents, or who have lost touch with the tasks they do enjoy. One caveat: Although these tests provide useful information, they should not be the last word in your decision-making.

Myers-Briggs Type Indicator (MBTI)

The MBTI, based on Carl Jung's theory of psychological types, is a personality evaluator that studies four sets of character traits, places you in one of 16 types, and draws conclusions about your preferences. The test has over 40 years of research, development and practical application behind it, including extensive use in Fortune 500 companies. According to studies, certain proclivities are shared by satisfied attorneys in different areas of the law, and this test can tell you whether you fit into the right pattern. It can also help you understand and deal more effectively with a difficult boss or colleague. For information about licensed MBTI administrators in your area, contact Consulting Psychologists Press, www.cpp-db.com; 3803 E. Bayshore Rd., PO Box 10096, Palo Alto, CA 94303; (415) 969-8901 or (800) 624-1765.

Do What You Are, Paul D. Tieger and Barbara Barron-Tieger. The authors' discussion of the test's implications for career choice is insightful and you'll be pointed in specific career directions. They also include a much simplified and probably not very accurate version of the MBTI. Paperback; Little Brown, 1995.

Gifts Differing, Isabel Briggs Myers. The test designer's explanation of her creation. Paperback; Consulting Psychologists Press, Inc., 1995.

LifeTypes, Sandra Hirsh and Jean Kummerow. A thorough and engaging study of the general characteristics, communication, relationship and work styles, careers and population statistics of the 16 MBTI types. Paperback; Warner Books, 1992.

Please Understand Me: Character & Temperament Types, David Kiersey and Marilyn Bates. These authors devised another version of the MBTI to come up with a "temperament sorter." (Again, their test is not a reliable substitute for the MBTI.) They then apply these personality types, identical to the MBTI, to preferences in employment, mating, parenting, leadership, and learning. Paperback; Prometheus, 1984.

"The Lawyer Types: How Your Personality Affects Your Practice," Larry Richard, *ABA Journal,* July 1993.

Type Talk: How the 16 Personality Types Determine Your Success on the Job, Otto Kroeger & Janet M. Thiesen. A rewrite of an earlier work, this book helps you understand your own and others' work styles. Paperback; Dell, 1993.

WORKTypes, Jean Kummerow, Linda Kirby and Nancy Barger. A practical guide to using the MBTI to recognize your work style, handle day-to-day tasks and adjust to constant changes in the work world. Paperback; Warner Books, 1997.

Johnson O'Connor Research Foundation

Established in 1939, the Johnson-O'Connor Human Engineering Laboratory is the nation's oldest center for the study of human aptitudes. Although anyone can learn to handle difficult tasks, the O'Connor Foundation asserts that true job satisfaction depends upon using those aptitudes (or natural talents and skills) with which you were born. Testing takes a day and a half and yields a useful and individualized job profile. Highly recommended for those who have lost touch with the range of tasks they enjoy, or suspect that they are leaving something out of their analysis. Check your local telephone directory or their website, http://members.aol.com/jocrf19, for the branch office nearest you. National headquarters are at 11 E. 62nd St., New York, NY 10021; (212) 838-0550.

JOB SEARCH RESOURCES

Complete Job Search Handbook, Howard Figler. A practical, clearly written overview of the job-hunting process. The author quickly gets to the bottom of career evaluation and planning, then concentrates mostly on "all the skills you need to get any job and have a good time doing it." Paperback; Henry Holt, 1988.

Dig Your Well Before You're Thirsty, Harvey Mackay. The author of *Swim with the Sharks Without Getting Eaten* explains how to and why develop and maintain contacts with others. Hardback; Doubleday, 1997.

How to Work a Room: Learn the Strategies of Savvy Socializing-for Business and Personal Success, Susan Roane. A humorous book chock full of helpful suggestions for breaking the ice at professional gatherings. Paperback; Warner Books, 1989.

It's Who You Know: The Magic of Networking in Person and On the Internet, Cynthia Chin-Lee. An easy to read and instructive guide to effective networking. Explains informational interviewing and how to overcome your barriers to meeting new people. Paperback;

Career Research Institute, 1991.

Knock 'Em Dead 1998, Martin Yate. Focuses primarily on getting and performing well in interviews. Check it out online at www.knockemdead.com. Paperback; Bob Adams, Inc., 1997.

Networking: Insiders' Strategies for Tapping the Hidden Job Market Where Most Jobs Are, Doug Richardson. The author, a former practicing lawyer who now works in outplacement and executive career coaching, wrote this book for the *National Business Employment Weekly.* Paperback; Wiley, 1994.

Rites of Passage at $100,000 Plus: The Insider's Lifetime Guide to Effective Job Changing and Faster Career Progress, John Lucht. A special job-search guide for those who are used to the status that comes with a higher income, but find themselves now wanting or needing another job. Written by a New York executive recruiter. Hardback; Viceroy Press, 1993.

Sweaty Palms: The Neglected Art of Being Interviewed, H. Anthony Medley. A former practicing lawyer wrote this interesting and comprehensive book on interviewing. Helpful, informative, and easy to read. Paperback; Ten Speed Press, 1992.

The Essential Book of Interviewing: Everything You Need to Know from Both Sides of the Table, Arnold B. Kanter. The author is a former law firm hiring attorney and author of the *Lawyer Hiring Handbook.* Written for both interviewer and interviewee. Paperback; Times Books, 1995.

Job-Search Secrets that Have Helped Thousands of Members, Kate Wendleton. An accessible and helpful job search guide with a good resource section. Paperback; Five O'Clock Books, 1996.

JOB SEARCH TIPS FOR OLDER WORKERS

40 Plus. Nonprofit organizations in cities across the country that provide job search assistance to displaced professionals age 40 or older. Most "clubs" offer job search classes and

access to fully-equipped office space to conduct your job search. Courses are taught by prior graduates. To find the closest office, check the website of 40 Plus of Greater Washington at www.fp.org/chapters.

A Winning Résumé: A Guide to Writing an Effective Résumé for Older Job Seekers, stock #PW4548 (293) D13961; and *How to Stay Employable: A Guide for the Midlife and Older Worker,* stock #PW4983 (1192) D14945. Two free booklets published by the AARP. Mail in your request, including stock numbers, to AARP Fulfillment, 601 E. St., NW, Washington, DC 20049.

Mid-Career Job Hunting: Official Handbook of the Forty Plus Club, E. Patricia Birsner. A former member of this national self-help group revised their guidebook. Prepares out-of-work, mid-life executives for re-entry into the job market. Paperback; Arco, 1991.

Over 40 and Looking for Work?: A Guide for the Unemployed, Underemployed and Unhappily Employed, Rebecca Anthony and Gerald Roe. Paperback; Bob Adams, 1991.

New Passages: Mapping Your Life Across Time, Gail Sheehy. Extended life expectancy has led to a new life stage: second adulthood. Sheehy, author of the groundbreaking *Passages,* tells you how to customize your life cycle and find deeper meaning, renewed playfulness and creativity after age 45. Paperback; Ballantine Books, 1995.

Retirement Careers: Combining the Best of Work and Leisure, DeLoss L. Marsh. Paperback; Williamson Publications, 1991.

RÉSUMÉS & COVER LETTERS

200 Letters for Job Hunters, William S. Frank. Inspiration for a wide range of marketing letters. Paperback; Ten Speed Press, 1993.

Dynamic Cover Letters, Katherine & Randall Hansen. How to sell yourself to an employer by writing a letter that will get your résumé read, get you an interview and get you the job. Paperback; Ten Speed Press, 1995.

Electronic Résumés: A Complete Guide to Putting Your Résumé Online, James & Wayne Gonyea. Paperback; McGraw Hill, 1996.

Résumé Power: Selling Yourself on Paper, Tom Washington, Mount Vernon Press, 1996.

The Damn Good Résumé Guide: A Crash Course in Résumé Writing, Yana Parker, Ten Speed Press, 3rd ed. 1996.

The New Perfect Résumé, Tom & Ellen Jackson. Helps you prepare a capabilities portfolio or an internal, external or electronic résumé. 50 sample résumés provided. Paperback; Doubleday, 1996.

JOB-FINDING ON THE INTERNET

America's Job Bank, www.ajb.dni.us. A nationwide selection of over 700,000 jobs with nearly 200,000 job seekers participating at any time.

Business Job Finder, www.cob.ohio-state. edu /~fin/osujobs.htm. Geared to accounting, financial and consulting fields. Job descriptions, employer profiles, job search aids, online job listings.

Career Magazine, www.careermag.com. Free access to job openings, employee profiles, interactive discussion groups, news and feature articles and a directory of executive recruiters. Many jobs in accounting, construction, computers and environment. Links to other career and employer websites.

Career Path, www.careerpath.com. Job listings from six of the country's largest newspapers.

CareerMosaic, www.careermosaic.com. Specific job openings with requirements and descriptions. Individuals can exchange e-mail with employees within a company. Many employers in high tech, financial, insurance, health care, retail and telecommunications.

CareerxRoads: The 1998 Directory to Jobs, Résumés & Career Management on the World Wide Web, Gerry Crispin & Mark Mehler. Best places to look for opportunities online. Updated online at www.careerxroads.com.

Paperback; IEEE, 3rd ed. 1997.

E-Span's Job Options, www.espan.com.

Guide to Internet Job Searching, 1998-99 Edition, Margaret Riley, Frances Roehm & Steve Oserman. A comprehensive guide to career-related websites and how to conduct an effective internet job search. Paperback; VGM Career Horizons, 1998.

Job Bank USA, www.jobbankusa.com. General job search site.

JobTrak, www.jobtrack.com. A job-listing service offered by a consortium of college and university careers centers and alumni associations.

Monster Board, www.monster.com/home.html. Free to job seekers. 50,000 job openings worldwide plus overview of employers. Mostly technical positions as well as some marketing, sales, multimedia and management. Résumé builder.

NationJob, www.nationjob.com. Online jobs database.

Online Career Center, www.occ.com. Careers resources including links to salary information. Job openings with special categories of healthcare, human resources and engineering.

PursuitNet, www.tiac.net/users/jobs. Free résumé match service.

Recruiter Online Network, www.ipa.com. Free résumé posting service to 6,000 registered recruiters, search firms and employment professionals.

Recruiting Links, www.recruiting-links.com. Links to employment announcements of participating companies.

Résumés in Cyberspace: Your Complete Guide to a Computerized Job Search, Pat Criscito. Paperback; Barron's, 1997.

The Riley Guide, www.dbm.com/jobguide. Employment opportunities and job resources on the Internet. Reputed to be one of the better online job search centers.

Virtual Job Fair, www.vjf.com. A high-tech career resource and résumé center.

OVERVIEW OF OTHER JOBS AND CAREERS

Occu-Facts: Information on 580 Careers in Outline Form, edited by Elizabeth Handville. Includes employment outlook, earnings range, suitable temperament, time demands and environment. Hardback; Careers Inc., 3rd ed. 1995.

Occupational Outlook Handbook 1998-99, U.S. Department of Labor. Describes over 250· career fields in detail, including skills demanded by the work, required educational background, range of opportunities and salaries. Paperback; VGM Career Horizons, 1998 or online at http://stats.bls.gov.

Occupational Outlook Quarterly, U.S. Department of Labor. Well-researched articles on labor force, industry and occupational projections, descriptions of particular careers and advice on educational opportunities. Available in public libraries or call the Superintendent of Documents at (202) 512-1800 to order a one-year subscription.

GENERAL RESEARCH RESOURCES

Almanac of American Employers 1998-99, Jack Plunkett. Compares the financial stability and benefit plans of major companies. Hardback; Plunkett Research, 4th ed. 1998.

Better Business Bureau. To determine the reputation of a potential employer, check to see what reports are available from the bureau in the city where a particular business is located.

Business Organizations, Agencies and Publications Directory, Jennifer Mast & Kimberly Hujt, editors. How to get facts on business concerns. Hardback; Gale Research, 9th ed. 1997.

Catapult Job Search & Industry Information, www.jobweb.org/catapult/emplyer.htm. Links to private, government and international websites with data on potential employers.

Chamber of Commerce. Check your local chamber for data on local organizations and employment fields.

Directories of Major Employers. May not have this precise title but generally list major regional employers alphabetically and by category. Provide name of company, address, phone number, key names, market area, number of employees, revenues, and industry. Produced by several different publishers. Available at most public libraries.

Encyclopedia of Associations: National Organization of the U.S. Over 23,000 associations in the United States, listed alphabetically and in 17 categories including, as examples, (a) trade, commercial and business; (b) legal, government, public administration and military; and (c) educational. Hardback, 3 vol. set; Gale Research, 33rd ed. 1997.

Encyclopedia of Business Information Sources, edited by James Woy. Hardback; Gale Research, 12th ed. 1998.

Great American Website, www.uncle-sam.com. Nongovernmental research firm provides access to every branch of government, from Library of Congress to NASA to the CIA. Recommends reasonable government sites containing statistical, marketing and business information and resources. Download and read the help files for each site you use. The best, the newest and most useful federal information website.

Hoover's Online, www.hoover.com. Extensive database of public, private and international companies.

International Directory of Company Histories. Detailed information about the development of the world's largest and most influential companies. 20 volumes published as of 1997. Hardcover; St. James Press.

Job Seeker's Guide to Private and Public Employers. Published in four regional volumes—West, Midwest, South and Northeast—in different years up to 1998. Hardcover; Gale Research.

Newsletters in Print, edited by Louise Gagne. An annually-updated descriptive guide to more than 10,000 subscription, membership, and free newsletters, bulletins, digests, updates, and similar serial publications issued in the US by business firms, associations, societies, institutions, and government agencies. Hardback; Gale Research, 11th ed. 1998.

NTPA 98: National Trade and Professional Associations of the US, Buck Downs, R. Willson Hardy & Nathan L. Cantor, editors. 6,250 entries including name, year established, name of chief executive, address and phone numbers of staff members. Paperback; Columbia Books, 33rd ed. 1998.

Professional's Job Finder 1997-2000, Daniel Lauber. A how-to book for professionals looking for work. Includes information about jobs and employers. Lists 3,003 sources of information to find private sector job vacancies including hotlines, websites, directories and job-listing resources. Paperback; Planning Communications, 1997.

Standard Periodical Directory. Covers United States and Canada. Available in most libraries. Hardback; Oxbridge Communications, 21st ed. 1998.

Switchboard, www.switchboard.com. Find the current e-mail address of any business or individual registered with this website. Access and registration are both free.

Ulrich's International Periodicals Directory. Annually updated. Available in most libraries. Hardback; R.R. Bowker, 36th ed. 1998.

Who's Who 1998: An Annual Biographical Guide. Useful information about persons with power to hire. Hardback; St. Martin's Press, 150th ed. 1998.

JOB OPTIONS

FOR LAWYERS

AND LAW SCHOOL

GRADUATES

This section lists job options, as well as resources to help you research positions, in the following fields:

Alternative Dispute Resolution
Arts and Entertainment
Bar Associations
Communications (publishing listed separately)
Consulting
Corporate, Business, Banking (law firms and real estate listed separately)
Counseling
Education
Entrepreneurial Ventures (consulting listed separately)
Environmental
Ethics
Foundations and Nonprofit Organizations (bar associations listed separately)
Government (law enforcement listed separately)
Healthcare
International
Judiciary
Labor Unions
Law Enforcement
Law Firms
Legal Information Science
Lobbying & Public Affairs
Publishing
Real Estate
Sports
Technology

Jobs in each category are listed under subheadings that identify types of employers and whether the positions involve the practice of law, are law-related or are considered non-legal. All positions referenced as practicing law require an active license to practice, though not necessarily in the same jurisdiction. Law-related positions are either in a legal setting, or demand skills that make a legal background desirable; but none of the law-related positions require an active license to practice law. Jobs listed as non-legal, or without any reference to the law, neither require a law degree nor specifically demand legal skills or knowledge.

Jobs followed by an asterisk (*) are briefly described in Appendix 5. Every job listed is now, or has been, held by a lawyer or law school graduate. Yet, with hundreds of positions identified, this list is merely an illustration of the wide range of opportunities available. Please do not limit yourself to consideration of only these jobs.

Related books, job banks, periodical publications, articles, bibliographies, websites and organizations are identified after each job category. Some of the printed material lists job descriptions or announcements. Most provide information about the work involved, or the names of individuals working in that employment field. Printed material, except where otherwise indicated, is generally available in either law school placement offices, law libraries, or larger public libraries. Paperback books, except those published by the American Bar Association, were all available in September, 1998, through Amazon.com.

Website addresses are provided whenever possible. (Assume http:// before any address that begins with "www.") You will be seriously hampered in your research if you do not use web-based research. Most sites contain a wealth of up-to-date information about the organization or industry, and often post job announcements. You'd be wise to start your research process by reviewing websites for professional associations of the fields that interest you. If you find the content interesting and the job announcements intriguing, take your research a step further by ordering one of their publications, "lurking" in an online discussion group or contacting a member in your area to get additional input about the field.

Use the information provided in this appendix as a starting point, and search for other leads from it. Remember that these are not the only jobs or resources available. All information was updated August to September 1998.

ALTERNATIVE DISPUTE RESOLUTION

Possible Employers:
colleges and universities

A NOTE ABOUT MEDIATION

Many lawyers today face significant barriers when they attempt to enter the mediation field. First, they often compete for business with free community- and court-sponsored programs founded to lessen the backlog of lawsuits and to remove from the legal system altogether matters involving small amounts of money or emotional issues like child custody and visitation. Competition is exacerbated by companies that retain retired judges to serve as mediators (although most actually conduct their sessions more like settlement conferences). Most important of all, interest in serving as a mediator continues to outpace consumer demand.

The combination of all three factors makes paying customers hard to come by. As a result, most lawyers who are drawn to mediation find they must mix a regular law practice with their mediation cases, or be paid to train others in the art of dispute resolution.

Lawyers who attract most of the mediation referrals usually have followed one of these paths:

■ They've established a reputation for fairness and competence as practitioners in such specialties as environmental, construction, personal injury or family law.

■ They retired from the trial court bench with reputations as effective settlement judges.

■ They combined their legal backgrounds with degrees in psychology, social work or counseling. Then, they networked with former colleagues to generate referrals and now focus primarily on mediating family or interpersonal disputes.

■ They operate an alternative dispute resolution service which handles all marketing and logistics, but they generally do not mediate the disputes themselves. Instead, they rely upon a panel of mediators (primarily those from the first three categories) to whom they pay a portion of the fees collected.

■ They volunteered for a well-regarded community mediation program long enough to develop a reputation for effectiveness, then let the agency know of their interest in receiving referrals of matters outside the agency's jurisdiction.

Considering these restrictions, it's difficult for all but the elite few in any area or field to obtain enough private mediation work to make a decent living. Fortunately, lawyers can obtain other positions which make use of their conflict resolution skills. The broadest range of opportunities fall under the categories of ombuds and grievance investigator.

An ombuds is a neutral party who investigates complaints, issues reports, and provides assistance in resolving disputes. A classical ombuds conducts formal investigations, often in a public setting, and has powers of subpoena; an organizational ombuds conducts informal interviews, preserving the confidentiality of those involved. An organizational ombuds may work internally, that is, as an employee of the company, or as an external consultant on an outsourced basis.

Most ombuds positions are found in large institutions (e.g., government, universities, hospitals, newspaper publishing, corporations) and deal with grievances filed by students, customers, citizens, suppliers or employees. This field has grown—and is likely to continue to grow—because businesses recognize the cost-savings and improved morale of avoiding litigation.

A similar role is that of a grievance investigator in a corporate, university or government environment. The ADA has triggered an enormous number of employee and student complaints of failure to accommodate their physical, mental or learning disabilities. In many environments, the human rights or equal opportunity department handles these complaints, but some organizations have moved the investigations to the risk management department. Investigators are hired, therefore, not only to get to the truth of the complaint, but to work with the complainant and respondent to resolve their differences amicably.

community dispute resolution boards or panels
corporations
court-sponsored programs
federal, state and local government
for-profit mediation services
labor unions
law firms
newspapers
nonprofit organizations
panels such as the American Arbitration
    Association
private solo practice

Common Subject Matters:
ADA complaints
boundary disputes
child custody/visitation
commercial litigation
construction disputes
dissolution of marriage
environmental compliance
insurance coverage
landlord-tenant disputes
partnership/business dissolution
personal injury claims

Service Positions:
ADR specialist*
arbitrator
contract mediator
creator of online mediation service
director of legal services

dispute resolution trainer*
employee grievance mediator*
mediator
ombuds*
settlement conference referee
staff mediator
volunteer mediator

Administrative Positions:
director/manager
director of training
marketing director
owner/founder
program administrator/coordinator
volunteer coordinator

Law-Related Resources
ABA Section of Dispute Resolution, abanet.org/dispute/home.html. Maintains a National Dispute Resolution Resource Center at 740 15th St., NW, Washington, DC 20005; (202) 662-1680. Publishes *Dispute Resolution Magazine,* containing updates on events and resources in ADR, three times annually.
Academy of Family Mediators, www.igc.apc.org/afm/; 5 Militia Drive, Lexington, MA 02421; (781) 674-2663. A national membership organization for lawyers and mental health professionals involved in the resolution of domestic relations issues. Publishes annual membership directory, and quarterly newsletter and

journal. Provides referral service to public.

American Arbitration Association, www.adr.org; 140 W. 51st St., New York, NY 10020; (212) 484-4000. Publishes the quarterly *Dispute Resolution Journal, Dispute Resolution Times,* and *ADR Currents.* Branch offices maintain panels of arbitration and mediation attorneys available for referral mostly in construction, securities, computers or commercial law disputes. You'll find branch office listings in your local telephone directory or check their website for a directory of regional offices organized by state.

Association of Family and Conciliation Courts, www.afccnet.org (under construction 9/98) c/o Ann Milne, Executive Director, 329 W. Wilson St., Madison, WI 53703; (608) 251-4001. An organization of judges, counselors, lawyers, mediators and others interested in the resolution of family disputes as they affect children.

BBB Dispute Resolution Services, Council of Better Business Bureaus, www.bbb.org; 4200 Wilson Blvd., Suite 800, Arlington, VA 22203; (703) 276-0100. You'll find a directory of their offices on their website, organized by state and zip code. Includes the Auto Line Program, a mediation and arbitration service for disputes between consumers and participating manufacturers.

CPR Institute for Dispute Resolution, www.cpradr.org; 366 Madison Ave., 14th Floor, New York, NY 10017; (212) 949-6490. Nonprofit organization of general counsel from major corporations, senior partners in leading law firms and legal scholars interested in installing ADR into the mainstream of corporate law departments and law firm practices.

Directory of Law School ADR Courses & Programs. Lists professors, course descriptions and teaching methods for ADR courses around the country. Available from the American Bar Association, www.abanet.org.

Federal Mediation & Conciliation Service, www.fmcs.gov; 2100 K St., NW, Washington, DC 20427; (202) 606-8100. A federal government agency which mediates labor disputes. Regional offices located nationwide. Check their website or your local telephone directory for contact information about local offices.

J.A.M.S. Endispute, www.jams-endispute.com; 1920 Main Street, Suite 300, Irvine, CA 92714; (800) 352-5267. A nationally-franchised alternative dispute resolution service which uses lawyers and retired judges as intermediaries. You can search for a local office or particular panelist on their website.

Journal of Dispute Resolution, www.law.missouri.edu/csdr/jdr.html. A semiannual magazine published by the University of Missouri-Columbia School of Law in cooperation with its Center for Dispute Resolution.

Martindale-Hubbell Dispute Resolution Directory, www.martindale.com/products/dispute_res.html. State-by-state listing of over 45,000 professionals participating in alternative dispute resolution.

National Institute for Dispute Resolution, www.crenet.org; 1726 M St. NW, Suite 500, Washington, DC 20036; (202) 466-4764. Posts employment and volunteer opportunities on its website. Circulates a catalogue of conflict resolution resources.

Society of Professionals in Dispute Resolution (SPIDR), www.spidr.org; 1621 Connecticut Ave. NW, Suite 400, Washington, DC 20009; (202) 265-1927. Organization of professionals and volunteers interested in alternative dispute resolution. Annual conference, newsletter, clearinghouse of information about dispute resolution in many arenas, annual membership directory. You'll find information about local and regional chapters on their website.

US Arbitration & Mediation, www.usam.com (under construction in September 1998); 800

Roosevelt Road, Suite A5, PO Box 2607, Glen Ellyn, IL 60138; (800) 318-2700. Franchise operation with offices in the US, Canada and abroad.

Contact local arbitration and mediation service providers. Listed in local telephone directories under "Arbitration Services" and "Mediation Services."

Negotiation Resources

Getting to Yes: Negotiating Agreement without Giving In, Roger Fisher and William Ury. Clearly explains the concept of principled negotiations on which the mediation industry is based. Paperback; Penguin Books, 1991.

The Negotiation Journal. A quarterly magazine containing articles on the subject of dispute settlement. Published in collaboration with the Harvard Law School Program on Negotiation, www.law.harvard.edu/Programs/PON. Available from Plenum Publishing Corp., www.plenum.com.

Ombuds Resources

"A Neutral Third Party," Minda Zetlin, *Management Review,* September 1992. An article about the corporate ombuds profession, published in the American Management Association magazine.

"Options, Functions and Skills: What an Organizational Ombudsman Might Want to Know," Mary P. Rowe, *Negotiation Journal,* April 1995.

The Ombudsman Association, www.igc.org/toa; 5521 Greenville Ave., Suite 104-265, Dallas, TX 75206; (214) 553-0043. Membership organization consisting of those currently involved as internal and external organizational ombuds, as well as those interested in the field. Publishes the *Ombudsman's Handbook,* and a code of ethics and standards of practice. Offers training programs. Free information packet available upon request.

ARTS AND ENTERTAINMENT

Practicing Law:
entertainment lawyer
First Amendment lawyer
in-house counsel for an arts organization
intellectual property lawyer

Law-Related Positions:
art sales to law firms
computer-aided trial exhibits designer*
consultant on visual aids for trial
producer, associate producer or assistant producer of a law-related television program
producer of a courtroom television program like People's Court
supervising producer of television program about lawyers

The Talent:
actor
classical musician
comedian
commercial voice talent (a.k.a. "voice over" work)*
composer
fashion model
film maker
furniture art designer
graphic artist
jazz band member
jewelry designer
lyricist
folk musician
lasso artist
painter
rock musician
sculptor
singer
songwriter
storyteller
woodworker

RELEASING THE ARTIST WITHIN

Barry held an enviable position as senior partner of a prestigious New York City law firm. After many years of working almost around-the-clock, his life had eased into a pleasant routine of practicing law by day and, in the evenings, painting and sculpting. When a voice inside him announced the time to follow his passion in art, Barry was attentive enough to finally leave the law.

Barry's Statement: I wish I'd left law sooner. But like everything else it happened at one of those times when I least expected it.

I was actually happier practicing law than I had been in years. My workload was much easier because I had more help. I was doing much more supervisory work rather than all the detailed stuff that used to consume me. Life was a lot better than it had been, but by then I had already crossed over the line.

I was on my way home from Norway where I had obtained lengthy affidavits for an international bankruptcy matter. It had been a wonderful week, full of intellectual stimulation. When I was on the plane home, all of a sudden, I had this overwhelming feeling that I had to stop practicing law. Before that moment one of my biggest barriers to leaving was that I could not walk away from my partners; that I owed it to everybody to stay put for the rest of my life. At that moment, though, it all became crystal clear; I knew exactly what I had to do, and how I would tell them. The relief was so great that I started to cry. That clinched it. There was no turning back.

When I practiced commercial law, I never had the sense I was doing anything of great social value. It was more a matter of getting satisfaction out of presenting the best legal case I could with the facts and legal precedent I had. Although the work was very challenging, it was also totally consuming. We were a very small firm and worked harder than everybody else because we had to make up for the lack of numbers. The workload was incredible: seven days and seven nights at the beginning. It was a grind.

After the first seven years, I started to question what I was doing. As a way of expanding my life, I invested in an art gallery with three others. I participated in the planning, visited artists' studios and helped to select artists to represent. On weekends, I would go down to see what was going on. Before long, I began to read and study obsessively about art.

About a year after we opened the gallery, I started drawing after I came home from work, sometimes feeling so driven that I was at it until almost dawn. A few hours later, I'd go back to the office. The more I indulged my interest in art, though, the more frustrated I got with the life I was leading as a successful commercial lawyer. Other lawyers in the firm seemed totally obsessed with practicing law, that being the major impulse in their lives. With only a few exceptions, it seemed they didn't resent the demands because they weren't actively involved in anything else. On the other hand, my life was becoming schizophrenic. I tried to put my energies into the law as fully as I could, but art engaged me more and more.

Initially, I was just discontent. Then I started to realize how I was not living the kind of life that I really wanted to live.

Deciding whether or not to leave presented a multi-faceted conflict. On the one hand, there were the non-material rewards—the excitement of cases; the intellectual challenge; the prestige of being with a successful firm; the good feeling of being accepted as a successful lawyer. There were also the material rewards. As unhappy as I was, those things were hard to give up.

One the other hand, I was really in love with, and excited by, painting and art, and I hadn't felt that way about law for a long time. I had this feeling that I could do something significant with my life by devoting myself to art. Sure, I had doubts about starting a new career. Was I fooling myself? Did I only want to escape from law, or did I truly believe that I could do something meaningful? Did I have enough money to make the change and still maintain a reasonable lifestyle until I established myself again? What would it mean to my family?

Most lawyers I know are extremely interested in hearing about others who have left the law because 95 percent of them have secret yearnings to leave themselves. The only advice I can give is that when you begin to be unhappy with what you are doing, take the time to isolate the reasons why. If you find that you can't change them, then leave.

People say I was courageous to do what I did. But leaving law was a necessity for me. It was like having an illness. The way I see it, I either had to cure myself, or watch a big part of me die.

The Business Angle:

art gallery owner

artist's agent or representative

assistant artistic director

associate producer

co-creator of television show

dance instructor

executive producer, major motion pictures

executive producer of television show

founder of recording company

literary agent*

manager for actors, musicians, or musical groups

managing director of theatrical production
    company

movie producer

museum curator

theatrical agent

theatrical producer

Law-Related Resources

Volunteer Lawyers for the Arts, 1 E. 53rd St., 6th Floor, New York, NY 10022; (212) 319-2787. Maintains an annually updated listing of affiliated groups across the country, called the *Volunteer Lawyers for the Arts National Directory.* A publications brochure is available upon request.

Art Resources

100 Best Careers for Writers and Artists, Shelly Field. Includes information about television, theater arts, fashion, film, advertising, marketing, journalism, publishing and more. Paperback, Arco Publications, 1997.

American Association of Museums, www.aam-us.org/AAM; 1225 Eye St., NW, Suite 400, Washington, DC 20005; (202) 289-1818. Website contains articles on issues of interest to the museum community (fair use, ADA, intellectual property as examples).

ArtSearch. A national employment service bulletin for the performing arts issued twice monthly except January. Covers positions in the areas of artistic, administrative, career development, production and education. Available at many public libraries or purchase a one-year subscription through TCG, attn.: Order Department, 355 Lexington Ave., New York, NY 10017; (212) 697-5230. Also available by e-mail.

Career Opportunities in Art, Susan Haubenstock and David Joselit. Provides realistic, detailed information on 75 specific job titles.

Summarizes duties, alternate titles, salary range, prospects for employment and advancement, and prerequisites. Appendices list trade periodicals, associations, and educational programs. Paperback; Facts on File, 1995.

Careers in the Visual Arts, Dee Ito. Surveys diverse fields in the visual arts and offers advice on getting started and getting ahead. Paperback; Watson-Guptill, 1993.

How to Survive and Prosper as an Artist, Caroll Michels. The author has been helping others succeed in the art world since 1978. Includes advice on getting your work exhibited, preparing résumés and presentations, applying for grants and awards as well as a resource guide. Paperback; Henry Holt, 4th ed. 1997.

Official Museum Directory. A descriptive guide to US museums. Paperback; National Register Publishing, 28th ed. 1998.

The Business of Art, edited by Lee Caplin & Tom Power. A look at the business aspects of both creating and dealing in art. Paperback; Prentice Hall in cooperation with the National Endowment for the Arts, 1998.

Arts Education Resource

Employment Opportunities. Monthly announcements of administrative openings in the field of community arts education available to members of the National Guild of Community Schools of the Arts, www.natguild.org; Box 8018, Englewood, NJ 07631; (201) 871-3337. The Guild focuses on nonprofit, non-degree granting community schools offering instruction in the performance and visual arts.

Music Resources

Career Opportunities in the Music Industry, Shelly Field. Job descriptions for over 80 jobs in the business, talent, editing and recording aspects of the industry. Paperback; Facts on File, 3rd ed. 1996.

Songwriter's Market: 2000 Places to Market Your Songs, edited by Cindy Laufenberg. An annual listing of potential markets for songwriters and lyricists. Paperback; Writer's Digest Books, 1997.

The Music Business: Career Opportunities and Self-Defense, Dick Weissman. For those who wish to join the music business as artists, managers, producers, music publishers and more. Explores opportunities, tells how to get started and explains how the business operates. Paperback; Three Rivers Press, 2nd ed. 1997.

The Music Business (Explained in Plain English): What Every Artist and Songwriter Should Know to Avoid Getting Ripped Off, David Naggar and Jeffrey Brandstetter. Paperback; Scb Distributors, 1996.

Performing Arts Resources

Actor's Equity Association Hotlines, www.actorsequity.org. A 24-hour recorded telephone service provided by the four regional Equity union locals offering information about regional auditions, workshops, and other drama-related items. Website also features "Casting Call," announcements for principal, chorus and stage management positions.

Back Stage Online, www.backstage.com/casting. Casting call notices organized by region. Also features directory of service providers for performing artists.

Career Opportunities in Theater and the Performing Arts, Shelly Field. Features 70 different jobs, both behind-the-scenes and performance. Outlines salary ranges, skill requirements and opportunities for advancement. Paperback; Facts on File, 1995.

Careers for Film Buffs and Other Hollywood Types, Jaq Greenspon. Details on jobs behind the camera like art direction, production assistant, script supervisor, animation, titling, sound mixing, film scoring, special effects, marketing, publicity, distribution and more. Paperback; VGM Career Horizons, 1993.

Opportunities in Performing Arts Careers, Bonnie Bekken. Describes jobs and job-finding for careers in music, dance, theater. Paperback; VGM Career Horizons, 1991.

BAR ASSOCIATIONS

Practicing Law:
disciplinary counsel
general counsel
lawyer referral service supervising attorney
lawyer referral service telephone intake attorney*
legal education staff attorney
professionalism counsel
volunteer legal service project intake or staff attorney
volunteer legal service project supervising attorney
See also positions under ethics at page 321.

Administrative and Program Positions:
admissions/licensing director
assistant director
continuing legal education director
convention planner
coordinator of Lawyer Helpline service
director, assistant director or program coordinator for CLE
director of Lawyers Concerned with Lawyers program
director of professional competence, planning & development
director, special funds
executive director
fee arbitration program director*
law-related education director*
lawyers' assistance program director*
legal information answer line coordinator*
legislative representative
membership services director*
program planning advisor
programming director
public affairs director*
publications manager*
special project coordinator

volunteer legal services project director
website developer

Law-Related Resources
ABA Job Opportunities, www:abanet.org/hr.home.html. Includes internships, full-time and part-time open positions.
American Bar Association, www.abanet.org; main headquarters, 750 N. Lake Shore Dr., Chicago, IL 60611; (312) 988-5000. Branch office at 740 15th St., NW, Washington, DC 20005; (202) 662-1000. Chicago offices include membership, communications, meetings, CLE, publishing and young lawyers as well as most sections and committees. The Washington, DC, offices include governmental affairs, ADR and public service departments.
Directory of Lawyer Referral Services, 1997-98. Programs in the US and Canada. Available from the American Bar Association, www.abanet.org.
Job Descriptions & Association Personnel Policies. A collection of over 100 sample descriptions of bar association positions from executive director to secretary. Spiral bound; American Bar Association, 1997.
Lawyer Referral Network. News briefs on issues relevant to state and local lawyer referral services, produced three times yearly by the ABA Lawyer Referral Network. Available free from the American Bar Association.
Legal Researcher's Desk Reference, edited by Arlene L. Eis. List law-related associations nationwide. See prior listing at page 266.
National Association of Bar Executives, www.nabenet.org; 541 N. Fairbanks Court, 14th Floor, Chicago, IL 60611; (312) 988-5360 or 5362. An organization of managing directors, public information officers, CLE directors, counsel and other professional staff of state, county and city bar associations. You can search their membership directory by state on their website. Lists bar association job openings

nationwide on its website at www.abanet.
org/barserv.jobannc.html.
National Organization of Bar Counsel,
www.nobc.org. A nonprofit group of 450+
current disciplinary counsel to state and
federal courts, and bar associations.
Membership directory online. Holds
semiannual conventions in February and
August, in conjunction with ABA meetings.
Contact state, city, specialty and other local bar
associations. Often post or publish current
job vacancies.

COMMUNICATIONS

Practicing Law:
defamation lawyer
First Amendment lawyer
intellectual property lawyer
in-house lawyer for media organization

Law-Related Positions:
account representative for PR firm working
    with law firms
crisis PR for law firms*
freelance writer for any legal magazine,
    newspaper, or newsletter
legal correspondent for television or
    radio network news*
reporter for legal newspaper*
reporter on legal issues for general circulation
    magazine or newspaper
scriptwriter for television program
    about lawyers
speaker on career issues for law students
staff writer or editor for a law book publisher
staff writer for legal magazine or journal
website developer or editor
writer for a law-related television program
writer of legal career books
writer of substantive law books

The Business Angle:
account executive for public relations company*
agent

associate publisher for children's newspaper*
business affairs manager at media company
corporate communications
    company president
literary agent*
ombuds*
radio adman
television broadcast sales*

Other Editorial Positions:
assistant editor for collegiate dictionary*
associate food editor for women's magazine
copy editor*
editor (book, magazine, newspaper, newsletter)
editorial page editor
industry newsletter editor*
proofreader
publications director
reader
walking editor of two health magazines

Talent:
advice columnist
author of nonfiction book
dance critic*
disc jockey
editorial columnist
essayist
fiction writer
food critic
freelance computer training manual writer
freelance corporate communications
freelance magazine article writer
freelance newspaper reporter ("stringer")
historical romance novelist
humor columnist
corporate communications specialist*
journalist
motivational speaker
newspaper columnist
newspaper or magazine reporter
news writer and producer for network
    television affiliate
playwright
public affairs producer*

EXPLODING THE MYTH ABOUT WRITING BOOKS

John Grisham can't write a book that doesn't sell millions of copies. Scott Turow negotiates multi-million dollar movie deals for his novels. Nina and Eugene Zagat eat out a lot in New York City, review the food and get rich off their restaurant guides. It seems that lawyer-writers have it made. If you could just find the time to write a book, you tell yourself, you'd be on easy street for the rest of your life.

Let me share with you the real truth: Most lawyers who write books never get them published. Those that do usually earn no more than a small advance, perhaps $5,000. With royalties averaging less than ten percent of the cover price and the vast majority of books selling fewer than 5,000 copies per year, being an author is not a reliable way to earn a living.

With few exceptions, the publishing success stories you read about occur when authors spend countless hours and their own money publicizing (and sometimes, like the Zagats, self-publishing) their books. They fund their own book tours, book their own television and radio appearances and pay private publicists to influence magazines and newspapers to publish articles or reviews. In fact, many non-fiction bestsellers—think Stephen Covey, Tony Robbins, Gail Sheehy, the *Chicken Soup for the Soul* guys—were written as promotion tools for existing management consulting or public speaking businesses.

There's the Catch 22: Most lawyers hate to sell, especially themselves.

Don't despair, though, if you want to make a living as a writer. Just let go of the fantasy of hitting it big with a book and explore one of the less glamorous ways to be paid for the written word. Look into openings as reporters or editors with legal newspapers, newsletters, reporting services or publishers. Check with the CLE or publications departments of local bar associations. Investigate public relations companies, especially those that represent law firms. Take a look a writing opportunities in corporations; positions abound like technical writer, corporate communications manager or employee communication specialist.

professional speaker*
published novelist
radio talk-show host
restaurant reviewer*
screenwriter*
self-published nonfiction author
sportscaster
stand-up comedian
syndicated columnist
talk show host
technical writer*
television news reporter
television scriptwriter
weekend television anchor
writer for "The Simpsons"

Law-Related Resources

Careers in Entertainment Law, William D. Henslee. What to expect as an entertainment lawyer, including recommended academic background and work experience (pre-technology). Paperback; American Bar Association, 1990.

Communications Lawyer. A quarterly newsletter produced by the ABA's Communication Law Section. Reviews significant activities and developments in communications law.

Creative Writing for Lawyers, Michael H. Cohen. Paperback; Citadel Press, 1991.

Forum on Communications Law, www.abanet.org/forums/communication/col

ead.html. Encourages discussion and information exchange relating to legal counseling of print media, the telecommunications industry and electronic media.

Legal Newsletters in Print, edited by Arlene Eis. Over 2,200 different newsletters listed, most of them with contact names and numbers, nature of the publication, and requirements for submissions. Paperback; Infosources Publishing, www.infosourcespub.com, 1997.

"Murder, They Write," Adrienne Drell, *ABA Journal,* June 1994. Features lawyers across the country who write mystery novels, as well as tips on how to get your work published.

"Outside Insight: Index of the Latest Law Firm Newsletters," *American Lawyer,* monthly through March 1993. From April 1993 on, this listing is available on Counsel Connect, www.counselconnect.com.

The Reporter and the Law: Techniques of Covering the Courts, Lyle W. Denniston. An insider's view of how the legal system and the press work together. Denniston, dean of the Supreme Court press, breaks through legalese, defines the jargon of both the legal and journalistic professions and explains how each discipline depends on the other. Paperback; Columbia University Press, 1992.

Advertising Resources

American Association of Advertising Agencies (The Four As), www.commercepark.com /AAAA; 405 Lexington Avenue, 18th Floor, New York, NY 10174; (212) 682-2500. A national trade association representing the advertising business. A roster of members is available online, as well as references to about 150 other publications on the advertising field.

Careers in Advertising, S. William Pattis. Describes such jobs as creative director, media buyer and researcher and how to get them. Paperback; VGM Career Horizons, 2nd ed. 1996.

How to Approach an Advertising Agency and Walk Away with the Job You Want, Barbara Ganim. An insider's perspective into what agencies are looking for and how you can offer what they want. Paperback; VGM Career Horizons, 1993.

Standard Directory of Advertising Agencies, National Register Publishing Co. Details about advertising agencies worldwide.

Broadcasting

Breaking into Broadcasting: The Fast Track to Landing Your First or Next On-Air Job in Television, Jon Kelley & Tom Zenner. Paperback; KasterZ Co, 1996.

Let's Talk Pay in Television and Radio News, Vernon Stone. A comprehensive guide to salaries and benefits in TV and radio news. Charts the trends of the past two decades and projects into the future. Hardcover; Bonus Books, 1993.

National Association of Broadcasters, www.nab.org; 1771 N Street, NW, Washington, DC 20036; (202) 429-5300. Representatives of radio and TV stations and networks; associate members include freelance producers. An extensive career center online lists both employee and employer job announcements and permits résumé posting.

Radio-Television News Directors Association, www.rtnda.org/rtnda; 1000 Connecticut Ave., NW, Suite 615, Washington, DC 20036; (202) 659-6510 or (800) 80 RTNDA. The trade association for the electronic journalism profession. Offers a 25-page booklet entitled *Careers in Radio & Television* as well as an annual salary survey.

Television Careers: A Guide to Breaking and Entering, Linda Guess Farris. The author has more than 20 years experience in television. Reveals how to break into local television, network, cable and television production companies, both behind the scenes and on camera. Paperback; Buy the Book Enterprises, 1995.

TV News: Building a Career in Broadcast Journalism, Ray White. Offers realistic, effective steps prospective journalists can take to build a career foundation. Paperback; Focal Press, 1990.

Entertainment Resources

Plunkett's Entertainment & Media Industry Almanac 1998, Jack Plunkett. Provides contact names, addresses and phone numbers for hundreds of companies. Hardback; Plunkett Research, 1997.

Working in Show Business: Behind-the-Scene Careers in Theatre, Film and Television, Lynne Rogers. An overview of backstage roles including background and education, training programs, earnings and resources. Paperback; Back Stage Books, 1998.

Public Relations & Business Communication Resources

International Association of Business Communicators, www.iabc.com; One Hallidie Plaza, Suite 600, San Francisco, CA 94102; (800) 776-4222 or (415) 433-3400. A professional association and information network for communication managers, public relations directors, writers, editors, audiovisual specialists and consultants. Publishes *Communication World* magazine, other books, a bibliography of communication-related books, and an annual directory of members. Offers an accreditation program. Many chapters operate job listing services which nonmembers may access for a nominal fee. Website provides a search mechanism and links to groups in your metropolitan area.

O'Dwyer's Directory of Public Relations Firms. Lists contact information, clients and geographic reach of over 1,900 US and Canadian public relations firm. Annually updated.

Opportunities in Public Relations, Morris B. Rotman. Includes an excellent overview of the industry. Paperback; VGM Career Horizons, 1995.

PR News Casebook, Gale Research. A collection of 1,000 studies of major public relations campaigns from *PR News,* a widely read public relations weekly. Deals with issues like downsizing, minority relations, plant closing, product tampering and stockholder relations.

PR Opportunities, www.careeropps.com/prcareer/index.html. A national listing of public relations openings.

Public Relations Society of America, www.prsa.org; 33 Irving Place, 3rd Floor, New York, NY 10003; (212) 995-2230. Publish a subscription database of current public relations opportunities that pay more than $35,000 annually. You can view a sample issue under "Career Opportunities." Publish *Careers in Public Relations,* an eight-page booklet, the *PRSA Salary Survey,* a *Green Book* identifying PR service companies nationwide and a *Red Book* identifying PR firms and consultants nationwide.

Speaking Career Resources

International Platform Association, www.internationalplatform.com; PO Box 250, Winnetka, IL 60093-0250; (847) 446-4321. Networking opportunity for professional speakers, musicians, actors, booking agents and lecture bureaus.

National Speakers Association, www.nsaspeaker.org; 1500 S. Priest Dr., Tempe, AZ 85281; (602) 968-2552. Publishes *Who's Who in Professional Speaking* and *Professional Speaker* magazine. Excellent mid-year and annual educational conferences as well as local chapter programming.

Toastmasters International, www.toastmasters.org. Thousands of groups operate all over the world to improve communication and leadership skills. To locate groups in your area, check your local telephone directory, contact the national headquarters at PO Box 9052, Mission Viejo, CA 92690; (949) 858-8255, or use the search mechanism in their website. Receive *The*

Toastmaster monthly as a benefit of membership.

Writing and Editing Resources

Association of American University Presses Directory 1997-1998. A directory of over 100 university presses in the US, Canada and overseas, including complete addresses, phone and FAX numbers, names and responsibilities of key staff members, subject guide to areas published, and advice to authors on submission of manuscripts. Paperback; The University of Chicago Press, 1997.

Be Your Own Literary Agent: the Ultimate Insider's Guide to Getting Published, Martin P. Levin. Paperback; Ten Speed Press, 1996.

Bourque Newswatch, www.bourque.org. Links to all online newspapers in the world, plus 40 news wires and radio stations.

Career Opportunities for Writers, Rosemary Ellen Guiley. An in-depth survey of nearly 100 separate job descriptions in media and information services, publishing, arts and entertainment, business communications and public relations. Paperback; Facts on File, 3rd ed. 1996.

Editor and Publisher's Classified Page, http://epclassifieds.com. Search a wide variety of writing and multimedia—but primarily editorial—job openings.

Encyclopedia of Associations: Association Periodicals, Gale Research.

Foundation Center's Guide to Proposal Writing. See listing at page 326.

Hudson's Subscription Newsletter Directory. Paperback; Newsletter Clearing House, 13th ed. 1996.

International Directory of Little Magazines and Small Presses. Over 5,000 presses and journals identified, with contact names and numbers, and manuscript requirements. Paperback; W. W. Norton, 34th ed. 1998.

Largest Newspaper Index on the Web, www.concentric.net/~stevewt/. Provides links to over 3,000 newspapers in more than 80 countries with websites established as of April 1997.

LMP 1998: Literary Market Place. A basic reference work for the publishing industry, issued annually. Includes information on over 3,300 publishers, including small presses, cross-referenced geographically and by subject areas. Also lists literary agents, book review media, typing and word-processing services and other services related to publishing. Paperback; R. R. Bowker, annually updated.

National Writers Association, 3140 S. Peoria #295, Aurora, CO 80014; (303) 841-0246. An association of freelance writers, editors and agents. Publishes *Professional Freelance Writers Directory* each March and the bimonthly *Authorship* journal. Subsidiary agencies include the Associated Business Writers of America, American Technical Writers, and National Writers Literary Agency.

Newsletters in Print. See prior listing at page 279.

Newspapers Career Directory: A Practical, One-Stop Guide to Getting a Job in Newspaper Publishing, edited by Bradley J. Morgan and Joseph M. Palmisano. Includes job search advice, employers and associations for reporting work. Hardback; Gale Research, 4th ed. 1993.

Society for Technical Communication, www.stc-VA.org; 901 N. Stuart St., Suite 904, Arlington, VA 22203; (703) 522-4114. An association of technical writers, editors, publishers, graphic designers and others whose work involves making technical information understandable to the general public. Members have access to their web-based job search database. Look at their website for links to local chapters and to download *Careers in Technical Communication* and recent salary surveys.

Writer's Guide to Book Editors, Publishers & Literary Agents, 1999-2000. Who they are, what they want, and how to win them over. Paperback, Prima Publishing, 1998.

Writer's Guide to Hollywood Producers, Directors, and Screenwriter's Agents, Skip Press. Hundreds of listings of those who might want to buy your screenplay. Summaries of what they want, what they've bought before and how to contact them. Paperback, Prima Publishing, 1998.

Writer's Market. 4,000 places to sell your articles, books, fillers, greeting cards, novels, plays, scripts and short stories. Annually updated. Paperback; Writer's Digest Books.

Writing for the Corporate Market: How to Make Big Money Freelancing for Business, George Sorenson. Tells you how to make contacts and what kind of products are marketable. Paperback; Mid-List Press, 1990.

Other Communications Resources

Directory of Publications & Broadcast Media, Gale Research. An exhaustive listing of media outlets, including legal publications. Available at most public libraries.

Make Money Reading Books: How to Start and Operate Your Own Home-Based Freelance Reading Service, Bruce Fife. Covers literary services, book reviewing, researching, translating, indexing, manuscript reading, literary representation and other opportunities. Paperback; Piccadilly Books, 1993.

News Media Yellow Book: who's who among reporters, writers, editors and producers in the leading national news media. Quarterly updates of a personnel directory of national news media organizations. Provides complete contact information, including direct-dial telephone numbers of more than 2,700 leading national news media organizations.

Pathways to Careers in Communications. A 20-page brochure (4th ed. 1995) which presents an overview of the role of communication in the US economy and tells how course work and background may contribute to various job options in the communication arts and sciences. Available from the National

Association of Communicators, www.natcom.org; 5105 Backlick Rd., Building F, Annandale, VA 22003; (703) 750-0533, a group of teachers, clinicians, consultants, students and others interested in the communication arts and sciences.

Society of Professional Journalists, www.spj.org; 16 S. Jackson, Greencastle, IN 46135; (317) 653-3333. Promotes journalism as a career. Maintains a placement service and publishes the *1997-98 SPJ Internship Directory* and the *1998-99 Writer's Guide to Magazine Editors and Publishers.* Membership includes lawyers interested in their Freedom of Information committee.

CONSULTING

Practicing Law:
appellate specialist*
consulting lawyer*
legal research & writing specialist*

With Law Firms, Lawyers and In-House Legal Departments:
associate training
automation*
building good client relationships
business acquisition
business valuations expert*
case management systems
communication with clients and juries
computer usage (systems purchase or training)
document assembly systems
document management systems
employee selection, both professional and staff
expert witness on business and real estate failures
expert witness on general/limited partnership disputes
expert witness on insurance coverage, bad faith and underwriting issues
expert witness on lawyer standard of care or legal ethics

improving the quality and effectiveness of
   inside counsel
increasing law firm profitability
interpersonal communication
jury selection
law firm management
law firm systems
lawyer training (a.k.a. professional development)
marketing and promotion
marketing coaching
market research
mergers and acquisitions
Myers-Briggs Type Indicator testing
quality of life
office space design
outsourcing legal services
network design
pension and profit-sharing plans
pricing legal services
relationship building
staffing
strategic planning*
stress reduction
structuring alternative fee arrangements
telephone systems selection
time management
trial preparation
trial strategy
visual aids for trial
wardrobe and personal appearance, especially
   for jury presentations
winning client competitions
writing

Law-Related Consulting with Other Types of Businesses:

acquisition consulting
advising veterinarians about legal/business
   aspects of their practices
consulting in cost, quality and effective use of
   legal services
designing corporate compliance programs
dispute resolution training
employment law/human resources
freelance negotiator

intellectual property protection systems design*
internal dispute resolution
international business
IRS compliance analyst
labor-management relations
litigation avoidance*
litigation management*
pension benefits programs
promotion of European investment
real estate syndication
seminars that teach law to non-lawyers
sexual harassment avoidance training*
telecommunications fraud*
training managers to avoid employee lawsuits

Non-Legal Consulting:

business & entrepreneurial coaching
business management
executive search
financing
human resources
human services*
humor in the workplace
international relations
political*
sports stadium construction

Law-Related Resources

Altman Weil Pensa, www.altmanweil.com; PO
   Box 625, Two Campus Boulevard, Newtown
   Square, PA 19073; (610) 359-9900.
   Management consulting exclusively to the
   legal profession. Website includes many
   articles on law firm management consulting
   topics. Branch offices in Milwaukee, WI,
   Orinda, CA, and Ft. Myers, FL.
"Dilemma: Who Will Teach Associates?," Mike
   France, *National Law Journal,* November 20,
   1995. An article about the use of outside
   professional development trainers.
"Expert Witness Directory," *California Lawyer,*
   annual.
Hildebrandt, Inc. Management Consultants,
   www.hildebrandt.com; 200 Cottontail Lane,
   Somerset, NJ 08873; (732) 560-8888.

Management consulting services exclusively for law firms, corporate law departments and others in the legal profession. Offer executive search services for their clients as well. Branches in Chicago, (312) 857-1424; Naples, FL, (941) 594-5516; and San Francisco, (415) 956-9191.

Law Practice Management (formerly *Legal Economics*). Often features articles contributed by consultants to the legal profession. Published eight times annually by the Law Practice Management Section of the American Bar Association. Back issues available in most law libraries.

TASA (Technical Advisory Services for Attorneys), www.tasanet.com; 1166 DeKalb Pike, Blue Bell, PA 19422-1853; (800) 523-2319. An expert referral service for lawyers which claims access to 24,000 experts, some of whom are non-practicing lawyers.

"Technology," *American Lawyer*, periodic. A special pullout supplement that lists consultants to law firms nationwide.

General Resources

Consultants and Consulting Organizations Directory, Gale Research. Provides contact information and service overview for about 18,000 national and international consulting operations in over 400 specialties. Annually updated and also available online.

Consultant's Calling: Bringing Who You Are To What You Do, Geoffrey M. Bellman. An excellent how-to guide for professional consulting. Covers the whole picture, from the practical to the psychological. Paperback; Jossey-Bass, 1990.

Consultant's News. A monthly newsletter of 12 pages available for a free 3-month trial period. Contact Kennedy Information, Inc., www.kennedyinfo.com; (800) 531-1026, for a subscription.

"Do-It-Yourself Job Creation," Anne Murphy, *INC.*, January 1994. An extensive article about the large number of ex-employees who are contracting with their former employers and others to provide a wide variety of lucrative consulting services.

Flawless Consulting: A Guide to Getting Your Expertise Used, Peter Block. Highly-rated. As relevant now as it was when it was written. Hardback; Pfeiffer, 1981.

"Free Agent Nation" and "Free-Agent Almanac," Daniel H. Pink, *Fast Company*, December/January 1998. A description and resource guide to becoming an independent contractor for corporate project work.

Going Solo: Developing a Home-Based Consulting Business from the Ground Up, William J. Bond. Includes lists of more than 350 specialized consulting areas to help shape a business. Paperback; McGraw-Hill, 1997.

How to Become a Successful Consultant in Your Own Field, Hubert Bermont. The director of the American Consultants League explains how to get started in self-employed consulting. Paperback; Prima Publishing, 1997.

Institute of Certified Financial Planners, www.icfp.org; 3801 E. Florida Ave., Suite 708, Denver, CO 80210; (800) 322-4237 or (303) 759-4900. Operates Certified Financial Planner Board of Standards which licenses financial planners who have earned their CFP. Also maintains a referral service and 75 local affiliates. You can request information about becoming a CFP by phoning the 800 number and requesting their booklet on the subject. Career center online posts job openings.

Management Consulting 1998 (Harvard Business School Career Guide), edited by Alex R. Miller. Brief summaries of consulting companies nationwide. Paperback; Harvard Business School Press, 1997.

"The Talent Market," Daniel H. Pink, *Fast Company*, August 1998. An article about the growing number of agencies that are helping independent professionals build their careers.

CORPORATE, BUSINESS AND BANKING

Practicing Law:
associate general counsel
department (tax, real estate, labor relations, contracts, public information, finance, acquisitions) legal advisor*
director, intellectual property
general counsel*
independent general counsel (see next page)
in-house insurance defense
in-house intellectual property auditor
litigation management
medical division counsel
part-time in-house counsel
patent attorney
tax department of public accounting firm
VP, legal administration

Law-Related Employers:
accounting firms
banks
collection companies
law firm consulting companies
insurance companies
legal publishers
management consulting companies
mortgage companies
public accounting firms
retailers of products or services for lawyers and law firms
Section 1031 exchange intermediaries
software developers for law firms
wealth management companies

Examples of Law-Related Products:
advertisements in legal newspapers and magazines
communications systems
computer animation/graphics
computer hardware/software
computerized legal forms
computer systems and components
corporate kits
educational videos

executive gifts (also known as premium sales)
forms
law books and directories
legal applications computer software
legal forms
mail order products with a lawyer theme
office furniture
office equipment
office supplies
printing
training films on legal ethics & overcoming discrimination
visual aids for trial

Examples of Law-Related Services:
accounting/bookkeeping
advertising
appraisals (personal property; residential and commercial real estate)
career and life planning for lawyers*
CLE-accredited seminars
completion of legal forms
computer-assisted research and retrieval
computer-generated accident reconstruction
contract lawyer placement
corporate communications
courier/messenger service
courtroom exhibit preparation and design
deposition and trial transcript summaries
expert witness clearinghouse and referral service
facilities management
graphic design
in-firm training programs
in-house continuing legal education
independent paralegal
insurance coverage, such as malpractice, office liability, disability, life, and health insurance
interactive CLE videos
investigator, criminal or civil
judgment purchase
language/interpretation services
legal research services
legal search consultant (also known as "headhunter")
linguistic analysis
litigation management

INDEPENDENT GENERAL COUNSEL OR PART-TIME IN-HOUSE COUNSEL

In the late 1980's, Michael came up with an idea for a new service. He'd act as in-house counsel for several corporations on a part-time basis, charging a reduced hourly rate in exchange for an as-needed office and occasional secretarial assistance. He contacted companies in his area that were too small to justify an in-house legal department but had enough legal expense to be interested in the cost-savings he was suggesting. Several bought the idea. One, as it expanded, eventually offered him a full-time position as general counsel.

Jerry's ten-year stint as house counsel for a real estate development company ended when the company went bankrupt. After some serious soul-searching, researching the market and discovering how slim were his prospects for another in-house position—and hearing Michael speak at a gathering of

disgruntled lawyers—Jerry copied Michael's idea. He marketed his services exclusively to privately-held property management and real estate development companies. His efforts resulted in relationships with four companies and an income which doubled the salary he lost.

Now, innovative law firms across the country market themselves as "independent general counsel." They take on routine corporate assignments for mostly new and emerging high-technology companies with little or no in-house staff. Firms that have done well enough to get in the news include the General Counsel Group in Pennsylvania; General Counsel Associates in Mountain View; The General Counsel, Ltd., in Minneapolis; the Association of Independent General Counsel in the Boston area; and Venture Counsel in Portland, OR.

litigation oversight
litigation research
litigation support
management consulting
market analysis
"mastery of practice" training seminars
medical illustration
medical research
office machine maintenance and repair
outplacement services
paralegal and clerical staff placement
paralegal services (e.g. document organization, indexing, and retrieval)
polygraphs
probate administration
professional development courses
public relations
research
storytelling for law firm social events
strategic automation

strategic planning retreats
systems integration
videotaping depositions, will-signings, accident scenes, etc.

Positions with Law-Related Employers:
acquisitions counselor
acquisitions evaluator*
adjuster in claims department of insurance company or self-insured corporation
attorney-pension operations for insurance company
attorney-underwriter
bank investment compliance officer
bank probate administrator*
bank regulation analyst*
bank trust department consultant (petroleum)*
bank trust officer
claims adjuster*
claims examiner*

client service representative for trust company

commercial loan administrator

contract lawyer placement specialist*

estate administrator

insurance claims representative

insurance/bonding specialist

loan administrator

life insurance agent

manager

prepaid legal plan administrator*

sales manager, national collection company

trust examiner

trust officer

vice-president, loan review

Law-Related Positions for Non-Legal Employers:

account executive for private wealth
   management group

ADA compliance specialist*

ADA coordinator

affirmative action director*

affirmative action officer

associate director of business affairs

chief operating officer (COO)

compliance officer

contract compliance administrator*

contract negotiator*

contract specialist

contracting director or staff

corporate quality and technical affairs director or
   staff

dispute resolution specialist

EEOC compliance officer

employee benefit plan administrator

employee benefit plan designer

employee benefit products and development
   director or staff

employee benefits analyst*

employee benefits consultant

employee relations officer

employee/labor relations director or staff

errors and omissions examiner

estate planning specialist

ethics officer*

human resources consultant

IRS compliance analyst*

labor administration

leasing contract administrator

legal compliance manager*

legal editor

legal translation specialist

litigation oversight

loan administrator

ombudsman

procurement analyst

product licensing director or staff

property protection specialist

purchasing director

regulation analyst

retirement plan consultant

risk management advisor*

SEC compliance monitor*

tax consulting

tax law analyst

training administrator*

workers' compensation claims examiner

Other Management Positions:

assistant manager of comic-book store

bookstore manager

CEO

chairman of the board

director of field human resources

manager of frame shop

manager of management practices

president of film distribution company

senior vice-president for
   business management

store manager

VP, job-placement firm

VP/manager, administration

VP/manager, business

VP/manager, community relations

VP/manager, development

VP/manager, financial planning

VP/manager, research

Other Sales Positions:

automotive sales

corporate marketing*
financial plans sales director*
financial products sales
institutional sales
insurance broker*
manufacturer's representative*
stockbroker*
VP, equity sales

Other Staff Positions:
actuary
airline pilot*
computer systems analyst*
conference planner*
convention planner*
director of field human resources
director of special projects
documentary producer
employee relations officer
employee relations representative
employee training
executive search consultant*
field education director*
human resources manager
human services consulting*
independent insurance adjuster*
international business development advisor
investment banking*
investment analyst*
investment strategist*
linguist
merchandising
mergers and acquisitions specialist
pension & profit sharing analyst
program development director at
    a health resort
public insurance adjuster
public relations director
purchasing agent*
risk arbitrage analyst
senior account manager
senior internal auditor
software design
supervising environmental scientist
trainer*

Law-Related Resources
1998 Directory of Trust Institutions,
    www.trustandestates.com/dir/dir.html.
    Provides location, contact person(s), trust
    assets and branches of trust institutions
    nationwide.
American Corporate Counsel Association
    (ACCA), www.acca.com; 1225 Connecticut
    Ave., NW, Suite 302, Washington, DC 20036;
    (202) 296-4522. An organization of 10,500
    attorneys employed in corporate law
    departments, with 41 chapters nationwide.
    Publishes a membership directory and in-
    house jobline on its website.
Careers in Finance & Banking. Pamphlet, National
    Association for Law Placement, 1998.
Directory of Corporate Counsel, Aspen Law &
    Business. A two-volume listing of in-house
    legal departments for major corporations,
    nonprofits, public utilities and universities
    nationwide. Available in many law school
    career services offices and law libraries.
"Don't Bank On It," Lisa Brennan, *National Law
    Journal,* July 6, 1998. The pros and cons of
    leaving private law practice for investment
    banking.
"Firms Find New Ways to Save: Outsourcing of
    Law Firm Support Services Spreads to New
    Areas," Martha Middleton, *National Law
    Journal,* January 24, 1994.
"Getting Those In-House Jobs," Lisa Brennan,
    National Law Journal, March 16, 1998.
House Counsel, a quarterly magazine dealing
    with concerns of in-house counsel, published
    by the Daily Journal Corporation.
JD Preferred, section on insurance and risk
    management. See prior listing at page 264.
Judgment Reversed. See prior listing at page 264.
Law Practice Management. Features articles on
    trends in the practice of law, including new
    products. See prior listing at page 299.
National Contract Managers Association
    (NCMA), www.ncmahq.org; 1912 Woodford
    Rd., Vienna, VA 22182: (703) 448-9231 or
    (800) 344-8096. An organization of contract

administrators, negotiators and others involved in contract management and procurement for private business and government. Website offers job announcements, information about the profession and links to regional and local chapters.

Ombudsman Association. See previous listing at page 287.

"NLJ Client List," *National Law Journal.* A listing of 250 industrial companies, featuring both numbers of outside counsel and the size of any in-house legal department. Periodically published, sometimes twice annually.

"They're Leaving for Wall Street: Bull market is luring associates out of law firms into the banks," Lisa Brennan, *National Law Journal,* May 25, 1998.

Check other magazines and newspapers for lawyers. State and local bar association publications, *ABA Journal, American Lawyer, National Law Journal* and others contain advertisements of companies that provide products to law firms and lawyers, articles on product trends in the profession and periodic special advertising sections.

Financial Services (Banking, Insurance, Finance) Resources:

American Bankers Association, www.aba.com; 1120 Connecticut Ave., NW, Washington, DC 20036; (202) 663-5000 or (800) 338-0626. Sponsors the Bankers News Executive Career Services online at www.exec-jobs.aba.com. (A job tips section was under construction at time of publication.)

American Banker Online, www.americanbanker. com. The website of this financial services daily includes a Career Zone with articles on employment issues and job announcements.

Plunkett's Financial Services Industry Almanac 1996-97, Jack Plunkett. Profiles of large financial services companies. Paperback; Plunkett Research, 1996.

Careers in Finance, Trudy Ring. Jobs in corporate and public finance from banks, to savings and loan and credit unions, to investment banking and futures trading. Paperback; VGM Career Horizons, 1993.

Financial Yellow Book: who's who at the leading US financial institutions. Features 41,000 top executives in areas such as investment, money management, insurance and underwriting. Also lists government financial institutions.

Harvard Business School's Career Guide for Finance, edited by Anthony L. Tillman. Describes current trends in finance, profiles of investment and commercial banks, and a glossary of finance terms. Paperback; Harvard Business School Press, 1999.

Best's Directory of Recommended Independent Insurance Adjusters. A guide to those who contract their claims investigation services to insurance companies and insureds with major losses.

Best's Insurance Reports, Property and Casualty. Operating statistics and financial data and names of officers in over 1,300 stock and mutual insurance companies plus summary information about 2,000 smaller companies.

Business & Finance Career Directory: One-Stop Guide to Getting a Job in Business & Finance, edited by Bradley J. Morgan. Job search assistance and databanks on such fields as stockbroker, insurance, management information, securities analyst, trading, banking, mortgage and savings and loans. Paperback; Gale Research, 2nd ed. 1992.

The Wall Street Journal Guide to Who's Who and What's What on Wall Street, editors of the *Wall Street Journal.* Explores the biggest companies on Wall Street and the regulatory agencies that impact them. Paperback; Del Rey, 1998.

Human Resources:

American Compensation Association, www.acaonline.org; 14040 N. Northsight Blvd., Scottsdale, AZ 85260; (602) 922-2020.

A nonprofit organization of human resources practitioners who design and manage employee compensation and benefit programs. Confers certified compensation and certified benefits professional designations.

Careers in Human Resources. Pamphlet, National Association for Law Placement, 1998.

National Association of Temporary & Staffing Services, www.natss.com; 119 S. Saint Asaph St., Alexandria, VA 22314; (703) 549-6287. An organization of 1,600 companies with 13,000 offices that supply workers on a temporary basis. You can download some informational pamphlets from their website.

Society for Human Resource Management, www.shrm.org, 1800 Duke St., Alexandria, VA 22314; (703) 548-3440. 100,000 members worldwide; membership directory available online. Access job listings for careers in personnel and industrial relations on their website or sign up for their free e-mail notification service.

Marketing and Sales Resources

American Marketing Association, www.ama.org; 250 S. Wacker Dr., Suite 200, Chicago, IL 60606; (312) 648-0536 or (800) AMA-1150. Publish many resources on marketing as well as an *International Membership Directory.* Their extensive website includes announcements of job vacancies around the country.

Making $70,000 Plus a Year as a Self-Employed Manufacturer's Representative, Leigh Silliphant, Shirley Myers Pierce and Sureleigh Silliphant. Paperback; Ten Speed Press, 1998.

The Green Book: International Directory of Marketing Research Companies and Services. Indexed by service, geography and alphabet and includes information about advertising research, concept development and testing, consumer research, interviewing service, name and package development and

product testing. Paperback; American Marketing Association, 1995

Opportunities in Sales Careers, James Brescoll and Ralph Dahm. Information about finding jobs in sales and sales management positions in retail, manufacturing and service. Paperback; VGM Career Horizons, 1995.

Organizational Development

Organizational Development Network, www.odnet.org; 71 Valley St., Suite 301, South Orange, NJ 07079; (973) 763-7337. Practitioners, academics, managers and students employed or interested in organizational development, a process of analyzing group psychology and assisting with change. Call the ODN Job Exchange at (609) 428-6762 for active job listings, or subscribe to a mailing service for $35 quarterly by sending your check to the OD Network Exchange, PO Box 242, Haddonfield, NJ 08033.

Trade Shows and Conventions

Trade Shows Worldwide, Gale Research. Profiles of almost 6,000 trade shows, 4,600 trade show organizers and sponsors, 700 convention centers, and over 400 industry suppliers.

Meeting Professionals International, www.mpiweb.org; 4455 LBJ Freeway, Suite 1200, Dallas, TX 75244; (972) 702-3000. An association of corporate, association and independent conference, retreat and convention planners. Publishes an annual directory. Chapters nationwide maintain job banks; membership also provides access to the organization's online Career Resource Service. Look at their Discussion Center online for information about current issues in meeting planning.

Training

American Management Association International, www.amanet.org; 1601 Broadway New York, NY 10019; (212) 586-8100. Focuses on development and training within the corporate environment.

American Society for Training and Development, www.astd.org; Box 1443, 1640 King St., Alexandria, VA 22313; (703) 683-8100. A national organization for professionals in business, industry, education, and government who concentrate on workplace learning and performance. Publishes *Who's Who in Training and Development, Training & Development* magazine, and *ASTD's Buyer's Guide and Consultant Directory.* Local chapters may have employment hotlines and are good networking groups.

Multidisciplinary Associations

Association for Quality and Participation, www.aqp.org; 801B W. 8th St., Suite 501, Cincinnati, OH 45203; (513) 381-1959. A group of managers, manufacturing executives, professionals in personnel relations, employee involvement professionals like trainers, facilitators and coordinators who promote quality and participation in the workplace. Operates nine regional groups and 80 active chapters; references available online. Members only access to career opportunities on their website.

Chamber of Commerce, www.uschamber.org. Local chambers provide good networking, educational and information gathering opportunities. Their website provides links to local organizations. The national headquarters at 1615 "H" St., NW, Washington, DC 20062; (202) 659-6000, publishes *Nation's Business,* a monthly magazine with an emphasis on small business.

General References

Corporate Jobs Outlook! A 40- to 50-page bimonthly newsletter which analyzes job prospects and provides complete reports on the nation's fastest growing corporations. Produced by Plunkett Research, www.plunkettresearch.com; PO Drawer 541737, Houston, TX 77254-1737; (713) 932-0000.

Business Phone Book USA 1998: The National Directory of Addresses & Telephone Numbers, Omnigraphics. Lists phone numbers and addresses for 115,000 businesses with more than 20 employees. Useful when you are trying to locate the home office of a company you've identified only by name.

Corporate Yellow Book: Who's Who at the Leading US Companies. A 1,250 page quarterly publication profiling over 1,100 companies and their 7,700 subsidiaries. Business descriptions and annual revenues plus names and titles of executives, addresses, telephone, fax and Internet addresses of corporate headquarters and government affairs offices.

Directory of Corporate Affiliations, National Register Publishing Co., Inc. Provides detailed information on the family tree of every major corporation.

Fast Company, www.fastcompany.com. A monthly magazine focusing on how today's smart businesses work. Highly-recommended for anyone seeking employment with progressive, start-up or technology-related companies.

Million Dollar Directory: America's Leading Public & Private Companies. Focuses on the top 50,000 firms with reported net worth greater than $500,000. Arranged alphabetically and by location. Entries include address, phone number, size, sales, products and key names. Available at most public libraries. Hardback; Dun's Marketing Service, 1991.

National Business Employment Weekly, 200 Burnett Road, Chicopee, MA 01020; (800) 562-4868. Published by Dow Jones, this weekly newspaper contains articles from the *Wall Street Journal* relating to employment, as well as classified ads from all regional editions of the *Journal.*

National Directory of Minority-Owned Business Firms. Hardback; Business Research Services, 9th ed. 1998.

National Directory of Women-Owned Business Firms. Hardback; Business Research Services, 8th ed. 1996.

National Job Bank 1999, Steven Graber, editor. Provides information on 10,000 US corporations. Includes name, address, business description, job categories and educational backgrounds sought. Hardback; Bob Adams, Inc., 1998.

New Rules of Business. A 1997 supplement to *Fast Company* magazine sponsored by Coopers & Lybrand. A terrific overview of the changing corporate structure, including sections on achieving personal success and new ways of working.

The Forbes 500. Almost 800 companies overall listed in rankings of jobs and productivity, sales, profits, market value and assets, with telephone numbers, addresses, websites and CEO names provided. Published annually in April by *Forbes* magazine.

The Fortune 500. A list of America's largest industrial and service companies, ranked by revenue, published annually in August by *Fortune* magazine.

The Job Seeker's Guide to Private and Public Companies, Gale Research. References to the largest, best of the small and fastest-growing companies in the US. Includes personnel names and sometimes toll-free and fax numbers. Listed by industry and geography in regional volumes.

The Job-Seeker's Guide to Socially Responsible Companies, Katherine Jankowski. Profiles 1,000 companies with high ethics, environmental consciousness, quality of life, fair hiring and profit sharing. Hardback; Gale Research, 1994.

US Industrial Directory. 50,000 company names, addresses, trade names and phone numbers plus local sales offices and distributors. Annually updated.

Wall Street Journal. Business news Monday through Friday. Features periodic special reports on industry leaders such as "The World's 100 Biggest Public Companies."

Ward's Business Directory of US Private and Public Companies 1998, Gale Research. Lists revenue, number of employees, and general information.

Web 100, www.w100.com. Offers links to the 100 largest (ranked by revenue) US companies on the Web.

Local libraries will also carry directories of state, county and sometimes city manufacturers and other business employers. These directories are produced by a variety of different publishers. They generally contain an extensive list of firms by company title, product(s) manufactured and location, and provide company address, size, sales market and key names.

COUNSELING

Practicing Law:
elder law lawyer*
estate planning lawyer
guardianship lawyer*
involuntary commitment lawyer
matrimonial (family law) lawyer*
probate lawyer

Law-Related Positions:
career counselor at a law school
career counselor for lawyers
family therapist specializing in child custody/divorce actions
forensic psychologist*
individual therapist specializing in lawyers and their families
lawyers assistance program counselor*

Other Counseling Positions:
after-care coordinator at residential treatment facility
career counselor
channeler
corporate counseling via a masters in applied behavioral science

employee assistance program (EAP) counselor *
experimental psychology and cognitive science
 via a doctoral degree
hypnotherapist
minister
personal coach
psychological counseling via a masters in
 psychology
psychological counseling via a Ph.D. in
 psychology
rabbi
shamanic counselor
social worker

Law-Related Resources

1998 Directory of Lawyer Assistance Programs,
 www.abanet.org/cpr/colap/assistance.html.
 Lists contact information for bar association
 committee chairs and program managers, of
 about 100 lawyer assistance programs in the
 US and Canada. Available online, or in print
 for a fee from the American Bar Association.
American Academy of Matrimonial Lawyers,
 www.aaml.org; 150 N. Michigan Ave., Suite
 2040, Chicago, IL 60601; (312) 263-6477.
 Publishes annual membership roster, journal
 and newsletter. Articles and a divorce manual
 accessible on their website.
"Beyond Ozzie & Harriet," Debra Baker, *ABA
 Journal,* September 1998. Domestic relations
 now includes nontraditional legal issues.
Commission on Lawyers Assistance Programs,
 www.abanet.org/cpr/colap; 750 N. Lake
 Shore Dr., Chicago, IL 60611; (312) 988-
 5359. The governing body for programs that
 assist lawyers with drug and alcohol
 problems; some programs also provide
 outreach to lawyers suffering from depression
 or other mental illness, and career
 dissatisfaction. You'll find announcements
 about open positions with lawyers assistance
 programs nationwide on their website. You
 can also purchase a 1997 survey about
 funding sources, budgets and personnel of
 lawyers assistance programs nationwide.

Family Advocate. A quarterly journal produced by
 the ABA Family Law Section. Contains
 information on current trends in divorce,
 mental health, custody, support and
 problems of aging.
National Association for Law Placement Bulletin. A
 monthly newsletter published by an
 organization that includes career services
 offices of all the accredited law schools. Posts
 job notices in every edition, many of them
 counseling-related. Available in your law
 school career services office or for $100
 annually from NALP, www.nalp.org.
"They're Psych Ph.D.s and JDs: Meet the new
 family law hybrids, loaded with credentials
 and empathy," Cynthia Cotts, *National Law
 Journal,* August 31, 1998.

General Resources

American Counseling Association,
 www.counseling.org; 5999 Stevenson Ave.,
 Alexandria, VA 22304; (800) 347-6647 or
 (703) 823-9800. Over 60,000 counseling and
 human development professionals in
 government, education, nonprofit, business,
 and private practice dealing with career,
 mental health, school and rehabilitation
 matters. Go to CTOnline Classifieds on their
 website to find some national employment
 announcements. Also publishes *Career
 Development Quarterly* through a division, the
 National Career Development Association,
 http://ncda.org, and the monthly *Counseling
 Today.* Another division, the National
 Employment Counseling Association,
 provides links to counseling organizations
 and other employers at www.geocities.com/
 Athens/Acropolis/6491/neca.html.
Career Planning and Adult Development
 Network, www.careertrainer.com/
 network.html; 4965 Sierra Rd., San Jose, CA
 95132; (408) 441-9100 or (800) 888-4945. A
 nonprofit professional organization of 1,200
 professionals who work with adults in job and
 career transition. Publishes a monthly

newsletter and a quarterly journal for members.

Employee Assistance Professionals Association (EAPA), www.eap-association.com; 2101 Wilson Blvd., Suite 500, Arlington, VA 22201; (703) 522-6272. 7,000 professionals who assist in identifying and resolving productivity problems caused by employee impairment from alcoholism, divorce, depression and other personal issues. 100 chapters worldwide. Publish an *Employee Assistance Law Book* and a member resource directory.

National Association of Social Workers, www.socialworkers.org; 750 First St., NE, Suite 700, Washington, DC 20002; (202) 408-8600 or (800) 227-3590 (membership). The largest organization of professional social workers with over 155,000 members. NASW JobLink online or at (303) 221-4970 lists jobs announcements. You'll also find links to other job listing websites, and information on developing a career in social work, on their website.

National Board for Certified Counselors, www.nbcc.org; 3 Terrace Way, Suite D, Greensboro, NC 27403; (336) 547-0607. Confers national certified counselor (NCC), national certified career counselor (NCCC) and certified clinical mental health counselor (CCMHC) designations. You can obtain a list of those among the 24,000 certified counselors who practice in your geographic area on their website or by calling (800) 398-5389.

Opportunities in Counseling & Development Careers, Mark Toch, Philip Perry & Neale Baxter. Describes and gives career advice for fields like school, mental health, alcohol & drug and rehabilitation counselor. Paperback; VGM Career Horizons, 1997.

EDUCATION

Possible Employers:
adult education companies
bar review courses
CLE providers
colleges and universities
community colleges
corporate training companies
corporations
court reporting schools
law schools
private schools
school districts

Practicing Law Positions:
general counsel
outside counsel
plaintiff's lawyer for ADA and other claims
in-house staff attorney

Teaching Law School:
adjunct professor*
director of law center
director/supervising attorney of clinical education program*
instructor
lecturer
legal writing instructor*
tenured professor
tenure-track professor
tutor

Law School Administrative Positions:
academic compliance manager
assistant dean
associate director, Center for Law and Entrepreneurship*
cooperative legal education director
dean
dean of students*
director or assistant director of admissions*
director of alumni affairs*
director of legal externship program
director or assistant director of career services, career development or placement*
director or assistant director of continuing legal education
director or assistant director of development or fundraising

BREAKING INTO LAW SCHOOL ADMINISTRATION

In the eight years after she graduated from law school, Sharon held four different jobs as a lawyer. She tried academia, public interest law, legal publishing and private practice. Her focus ranged from counseling to administration; from litigation to legal research and writing; from day care regulation to school bond issues. None of it, though, complemented her roles as wife and mother until she moved into law school administration. Here's her story of how she made the switch and what her job now entails.

Sharon's Statement: I'm one of those people who was headed for an academic career and then shifted when it seemed that teaching English at the college level full time had become an impossibility. I always knew that I was going to do something serious—whatever that means—so when the time came to take the next step, I went into law.

My first job as a practicing attorney—director of a public interest project devoted to children's issues—was originally set up as a 30-hour per week commitment. I noticed a huge difference between being a law student with three young children and being an attorney with three young children. As a student, I could do what I needed to do fairly easily. As a lawyer, it was very hard. I was always frantic and conflicted, thinking, "I should be home with the children; I should be here at work." Everything had to be so carefully calculated in terms of time and who was responsible when. It seemed that there was a constant crisis or near-crisis all of the time. I was always juggling too many things.

I was dedicated to a part-time arrangement. But the conventional wisdom was that practicing law part-time could not be done if you wanted to have a serious

practice. So, after the first year, the board voted to switch my position to full time with a proportionate increase in income. I fought the decision long and hard but eventually lost.

It was not a good trade-off for me. Full-time practice meant spending all day in the city, bringing a lot of work home, attending many night meetings and sometimes working through the weekend. I had to do all of the fundraising, manage the office, and take care of the clients. It was much more than I could handle given that it didn't pay enough for me to have the amount of child care I really needed. When I look back at what made me leave the children's rights project, it was, ironically, the demands of my own family.

When I am under a lot of stress, I wake up at two in the morning and can't go back to sleep. Back then, I was doing it constantly. At one point, I had a serious bout of pneumonia, which I am sure was 90 percent stress-related. I got to thinking that there had to be a better way to live.

Fortunately, my husband got a job offer in Denver. It was a difficult decision, but we were both ready for a change. We thought a less high-powered environment would make our marriage work better.

I worked for a midsize Denver firm for a year, slowly working into advising school districts on their elections. We did some corporate work for hospitals. The firm was generous in paying for the bar, and giving me a month off with salary to study for it.

I thought I had actually achieved a balance among my obligations. But the moment I was to take the bar, my husband told me that he was moving back to Illinois—whether or not I wanted to come—and that he was inviting our teenage kids to return to the Chicago area with him. We moved back together, but that episode finished our marriage.

After my husband moved out, I took a job with a legal publisher. I wondered if I would be happier in a job with less stress and excitement, and with regular hours. All I discovered was that working at something too easy and boring has its own stresses.

At some point, I began to make lists of what I liked and didn't like. By conducting some research, I figured out that my lists pointed to university administration of one sort or another. I applied for a position as a placement director at a local law school and called the director of career services at my alma mater to tell her what I was doing and ask if she would write a letter of reference. She told me in confidence that she was about to leave her job and would love to recommend me as a replacement.

In my present job at the law school, I do a lot of individual student counseling and some teaching about careers and job hunting. I've written handouts and guides on different types of legal careers and how to go about preparing for and finding those jobs. I'm working in a legal environment, but my schedule is manageable and predictable. The summer, when my children are on vacation, is quiet; a time for me to catch up and reassess what I am doing. The upside of the job is that I have a lot of autonomy. The downside is the isolation; I'm not faculty and there is no one at the law school at my level who is working with the same issues and concerns.

People often ask if I'm ever going to go back into practice. The answer is yes, probably. But not until I feel less of an obligation to be available to my last child at home and very likely, even then, on a volunteer basis only. You see, to be truthful, I do not miss the practice of law at all.

director or assistant director of community relations
director or assistant director of marketing
director or assistant director of student affairs
faculty computer consultant
law librarian
publication support specialist

Other Law-Related Administrative Positions:
affirmative action/EEO officer
bar review course administrator*
director or assistant director of the office of technology transfer*
campus ombuds
campus security/compliance officer
coordinator for a CLE provider
course designer for a CLE provider*
contract staff analyst

corporate liaison officer
director of federal/state relations
director of a legal assistant/paralegal program
director or assistant director of legislative and regulatory affairs
director of cooperative legal education
director of planned giving
diversity management director
equal opportunity officer
executive director or manager of CLE provider
executive director, center for law-related education
faculty director of master's degree in dispute resolution
investigation and resolution specialist*
planned or deferred giving officer or director*
pre-law advisor
risk management director (see risk management consultant*)

special assistant to the president

technology licensing associate

Law-Related Subject Matters

business ethics

business law*

constitutional law

criminal justice

juvenile justice

dispute resolution

environmental law or policy

estate planning

labor relations

law and society

legal studies*

marketing for lawyers

negotiation

paralegal education

political science

real estate law

securities law

sexual harassment avoidance

tax

Law-Related Teaching Positions:

bar review course instructor

bar review tutor

community college instructor

corporate trainer

full or associate professor

instructor

lecturer

Other Administrative Positions:

administrative vice chancellor and CFO

assistant dean of students

assistant to the President or Dean

assistant director of office of technology transfer

dean

dean of students

director of alumni affairs

director, professional development centers and
institutes

program coordinator of academic support

provost for faculty recruitment and retention

researcher, educational "think tank"

university administrator*

vice-president., community college
academic services

Other Teaching Positions:

elementary school teacher

facilitator of personal growth or transformational
seminar

high school teacher

junior high school teacher

instructor, college prep course offered on-
site in a corporation

instructor, professional writing skills for trainers

"New Age" seminar facilitator

outdoor leadership instructor

professor at an art academy

secondary-education teacher

team-building & leadership instructor

Law-Related Resources

1998-99 National Directory of Law Schools.
Contact information, program descriptions
and other information about the ABA-
accredited schools. Paperback; National
Association for Law Placement, 1998.

AALS Faculty Recruitment Conference. An annual
Fall recruitment program held in Washington,
DC, in which law schools interview
prospective candidates for upcoming faculty
openings. Interviewees submit one application
form which is circulated to all ABA-approved
law schools. Interested schools make
appointments to meet with you and other
candidates at this conference. For information,
contact the American Association of Law
Schools (AALS), listing below.

ABA-Approved Law Schools. Statistical information
about all accredited law schools. Paperback;
ABA/MacMillan, 1998.

Academy of Legal Studies in Business (formerly
American Business Law Association),
http://miavx1.muohio.edu/~herrondj/about.
html; c/o Professor Dan Herron, ALSB
Executive Secretary, 120 Upham Hall,

Department of Finance, Miami University, Oxford, OH 45056; (800) 831-2903. An organization of over 1,000 teachers and scholars (primarily in schools of business) who work in the field of business law, legal environment and law-related courses outside of professional law schools. Publishes a newsletter three times annually which contains job listings, the quarterly *American Business Law Journal* and the *Journal of Legal Studies in Education* twice yearly. Networks with 11 regional associations. Professor Herron welcomes inquiries about the educational job market, job search and drafting an effective résumé.

ALI-ABA Committee on Continuing Professional Education, www.ali-aba.org; 4025 Chestnut St., Philadelphia, PA 19104; (800) CLE-NEWS or (215) 243-1600. Assists in the development, organization and implementation of educational tools for lawyers, including a satellite broadcast network, publications and live programs.

American Association of Law Schools (AALS), www.aals.org; 1201 Connecticut Ave., NW, Suite 800, Washington, DC 20036; (202) 296-8851. Website lists current faculty as well as faculty, administrative and law library job openings at US law schools. You can also receive these postings through the *AALS Placement Bulletin,* published three times a semester.

American Association for Paralegal Education, www.aafpe.org; PO Box 40244, Overland Park, KS 66204; (913) 381-4458. An association of paralegal educators and institutions of higher learning offering paralegal programs. Publishes an annual directory of members.

American Institute for Law Training Within the Office (AILTO), www.aliaba.org/aliaba/ailto.htm; 4025 Chestnut St., Philadelphia, PA 19104; (800) CLE-NEWS or (215) 243-1614. A project of ALI-ABA in cooperation with the ABA Standing Committee on Continuing Education of the Bar. Assists law firms in establishing in-firm training programs for lawyers.

Association of Continuing Legal Education (ACLEA), www.aclea.org; c/o Donna Passons, Executive Director, PO Box 4646, Austin, TX 78765; (512) 453-4340. Coordinating group for CLE providers (nonprofit and profit-making) across the country. Membership open to bar associations, law schools, legal publishers, for-profit companies, adult education specialists, editors, publishers, marketing and media specialists and in-house educators that present a minimum number of CLE-accredited programs annually. Publishes a quarterly newsletter and holds annual and mid-year conferences, often in conjunction with ABA meetings.

Breaking into the Academy: The 1998-2000 University of Michigan Journal of Race and Law Guide to Programs for Aspiring Law Professors, Gabriel J. Chin and Denise Morgan, editors. Designed to help law students and lawyers break into legal academia. Contains advice on negotiating the application process, references to law teaching organizations and lists of fellowship programs, graduate law degree programs and legal methods teaching programs. For more information or to order, contact Maureen Bishop, Administrative Associate, Michigan Law School Publications Center, B10-C Hutchins Hall, Ann Arbor, MI 48109-1215; (734) 763-6100.

"Campus Legal Posts Sinecures No More: Only top notch and versatile need apply for fun but demanding jobs," Victoria Slid-Flor, *National Law Journal,* August 26, 1996.

Directory of Law School ADR Courses & Programs. See prior listing at page 286.

Directory of Paralegal Training Programs. Available free on the net, accessible state-by-state, or for $15 by mail from the National Federation of Paralegal Associations, www.paralegals.org; PO Box 33108, Kansas City, MO 64114; (816) 941-4000.

Law School Career Services Survey. Detailed job responsibilities and salary information for law school career services employees. Periodically published by the National Association for Law Placement, www.nalp.org.

National Association for Law Placement (NALP), www.nalp.org; 1666 Connecticut Ave., Washington, DC 20009; (202) 667-1666. An organization of law school career services offices and law firm recruiters. Monthly *NALP Bulletin* posts job notices for law school career services positions in every edition. Available in your law school career services office.

National Association of College and University Attorneys (NACUA), www.nacua.org; One DuPont Circle, Suite 620, Washington DC 20036; (202) 833-8390. Attorneys representing about 1,400 US and Canadian college and university campuses in legal matters. You'll find a good summary of the legal issues involved in university representation on their website under the heading "What's New?"

NSBA Council of School Attorneys, www.nsba.org/cosa; 1680 Duke St., Alexandria, VA 22314; (703) 838-6722. About 3,000 members nationwide, primarily private practitioners representing school districts. 35 affiliated state groups. Employment opportunities posted online. Website offers insight into the legal issues facing those who represent school districts.

General Resources:

Academic Employment Network, www.academploy.com. Lists available positions across the country in colleges and primary and secondary institutions for faculty, staff and administrative professionals.

Academic Job Search Handbook, Mary Morris Heiberger and Julia Miller Vick. A practical, step-by-step guide to getting a job in academia. Paperback; University of Pennsylvania Press, 2nd ed. 1996.

American Association for Adult and Continuing Education, www.albany.edu/aaace; 1200 19th St., NW, Suite 300, Washington, DC 20036; (202) 429-5131. A group of administrators and professors involved in adult education programs. Publish three well-respected periodicals on education and training: *Adult Learning* magazine, *Adult Education Quarterly,* and *Adult Basic Education.*

American Association for Employment in Education, Inc., www.aaee.org; 820 Davis Street, Suite 222, Evanston, IL 60201; (847) 864-1999. Publishes the *National Directory for Employment in Education* (a directory of member schools) and the *National Directory of Job & Career Fairs for Educators.*

American Association for Higher Education (AAHE), www.aahe.org; One Dupont Circle, Suite 360, Washington, DC 20036; (202) 295-6440. Membership organization that addresses the needs of individuals and institutions in higher education.

American Association of Community Colleges, www.aacc.nche.edu; c/o National Center for Higher Education, One Dupont Circle, Suite 410, Washington, DC 20036; (202) 728-0200. Website includes job listings at "Careerline" and a membership directory.

American Society for Training and Development. Educators working primarily in corporate environments. See prior listing at page 306.

Careers in Education, Roy A. Edelfelt. Surveys jobs in administration, teaching and social services. Paperback; VGM Career Horizons, 1997.

Chronicle of Higher Education, www.chronicle.com. A weekly publication with an extensive listing of education-related positions (online at /jobs/). Available in many public libraries.

Education World, www.education-world.com. Posts K-12 teaching job openings.

Educator's Job Search: The Ultimate Guide to Finding Positions in Education, Martin Kimeldorf. Paperback; National Education Association, 1993.

Inside Secrets of Finding a Teaching Job, Jack Warner, Diane Warner & Clyde Bryan. How to distinguish yourself from the competition in today's job market. Paperback; Park Avenue Productions, 1997.

Mining's Private School Listings, http://private school.miningco.com/sub7.htm. Links to more than a dozen websites listing private-school job openings worldwide.

National Association of Student Personnel Administrators, www.naspa.org; 1875 Connecticut Ave., NW, Suite 418, Washington, DC 20009, (202) 265-7500. The leading national association for college and university student affairs administrators (like dean of students). Jobs Link announcements online or at (202) 234-2600 (password found on their website).

National Educators Employment Review, www.thereview.com/neer_main.htm. Job announcements nationwide for K-12 teachers, specialists, administrators and superintendents.

On the Market: Surviving the Academic Job Search, Christina Boufis & Victoria Olsen, editors. A collection of articles that reveal successful strategies for getting teaching and research positions in colleges. Offers advice about the value of earning a Ph.D. Paperback; Riverhead Books, 1997.

Teacher Job Links, www.geocities.com/Athens/Forum/2080. Links to national and international teaching jobs; updated weekly. Adding community and technical college openings by November 1998. Also provides information about and references for alternative certification methods.

Training and Development Organizations Directory, Janice McLean, editor. Descriptions of over 2,400 companies that produce workshops, seminars, videos and other programs that contribute to skills enhancement and personal development. Hardcover; Gale Research, 6th ed. 1994.

ENTREPRENEURIAL VENTURES

Practicing Law:
consulting lawyer*
contract or temporary lawyer
partner in a start-up firm
solo practitioner
solo practice with direct client contact
solo practice as consulting expert (e.g., appellate work, subject matter specialist)

Law-Related Service Businesses:
consumer advocate
contract lawyer placement
dispute resolution training
diversity training
ghost-writing and providing legal background for news reports, newspaper & magazine articles, and novels containing legal issues
heirfinder*
legal headhunting
mediation
nonprofit lawyer selection service
private investigation
sexual harassment avoidance training
training in the law for therapists working with divorcing clients

Law-Related Manufacturing Businesses:
do-it-yourself divorce books/software
do-it-yourself probate books/software
do-it-yourself will writing books/software
interactive computer-based legal compliance training program
self-help law book publisher*
legal information to non-lawyers
court coach

Law-Related Design Business:
bankruptcy software
cartoons
legal trivia game*
office space planning
trial exhibits

THE LAWYER-ENTREPRENEUR

Earl expressed a strong entrepreneurial spirit from the moment he left the Air Force in 1973. He put himself through law school by making wind chimes, then founded a general law practice when he graduated and later narrowed it into the first bankruptcy law clinic in his area. In the early 1980's, he decided to get out of law by getting back into crafts. His ceramic Christmas tree ornament business netted close to $100,000 a year. When the market dropped for that product, he designed well-received bankruptcy software for the Macintosh platform, and later, for Windows. Here is his story about becoming an entrepreneur, and his suggestions for how other lawyers can follow in his footsteps:

Earl's Statement: In 1982 I happened to see some ceramic Christmas tree ornaments that appealed to me. I knew nothing about the technique of making them, but I bought one anyway and went around to ceramics stores and crafts outlets, trying to figure out what glaze was used and how the colors were applied.

After hundreds of false starts, I made a small run of my own ornaments. They sold pretty well. The following spring, my wife and I entered ourselves in a gift show and got a sales rep. A few months later, I was already spending far more of my time making Christmas ornaments than practicing law. Ceramics became my first priority. I told the secretaries that if I was on the phone talking about selling the ornaments, I didn't care if a Supreme Court Justice called, everything else went on hold. It got to the point where I was working at the law office only as long as the parking meter would last—120 minutes at a time. I went in and moved through all of my

work as fast as I could. I booked clients every quarter hour. The minute it looked like bankruptcy wasn't an appropriate option, I sent them out the door. I wasn't there serving coffee to people.

I cut out every ounce of dead weight. Every minute at the office was productive so I had big blocks of time to devote to the ornaments. By the Fall, it looked like the business would fly and we packed up our office and left.

Those ornaments gave us a good ride for six years. We were able to make a killing in the crafts business for the simple reason that we regarded it as a business, not a hobby or an artistic endeavor. As in any business, though, you have to keep creating new products in order to survive. I did at first, but then I lost interest. Computer programming hooked me instead.

That's where I was able to combine my legal background with a nonlegal venture. I designed a software program that took all the effort out of bankruptcy filings. It took a while to get the bugs out, but now it's selling well and paying off.

After 25 years of personal experience, I've learned a lot about how lawyers become successful entrepreneurs.

1. Be on the lookout for opportunities. You need to be in the right frame of mind for a fairly long period so that you view opportunities that come your way with a different mind than you would if you were committed to your current position. One of the common fallacies is that if it's such a good idea, why hasn't someone else done it? Look at the converse of that right in the legal profession. How can so many people who are so smart do something that makes them so unhappy?

The reason is inertia, or they don't understand how to implement a change, not that it's a bad idea.

2. Set aside some serious non-law time to coming up with something that will work. Get out of the office and look at ideas. See what's out there. Go to suppliers and see what can be made. Go to stores to see what people are buying. Ask questions.

3. Pick a product or service with a big margin. That way you can make lots of mistakes. It lets you be very generous with everybody. You can treat them to generous terms, give discounts, pay for shipping.

4. Research, research and research some more. If somebody came to you with a contract problem, you would do what you could to understand their business in order to write the contract. With lawsuits, you do the same thing. Why can't you use the same skills for your own benefit?

5. Build your new business little by little. You don't have to shut down your practice and devote all your time to the new. You can see what happens with a smaller effort, then make some hard decisions.

6. Write up a business plan. What do potential customers need? Where do you want to be in three to five years? How can you win the market? Project revenues and expenses.

7. Stop thinking like a lawyer. Lawyers are extremely pessimistic people, always looking for what can go wrong. Business people don't care. Their thinking is, "Try to do it; what have you got to lose?" Consider what you've got to lose, do it and try to minimize the losses.

8. Lawyers are used to delaying gratification. You do it all the time by waiting for the big one to come in the door, or for the next case to settle. You can't do that. Take a lesson from your clients. Get a little flaky. Do it now.

9. Lawyers are aggressive; aggression doesn't work in the business world. It scares people. They think you're pushy. You have to be a nice, honest, hand-shaking sort of person. A good example is contracts. Business people think that contracts are either for sissies or crooks. You don't need contracts unless you're going to pull a fast one on somebody.

10. Lawyers are always obsessed with details. There's no time for that when you're in business. You can't worry about the small stuff. You have to accept and trust people and go with the flow.

Law-Related Retail Businesses:
catalogue sales
law office software

Other Service Businesses:
accounts payable auditing
ballet school
business coach
catering
channeling seminars
consumer advocacy
desktop publishing

film financing
fitness trainer
hair salon
horse trainer
licensing agency
landscape gardener
massage therapist
mountain trek company using llamas
personal fitness trainer
personal growth seminars
self-defense training
seminars

social matchmaker

telemarketing

training and placing hearing and service dogs

venture capital firm

yacht parties

Retail Businesses:

aircraft leasing

automobile dealership

bakery franchise

beach resort

bed-and-breakfast

careers & job-finding resources catalogue

commercial airline

computerized information services

custom pottery painting store

fast food franchisee

fishing tackle and other equipment

frozen yogurt franchise

high-end gadgets

indoor playground for children

jazz club

laundry owner

maps to on-location production sites in Hollywood

multi-level marketing

night club owner

paper ephemera

restaurant chain owner (California Pizza Kitchen)

restaurant owner/operator*

sail boat broker

semi-professional and professional baseball teams

sex boutique

ski resort

small hotel

sofabeds

travel store

Wholesale Businesses:

cattle ranch

evergreen tree farm

horse farm

imported specialty items

paper goods

puka shell products

wine importing

Manufacturing (and Design):

acne drug

alternative baseball magazine

audio and videotape course instruction*

beer

bread

ceramic Christmas tree ornaments

direct mail marketing*

educational and entertainment software

furniture art

jewelry

non-fiction books

organic baby food

records and tapes

restaurant and hotel guides

surfing machine

tennis cards

tomato sauce for pizza restaurants

toy that teaches phonics

video lectures

wine

Law-Related Resources

"Bullish on Spinoffs," Darryl Van Duch, *National Law Journal,* August 10, 1998. An article on the ethical ramifications of nonlegal business subsidiaries operated by law firms including training, real estate, bankruptcy claim recovery, software, public relations and product development.

Flying Solo: A Survival Guide for Solo Lawyers. A 320-page publication in which successful solo practitioners share their methods and systems. Paperback; American Bar Association, 2nd ed. 1994.

How to Start & Build a Law Practice, Jay G. Foonberg. Contains chapters on marketing, automation, client development and relations, and staffing. Hard or soft cover; American Bar Association, 3rd ed. 1991.

Opening a Law Office Handbook, California Young Lawyers Association. Offers step-by-step guidance in topics like client billings, employing staff, office technology and client relations. Available for $25 (check or money

ARE YOU CUT OUT TO BE AN ENTREPRENEUR?

Successful entrepreneurs:

- ☞ Are very realistic;
- ☞ Possess superior conceptual abilities and the broad thinking of a generalist;
- ☞ Bristle against standard operating procedures;
- ☞ Don't make good team players;
- ☞ Are willing to gamble their own money on a great idea;
- ☞ Like to get something going much more than maintaining it once it's established;
- ☞ Possess above-average energy and persistence;
- ☞ Often neglect their personal lives;
- ☞ Will readily "steal" the ideas of others and improve upon them;
- ☞ Invest in substantial market research before launching their business;
- ☞ Are highly ethical and trustworthy;
- ☞ Are confident enough to make mistakes . . . and often do!

order made payable to the State Bar of California) from CYLA, 555 Franklin Street, San Francisco, CA 94102; (415) 561-8833.

"Outsourcery," Penny Arevalo, *House Counsel,* Fall 1996. An article on the ethics of in-house legal departments contracting out research to legal research businesses.

"Owning Your Own Firm: Is It for You?," Edna R. S. Alvarez and Demetrios Dimitriou, *ABA Journal,* May 1990.

The Compleat Lawyer. Published quarterly by the General Practice Section of the ABA. Includes a practice management section addressed to solo practitioners.

Running a Law Practice on a Shoestring, Theda C. Snyder. Cost-cutting techniques for the thrifty or new practitioner. Paperback; American Bar Association, 1997.

General Resources

Creative Cash: How to Profit from Your Special Artistry, Creativity, Hand Skills and Related Know-How, Barbara Brabec. Includes a resource chapter of 200 of the best arts-and-

crafts marketing resources. Annually updated. Paperback; Prima Publishing, 1998.

Entrepreneur and Small Business Marketing Problem Solver: An Encyclopedic Reference & Guide, William Cohen. How to introduce, price and sell products and services. Paperback; John Wiley, 2nd ed. 1990.

Generation E: The Do-It-Yourself Business Guide for Twentysomethings and Other Non-Corporate Types, Joel and Lee Naftali. Helps you develop a blueprint for a perfect business with a directory of 300 business ideas and other entrepreneurial start-up advice. Paperback; Ten Speed Press, 1997.

Growing a Business, Paul Hawken. The founder of Smith and Hawken, a mail-order garden supply company, discusses the fundamental ethical questions everyone should ask when starting a business. Profiles successful businesses like Ben & Jerry's, Esprit and Patagonia. Highly-rated. Paperback; Simon & Schuster, 1987.

Homemade Money: How to select, start, manage, market and multiply the profits of a business at home, Barbara Brabec. An entrepreneur's survival guide with over 100,000 copies in print. Paperback; Betterway Publications, 5th ed. 1997.

Running a One Person Business, Claude Whitmyer and Salli Rasberry. Covers topics such as time management, marketing and financial strategies. Paperback; Ten Speed Press, 1994.

Service Corps of Retired Executives (SCORE), www.score.org. A group of over 12,000 volunteer retired business professionals with an average of 35 years experience who provide free business counseling, e-mail consulting, workshops and other assistance. 400 chapters in 750 locations nationwide. Contact their website, the SBA office in your area or your local telephone directory for the location of the office nearest you.

Small Business Administration (SBA), www.sba.gov. Federal government assistance for America's small businesses. The website offers extensive information organized at www.sba.gov/map.html. Scroll down to Opportunities, Online Library and Starting, Financing and Expanding Your Business. You can also find the address and phone numbers of local offices on that page under Local Information and SBA offices. You can also access the SBA Resource Centers; these offices offer a wide-range of assistance to entrepreneurs through publications and videotapes on all aspects of starting and running a small business, workshops and the latest computer technology, computer databases, tutorials and interactive media. You'll find locations online, in your local telephone directory, or by phoning (800) 827-5722. SBA Small Business Development Centers provide personal one-on-one counseling to entrepreneurs who cannot afford the services of a private consultant, education, seminars, conferences, networking, and reference books. 1,000 locations at college campuses across the US. Check their website or your local telephone directory for the Development Center nearest you.

Small Business Profiles. A guide to top opportunities for entrepreneurs. Paperback; Gale Research, 3rd ed. 1999.

Start-Up Guide: A One-Year Plan for Entrepreneurs, David H. Bangs, Jr. Step-by-step instructions in workbook form to help you create a timetable for organizing a business. Paperback; Dearborn Trade, 1996.

Working Solo: The Real Guide to Freedom & Financial Success with Your Own Business, Terry Lonier. Paperback; John Wiley & Sons, 1998.

Working Solo Online, www.workingsolo.com. A website for current or future solo business people. Includes access to the *Working Solo Sourcebook,* a guide to 1,200 business resources.

ENVIRONMENTAL

Practicing Law:
environmental lawyer in private practice
environmental specialist for government
environmental specialist for in-house corporate legal department
litigator for environmental public interest group
real estate lawyer for preservationist organization

Law-Related Positions:
environmental and energy policy manager for corporation
environmental consulting*
environmental policy analyst
environmental protection specialist*
environmental regulation/compliance analyst
landman*
negotiator for preservationist organization

Non-Legal Positions:
managing director of multinational alternative energy company
recycling coordinator for local government*
secretary, Environmental Regulation Department
waste reduction and recycling supervisor for local government*
waste management planning*

Law-Related Resources

American Association of Professional Landmen, www.landman.org; 4100 Fossil Creek Boulevard, Fort Worth, TX 76137; (817) 847-7700. A group of law school graduates and others who negotiate mineral rights and exploration agreements for energy companies. Maintains a private job bank listing service for members only.

Careers in Natural Resources and Environmental Law, Percy R. Luney, Jr. In 300 pages, this publication discusses preparation and opportunities for advancement in the field. Paperback; American Bar Association, 1987.

Directory of Environmental Attorneys, published by Prentice Hall (now Aspen) Law & Business and issued annually until 1994.

Environmental Law Careers Directory. Lists private law firms, as well as nonprofit organizations and government agencies, providing opportunities for the environmental lawyer. Annually updated. Available for $10 from the Ecology Law Quarterly, Simon Hall Room 493, Boalt Hall School of Law, University of California, Berkeley, CA 94720; (510) 642-0457.

Natural Resources and Environment. A quarterly magazine on the latest developments in the field published by the American Bar Association Natural Resources, Energy and Environmental Law Section.

General Resources

Careers in the Environment, Michael Fasulo & Paul Walker. Paperback; VGM Career Horizons, 1995.

Econet, www.econet.apc.org/econet/. Links to environmental activity on the net. You can obtain access to their environmental job postings (found on their web page under Econet Resources) by joining their parent organization for a small fee.

Envirolink, www.envirolink.org. An online environmental community. Website includes

"green internships" and "green dream jobs" in consulting, universities and at the executive, mid-career and entry levels.

Environmental Career Opportunities Newsletter, www.ecojobs.com; (800) 315-9777. You can get samples of their advocacy, policy and education job announcements on the Web but you have to order the newsletter to get all the listings.

Gale Environmental Sourcebook, Donna Batten, editor. Full contact information about over 8,000 environmental organizations, information services, programs and publications. Hardback; Gale Research, 2nd ed. 1994.

Opportunities in Environmental Careers, Odom Fanning. Covers such fields as land use and urban planning, along with more technical positions. Paperback; VGM Career Horizons, 1996.

The Environmental Career Guide: Job Opportunities with the Earth in Mind, Nicholas Basta. A thoughtful overview of the environmental field. Paperback; Wiley, 1991.

The Job Seeker, www.tomah.com/jobseeker; 28672 County Rd EW, Warrens, WI 54666-9501; (608) 378-4290. A newsletter of environmental jobs, careers and business opportunities in 1,000's of companies, professions, nonprofits and government agencies throughout the US.

The New Complete Guide to Environmental Careers, edited by John Cook & Bill Sharp of the Environmental Careers Organization. Describes jobs and gives advice about getting them. Paperback; Island Press, 1993.

ETHICS

Practicing Law:

complaint audit and review for bar association defense counsel
disciplinary proceedings prosecutor for bar association*
state bar court staff

Law-Related Positions:

associate director, AMA division on medical ethics
bioethicist*
business ethics instructor
corporate or governmental ethics officer
ethics officer*
ethics professor at law school
ethics instructor or professor at collegiate level

Law-Related Resources

Academy of Legal Studies in Business. JD's who
teach ethics (among other subjects) in the
university setting. See prior listing at page 313.

Association of Professional Responsibility
Lawyers, c/o Kirsten Dell, Administrator, 150
E. Wilson Bridge Rd., Suite 200, Worthington,
OH 43085; (614) 436-2750. A young but
fast-growing organization of consultants,
teachers and practitioners in attorney
discipline, ethics and risk management.

Careers in Ethics & Professional Responsibility. A
section of *JD Preferred* (see prior listing at
page 264) available for separate purchase.
Looseleaf; Federal Reports, Inc., 1996.

*Directory of Lawyer Disciplinary Agencies and
Client Protection Funds,*
www.abanet.org/cpr/disciplinary.html. A
state-by-state listing put together by the ABA
Center for Professional Responsibility

"Playing God," California Lawyer, November
1989. An article on bioethicists.

The Professional Lawyer. A quarterly magazine
produced by the ABA Center for Professional
Responsibility that examines professionalism,
regulation and ethical issues impacting the
legal profession.

General Resources

Applied Ethics Resources on WWW,
www.ethics.ubc.ca/resources. Links to ethics
websites in the fields of healthcare, business,
high technology, environmental, media,
animal welfare, professionals and more.

Association for Practical and Professional Ethics,
http://php.indiana.edu/~appe/home.html;

618 E. Third St., Bloomington, IN 47405;
(812) 855-6450. An organization of scholars
and professionals interested in practical and
professional ethics. Profiles in Ethics online
offers a comprehensive list of member ethics
centers.

Council on Governmental Ethics Laws,
www.cogel.org; 10951 W. Pico Blvd.,
Suite 120, Los Angeles, CA 90064; (310)
470-6590. An organization for government
agencies, organizations and individuals with
responsibilities or interests in governmental
ethics, elections, campaign finance, lobby
law and open public meetings and records
regulation. Individual associate membership
available. Publishes guidebooks to such
governmental ethics issues as campaign
finance, lobbying and freedom of information.

FOUNDATIONS AND NONPROFIT ORGANIZATIONS

Practicing Law:

directing attorney
director of law firm pro bono work
director of legal affairs
director of legal project
fundraising counsel
litigation coordinator
special counsel to the president
staff attorney
staff researcher
supervising attorney*

Law-Related Organizations:

legal foundations
legal services offices
public defender offices
public interest law centers

Law-Related Positions:

development officer*
director of development
director of education, effective incarceration
project

GETTING INTO NONPROFIT WORK

The road from law school or law practice to nonprofit employment is a relatively easy one: Just be a committed volunteer. Catherine worked as both a legal services lawyer and solo practitioner in Michigan before moving into nonprofit management. Here is her story, and her advice about making your own transition.

Catherine's Statement: All the time I practiced law I was angry. I was angry when my clients were evicted. I was angry when my clients were arrested (even though they were usually guilty). I was even angry when I managed to protect a client, or get a good result for one, because I knew that my clients needed money or a social worker a lot more than they needed me. Before long, I realized that practicing law was encouraging certain, maybe primal, anger in me. It encouraged me to be fairly pugnacious about almost everything. I wasn't sleeping well. I worried about my clients; but I worried more about losing.

At the same time that I was practicing law, I was volunteering at the local animal shelter. I started out cleaning kennels, working in the front office, doing anything and everything the staff asked me to do. I put in a lot of time and made it clear that I was willing to learn. Eventually, I was asked both to sit on the Board of Directors and to do some legal research on antivivisection statutes for a number of national organizations. I came away from all of those experiences feeling up, excited and almost never being angry or losing any sleep.

Opportunity knocked when the current executive director resigned and there was an opening. I was on the search committee and as I reviewed candidates, I realized that none

of them were as well-qualified as I thought I was. So I resigned from the Board and applied for the job. They had known me for several years and liked me, as well as my credentials. It was a small organization without a lot of credibility in the community and they thought my legal background would boost their image.

They hired me. It was an easy transition in some ways, but a difficult one in that I had to give up a dream. I was the youngest of seven children of an immigrant family. My family was very proud of my accomplishments and that felt really good. I also liked the idea of being empowered as a professional, of having the opportunity not only to earn a good living but to do something important. I had to leave that dream behind when I made the transition. Even now, I have some misgivings when I look at my paycheck, but never when I look at my life.

Only in retrospect, though, do I feel bad. My work in animal welfare has always been very absorbing. I started out with strong feelings for animals and their welfare. But I didn't know much about running a business, or about animals, and I had to learn very fast. I spent two years at the humane society in Michigan. That gave me the background to get a position as executive director of a much larger, very prestigious and influential humane society in California.

Some of the things I do in my current job I could not do as well if I had not been to law school or practiced law for five years. I negotiate contracts with dealers for fleet automobiles, with counties and cities to provide animal services, and with private citizens for the purchase and sale of property. I deal with lawyers on trust and estate issues. I talk to legal groups about encouraging clients to provide for animal welfare organizations in their estate planning. I work on planned giving programs. One of the skills I use most often from practicing law is problem solving, looking at issues and developing a strategy. At the same time I find the experience significantly different from practicing law because I am working with a team within a community effort.

Being connected to an organization or a cause is essential to getting a job in a nonprofit. I would be very suspicious if I got a résumé from a lawyer I didn't know. I would suspect the applicant was a self-centered, egotistical, difficult person who was trying to escape to something less stressful. It would be different if the person had volunteered for our organization and I could see that he was a genuinely committed person with good people skills on top of being well-educated. You need to volunteer, get on the board, offer to help free of charge so that you have a relationship with a particular organization or the substantive community. At least three-quarters of the executive directors of nonprofits in my area volunteered for those organizations before their appointment. It's the single most important key to getting a paid position.

director of governmental relations
director of national training project
director of planned giving*
director or assistant director
executive director
freelance development/fundraising assistant
government relations assistant
intake worker
legal information answer line coordinator*
legal outreach program developer*
organizer for law-related organization
pro bono foundation (IOLTA) administrator
pro bono foundation (IOLTA) director*
program developer*

Non-Legal Positions:
administrator of small agency
campaign director
CEO of public policy think tank
consumer advocate
director
director of awards programs
director of the National Endowment for the Arts
director of planning
director of private family charitable foundation
eligibility investigator for the NCAA
executive director*

founder & executive director of nonprofit
    focusing on dating violence prevention
fundraiser*
grant writer*
organizer
Outward Bound facilitator
president, amateur athletic foundation
president, regional trade association
project director
publications director for theater
public information officer
regional coordinator
regional director
secretary of the Smithsonian Institution
vice-president, community relations
vice-president, donor and board relations
wish director for Make-A-Wish Foundation

Law-Related Resources
ABA Awards and Grants Listing. A 1997, 28-page guide to seed moneys available from the ABA including sponsoring entity, description, criteria, eligibility, application deadline and contact information.
American Civil Liberties Union (ACLU), www.aclu.org; national office, 125 Broad St., 18th Floor, New York, NY 10004; (212)

549-2599. Read about current constitutional issues or locate the affiliates in your state on their award-winning website.

Directory of Public Interest Law Centers. 200 public interest law centers indexed by state and subject area. Last update 1996. To order, mail a check for $10 to the Alliance for Justice, www.afj.org; 2000 "P" St., Suite 712, Washington, DC 20036; (202) 822-6070.

"Full-Time Do-Gooders a Rarity But on the Rise," Wendy R. Leibowitz, *National Law Journal,* August 19, 1996. An article about the move for larger law firms to employ one lawyer on a full-time basis to seek out, assign and supervise pro bono representation.

Lawful Pursuit: Careers in Public Interest Law, Ronald W. Fox. An overview of career paths in public law firms, nonprofit organizations and private law firms. Paperback; American Bar Association, 1995.

National Clearinghouse for Legal Services, Inc. Website, www.nclsplp.org. Links to other legal services and bar association websites.

National Association for Public Interest Law (NAPIL), www.napil.org; 2120 "L" St., NW, Washington, DC 20037; (202) 466-3686. A national coalition of student groups from about 80 percent of all ABA-approved law schools. Publishes *NAPIL Public Interest Career Resources Guide* and the *Yale Law School Public Interest Fellowships Guide.*

National Conference of Bar Foundations, www.abanet.org/barserv/ncbf/home.html; c/o American Bar Association, Division for Bar Services, 541 N. Fairbanks Court, 14th Floor, Chicago, IL 60611; (312) 988-5354. You'll find a list of member foundations online.

National Legal Aid & Defender Association, www.nlada.org; 1625 "K" St. NW, Suite 800, Washington, DC 20006; (202) 452-0620. Publishes the *Directory of Legal Aid and Defender Offices in the US* biennially (last ed. published June 1998). Employment opportunities are listed in *NLADA's Cornerstone* newsletter, published quarterly.

PIES (Public Interest Employment Services) Job Alert! Nationwide job listings in public interest law published the second and fourth Tuesday of each month. Call the Public Interest Clearinghouse, 100 McAllister Street, 2nd Floor, San Francisco, CA 94102-4929; (415) 255-1714, for current price information.

Public Service JobNet, www.law.umich.edu/ academic/opsp/jobsalert. An online database of public interest jobs by location, practice area, eligibility and type of position.

The Public Interest Job Search Guide: Harvard Law School's Handbook & Employer Directory for Law Students & Practitioners Seeking Public Service Work. Issued annually, provides information about finding and applying for public interest positions, and includes directories of public interest fellowships and employers. Contact the Public Interest Office, www.law.harvard.edu/students/opia/pig.htm; Harvard Law School, Pound Hall, Room 328, Cambridge, MA 02138; (617) 495-3108, for current ordering information.

General Resources

ACCESS: Networking in the Public Interest, www.communityjobs.org; 1001 Connecticut Ave., NW, Suite 838, Washington, DC 20036; (202) 785-4233. This nonprofit organization offers career consulting and job leads to those interested in working for nonprofits. Publishes *Community Jobs: The National Employment Newspaper for the Non-Profit Sector,* a subscription job register updated monthly with hundreds of job-listings from nonprofit organizations around the country. Also features resource lists, book reviews and profiles of nonprofit organizations. Available online, in college career centers, public libraries and other referral centers.

American Society of Association Executives (ASAE), www.asaenet.org; 1575 Eye St., NW, Washington, DC 20005; (202) 626-2734. A professional society of paid executives of national, state and local trade, professional and philanthropic organizations. Publishes *Who's Who in Association Management*. Offers a certified association executive program, and other education on effective association management. Their website includes a "Careers in Associations" page that describes types of jobs and salaries.

America's New Foundations 1998: The Source Book on Recently Created Philanthropies. Provides contact information and an overview of 3,500 private, corporate and community foundations created since 1990 with assets or annual giving of $100,000 or more. Paperback; Soho Press, Inc., 12th ed. 1997.

Annual Directory of Grant Support 1998: A Directory of Funding Sources. Hardcover; R.R. Bowker, 31st ed. 1997.

"Asking for a Fortune," Susan E. Tifft, *Working Woman,* November 1992. An excellent article on opportunities in planned giving and development work.

Associations Yellow Book: who's who at the leading US trade and professional associations. Profiles more than 1,175 associations with budgets over $1 million. Lists their headquarters and branches, board of directors, committees and chairs, PACs, foundations and publications, including editors.

CareerOpps: Association/Nonprofit Jobs, www.careeropps.com/newsltrs.htm. A website sponsored by ASAE (see above) offers information on career paths in associations, including salary surveys. Posts CEO and senior staff job announcements.

Careers for Dreamers and Doers: A Guide to Management Careers in the Nonprofit Sector, Lilly Cohen and Dennis Young. An anthology of articles with a practical focus on employment opportunities and career profiles in such areas as philanthropy, fundraising, marketing and service providers to the sector. Paperback; The Foundation Center, 1989.

Careers for Good Samaritans and Other Humanitarian Types, Marjorie Eberts and Margaret Gisler. An overview of opportunities in social service, government, healthcare, religious organizations and volunteering. Paperback; VGM Career Horizons, 1998.

Chronicle of Philanthropy. A biweekly periodical on the nonprofit and fundraising fields.

Corporate Foundations Profile. Information on 195 of the largest US corporate foundations. Hardback; The Foundation Center, 10th ed. 1998.

Corporate Giving Yellow Pages 1998: Guide to Corporate Giving Contracts, Laura Wisner-Broyles, editor. Contact names and numbers for more than 3,900 corporate giving programs and corporate foundations. Paperback; Taft Group, 13th ed. 1997.

Council on Foundations, www.cof.org; 1828 "L" St., NW, Suite 300, Washington, DC 20036; (202) 466-6512. This association of grant-making foundations and corporations publishes a membership list, newsletter and journal. Their website offers information on foundation basics.

Cyberhound's Guide to Associations and Nonprofit Organizations on the Internet, Amanda M. Moran. A huge directory of internet sites for over 2,500 nonprofit and professional associations. Available in most public libraries. Hardback; Gale Research, 1997.

Doing Well by Doing Good: The First Complete Guide to Careers in the Nonprofit Sector, Terry McAdam. A highly recommended book which evaluates the attraction of and suitability to nonprofit employment, provides an overview of options, profiles those working in the area, and outlines preferred skills and education for obtaining employment. Hardback; Fundraising Institute, 1991.

Essential Information, www.essential.org. Links to nonprofit organizations.

Foundation Center's Guide to Proposal Writing. Includes sample proposals and advice for pre-proposal planning. Paperback; The Foundation Center, 2nd ed. 1997. You can find an abbreviated version of this book online at www.fdncenter.org.

Foundation Directory. A detailed listing of the 8,600 largest US foundations, annually updated. Hardback; The Foundation Center, 1998.

Foundation Directory Part 2. Provides contact information for 4,900 mid-sized foundations. Hardback; The Foundation Center, 1998.

Goodworks: A Guide to Careers in Social Change, edited by Donna Colvin. A national directory of over 1,000 nonprofit organizations, their staff positions and salaries. Paperback; Barricade Books, 5th ed. 1994.

Goodworks, www.essential.org/goodworks/ jobs/map.html. Job listings from the national public interest community. You can also access www.essential.org for other information about public interest organizations.

Guide to US Foundations: Their Trustees, Officers and Donors. A two-volume source of data on all active grant-making foundations, over 40,000. Paperback; Foundation Center, 1997.

Jobs and Careers With Nonprofit Organizations: Profitable Careers in Nonprofits, Ronald L. Krannich. Advice in selecting a role in and finding jobs in the nonprofit sector. Paperback; Impact Publications, 1998.

National Committee on Planned Giving, www.ncpg.org; 233 McCrea St., Suite 400, Indianapolis, IN 46225; (317) 269-6274. A group of those involved in fundraising, accounting, estate planning and insurance who specialize in developing charitable gifts through bequests, trusts, annuities, life insurance and real estate. Operates local groups. Publishes the *Directory of Counsel Members.*

National Directory of Corporate Giving. 2,900 corporate foundations and direct-giving programs. Includes names of key personnel. Hardback; The Foundation Center, 5th ed. 1997.

National Directory of Nonprofit Organizations 1998. Provides annual income figures and contact names and numbers for over 250,000 organizations with annual income of $25,000 or more. Paperback in 3 volumes; Soho Press, Inc., 1997.

National Society of Fundraising Executives, www.nsfre.org; 1101 King St., Suite 700, Alexandria, VA 22314; (800) 666-FUND or (703) 684-0410. Contact information for 145 local groups listed online. Publishes the *ESS Employment Opportunities Newsletter,* available only to members, the *NSFRE Fund-Raising Dictionary* (definitions for 1,400 terms used in the fundraising field) and other books about the industry. Offers courses like "First Course on Fund-Raising" as well as certification in fundraising.

Nonprofit Entrepreneur: Creating Ventures to Earn Income, edited by Edward Skloot. How nonprofits can launch successful enterprises without compromising their missions. Gives you ideas about marketing new programs you could be paid to run. Paperback; The Foundation Center, 1988.

Non-Profits & Education Job Finder 1997-2000, Daniel Lauber. Lists over 2,200 resources in education, social services, legal aid, the arts, advocacy, environment, religion, research, fundraising, foundations, housing, community development, public interest, child care, adult care, disabilities, museums and other specialties. Paperback; Planning Communications, 1997.

Society for Nonprofit Organizations, http://danenet.wicip.org/snpo; 6314 Odana Rd., Suite 1, Madison, WI 53719; (800) 424-7367 or (608) 274-9777. Publishes bimonthly *Nonprofit World,* a leadership and management magazine for the nonprofit sector. Articles on the legal, legislative, marketing, fundraising and planning aspects of nonprofit management online.

Successful Grantsmanship: A Guerrilla Guide to Raising Money, Susan L. Golden, Alan

Schrader, editors. Paperback; Jossey-Bass, 1997.

The Foundation Center, www.fdncenter.org; 79 Fifth Ave., New York, NY 10003; (800) 424-9836 or (212) 620-4230. A national nonprofit clearinghouse of information on foundations, grants and corporate giving. Maintains an extensive resource library in New York, fully-staffed branch libraries in San Francisco, Washington, Atlanta and Cleveland, and 180 cooperating collections nationwide. Their online library includes a short course on proposal writing as well as regional and international directories.

GOVERNMENT

Practicing Law in the Federal Jurisdiction:
administrative law judge in agency or department*
attorney advisor
circuit mediator for US Court of Appeals*
deputy general counsel, US Sentencing
    Commission*
deputy US attorney
federal public defender
Judge Advocate General (JAG) in any military
    branch, active or reserve*
staff attorney in agency or department
technology licensing
US Attorney
US trustee in bankruptcy*

Practicing Law in State Jurisdiction:
administrative law judge
attorney general
chief legal counsel for State Ethics Board
condemnation specialist
deputy attorney general
deputy chief counsel for coastal commission
hearing officer for agency or department
legislative analyst
probate referee
program advisor
staff attorney for agency or department

Practicing Law in Local Jurisdictions:
chief or supervising public defender
city attorney
city or county council legal advisor*
deputy city attorney
deputy district/prosecuting attorney
deputy public defender
district/prosecuting attorney
hearing officer or administrative law judge*

Law-Related Positions:
ADA investigator*
bank fraud investigator*
child support enforcement case analyst
claims officer
code research analyst (a.k.a. code reviser)*
commissioner, anti-discrimination commission
community relations coordinator*
complaint investigator
condemnation specialist
congressional aide*
contract compliance administrator*
crime prevention coordinator
criminal investigator
deputy planning commissioner
director of Capital Punishment Resource Center
director of ethics commission
director of human relations commission*
elected official
ethics officer
executive assistant to Director of Natural
    Resources
forensic investigator
human relations coordinator for Office of
    Women's Rights
immigration inspector
insurance regulation analyst*
international or interstate trade relations
    specialist*
investigation & resolution specialist*
land use examiner*
legal documents officer
legal investigator
legislative director
lobbyist

FINDING OUT ABOUT GOVERNMENT AND INSTITUTIONAL JOB VACANCIES

Many government jobs are not posted in public, or they are posted long after the hiring person has already informally decided who is going to get the job. As in all other job searches, therefore, it's better to access the system from within.

One successful government job finder called his contacts "inside" every two weeks to find out about upcoming openings. If you have advance notice that there is about to be an opening, you can set up an introductory interview with the hiring person. Sometimes, the job is one that did not previously exist and the agency has to get budgetary approval to add it to its permanent employment roster. Someone may have the temporary position now and not want to

continue as a permanent employee. Or, you might approach the department soon enough to be hired for the temporary slot, taking the chance that approval for permanent funding will be forthcoming and you'll be the one who gets the job.

You can identify those in the agency who might be helpful and keep in regular contact with them, or religiously check public job announcements. Until you develop contacts on the "inside," work the outside by checking postings every Monday or Friday. Most jobs are advertised for only two weeks. Within that time, you must spot the posting, prepare your application, line up any necessary references and get your papers filed in the right place.

Medicaid/Medicare fraud investigator
member of Labor Relations Board
ombudsman
postal inspector*
program advisor*
public disclosure commission director*
purchasing agent*
regulation analyst
research staff for congressional committee
retail application analyst for state lottery
supervisor of public trust accounts*
victim's compensation investigator or advocate*
waste fraud abuse

Non-Legal Positions:
bus driver
campaign manager*
city/county clerk
city manager*
city parks landscape laborer
director of commission or agency
director of human relations commission*
elected official

executive director of the governor's council on
    disabilities
fund-raiser
human services project manager
mail carrier
mayor
special project administrator

Law-Related Resources
Air Force Attorney Recruiting Office,
    www.jagusaf.hq.af.mil. Contact Capt. James
    Durant at (800) 524-8723.
American Association of Public Welfare
    Attorneys, www.aphsa.org/affiliat/affiliat.htm;
    810 First St. NE, Suite 500, Washington, DC
    20002; (202) 682-0100. A division of the
    American Public Human Services Association.
    Provides a forum at the national, state
    and regional levels for discussion of legal
    matters pertaining to public welfare on their
    website at www.aphsa.org/netforum/
    lawyers/a.cgh/1.
Army Civilian Attorney Program; Recruiting

Office, (703) 588-6773. Ask for Mr. Roger Buckner.

Army JAG Corps Recruiting & Placement Office, www.jagcnet.army.mil/recruit.nsf. Contact Capt. Toby McCoy at (800) 336-3315.

Department of Justice, www.usdoj.gov/careers/ oapm. Posts current job openings in US Attorney offices nationwide and in DC.

Federal Job Application (SF-171) Instruction Kit. Includes 41-page *Guidelines for Completing the SF-171 ("Application for Federal Employment")* designed for lawyers, sample completed SF-171, blank application forms, information on the Federal Senior Executive Service (SES) and SES application procedures, and a Federal Job Information Center list. Pamphlets and forms; Federal Reports, Inc.

Federal Law-Related Careers. Job descriptions and contact information for over 140 positions in the US government that are not designated "attorney" but which require a strong legal background. Paperback; Federal Reports, Inc., 3rd ed. 1994.

Lawyers Job Bulletin Board, www.fedbar.org. Monthly job listings in federal government nationwide, plus occasional other job tips, published by the Federal Bar Association, 1815 H St., NW, Suite 408, Washington, DC 20006; (202) 638-0252. Fee subscription only.

Marine JAG Recruiting Office, www.usmc.mil/JA; (703) 614-1242.

Military Lawyers Conference, www.abanet.org;govpub/milcon1.html. An organization of active, reserve and retired military lawyers. Annual conference held in conjunction with the American Bar Association annual meeting. Publishes a newsletter, *Reveille.* Membership through the Government & Public Sector Lawyers Division of the American Bar Association, 740 15th St., NW, Washington, DC 20005-1022.

Most Frequently Asked Questions about the Navy Judge Advocate General Corps, www.finifter.com/jag/jag-faql.html.

Navy JAG Recruiting Office, c/o Officer Recruitment Program, www.navykc.com/ oprogrm; (800) 634-9407. Information about both law student recruitment and direct commissions for experienced lawyers.

Now Hiring: Government Jobs for Lawyers, edited by Abbie W. Thorner. A directory of agencies that hire lawyers. Geared to law students, or entry-level positions in the executive, legislative and judicial branches, and in independent agencies of federal government. Paperback; American Bar Association, 1995.

State and Local Law News. A quarterly newsletter published by the ABA State and Local Government Law section.

The OF-612 and Resume-Plus Kit: New Federal Job Application Procedures Kit for Attorneys. Federal government hiring practices changed in 1995. This resource explains the new procedures. Looseleaf; Federal Reports, Inc.

US Coast Guard Direct Commission Lawyer Program, www.uscg.mil/hq/g-lgl/lpd/dc/index. Information about requirements and application procedures, as well as duties, salary and assignments.

Contact city attorney offices. Established— sometimes with outside counsel—in all incorporated communities. Call personnel/human resources office for current job openings and application procedures.

General Resources

Army Civilian Personnel Online, www.cpol.army.mil/home.

Career America Connection. A telephone system of worldwide federal job opportunities. Online information and application packages mailed to you. Salaries and employee benefits information. Special recruitment messages. Available worldwide 24 hours a day, 7 days a week. Phone (912) 757-3000.

Complete Guide to Public Employment, Ronald and Caryl Krannich. A comprehensive collection of information on public employment, including advice on shifting government skills

SPECIAL HELP FOR FEDERAL JOBS

All governmental systems tend to be complex and hard to access. But as the federal government has grown larger, its application processes have become even more complicated and confusing.

The federal government provides some assistance in the form of Career America Connection, the US government's official employment information service. You can dial (912) 757-3000 or get the local access number by checking your local telephone directory under "Personnel Management Office automated telephone-based system, local access." You'll reach an automated information service through which you can investigate current job openings by title, at your educational level, in your area, nationally, or in certain broad job categories. You can also find out about application procedures and request employment forms.

Similar information can be obtained online at FedWorld Information Network or the Office of Personnel Management Website (see addresses in this section's resources).

Be sure to request a description of hiring practices from any agency that interests you. You'll want to know whether they hire directly or use the central registry; whether they handle vacancies through one nationwide personnel office or separately in each region, district or city; and about any current openings.

Because of the complexity of the federal system, many businesses have developed to help you find openings and comply with filing procedures. You'll find references to those groups in this section's listings.

---

into related nonprofit and private organizations. Paperback; Impact Publications, 3rd ed. 1994.

Congressional Staff Directory. Provides detailed information about all congressional offices, including biographies of all congressmen. Updated semi-annually. Paperback; Staff Directions, Ltd., 53rd ed. 1998.

Congressional Yellow Book: who's who in congress, including committees and key staff. Fully updated quarterly publication provides current contact information on all Senate and House officials, including committees, task forces and key staff as well as information on resignations and retirement.

County Directory. A semiannual listing of significant employees of 3,100 counties, boroughs and parishes in the US. Available in most libraries in hardcover or on the Carroll Publishing Company webpage, www.carrollpub.com.

Directory of Federal Jobs & Employers, Ronald and Caryl Krannich. Job hotlines and contact information for personnel offices in agencies in all three branches of federal government. Paperback; Impact Publications, 1996.

Federal Career Opportunities. Biweekly listings of federal job openings nationwide, arranged by occupational group and GS series. Available for a fee from Federal Research Service, Inc., 370 Maple W., Vienna, VA 22183; (703) 281-0200 or (202) FED-JOBS.

Federal Directory. A bimonthly listing of all legislative, judicial and executive branch employees available in most libraries in hardcover or on the Carroll Publishing Company webpage, www.carrollpub.com.

Federal Jobs Digest. A bimonthly newspaper listing all current federal job vacancies in the US and abroad. The publisher claims that this list is not available from any single government source. Telephone

(800) 824-5000 to order.

Federal Regional Yellow Book: who's who in the federal government's departments, agencies, military installations, and service academies outside of Washington, DC. Twice yearly updates of federal decision-makers nationwide.

Federal Regulatory Directory. Provides organizational charts, employee listings, publications, projects, authority of all federal regulatory agencies. Hardcover; Congressional Quarterly, 8th ed. 1996.

Federal Yellow Book: who's who in federal departments and agencies. Lists over 40,000 federal officials, including executive offices, cabinet-level federal departments, 70+ independent agencies and appointed officials.

FedWorld Information Network, www.fedworld.gov. Job postings from the federal government.

GovBot, http://eden.cs.umass.edu/Govbot/. The Center for Intelligent Information Retrieval's site provides access to nearly 850,000 US government and military websites. Friendly search screen and single-page help/tips file.

Government Job Finder 1997-2000, Daniel Lauber. Cites over 2,000 books, newsletters, job listings and other resources to help you locate jobs in local, state and federal government. Paperback; Planning Communications, 3rd ed. 1997.

Great American Website, www.uncle-sam.com. The best, the newest and most useful federal information website.

Military Facilities Directory. A semiannual listing of information about military installations throughout the US. Available in most libraries in hardcover or on the Carroll Publishing Company webpage, www.carrollpub.com.

Municipal Directory. A semiannual listing of significant employees of 7,800 cities and towns in the US. Available in most libraries in hardcover or on the Carroll Publishing Company webpage, www.carrollpub.com.

Municipal Yellow Book: who's who in the leading city and county governments and local authorities. Lists names, titles, addresses, telephone and fax numbers of elected and administrative officials of the largest 100 cities and counties.

Office of Personnel Management Website, www.usa.jobs.opm.gov/a.htm. Lists all current federal government openings handled through OPM.

Official Congressional Directory 1997-98. An annually updated resource, listing biographies of all members of Congress, committee assignments, diplomatic offices and representatives, the executive branch and the judiciary. Paperback; Bernan Press, 1997.

State Directory. A bimonthly listing of legislative, judicial and executive branch employees from all 50 states. Available in most libraries in hardcover or on the Carroll Publishing Company webpage, www.carrollpub.com.

State Yellow Book: who's who in the executive and legislative branches of the 50 state governments. Quarterly publication lists current administrators and legislators at all levels of state government. Includes DC and the four insular US territories.

Personnel/human resources office in your city, county seat or state capitol will have information about current job openings, upcoming state professional and attorney examination dates, and application procedures.

HEALTHCARE

Practicing Law:
in-house hospital lawyer
managed care attorney*
medical malpractice lawyer
outside counsel for healthcare organization

Law-Related Positions:
bioethicist
compliance officer

TIPS FOR GETTING INTO HOSPITAL LAW

Suzanne Mitchell, former assistant dean for Career Services at the University of Chicago Law School, spent many years as a hospital lawyer before entering career services, and returned to that milieu in 1998. She cautions those aspiring to this work to expect an extremely tight and demanding market. Most hospitals will not hire inexperienced law school graduates because they are:

- too small to devote any resources to training a new lawyer;
- too busy to hire anyone who needs supervision or orientation; and
- too under-funded to maintain an adequate library for the lawyer who needs to research before issuing an answer.

Consider the following positions as a career path into a hospital position, says Mitchell:

- a law firm with a healthcare, general corporate, medical malpractice, labor and employment, tax or real estate practice;
- federal or state health, human services, or social services agencies;

- managed care companies;
- insurance companies;
- nonprofit organizations with a health and human services focus.

In addition, consider:

- volunteering in a hospital legal office, or health-related agency (e.g. providing legal advice at a clinic for AIDS patients, working at Planned Parenthood);
- joining the American Health Lawyers Association (see reference under law-related resources);
- joining local, state and national associations with sections that pertain to health law;
- applying for law-related positions like human resources manager, regulatory compliance, or grants, contract or risk management.

"One last bit of advice," says Mitchell. "The healthcare field is not the place for people who like to master a body of law in a relatively short period of time. This is an area where the issues—political, legal, economic and ethical—change rapidly."

---

director of corporate integrity & compliance
editor for health law digest
healthcare licensing manager
managed care specialist
risk management advisor*
telephone triage trainer

Management Positions:
assistant to the president of a community
 hospital
hospital administrator
marketing director for private health-care
 provider
vice-president, corporate finance

Other Positions:
massage therapist
veterinarian

Law-Related Resources
The Health Lawyer. A periodic newsletter
 published by the ABA Health Law Section on
 current trends in health law.
American Health Lawyers Association,
 www.healthlawyers.org; 1120 Connecticut
 Ave., NW, Suite 950, Washington, DC 20036;
 (202) 833-1100. An organization of health
 lawyers and their clients formed in a merger
 of the National Health Lawyers Association

and the American Academy of Healthcare Attorneys. Website includes a national job bank and links to other related websites.

General Resources:

American Academy of Medical Administrators, www.aameda.org; Congress Building, 30555 Southfield Rd, Suite 150, Southfield, MI 48076; (248) 540-4310. An umbrella organization for administrators in managed care, healthcare information, home health, oncology and cardiovascular clinics. Publishes *AAMA Executive,* a bimonthly newsletter which contains advertisements for administrative positions.

American Association of Health Plans, www.aahp.org; 1129 20th St., NW, Suite 600, Washington, DC 20036; (202) 778-3200. National trade association for HMO's, PPO's and other network-based plans. Publishes *Healthplan Magazine* containing articles about healthcare trends and *Managed Care Careers* newsletter which contains ads for directors, executives and administrators in sales, marketing, research, projects and personnel. You can order a free sample copy of the newsletter on their website.

American College of Healthcare Executives, www.ache.org; 1 N. Franklin St., Suite 1700, Chicago, IL 60606; (312) 424-2800. Publishes *Career Mart: Executive Employment Newsletter* with 200+ ads for open positions monthly; subscriptions available to members only. You can find sample positions online by clicking on Career Mart. A career services section on their website is accessible only to members.

American Medical Group Association, www.amga.org; 1422 Duke St., Alexandria, VA 22314; (703) 838-0033. A group of about 200 medical groups nationwide that focus on the business aspects of medical group practice.

Exploring Healthcare Careers: Real People Tell You

What You Need to Know, edited by David Hayes. Two volumes and 944 pages of information about careers in medicine, medical technology, hospice work, healthcare management, acupuncture, nursing, therapy and more. Hardback; Ferguson Publishing, 1997.

Healthcare Financial Management Association, www.hfma.org; 2 Westbrook Corporate Center, Suite 700, Westchester, IL 60154; (708) 531-9600 or (800) 252-HFMA. An organization of CEOs, CFOs, controllers, patient accounts managers, information management specialists, consultants and others involved in the financial management of integrated health systems and other healthcare organizations. You'll find national job announcements on their website.

JobBank Guide to Health Care Companies. A guide to over 2,500 health care employers. Paperback; Adams Media, 1998.

Modern Healthcare, www.modernhealthcare.com. A weekly newsmagazine covering federal and state legislation and regulations, political activity and financial news of interest to healthcare organizations. Available from Crain Communications, 740 N. Rush St., Chicago, IL 60611; (312) 649-5341.

Medical & Health Information Directory, K. Bottden, editor. Organizations, agencies, institutions, services and information sources in medicine and health-related fields. Hardcover; Gale Research, 1996.

Planning Your Career in Alternative Medicine, Dianne Lyons. A how-to and resource guide to degree and certificate programs in massage, homeopathy and other alternative medical fields. Paperback; Avery Publishing Group, 1997.

Plunkett's Healthcare Industry Almanac 1997-98, Jack Plunkett. Profiles 500 firms and discusses career trends, job opportunities and types of careers. Paperback; Plunkett Research, www.plunkettresearch.com, 1996.

INTERNATIONAL

Practicing Law:
immigration lawyer
international transactions lawyer
in-house counsel for multi-national company
US counsel for foreign companies or investors

Law-Related Positions:
business agent for import/export company*
executive director, International Development
    Law Institute
international trade development
international trade services (duty drawback;
    country-of-origin verification & ISO 9000
    consultation)
legal translator for foreign law firm
underwater diver planner

Non-Legal Positions:
adventure travel leader
bicycle tour organizer and leader
foreign service officer
international or interstate trade relations
    specialist*
leader of scuba diving trips to Southeast Asia
managing director of an alternative energy
    company
program developer for trade education
    foundation

Law-Related Resources
ABA Guide to Foreign Law Firms, edited by James
    R. Silkenat & Howard B. Hill. Contains listings
    of law firms in over 90 foreign jurisdictions.
    Spiral bound; American Bar Association,
    1993.
American Immigration Lawyers Association,
    www.aila.org; 1400 Eye St., NW, Suite 1200,
    Washington, DC 20005; (202) 216-2400. A
    group of lawyers who specialize in assisting
    families and businesses with immigration
    issues. Website includes information about
    immigration law and a chapter index.
American Society of International Law,

www.asil.org; 2223 Massachusetts Ave., NW,
    Washington, DC 20008; (202) 276-2400.
    Publishes the *1998 International Law Career
    Guide* with information on international
    careers in human rights, international trade,
    environment, telecommunications, finance &
    banking, international development and
    dispute resolution. Also publishes an annual
    membership directory.
Careers in International Law, edited by Mark W.
    Janis. Covers basic considerations for anyone
    contemplating a career in international law.
    Describes preparation needed in various
    sectors, and suggests means to obtain
    specific jobs. Paperback; American Bar
    Association, 1993.
Directory of Opportunities in International Law,
    edited by Rasmani Bhattacharya. This
    directory lists domestic and international law
    firms with international practices,
    government opportunities in international
    law, and educational programs. Organized by
    state and country. Available for $20 ($10 for
    students) through John Bassett Moore
    Society of International Law, University of
    Virginia School of Law, Charlottesville, VA
    22901; (804) 924-3087.
International Lawyer's Newsletter. A 24-36 page
    bimonthly issue-oriented publication for
    lawyers interested in international law. Each
    issue contains job announcements, and
    references to international employment
    placement agencies. For more information,
    contact Kluwer Law & Taxation Publishers,
    www.kluwerlaw.com; 675 Massachusetts
    Ave., Cambridge, MA 02139; (617)
    354-0140.
International Lawyer. A quarterly journal
    produced by the ABA International Law and
    Practice Section. Contains articles for lawyers
    with an interest in international business
    transactions, public international law, and
    comparative law.
Martindale-Hubbell International Law Directory. A
    4-volume listing of 8,000 firms and 100,000

WORKING ABROAD

Ahhh, the romance of a job overseas. Wouldn't it be nice to study French for six years, catch the travel bug on a post-college tour of Europe, and snag a job in a French law firm upon graduation from law school? It's a wonderful fantasy, but far from the reality of obtaining international positions.

The most common way for a law school graduate to work abroad as a lawyer is to get hired by the international law department of a large, big city law firm and be assigned to a foreign locale for a year or so. European placements out of New York City and Asian placements out of Los Angeles, San Francisco and Seattle, are customary under those circumstances. If you practice any place else, finding well-paid work in a foreign country will be a tremendous challenge.

Notice that I said "well-paid" work. Most law school graduates without a law firm or business affiliation who end up working abroad start out with volunteer work, internships or acting as interpreters for foreign law firms. One graduate of the University of South Carolina School of Law who was fluent in French and Spanish got a job in Italy by offering to work unpaid to get the experience, telling them she was going to be living there anyway. A University of Texas graduate obtained a position in a German law firm translating English contracts into German and vice versa. She could not practice law, and as a result, her position was low paid with no prestige, but she did gain valuable experience in the international arena.

If you really want to practice law abroad and aren't qualified for employment with the international law department of a major US firm or the in-house legal department of a multinational company, move to the country of your choice and start making contacts!

lawyers in 150 countries who work in international law.

Public Service and International Law: A Guide to Professional Opportunities in the US and Abroad. Good inside scoop on hiring practices of such employers as the UN, the World Bank and many government agencies. Available for $30 by calling (617) 495-3108. Paperback; Yale & Harvard Law Schools, 3rd ed. 1998.

General Resources

Careers in International Affairs, GU School of Foreign Service. A 320-page resource guide to international careers. Paperback; Georgetown University Press, 1996.

Directory of American Firms Operating in Foreign Countries. Hardcover 3 volumes; Uniworld Business Publications, Inc., 15th ed. 1998.

Foreign Service Exam. Contact The State Department, Recruitment Division - FSWE, PO Box 12226, Arlington, VA 22219, for information about testing dates and requirements.

How to Get a Job in Europe, Robert Sanborn. Over 450 pages of detailed information, including 12 specific steps to take, the easiest jobs to find and the least promising areas, country-by-country listings of temporary and summer jobs, how to use international placement agencies and more. Paperback; Surrey Books, 3rd ed. 1995.

Human Rights Organizations and Periodicals Directory 1998. Describes 1,100 organizations and periodicals dealing with civil rights issues worldwide. For more information, contact Meikeljohn Civil Liberty Institute (website due in 1999), PO Box 673, Berkeley, CA 94701-0673; 510-848-0599.

International Career Employment Center, www.internationaljobs.org. A biweekly publication listing over 600 open positions with international health and welfare organizations, state governments, universities, federal agencies, government contractors, corporations involved in international trade and finance, export management firms, engineering companies, associations, foundations, student exchange organizations and international government agencies including the UN. Also includes profiles of major employers. Available on the website or by subscription from The Carlyle Corp., 1088 Middle River Road, Stanardsville, VA 22973; (804) 985-6444 or (800) 291-4618.

International Job Finder: Where the Jobs Are Worldwide, Sue Cubbage & Marcia Williams. Contains references to online databases, résumé banks and databases of employers plus advice on visas, work permits and other practical tips. Paperback; Planning Communications, 1998.

International Jobs Directory: 1001 Employers and Great Tips for Success!, Ron and Caryl Krannich. Contact information for international employers including businesses, government agencies, executive search firms, associations, research institutes, consulting firms, universities and other international organizations. Paperback; Impact Publications, 1998.

International Jobs: Where They Are, How to Get Them, Eric Kocher. A comprehensive guide (over 500 opportunities listed) to careers in law firms, businesses, publishing and more. Paperback; Perseus Press, 1993.

Jobs in Paradise: The Definitive Guide to Exotic Jobs Everywhere, Jeffrey Maltzman. Lists more than 100,000 jobs in the US, Canada, the Caribbean and other countries that allow Americans work permits. Shows how to find jobs and the perks and drawbacks of each job. Paperback; Harperperennial, 1993.

National Council for International Health, www.ncih.org; 1701 K St., NW, Suite 600, Washington, DC 20006; (202) 833-5900. Publishes *Career Network,* a monthly job bulletin listing positions worldwide with such organizations as the International Red Cross, Peace Corps, CARE and WHO. Get it on their website or by mail.

Now Hiring! Jobs in Asia, Jennifer DuBois, Steve Gutmann and Clarke Canfield. Seasonal and year round employment in Japan, Taiwan and South Korea. Paperback; Perpetual Press, 1994.

Now Hiring! Jobs In Eastern Europe, Clarke Canfield. A guide to working and living in the Czech Republic, Hungary, Poland, and Slovakia. Paperback; Perpetual Press, 1996.

Ulrich's International Periodicals Directory 1998. Annually updated. Available in most libraries. Hardcover; R. R. Bowker, 36th ed. 1998.

United Nations Website, www.un.org. Current employment openings are posted at www.un.org/Depts/OHRM/.

Work Abroad, Clayton Hubbs & Jason Whitmarsh. The publishers of *Transitions Abroad* magazine offer advice and resources on all aspects of international work. Paperback; Transitions Abroad Publishing, 1997.

JUDICIARY

Possible Jurisdictions:
county trial court system
federal court of appeals
federal district court
government agency or department
municipal or small claims court
state appellate court system
US Supreme Court

Positions Practicing Law:
central research staff*
staff attorney*
hearing officer or administrative law judge
judge or justice

SWITCHING CELLS

A seat on the bench is an attractive way to avoid many of the stresses that plague the general practitioner. Although some attorneys forsake high incomes for an appointment to the judiciary, judges still earn comfortable salaries and in most jurisdictions receive generous retirement benefits. They never have to worry about billing clients or collecting fees, nor about rising overhead. The cases judges decide have beginnings, middles and ends that generally occur over the span of a few days. Most importantly, they exercise the power to bring closure to those conflicts.

The choice to move to the bench is not, of course, available to every practicing lawyer. The lawyer must either be well-respected among those with the power to make appointments, or capable of waging a campaign and winning an election for the seat. More significantly, judges must find enough value in the adversarial system to tolerate sitting in the middle of argument and hostility. And, they must learn to endure constant public scrutiny, second-guessing and criticism.

Judge Smith entered the profession at a time when there were few women lawyers, and female litigators were even rarer. In defense against anonymity, she resorted to wearing loud hats and eccentric clothing in court, and brandishing her advocacy like a weapon. But as her legal reputation grew, she gradually relaxed and started each lawsuit in a novel fashion: by agreeing with opposing counsel to avoid mutual hostility. Eventually, she wearied of private practice. After four years of active lobbying, she was appointed to the state trial court bench.

Judge Smith's Statement: Back in 1970, the senior partner of the firm I joined said to me, "Someday you're going to be on the bench." I laughed it off because that was not what I saw for myself. I saw myself as a fire-breathing litigator.

In my first four years of practice, it was my goal to do every kind of proceeding and action at least once. What I ended up enjoying most was the trial work. As a woman lawyer in the early 1970's, I didn't have many examples to follow. At one extreme, there were women lawyers in title companies, and at the other, there was "Bernice the Bitch." By the time I was ready to go out on my own, I decided that if I had to choose one image, I'd be like Bernice, which in those days meant being pretty abrasive and strident. But remember. Back then, a woman got run over if she didn't throw down the gauntlet right away.

I worked horrendous hours, because when men opposed me (which was almost all the time) they tended to prepare harder. They took it very personally if they lost a case to a woman, as if it was somehow a challenge to their manhood. Fortunately, as my reputation preceded me, men expected a female barracuda, and I could afford to be nicer.

As I became more experienced, the first thing I would do in almost every major case was to take the opposing counsel to lunch. I spent half the time talking about the case and the other half speaking personally, finding out whether the lawyer was married and had kids, what his hobbies were, what other pressures he might be experiencing in addition to the case we had in common, and how all these factors might affect the progress of our case. If possible, I'd make a little pact to avoid hostility between us even as we advocated the clients' hostilities.

As the years went by though, I noticed that attorneys were becoming less and less cooperative. There was no such thing as settling a case over a cup of coffee. It was all so stress-producing that I used to come home like a helicopter setting down. I was all wired up, outraged and upset. In time, all that combat steered me into the judiciary.

I still feel the wear and tear of the adversarial system. In fact, the hardest adjustment in moving to the bench was shedding the adversarial role. As a judge, you have to sit back and wait for the other side to wage their attack. With my background as a litigator, that was difficult. I would listen to one side's arguments and force myself not to cut in and say, "Well what about this?" and "What about that?" and Gee, haven't you considered this, this and this?" I had to

consciously jump back from an adversarial orientation to become the decider. That's turned out to be the best thing about being a judge—the opportunity to do what I think is right. And, in some ways, it's the worst too, because it is an awesome challenge.

There are downsides to being a judge. First of all, the loneliness of the judiciary is not overrated. I'm definitely more restricted in my public interaction, having to watch what I say about everything. I'm never sure if some inadvertent statement I make is going to end up being lambasted on the front page of the newspaper.

All in all, though, I find this very satisfying. My years on the bench have been the best of my life.

justice of the peace
law clerk
court commissioner/magistrate*
pro-tem judge
supervising staff attorney

Law-Related Positions:
bankruptcy administrator
bankruptcy case administration manager
bankruptcy examiner
circuit mediator*
court administrator
court clerk
court interpreter*
director of training for judicial district*
guardianship clerk
probate clerk

Law-Related Resources
ALJ Handbook: An Insider's Guide to Becoming a Federal Administrative Law Judge. Describes the examination process and contains tips on completing the application documents, negotiating the different examination

elements, key qualification factors, how agencies select from the register, average scores for each exam component and what happens if an offer is rejected. Paperback; Federal Reports, Inc., 3rd ed. 1997.

"An Uncomfortable Distance: Being a judge often means choosing between what society expects and what life has to offer," Barbara L. Morgenstern, ABA Journal, July 1994.

BNA's Directory of State and Federal Courts, Judges and Clerks 1998, compiled by Judith A. Miller. A state-by-state and federal listing of names and contact numbers for all judicial staffs. Paperback; BNA, 1997.

Council of Appellate Staff Attorneys (CASA), www.abanet.org;jd/casaweb.html. A subdivision of the Judicial Division of the American Bar Association, consisting of about 300 lawyers who work as permanent staff lawyers for appellate courts nationwide. Publishes the CASA Quarterly, a newsletter, and a Directory of Appellate Central Staff Counsel.

Federal and State Judicial Clerkship Directory.

Application procedures, hiring criteria and
employment opportunities for hundreds of
federal and state court judges. Paperback;
National Association for Law Placement,
annually updated.

Federal Judiciary Home Page, www.uscourts.gov.
Posts employment opportunities online for
many, but not all, federal courts. Also
publishes *The Third Branch,* a monthly
newsletter which includes periodic inserts
that announce vacancies in magistrate and
judicial positions.

Judicial Fellows Program. One-year appointment
working on projects concerning the federal
court system and the administration of
justice. Requires 2+ years professional
experience with a record of high
performance. Paid as federal employee.
Application deadline mid-November every
year. Contact the Administrative Director,
Judicial Fellows Program, Room 5, Supreme
Court of the US, Washington, DC 20543;
(202) 479-3415.

*Judicial Yellow Book: who's who in federal and state
courts.* Profiles more than 2,000 federal
judges and 1,200 state appellate court
judges, as well as complete staff for each
judge's chambers, and administrative staff for
each court.

National Association of Administrative Law
Judges, www.aalj.org. Nonprofit group
dedicated to promoting the legal education,
training and professional standing of social
security administrative law judges. Members
include anyone appointed to the position of
administrative law judge. Website offers links
to social security offices, federal courts, and
other related sites.

National Association of Hearing Officials,
www.aphsa.org/affiliat/nahopage.htm. An
affiliate of the American Public Human
Services Association consisting of attorney
and non-attorney hearing officials, ALJ's and
managers in the resolution of human
services-related administrative matters.

National Conference of Appellate Court Clerks,
www.ncsc.dni.us/NCACC; 300 Newport
Avenue, PO Box 8798, Williamsburg, VA
23187; (757) 253-2000. An organization of
court administrators. Publishes a bimonthly
newsletter.

"So You Want to Become a Federal Judge by
35?," Alex Kozinski, *National Law Journal,*
August 19, 1996.

Want's Federal-State Court Directory 1998, edited
by Robert S. Want. Lists federal, state, and
local judges, attorney general offices and
more for all 50 states and Canada.
Paperback; Want Publishing Co., 1997.

Contact state and local bar associations. Often
publish membership directories which
include current listings of court personnel.

LABOR UNIONS

Practicing Law:
grievance counsel for union member
in-house labor counsel for employer
in-house lawyer for labor union
outside counsel for labor union
outside counsel for employer

Law-Related Positions:
administrator/manager
labor mediator
labor negotiator*
union representative*

Law-Related Resources:
Careers in Labor Law, Ellen Wayne. Describes
options in the labor law field, typical duties of
labor lawyers, and sources for more
information from both management and
labor perspectives. Paperback; American Bar
Association, 1985.

*Directory of Subscribers to the AFL-CIO Lawyers
Coordinating Committee.* A state-by-state
listing of counsel, both private and in-house,
for the AFL-CIO. Available only to member
attorneys (those who verify by letter that

50 percent or more of their practice consists of union-side representation).

General Resources

Directory of US Labor Organizations, edited by Courtney Clifford. 200 national unions, professional and state employee associations engaged in labor representation. Paperback; Bureau of National Affairs, 1998.

Encyclopedia of Associations, "Section 15: Labor Unions, Associations and Federations." Over 200 national collective bargaining groups listed. Hardback; Gale Research, annual.

LAW ENFORCEMENT

Practicing Law:
criminal defense lawyer in private practice
criminal prosecutor
department legal advisor
law enforcement legal advisor*
legal counsel to sheriff's office
public defense lawyer

Law-Related Positions:
CIA agent
court bailiff
customs inspector
DEA agent*
FBI agent
fines, penalties and forfeiture specialist
immigration inspector
juvenile justice
ombudsman
parole officer
police administration
police officer
postal inspector
special agent with the Department of Justice (customs, narcotics, US Marshall service, border patrol, secret service)
state patrol chief

Law-Related Resources
Association of Trial Lawyers of America (ATLA),

www.atlanet.org; 1050 31st St., NW, Washington, DC 20007; (202) 965-3500. An organization of lawyers, law professors and law students interested in criminal defense advocacy. Publishes an annual directory of members and various journals. Affiliated regional associations operate nationwide.

Criminal Justice. A quarterly ABA magazine providing practical treatment of aspects of criminal law.

National Association of Criminal Defense Lawyers, www.criminaljustice.org; 1025 Connecticut Ave., NW, Suite 901, Washington, DC 20036; (202) 872-8600.

National Directory of Prosecuting Attorneys. Identifies prosecuting attorneys and assistant prosecuting attorneys nationwide, as well as providing a guide to each state's prosecution system. Published annually. Available for $50 ($35 to members) from the National District Attorneys Association, www.ndaa-apri.org; 99 Canal Center Plaza, Suite 510, Alexandria, VA 22314; (703) 549-9222.

National Legal Aid & Defender Association, www.nlada.org. An organization of public defense organizations. See prior listing at page 325.

General Resources
100 Best Careers in Crime Fighting: Law Enforcement, Criminal Justice, Private Security & Cyberspace Crime Detection, Mary Price Lee, Richard S. Lee, Carol Beam & Carol Dilks. In-depth descriptions of career areas, employment opportunities, earnings and education & training requirements. Paperback; Macmillan, 1998.

Federal Jobs in Law Enforcement, Ross Smith, Ph.D. Lists job descriptions, activities of each office, how to qualify and where to apply. Paperback; Macmillan, 1996.

Guide to Law Enforcement Careers, Donald B. Hutton & Anna Mydlarz. Paperback; Barron's, 1997.

LAW FIRMS

Positions Practicing Law:
contract (temporary or freelance) lawyer*
department manager
managing attorney
managing partner
non-equity partner
participating attorney
partner
partnership-track associate
of counsel
public, pro bono or public service counsel
referral attorney
regional partner
senior attorney
staff attorney
special counsel

Areas of Practice:
administrative
adoption*
agricultural
alternative-dispute resolution
antitrust
appellate
banking
bankruptcy
biomedical issues
bond
business organization
commercial finance
commercial litigation
commercial banking
communications
computer
constitutional
construction*
copyright
corporate
corporate reorganization
disciplinary action by licensing boards
discrimination
domestic relations
elder*

employee benefits
employment
employment relations
energy
entertainment
environmental
estate planning
family*
franchising
general practice
governmental relations/ lobbying
guardianship
healthcare
immigration*
insurance
insurance defense*
intellectual property*
international finance
international
labor
litigation
lobbying
matrimonial*
mergers & acquisitions
natural resources
patent
pensions
probate
public contracts
public utility
real estate
social security
sports
taxation*
trademark
transportation
trust
workers' compensation

Law-Related Positions:
client services manager*
director of business development*
director of client relations
director of legal information services*
director of management and

INTELLECTUAL PROPERTY LITIGATION: A "GENTLY ADVERSARIAL" PRACTICE

Many lawyers who tire of conflict and hostility neither want to nor feel able to walk away from the profession. Concerned that they give their career every consideration, they trade one job for another within the profession until they find the right niche. Some move from private practice to public practice or corporate counsel; others from one area of law to another. With enough exploration and persistence, many settle into a less adversarial alternative.

Tom made two mistakes in getting his legal career off the ground. First, he went to law school before he was ready to make a commitment to the profession. Then, when he finally decided to take his degree seriously, he accepted the first job he was offered without exploring whether the subject matter, or style of his employer, suited his talents and personality. As a result, he was pigeonholed for five years in an intolerable environment. Only through a series of lucky breaks did he finally discover a specialty he now finds thoroughly enjoyable.

Tom's Statement: I went to law school without any expectation of ever practicing. I just wanted to stay out of the Army. Once I accomplished that, I didn't take my career seriously until almost 10 years later.

When I got married, I approached a solo practitioner for a job as an associate. I walked in, said "Here I am," and he said, "Okay. You're hired." The next four years consisted of a series of emergencies. It was Band Aid law; I was always patching up this guy's mistakes. I learned a little bit about all of his work, mostly personal injury lawsuits with some real estate, probate and misdemeanors thrown in. But I never felt comfortable with any of it.

Once, I quit to write science fiction for a few months. For the first time in years, I felt I was doing the right thing. But then we needed money and I didn't know how else to earn it. So I went back to work for him again. By the time I left for good, I had two children and didn't see fiction writing as a viable option to support them. Instead, I advertised in the legal newspapers for work assignments from other attorneys, set up an office in my home and waited for the calls to come in.

Rather than generating freelance work, the advertisement led to my next job. A three-person firm handling a huge patent case was facing three firms on the other side and was dying for help. I joined them on a provisional basis to write responses to summary judgment motions. They liked my work so well that I was asked to join the firm.

That was where law opened up for me. There was a whole new area to explore—patents, copyrights, trademarks—and I was pleasantly surprised to discover how well it suited my style. The litigation moves more slowly. Writing is very important. Cases are often won on the briefs I produce.

I worked for six years as part of that firm. Now, I do the same kind of work as an independent contractor for one of the partners, but the bulk of my practice is with my own clients. I emphasize "own," because this is where the satisfaction comes: from making the decisions, being the one in charge, taking the risks and reaping the rewards myself.

I still consider getting out of law every once in a while. The last time was about a year ago when we were in the middle of a big trade secrets lawsuit. The case took on a terribly combative tone, and it drove me crazy. At first, it was horrible waking up Monday morning. Pretty soon I contracted "Sunday Syndrome," dreading Monday when I awoke on Sunday. Eventually, the only good time of the week was Friday night because I still had all of Saturday before I felt that dread of heading back to the office again.

Other lawyers might crave winning; speaking the loudest and the most quickly to get the judge to believe them. But that's not for me. I've set limits now on my practice. When I accept a big litigation case, I associate a trial counsel to handle the things I don't like, leaving me to do what I enjoy most: the client contact, research, motion and appeals practice, being the lead counsel. My practice is gently adversarial and scholarly, and I no longer feel any pressing urge to flee.

legal information services
director of practice development
director of professional development*
director of training (clerical/paralegal)
firm manager
in-house corporate communications
in-house editor*
law firm administrator*
law librarian*
legal assistant manager
marketing manager*
paralegal/legal assistant
personnel director
professional development training officer*
public relations director
recruiting administrator/director*
strategic planner

Law-Office Management Resources

Altman Weil Pensa Website,
www.altmanweil.com. Articles available online on law firm management topics like strategic planning and human resources.

Altman Weil Pensa's Survey of Law Firm Economics, www.altmanweil.com. An overview of median salaries nationwide for law firm support staff. Annually updated.

Association of Legal Administrators,
www.alanet.org; 175 E. Hawthorn Parkway, Suite 325, Vernon Hills, IL 60061-1428; (847) 816-1212. Local chapter contacts listed on their website. ALA Management Connections offers a nationwide job bank, accessible

online at www.alanet.org/jobs/index.html, or by 24-hour voice mail at (708) 445-6777. Also offers Career Talk, a series of career development articles. Publishes the *Biographical Directory of Legal Administration Professionals.*

Law Partnership: Its Rights and Responsibilities, George H. Cain. Offers advice on drafting an effective agreement, legal requirements in the relationship of partners to associates, potential difficulties brought by dissolution and retirement. Paperback; American Bar Association, 1995.

Law Practice Management section of the American Bar Association, www.abanet.org/lpm/home.html. One of the better organized and most active sections of the ABA. Publishes the excellent *Law Practice Management* magazine.

"Legal Administrators: Can a Lawyer Run a Law Firm as Well as an Administrator Can?," *National Law Journal,* May 3, 1993.

Making Partner: A Guide for Law Firm Associates, Robert M. Greene. Includes a five-year plan for making partner and a list of questions to ask prospective employers. Paperback; American Bar Association, 1992.

"Managing Partner: The Tender Trap," Mike France, *National Law Journal,* February 6, 1995.

National Law Firm Marketing Association, www.legalmarketing.org; 401 N. Michigan Ave., Suite 2200, Chicago, IL 60611; (312)

245-1592. Maintains a job bank of marketing positions. Publishes *Strategies: The Journal of Legal Marketing, The View from Within: A National Survey of Legal Marketing Directors* and the *1996 Compensation & Benefits Survey.*

"The Quality of Life Among Legal Administrators, Sylvia Lurie, *Legal Management,* September/October 1994.

Survey of Legal Recruitment & Attorney Management Personnel. Job responsibilities and salaries of legal recruitment administrators and legal personnel directors. Photocopied; National Association for Law Placement, 1996.

Subject Matter Specialty Resources

American Bar Association, www.abanet.org; 750 N. Lake Shore Dr., Chicago, IL 60611; (312) 988-5522. Special interest sections and committees include administrative law & regulatory practice; affordable housing and community development law; air and space law; antitrust; business law; children and the law; communications law; construction industry; criminal justice; disability law; dispute resolution; domestic violence; entertainment and sports industries; family law; franchising; general practice; health law; individual rights and responsibilities; intellectual property law; international law and practice; labor and employment; law practice management; legal problems of the elderly; litigation; natural resources, energy and environmental law; public contract law; public utility, communication and transportation law; real property, probate and trust law; science and technology; state and local government law; tax; and tort and insurance practice. Many sections and committees publish periodic newsletters and journals. You'll find complete information on the ABA website.

"A Niche in Time," Kate Callen, *California Lawyer,* May 1996. Developing an off-beat specialty can be a smart survival tactic.

Guide to Law Specialties. Descriptions of the day-to-day work of lawyers in a wide variety of practice fields. Discusses typical cases, skills required and career paths. Paperback; National Association for Law Placement, 1996.

National Law Journal. Publishes periodic special pullout sections on various specialty areas (e.g., sports law, intellectual property, corporate law, employment law, technology).

Careers in Admiralty & Maritime Law, Robert M. Jarvis. Basic information about this practice field. Pamphlet; American Bar Association, 1993.

Air and Space Lawyer. A quarterly newsletter on significant developments in the field produced by the ABA's Air and Space Law Section.

Lawyer-Pilots Bar Association, www.lpba.org; PO Box 685, Poolesville, MD 20837; (301) 972-7700. For lawyers who are licensed pilots or engaged or interested in aviation law. You can find names of regional and state chapter leaders on their website.

Antitrust. A magazine on developments in antitrust law produced three times a year by the ABA's Antitrust Law Section.

Arts & Entertainment. See resources at pages 289 and 293.

National Association of Bond Lawyers, www.nabl.org; 1761 S. Naperville Rd. Suite 105, Wheaton, IL 60187 (630) 690-1135. Lawyers involved with state and municipal bond work. Website includes a job service and interactive news groups.

American Association of Attorney-CPAs, 24196 Alicia Parkway, Suite K, Mission Viejo, CA 92691; (714) 768-0336. Publishes an annual membership directory and a quarterly newsletter, *The Attorney-CPA.* To join, must be licensed both as a lawyer and a CPA, or be licensed in one and in the process of obtaining a license for the other.

Business Law Today. A bimonthly magazine produced by the ABA Business Law Section.

Features substantive articles, lifestyle pieces on being a business lawyer and practice forms.

Directory of Bankruptcy Attorneys. Annually issued until 1995; discontinued thereafter. Past editions may be available in law libraries or career services offices.

Communications. See resources at page 293.

National Academy of Elder Law Attorneys, Inc., www.naela.org; 1604 N. Country Club Rd., Tucson, AZ 85716; (520) 881-4005. Lawyers nationwide with practices involving estate planning, probate and guardianship, nursing home placement, public benefits planning, trusts, healthcare and other issues involving legal services to the elderly and disabled. Publish *NAELA Experience,* a registry of members, including areas of expertise, and a law and aging series of pamphlets.

"With Longer Lives, A Field of Legal Need," Robert W. Stock, *New York Times,* August 29, 1996. An article on the expected growth of elder law.

National Employment Lawyers Association, www.nela.org; 600 Harrison St., Suite 535, San Francisco, CA 94107; (415) 227-4655. An organization of over 3,000 lawyers who represent employees in employment discrimination, wrongful termination, employee benefits and other actions against their employers. Promotes professional development of members through networking, publications, technical assistance and education. NELA affiliate organizations nationwide.

Entertainment and Sports Lawyer. A quarterly newsletter of the ABA Entertainment and Sports Industries Forum.

Environmental. See resources at p. 321.

Family Law. See resources at p. 308.

Healthcare. See resources at p. 333.

American Association of Nurse Attorneys, www.taana.org; 3525 Ellicott Mills Drive #10, Ellicott City, MD 21043; (410) 418-4800. Acts as an employment network and assists new nurse attorneys. Publishes quarterly *Inside TAANA* and annual membership directory. Chapter directory online.

Labor Unions. See resources at p. 340.

Probate and Property. A bimonthly magazine aimed at lawyers who devote a large part of their practice to real estate law or wills, trusts and estates. Published by the American Bar Association.

School Law. See resources at page 312.

Directory of Intellectual Property Attorneys. Annually issued until 1995; discontinued thereafter. Past editions may be available in law libraries or career services offices.

Section of Taxation Newsletter. A quarterly publication of the ABA Taxation Section. Updates current tax developments and reports on work of the section.

Transportation Lawyers Association, PO Box 15122, Lenexa, KS 66285-5122; (913) 541-9077. Publishes biennial roster of members (available to members only) and *Transportation Lawyer* five times annually.

American College of Trust & Estate Counsel, www.actec.org; 3415 S. Sepulveda Blvd., Suite 330, Los Angeles, CA 90034; (310) 398-1888. A national group of 2,700 lawyers who have been invited to be members due to their high standards of practice. Check their website for links to trust and estate related websites.

Complete Guide to Contract Lawyering: What Every Lawyer & Law Firm Needs to Know About Temporary Legal Services, Deborah Arron & Deborah Guyol. How to hire and work with, and how to practice as, a lawyer on a temporary or freelance basis. Paperback; Niche Press, 2nd ed. 1999. See order information at end of this book.

"Full-Time Do-Gooders a Rarity But on the Rise," Wendy R. Leibowitz, *National Law Journal,* August 19, 1996. An article about the move for larger law firms to employ one lawyer on a full-time basis to seek out, assign and supervise pro bono representation.

THE LAWYER TYPES

Here's a simple sort mechanism to help students identify an initial career direction, and lawyers evaluate how well suited they are to the practice of law. Begin by answering these three simple questions:

1. *Are you more drawn to issues involving people and human behavior, or to financial, technical, scientific or business matters?*

2. *Are you more excited by solving problems or analyzing issues?* "Problem solvers" prefer the practical; "analyzers" the theoretical. "Problem solvers" like to focus on concrete issues with a good chance of closure. "Analyzers" prefer to explore complex issues; they often don't care if they find an absolute answer or conclusion as long as they've evaluated the situation thoroughly and correctly.

3. *Do you prefer to communicate and investigate orally or through the written word?* This is usually the hardest to answer, since most who choose law school enjoy communicating and are proficient both orally and in writing. Ask yourself which comes more easily to you. As a law student, thriving in the library or when you prepare class notes is a good clue that you tend to prefer writing. Enjoying your study group experiences or loving moot court and clinical education classes means you're happier when you're talking. In practice, if you most enjoy tasks like meeting with clients, talking on the telephone, attending depositions and appearing in court, you probably prefer oral communication and investigation. If instead, you'd rather be researching and writing briefs, composing letters and

settlement proposals, and communicating by e-mail, you'd prefer written communication. You might also ask yourself whether your best ideas and insights emerge when you're speaking or when you're writing, or whether you like to investigate by talking to people or by using the library and the Internet. Looking at it from the negative, which tasks are you facing when you procrastinate? Are they those done orally or in writing? You may not have a strong preference either way, but most of us lean to one side or the other.

Now that you've declared yourself, let's explore what each choice means.

People and human behavior v. financial, technical, scientific or business: Law is by its nature mostly a process of evaluating data and numbers, and exploring systems and ideas. In certain areas of law, the data and ideas spring directly from human behavior and the problems that are solved directly impact people rather than businesses, systems or processes. People-oriented areas of practice include criminal and juvenile law, domestic relations, guardianship, elder law, adoption, employment law, professional liability or license revocation, immigration, and personal injury. Other areas of law typically involve some people contact, but the issues themselves are more removed from human foibles. Those areas include corporate and international transactions, commercial litigation, insurance coverage, real estate, construction, employee benefits work and creditor representation in bankruptcy. A few areas, like consumer bankruptcy and estate planning, are hybrids, but legal work still involves more financial and technical analysis than people understanding.

Solving v. analyzing: The goal in law is eventually to achieve closure, usually by proving a point or winning. Working to create agreement and therefore solve the problem typically comes after a protracted process of analysis and posturing. This is especially true with complex litigation—class actions, antitrust, products liability, medical malpractice, employment claims, commercial transactions, construction disputes—and transactions involving significant sums of money. Lawyers who like to solve problems more than analyze them should focus on matters requiring faster turnaround and involving smaller amounts of money— consumer disputes, simple estate planning, adoption, employment law advising, residential real estate, and consumer bankruptcy as examples.

Speaking and investigating v. writing and researching: At the beginning of your legal career, you won't have much opportunity to communicate orally unless you choose a general practice, criminal or quasi-criminal advocacy, or litigation in a law firm that handles small matters. For the most part, you'll be learning the ropes by spending considerable time researching and writing briefs and memoranda and drafting pleadings and contracts. Later in your career,

especially if it's up to you to maintain client relationships, you'll find it hard to concentrate on research and writing unless you develop a career in appellate work, insurance coverage, intellectual property, employee benefits or complex business transactions.

Overall, you'll find much to commend itself in the practice of law if you prefer to analyze problems rather than solve them, written communication, and if you build your practice in a subject matter that reflects your preference as to focus (i.e. people issues v. technical matters). Those who like to solve problems, to communicate orally and to deal with people issues will have be very selective in developing their legal careers. First and foremost, target one of the practice areas where you'll be working with a variety of individuals on short-term projects: general practice, domestic relations, criminal prosecution and defense, adoption, immigration, elder law including simple estate planning, and employment law advising as examples. If those areas of practice hold no appeal to you, look outside the conventional practice of law to positions in bar association or law school administration, training, customer service (perhaps for a legal publisher), public relations, human resources, information and referral, or investigative functions.

"Paralawyers?," Eric Jansen, *California Lawyer,* May 1996.

Litigation Practice Resources
Defense Research Institute, www.dri.org; 750 North Lake Shore Drive, Suite 500, Chicago, IL 60611; (312) 944-0575. An organization for insurance defense lawyers. Member directory online as well as expanded attorney profiles and links to state and local defense organizations.

Association of Trial Lawyers of America (ATLA), www.atlanet.org; 1050 31st St., NW, Washington, DC 20007; (202) 965-3500 or (800) 424-2725. An organization of lawyers, judges, law professors and law students interested in civil plaintiff and criminal defense advocacy. Job bank found online in "About ATLA" category. Affiliated regional associations operate nationwide.
Careers in Civil Litigation, Monica Bay. What to expect from a career in litigation. Paperback;

American Bar Association, 1990.

Directory of Litigation Attorneys. Annually issued until 1994-1995; discontinued thereafter. Past editions may be available in law libraries or career services offices.

"Driven to Defection: Fed up with insurers' auditors, defense lawyers go to work for plaintiffs," Lisa Brennan, *National Law Journal,* May 18, 1998.

The Brief. News and feature magazine on current events in the fields of tort and insurance law. Produced quarterly by the ABA Tort and Insurance Practice Section.

Litigation. A quarterly journal in the style of a magazine which focuses on a specific trial practice topic in each issue. Produced by the ABA Litigation Section.

General Resources

1998 Associate Salary Survey. Based on a survey of law firms nationwide, this report details salary ranges for associates through the 8th year, bonus structures and timing of salary increases by firm size. Spiral bound; National Association for Law Placement, 1998.

American Lawyer. A weekly newsmagazine focusing on the legal profession, especially from a large law firm perspective. Publishes lists of law firms by specialty, size or other category and special features on different areas of law. Available at many law libraries. Annual subscriptions available by calling American Lawyer, 600 Third Ave., New York, NY 10016; (212) 973-2800.

Christian Legal Society, www.clsnet.org; 4208 Evergreen Lane, Suite 222, Annandale, VA 22203; (703) 642-1070. A national organization of lawyers, judges, law professors, students and non-lawyers founded in 1961. Free e-mail referrals to Christian lawyers in your area.

Directory of Legal Employers 1998-99. An extensive compilation of information on law firms, referencing size, hiring practices, specialties, partner/associate ratios, and salary and benefits. Paperback; Harcourt Brace, 1998. Also on CD-ROM.

Explaining the Inexplicable: The Rodent's Guide to Lawyers, The Rodent. A tongue-in-cheek though truthful look at large law firm life by one who's been there. Paperback; Pocket Books, 1995.

Guide to Small Firm Employment. A booklet addressing the advantages and disadvantages of small firm employment, including methods and resources for the job search. Brochure, National Association for Law Placement, 1998.

International Alliance of Holistic Lawyers, PO Box 753, Middlebury, VT 05753; (802) 388-7478. A nonprofit association of lawyers interested in supporting each other in practicing law from a whole systems approach, increasing their career satisfaction, and transforming the nature of conflict resolution in the US. Emphasizes personal and professional change through educational outreach.

Law Firm Partnership Agreements, Leslie D. Corwin and Arthur J. Ciampi. A detailed study of law firm partnership, including sample agreements. Looseleaf; Law Journal Seminars Press, 1998.

Law Firm Partnership Guide: Getting Started: Basics for a Successful Law Firm, Arthur C. Greene, editor. Covers the life cycle of the law firm, characteristics of successful practice arrangements, ownership options, content of partnership agreements and financing the new law firm. Paperback; American Bar Association, 1996.

Law Firms Yellow Book: who's who in the management of the leading US law firms. Names, titles, addresses and telephone numbers of over 17,000 managing attorneys and administrators at over 700 leading national law firms. Also lists practice groups, committees, administrative departments, office managers and law librarians as well as subsidiaries owned like economic consulting, public affairs and communication.

Lawyer's Weekly USA, www.masslaw.com. A 40-page tabloid for small firm lawyers.

Martindale-Hubbell Law Directory. Published in 26 volumes and annually updated. Identifies over 700,000 lawyers, law firms and corporate legal departments in the US, Canada, and the international community. Extensive biographical and practice information for law firms which pay for a listing; others referenced in brief. Published in CD-ROM. Accessible on Lexis-Nexis or at www.martindale.com/locator/home.html.

NLJ 250: Annual Survey. An overview of the 250 largest law firms in America. Includes locations and sizes of branch offices, associate/partner ratios and starting salaries for new associates. Published annually in the Fall.

Of Counsel 700. Aspen Law & Business' annual listing of the 700 largest US law firms, looking at size, partner-to-associate ratio, lateral hiring, non-equity partners, staff attorneys and more. For information, phone (800) 447-1717.

"Of Counsel: It's not just for retiring, anymore," Barbara B. Buchholz, *ABA Journal,* October 1995.

Presumed Equal: What America's Top Women Lawyers Really Think About Their Firms, Suzanne Nossel & Elizabeth Westfall. Paperback; Career Press, 1997.

Survival Skills for Practicing Lawyers, Theodore P. Ovenstein. A compilation of 29 articles from *Law Practice Management* magazine. Paperback; American Bar Association, 1994.

"Small Firms, Big Clients," Kerry Klumpe, *ABA Journal,* January 1995.

"The Am-Law 100," *American Lawyer.* Gross revenues, profits, pro bono grades and other information about American's highest grossing firms.

The Insider's Guide to Law Firms, Sheila Malkani and Michael Walsh. Evaluates the personalities and policies of large law firms

nationwide from the perspective of summer clerks and associates. Paperback; Mobius Press, 3rd ed. 1997.

The Of Counsel Agreement: A Guide for Law Firm & Practitioner, Harold G. Wren & Beverly J. Glascock. A 97-page examination of various of-counsel arrangements, including sample agreements. Paperback; American Bar Association, 1991.

Contact state and/or local bar associations. Most maintain special interest sections and produce newsletters and other publications.

LEGAL INFORMATION SCIENCE

Possible Employers:

corporate libraries
court libraries
data management companies
government agencies
law firms
law schools
public libraries
publishers

Possible Positions:

director of legal information services*
independent law librarian
law librarian*
manager of information systems
staff attorney for municipal research service*
vice-president for information services

Law-Related Resources

American Association of Law Libraries, www.aallnet.org; 53 W. Jackson Blvd., Suite 940, Chicago, IL 60604; (312) 939-4764. Librarians for courts, bar associations, law schools, private law firms, corporations and government. Publishes a monthly newsletter which contains job announcements. Operates a 24-hour Career Hotline at (312) 939-7877 which is updated Friday of each week. Online database of members and biennial salary survey.

General Resources

American Library Association, www.ala.org. Lists accredited library schools at www. ala.org/alaorg.oa/lisdir.htm.

American Society for Information Science, www.asis.org; 8720 Georgia Ave., Suite 501, Silver Spring, MD 20910; (301) 495-0900. Multidisciplinary organization of those interested in the way society stores, retrieves, analyzes, manages, archives and disseminates information. Maintains a placement service for information specialists, librarians, social scientists and others interested in recorded information. Also publishes a monthly *Jobline.*

Opportunities in Library and Information Science Careers, Kathleen de la Pena McCook and Margaret Myers. Describes the field and assesses the employment outlook. Paperback; VGM Career Horizons, 1996.

Research Centers Directory, Anthony L. Gerring, editor. A digest of information on types, location and activities of university-based and independent nonprofit research centers, indexed by subject matter. Hardback; Gale Research, 23rd ed. 1998.

LOBBYING & PUBLIC AFFAIRS

Practicing Law:

administrative law attorney
governmental relations lawyer
regulatory lawyer

Law-Related Positions

corporate director, federal affairs*
director of corporate affairs
fundraiser
governmental relations assistant*
lobbyist*
policy and legislative affairs director or staff *
public relations or public affairs for a
   bar association
regional marketing director

Other Positions:

campaign manager
political campaign planning
political consultant*
public affairs officer
public affairs producer*
public affairs director or staff
public information officer
VP/manager, public affairs

Law-Related Resources

ABA Legislative & Government Advocacy, www.abanet.org/legadv/home.html. The lobbying arm for the American Bar Association.

American Lobbyists Directory 1990, Robert Wilson, editor. A guide to more than 65,000 registered federal and state lobbyists and the businesses, organizations and other concerns they represent. Paperback; Gale Research, 1989.

Associations Yellow Book: who's who at the leading US trade and professional associations. See prior listing at page 326.

Corporate Yellow Book: Who's Who at the Leading US Companies. Provides contact information for government affairs offices of over 1,100 companies and their 7,700 subsidiaries.

Cyberhound's Guide to Associations and Nonprofit Organizations on the Internet. See prior listing at page 326.

Government Affairs Yellow Book: who's who in government affairs. Lists over 20,000 government affairs experts—both in-house and outside lobbyists—for the nation's leading business, government and professional organizations. Details issues they contest like taxation, health, environment or regulatory matters, and the coalitions they form to advance their legislative agendas.

Lobbying Manual: A Compliance Guide for Lawyers and Lobbyists. Real-world examples demystify complex world of federal lobbying laws. Paperback; American Bar Association, 2nd ed. 1998.

Opportunities in Public Affairs. A bimonthly list of job openings in public affairs, government affairs, legislation, print & broadcast journalism on Capitol Hill, and in nonprofits, corporations and federal agencies nationwide. Contact Brubach Enterprises, Inc., www.brubach.com; PO Box 34949, Chevy Chase/Bethesda, MD 20827-0949; (301) 571-0102.

National Directory of Corporate Public Affairs 1998, Valerie Steele. Lists public affairs programs including political action committees, public information services, or corporate giving programs. Paperback; Columbia Books, 16th ed. 1998.

NTPA 98: National Trade & Professional Associations of the US. See prior listing at page 279.

1998 Washington Representatives, Valerie Steele, editor. Lists lobbyists and others representing business, nonprofits and government interests in the nation's capitol. Paperback; Columbia Books, 22nd ed. 1998.

PUBLISHING

Practicing Law:
author representation
defamation lawyer
First Amendment lawyer
in-house counsel for publishing company
outside counsel for publishing company

Management Positions with Legal Publishers:
acquisitions director*
editor of legal magazine, newspaper or journal
manager, educational services
publisher of career books for lawyers
publisher of marketing books for lawyers
vice-president for governmental relations

Staff Positions with Legal Publishers:
access specialist
account representative

applications consultant
client support specialist*
computer-aided legal research trainer*
copy editor*
database development
developing Internet tools for lawyers
documentation specialist
legal reporting
legal research & writing
marketing specialist
purchasing
quality assurance
reference attorney
research associate
sales representative*
search representative
service representative
software development

Non-Legal Positions:
associate publisher of children's newspaper*
author's agent
independent publisher
publisher
publisher or editor of an industry newsletter
publisher or editor of an investment advisory
   newsletter
publisher of a city magazine
owner and publisher of a neighborhood weekly
   newspaper

Law-Related Resources
Please Note: The legal publishing market experienced both massive consolidation and an explosion in new ventures in the last decade. This listing is intended to identify the largest legal publishers, a sampling of the mid-sized organizations, and references that will help you identify the other players in your geographic area.

Aspen Publishers, www.aspenpub.com; 7201 McKinney Circle, Frederick, MD 21704; (301) 698-9100 or (800) 223-0231. Job opportunities posted online or accessible through their job line at (301) 417-7606.

MAKING MONEY ON SELF-HELP LAW

Ralph Warner was a self-described "quintessential hippie lawyer" who went to law school to change the world. When he became disillusioned with the law's ability to change anything, he dropped out of lawyering without sacrificing his notion of making a significant contribution to society. What began as a service to the poor evolved into a thriving legal self-help publishing company, Nolo Press, which offers affordable legal information and advice to the average citizen. This is his story:

Warner's Statement: I went into law because I somehow saw it as a way to make money while, at the same time, doing good. Since then, I've learned that life doesn't compensate poets well.

After graduation, I ran out and did what a whole lot of other people did: I joined Legal Aid and immediately filed a bunch of court actions against all of these huge and gross unfairnesses. We were able to shift some money from here to there; to win some individual cases. But I saw so many of these cases as merely winning $30 million here and moving it there without any more money being spent on the poor. The federal courts didn't make the poor less poor. They just took money away from somebody else who needed it just as badly so the game could go on forever. It got to the point that I couldn't write another grant, or go before another unresponsive legislative committee, or file another court action that was going to be buried.

After five years, most of the people who went into law for altruistic reasons—myself included—were burned out and unhappy. I looked very hard for another way to live because it seemed that law didn't work. It

produced a certain amount of money, but it didn't produce any poetry. And I really wanted to do something to change things for the better. Why? Because I was one of the people for whom the whole American dream worked: I grew up in the suburbs, passed all the SATs with flying colors, went to exactly the right schools, and got all the right degrees. But by the time I was 25 years old, I felt like I had done it all. At age 28, I quit everything.

Ed Sherman, my former partner here at Nolo Press, worked with me at Contra Costa Legal Services and quit about nine months before I did. Between the two of us we had five kids, and neither he nor I knew what to do next. So we ran a legal clinic out of the backyard. While running this clinic, Ed and I realized that half of the employees at Legal Aid only existed to tell people they weren't poor and miserable enough to qualify for free legal services. And yet those people had no other place to go. At some point, Ed wrote instructions to do your own divorce, put some staples in the side of it and ran it off as a quasi-book. It sold 500 copies.

Fortunately, the bar association attacked it as dangerous without ever having read it. What luck! Suddenly we were selling a couple thousand copies a month. Since then, we've sold more than 500,000 copies of the divorce book in California, and 35 percent of the population handles their own divorces. Now, twenty-seven years after we started writing plain-English law books for non-lawyers, Nolo Press publishes more than 120 titles—books, software, legal forms, audio and video tapes—and has over five million copies in print. Our products have helped more people take care of their legal work than any lawyer or law firm in history.

I don't have a grand plan in running this business, but I do have my own personal plan. I don't want to commute. I don't want to work 90 hours a week. I don't want to be too greedy. I want to continue to have fun. What appeals to me is the notion of empowering people with the tools to represent themselves. It satisfies a part of me that needs to be on the right side of the world.

I don't know that anybody is ever going to change the world's view about sharing everything. We are basically pretty greedy monkeys and the world's always been a pretty unfair place. But to the extent that anybody changes anything, they get there by walking step by step from where they are to where they want to be.

Talking about it, arguing in court, filing papers doesn't change it. Doing it changes it. In that sense, I hope my experience with Nolo serves as a model for others.

Bureau of National Affairs, Inc. (BNA), www.bna.com; 1231 25th St., NW, Washington DC 20037-1165; (202) 452-4200. Employment openings listed on their website.

Careers in Legal Publishing. Describes typical employers and positions, and lists resources. Brochure, National Association for Law Placement, 1998.

Commerce Clearinghouse, www.cch.com; 4025 W. Peterson Ave., Chicago, IL 60646; (312) 583-8500. Publish tax and business law information. Current career opportunities listed on their website or accessible on their job line at (800) 254-7772.

James Publishing, www.jamespublishing.com; 3505 Cadillac Avenue, Suite H, Costa Mesa, CA 92626; (800) 440-4780 or (714) 755-5450. Publishes substantive books as well as *Law Office Computing, Legal Assistant Today* and other law-related magazines.

Law Books & Serials In Print 1998. Three-volume set. Hardback; R. R. Bowker, 1997.

Legal Researcher's Desk Reference. Lists over 350 publishers of legal and law-related materials, including state codes, as well as online research services. See prior listing at page 266.

Lexis/Nexis, www.lexis-nexis.com/; PO Box 933, Dayton, OH 45401; (513) 865-6800. A division of Reed Elsevier. Employment

opportunities and recruiting brochure available on their website.

Lexis Law Publishing (formerly The Michie Company), www.lexislawpublishing.com; PO Box 7587, Charlottesville, VA 22906-7587; (804) 972-7600. A division of Reed Elsevier. Employment opportunities posted at www. lexislawpublishing.com/about/employment .html or on their job line at (804) 961-5555.

Martindale-Hubbell, www.martindale.com; 121 Chanlon Rd., New Providence, NJ 07974; (908) 464-6800 or (800) 526-4902. A division of Reed Elsevier.

Matthew Bender & Co., www.bender.com; 11 Penn Plaza, New York, NY 10001; (212) 967-7707 or (800) 833-9844. Two other locations in New York plus one in San Francisco.

Nolo Press, www.nolo.com; 950 Parker St., Berkeley, CA 94710; (510) 549-1976. See founder's profile on this page.

Reed Elsevier New Providence (formerly R. R. Bowker), www.reedref.com; 121 Chanlon Rd., New Providence, NJ 07974; (908) 464-6800 or (800) 521-8110. Current job openings posted on their website.

RIA Group, www.riag.com, and Research Institute of America, www.riatax.com; 90 Fifth Ave., New York, NY 10011; (212) 645-4800, and Warren, Gorham & Lamont, Inc., www.wgl.com; Park Square Building, 31 St. James Ave., Boston, MA 02116; (617) 423-2020. Employment opportunities posted at www.riag.com/jobs/index.html.

Shepard's/McGraw-Hill, Inc., www.shepards.com; 555 Middle Creek Parkway, Colorado Springs, CO 80921; (719) 481-7431 (human resources). Employment opportunities posted on their website.

Thomson Corporation, www.thomcorp.com; The Metro Center, One Station Place, 6th Floor N., Stamford, CT 06902, (243) 328-9400. An international publishing conglomerate. Sales representatives and editorial offices throughout the US selling books under the names of Clark Boardman Callaghan, Gale Research, The Taft Group, Bankcroft Whitney, Lawyer's Cooperative, West Group and many others. Employment matters handled separately in each subsidiary and at each location.

Thompson Publishing Group, www.thompson.com; 1725 K St., NW, Suite 700, Washington, DC 20006; (202) 872-4000. Current job announcements posted on their website.

VersusLaw, www.versuslaw.com; 2613 151st Pl. NE, Redmond, WA 98052; (425) 250-0142. Internet legal research provider. Employee web pages on the company website tell you something about who works there.

West Information Publishing Group, www.westgroup.com; PO Box 64526, St. Paul, MN 55164; (612) 687-8980 (human resources). A subsidiary of the Thomson Corporation. Branch offices throughout the US. Tends to hire law school graduates in a broad range of sales, editorial, acquisitions and training positions. You'll find employee profiles and job openings at http://jobs.westgroup.com/makemark.html. You can also build your résumé on their site.

General Resources

Complete Guide to Self-Publishing, Tom and Marilyn Ross. Tells you everything you need to know to write, publish, promote and sell your own book. Paperback; Writer's Digest Books, 1994.

Making It in Book Publishing: An Insider's Guide to Career Opportunities, Leonard Mogel. Who does what in the industry, earnings and career paths. Paperback; Macmillan, 1996.

Newsletters in Print. See prior listing at page 279.

Publishers Directory. Contact information and descriptions of specialties and imprints of 18,000 US and Canadian book publishers and 600 distributors, wholesalers and jobbers. Hardback; Gale Research, 19th ed. 1998.

Success in Newsletter Publishing: A Practical Guide, Frederick D. Goss. Paperback; Newspaper Publishers, 4th ed. 1993.

Newsletter Publishers Association, www.newsletters.org; 1501 Wilson Blvd., Suite 509, Arlington, VA 22209; (703) 527-2333 or (800) 356-9302. An organization of firms that publish for-profit, subscription-based commercial newsletters. Publishes a directory of members and of industry suppliers, as well as *How to Launch a Newsletter.*

REAL ESTATE

Practicing Law:
associate counsel for real estate association
construction lawyer
in-house lawyer for real estate company
in-house lawyer for closing company
in-house lawyer for mortgage company
real estate lawyer

Law-Related Positions:
land use examiner*
real estate law newsletter editor
title examiner*
zoning and short-platting specialist*

Non-Legal Positions:
carpenter
commercial property manager*

THE ROAD TO REAL ESTATE DEVELOPMENT

Law is a profession of abstractions and vicarious involvement. Real estate development couldn't be more different; it's hands-on, risky and at the end of the project, you can see the results of your labor.

Alan practiced law for 12 years before founding his own real estate development company. He loves what he is doing; it is his passion. Not only does he have time to enjoy his family, but he gets a kick out of the characters who inhabit the industry. More rewarding to him, though, is the challenge that comes from investing his creativity, time and ingenuity where the potential for a large financial return is so great. This is his story:

Alan's Statement: I don't regret having gone into the practice of law, or even having stayed long enough to get some sense of what it was about. And I have no regrets about leaving. None. Not for a minute.

What I do regret is having practiced for as long as I did. It irritates me that, in 10 or 11 years of practice, I probably put in four or five years too many.

What tied me to the law for so long? My perception is that people either have stable relationships or they don't. I've been married for almost 20 years. I worked with lawyers I liked. No one was driving me away from law. I was under no compulsion to get out of the practice. Unlike some of my friends, I was not unhappy. But I didn't feel great about practicing law. It wasn't fulfilling. And it got boring.

Before I entered law school, I had no idea what lawyers did. I had no lawyer-mentors or other examples to follow. My mentor was my father. He was a good businessman in a small town sort of way; he ran a garage and fixed cars. I remember when I was a kid, my father asked if I wanted to go into his auto repair

business with him. Even though I loved fixing cars, I said no. I was too young to be asked the question, and too stupid to realize I'd answered too quickly.

Thereafter, it was generally accepted that I was going to do something of a professional nature; something that would help me avoid what my parents saw as the hardship in their own lives. I didn't want to be a doctor. What I looked forward to was law school and then going into business.

As time went by, I lost sight of the fact that I never intended to be a lawyer in the first place; that I'd gone to law school only as a means of learning how business is done. And while practicing, I fooled myself into believing that I was participating in my clients' businesses, and was therefore a businessman myself.

What I've learned since is that when a client called me to do what I thought of as initiating a transaction, he was really calling me to finish it. You see, to me that phone call was the beginning of the excitement. To the client, it was the end of it. He'd been pursuing the deal for a long time, and finally he had it put together. All he wanted me to do was to get it in writing and not screw it up in the process. The client didn't want to hear from me six reasons why he couldn't, or shouldn't, complete a deal. He just wanted to be told where to sign. As a lawyer, I wasn't really involved in their businesses. I only handled their legal matters. One day, I woke up and realized that I was just kidding myself if I thought that somehow I would get more involved in a business way with some of my clients.

I spent nearly a year wrestling with how I could both develop real estate and practice law. I wanted to structure an arrangement that my partners would find acceptable and, at the same time, give me enough latitude to pursue my real passion. What finally helped me make my break was the realization that I could not wear two hats effectively.

Practicing law was in some ways easier than what I am doing now. Friends of mine who are happy as lawyers wouldn't be able to stand the risky, episodic and uncertain nature of what I do. Law may have been more intellectually challenging in an abstract way, but I actually find real estate problems to be much more stimulating. The builder calls and says there is a problem with the plan—a wall is supposed to be somewhere that conflicts with something else—and we figure out a solution. You don't have to be a genius to do that, but I like that kind of practical, structural problem solving.

I also meet a lot of characters in this business; you don't find your average securities lawyer in real estate development. Many of these men couldn't write a single sentence in correct English, but they are very good at what they do. I also like the fact that there's more independence than being a lawyer. You are driven by vicissitudes within the business, but you make your own choices along the way.

I'm much more satisfied with the buildings I construct than I ever was drafting a contract, no matter how brilliantly I might have conceived it. To build this last building took gasping at the price of paying for the land, then going through the approval process for a year with delay after delay, and then more problems of this and that, but ultimately the building is up. I take pride in knowing that what I have accomplished over the years, I've done by sticking it out, working hard, taking the bad news and rolling with it, and staying in.

commercial real estate broker*
co-founder and CEO of national resort
    communities development company
developer of affordable housing for the elderly
director of development company building
    housing for the homeless
director of human relations commission*
director of planning, community redevelopment
    project*
head of real estate subsidiary of major
    corporation
house painter
independent commercial real estate developer
independent residential real estate developer
on-site condominium sales
project manager for residential real estate
    development
real estate developer*
real estate licensing course instructor*
residential property manager

residential real estate agent or broker
residential rehabilitation
residential remodel contractor*
restoration specialist
unimproved property management

Law-Related Resources

American College of Real Estate Lawyers,
    www.acrel.org; One Central Plaza, 1300
    Rockville Pike, Suite 903, Rockville, MD
    20852; (301) 816-9811. An organization of
    real estate lawyers invited to be members
    because of their reputation for high quality
    legal work. Publishes a member roster.
    Website includes links to other real estate
    related websites.
Probate and Property. See prior listing at page 346.
The Construction Lawyer. A quarterly newsletter
    produced by the ABA Forum on the
    Construction Industry containing articles on

recent developments in the construction industry as well as announcements of organizations in the field..

General Resources

National Association of Women in Construction, www.nawic.org; 327 S. Adams St., Ft. Worth, TX 76104; (817) 877-5551. More than 200 local chapters nationwide provide networking and information gathering opportunities. Job Bank online accessible by members only.

Real Estate Careers: 25 Growing Opportunities, Carolyn Janik & Ruth Rejnis. How to succeed as a broker, appraiser, manager or agent. Paperback; Wiley, 1994.

Real Estate Career Starter: Launch a Lucrative & Fulfilling Career, Mary Masi. Paperback; Learning Express, 1998.

Realtors National Membership Directory. Published by the National Association of Realtors, www.realtor.com; 430 N. Michigan Ave., Chicago, IL 60611; (312) 329-8200 or (800) 874-6500. Look in your local telephone directory for local realtors associations.

Society for Marketing Professional Services, www.smps.org; 99 Canal Center Plaza, Suite 250, Alexandria, VA 22314; (703) 549-6117. Business development for design- and construction-related firms. Publishes *1998 Marketing Salary & Expense Survey.* Job postings online accessible to members only.

Your Successful Real Estate Career, Kenneth Edwards. Soup-to-nuts advice about entering and thriving in a real estate career. Paperback; Amacom, 3rd ed. 1997.

SPORTS

Practicing Law:
in-house counsel for league
in-house counsel for player's association
sports lawyer in private practice (i.e. outside counsel for leagues, unions or players)
team lawyer

vice-president & general counsel for professional football team

Law-Related Positions:
instructor in sports management
manager, Major League Baseball Properties
player's agent

Other Positions:
business manager for sports network
director of the NCAA awards program*
manager of a professional or semi-professional athletic team
"scout" for professional athletic team
sportscaster
sports stadium development consultant

Law-Related Resources

Careers in Sports Law, Kenneth L. Shropshire. What to expect from a career as a sports lawyer. Paperback; American Bar Association, 1990.

Directory of Entertainment & Sports Lawyers. Annually updated until 1995 by Prentice Hall Law & Business; discontinued thereafter. Past editions may be available in law libraries or career services offices.

"Sports Law Practice Is No Slam Dunk," Andrew Blum, and "Who's Who in the Wide World of Sports Law," *National Law Journal,* July 22, 1996.

Sports Lawyers Association, www.sportslaw. org/sla; 11250 Roger Bacon Drive, Suite 8, Reston, VA 20190; (703) 437-4377. An international educational nonprofit devoted to the understanding, advancement and ethical practice of sports law. Publishes *The Sports Lawyer,* a bimonthly newsletter, and the annual *Sports Lawyers Journal.*

General Resources

A Guide to Careers in Sports, Leonard Karlin. Where the jobs are off the field. Paperback; E. M. Guild, 1997.

Career Opportunities in the Sports Industry: A

JOINING THE TECHNOLOGICAL REVOLUTION

The lure of big bucks and working on the cutting edge make careers in technology attractive to many lawyers. Some lawyers apply as programmers and systems designers. Even more enter in market development, sales and other management functions. When lawyers make the switch, it's a win-win situation for both sides; software companies are hungry for the kind of logical thinking and self-motivation so well-honed in law school and practice.

After suffering frustration for over seven years in the bankruptcy departments of three high-pressure Manhattan firms, Rees took advantage of a chance meeting on a commuter train to shift his career into technology. By moving into sales with a legal software company, he was able to exercise his creative problem-solving skills, imagination and willingness to risk.

Rees' Statement: The law fits people who are comfortable with hierarchies, and who enjoy focusing intensely and deeply on certain problems. I moved from law school to the bankruptcy department of a large New York City firm because I thought helping businesses get back on their feet would be the most creative area of law. As a low-level associate, though, I wasn't paid to be creative. There were certain things I could and couldn't do; I had to keep to the tried and true forms. It was all so confining. With hindsight, I can see that I didn't fit in.

In business, on the other hand, there's no such structure and I love it. I try to think of what's the best thing to do in the unknown situation. I find that completely challenging. There are no answers. You're scared, and you do what you think is reasonable.

Throughout seven years of practicing law,

my insecurity ran rampant. For years, I had a complex that I was a fraud, an impostor, and in just a matter of time, I was going to be discovered. Yes, I was a National Merit Scholar; yes, somehow I got into Harvard; yes, Columbia Law School took me on a scholarship and I clerked for a prestigious firm. But somewhere I had the feeling it was going to catch up with me. At different times, I went to three therapists who all took me in different directions. Nothing helped.

Fortunately, while working at the third firm, I was asked to write a book on business opportunities in bankruptcy. I bought a laptop computer to work on it and was instantly smitten with technology. I liked figuring out what the computer could do so much that I joined lawyer computer user groups to learn more.

One day, I was standing at a train station, carrying my laptop computer, when I got to talking with another computerized commuter. He introduced me to a small legal software firm that thought I'd be perfect in sales. It was something I had absolutely no experience with and didn't know anything about. But it appealed to me from the very beginning.

My first employer essentially paid to train me. It was a big risk for them, because they were investing a fair amount of money in someone who'd never sold anything, and who didn't know much about software. But I did well enough for them that, three years later, I was recruited by a smaller company and offered an equity position.

My fear of being discovered disappeared the minute I stopped practicing law. Funny, isn't it?

When I practiced law, I probably spent more hours at the office than I do here. But, because I was unhappy, I would walk out of the door and try to forget about it. Now, I'm much more committed to my work. I go home at night, and after my son goes to bed, I turn on the computer. My work and my play cross over.

Most people look at the law as a lucrative profession. When the median income in the United States is $30,000, a lawyer making $80,000 a year looks really good. But there are true income limits to being a lawyer. Even the top lawyers, the freaks in a sense, make under a million dollars. In business, if you're successful and go public, as Bill Gates of

Microsoft did, you could be 31 years old and a billionaire.

Money is a motivator to me. But I hope I have enough sense to see that pursuing the dollar for its own sake drives you crazy. I make a lot of money in what I'm doing here; I'm not complaining. But more importantly, I like knowing that if I work hard, and if we get some more people to do well, we may go public. Who knows? Maybe at 40 I'll be able to retire. In which case the real question is: What would I do if I retired?

The answer is easy: I'd keep doing this.

Comprehensive Guide to Exciting Careers Open to You in the Sports Industry, Shelly Field. Paperback; Facts on File, 2nd ed. 1998.

Careers for Sports Nuts & Other Athletic Types, William R. Heitzmann. Explores careers in sports marketing, equipment sales, management, talent scouting and more. Paperback; VGM Career Horizons, 1997.

Chronicle of Higher Education, athletic job opportunities section. See listing at page 314.

How to Get a Job in Sports, Dale Ratermann & Mike Mullen. Specific paths outlined as well as stories of how others got their first jobs. Paperback; Masters Press, 1995.

Institute for Sports Advancement, www.ejkrause.com/sports/isa_home.html; 7315 Wisconsin Avenue, Suite 450N, Bethesda, MD 20814; (301) 986-7800. An annual conference held in New York City in January to assist individuals interested in gaining employment in the sports industry.

1998 Sports Summit Sports Business Directory. Contains company profiles, executives, addresses and other key information for every team, conference, venue, sports marketing organization, equipment manufacturer, agent and sports lawyer in the country. Paperback; E. J. Krause, www.ejkrause.com; or (301)

493-5500 (ask for Mike Patino).

Sports Careers and CBS Sportsline, www. sportscareers.com. A career development organization that focuses exclusively on jobs within the sports industry including special events, TV and cable, sporting goods, colleges/universities, facilities management, corporate sponsorship, athletic representation, front office, print and radio, and health and fitness. Publishes (through Franklin Covey) the *Sports Market Place Directory,* a detailed list of over 27,000 national and international sports contacts and *Career Connections,* a semi-monthly newsletter with listings of job opportunities and market research on major career paths. Job listings also posted online by subscription only. CBS Sportsline offers a free 30-day trial. For information, call (800) 776-7877 or (602) 954-8106, or write PO Box 10139, Phoenix, AZ 85064.

The 50 Coolest Jobs in Sports: Who's Got Them, What They Do & How You Can Get One!, David Fischer. Detailed descriptions of positions in pro sports. Good for those who know they want to work in sports but don't know where to start. Paperback; Arco, 1997.

Ultimate Guide to Sport Event Management & Marketing, Stedman Graham, Joe Jeff

Goldblatt, and Lisa Dephy. Intended for those breaking into the field, this thorough book provides an overview of the administration, coordination and evaluation of any type of event related to sports. Includes lists of career opportunities, corporate sponsors and selected sport event leagues and organizations. Hardback; Irwin Professional Publications, 1995.

You Can't Play the Game If You Don't Know the Rules: Career Opportunities in Sports Management, David Carter. Concentrates on the business of sports, with in-depth looks at college and university athletic departments, agencies, franchise management, media positions and sports management companies. Paperback; Impact Publications, 1994.

TECHNOLOGY

Practicing Law:
computer law specialist
intellectual property auditor*
IP (intellectual property) lawyer*
patent lawyer

Law-Related Positions:
co-designer of Web-based communication
    systems for lawyers
consulting Webmaster to law firms
designer & seller of a bankruptcy program
in-house law firm technology adviser
intellectual property protection systems design*
manager of intranet site development for law
    firm
selling customized Web-links to law firms
software development intern
telecommunications fraud consultant*
VP of sales, legal accounting software company

Non-Law Positions:
director of marketing & sales for ISP
freelance computer training manual writer
program manager

regional sales coordinator
systems analyst*
software designer*
software development
technical writer*
website project manager

Law-Related Resources
American Intellectual Property Association, www.aipla.org, 2001 Jefferson Davis Highway, Suite 203, Arlington, VA 22202; (703) 415-0780. More than 10,000 lawyers nationwide specializing in the practice of intellectual property law.

Attorneys and Agents Registered to Practice Before the US Patent & Trademark Office. An annual publication of the US Patent & Trademark Office; (800) 786-9199 or (703) 308-4357.

Careers in Intellectual Property Law, www.abanet. org/intelprop/careers.htm. An overview of the intellectual property law field, including preparation and employment opportunities.

Computer Law Association, www.cla.org; 3028 Javier Rd., Suite 402, Fairfax, VA 22031; (703) 560-7747. An international organization of technology lawyers. Current job openings posted on website; blind listings of availability for employment may also be posted by members.

"Covering Your Assets," Di Mari Ricker, *California Lawyer,* June 1996. An article about the new growth area of intellectual property auditing, where lawyers pick through a company's portfolio looking for cross-marketing or licensing potential.

International Trademark Association, www.inta.org; 1133 Avenue of the Americas, New York, NY 10036; (212) 768-9887. Members include trademark holding companies and intellectual property lawyers, among others. Extensive publication list on international and US trademark issues.

"Lawyers Thriving in 'Net Businesses," Wendy R. Leibowitz, *National Law Journal,* October 19, 1998.

General Resources

100 Jobs in Technology, Lori Hawkins & Betsy Dowling. Descriptions and profiles of entry-level positions with technology companies. Paperback, Macmillan, 1997.

Association for Multimedia Communications, www.amcomm.org; PO Box 10645, Chicago, IL 60610: (312) 309-1032. An organization of individuals, small businesses, corporations and educational institutions interested in interactive multimedia and the Internet as communications tools. Job opportunities posted on their website.

Career Renewal: Tools for Scientists and Technical Professionals, Stephen Rosen and Celia Paul. A comprehensive career evaluation and job search guide for those working in technical fields. The individual profiles offer an inside look at the technical work environment. Paperback; Academic Press, 1998.

Careers in Multimedia: Roles and Resources, Hal Josephson & Trisha Gorman. Profiles of those working in multimedia, including how they got the job and what they do on a daily basis. Paperback; Books/Cole Publications, 1996.

Careers for Cybersurfers & Other Online Types, Marjorie Eberts and Rachel Kelsey. Descriptions of jobs in Internet technology. Paperback; VGM Career Horizons, 1998.

Fast Company, www.fastcompany.com. This monthly magazine is an essential resource for anyone seeking work with technology companies. Tells you "how smart business works" in terms of customer service, employee development, leadership, competition, management and more.

International Interactive Communications Society, www.iics.org; 39355 California St., Suite 302, Fremont, CA 94538; (510) 608-5930. An organization of those who work in a full spectrum of new media discipline. Job listings on their website.

Making Money in Technical Writing: Turn Your Writing Skills into $100,000 a Year, Peter Kent. Information about training, freelancing, setting rates, evaluating contracts and generating more business. Paperback, Arco, 1997.

NASPA, Inc., www.naspa.net; 7044 S. 13th St., Oak Creek, WI 53154; (414) 768-8000. An association of corporate computing technical professionals. Membership includes a copy of *Technical Support* monthly. Free online job bank with more than 5,000 positions at any one time. New jobs posted daily.

Opportunities in Desktop Publishing Careers, Kenny Schiff. Paperback; VGM Career Horizons, 1993.

Opportunities in Telecommunications Careers, Jan Bone. Information about Internet, cellular, education and training, e-mail and telemarketing jobs. Paperback; VGM Career Horizons, 1996.

Plunkett's Infotech Industry Almanac 1999-2000, Jack Plunkett. 500 one-page profiles of industry leaders, plus trends and emerging markets. Paperback; Plunkett Research, 1998.

Society for Technical Communication. See prior listing at page 296.

Software Publishers Association, www.spa.org; 1730 M. St. NW, Suite 700, Washington, DC 20036; (202) 452-1600. A full service association for software publishers and developers; associate members include law firms that represent software companies. Publishes *SPA Guide to Contracts and the Legal Protection of Software.* SPA's Jobwire lists current job openings online.

Telecommunications Directory 1998: An International Guide to Electronic Transmission of Voice, Image & Data. National and international associations, consultants, law firms, publishers, regulatory bodies, training organizations and businesses involved in voice and data communications, local area networks, teleconferencing facilities, videotex and teletext operations or providing electronic mail, facsimile, telegram and telex, voice processing and response, and satellite-related services and products. Hardback; Gale Research, 9th ed. 1997.

SELECTED

JOB

DESCRIPTIONS

account executive for public relations company: Help businesses, nonprofit organizations and individuals create a positive public image. Design a campaign intended to generate positive media coverage, sometimes in response to an attack. Prepare press releases, articles; arrange interviews, public speaking engagements, receptions, seminars and other events that expose clients to the right audiences.

acquisitions director for legal publisher: Negotiate for new writings (articles, books) to be published via hard copy, CD-ROM or other electronic means. Coordinate between author and publishing company to have a final product created. Responsible for tracking and predicting market trends and demands for maximum sales of published materials. Often communicate with the leading experts in certain subject areas.

acquisitions evaluator: Evaluate the desirability of purchasing a business or other significant asset by a corporation. Involves investigation, analysis, review of information, calculations, and making recommendations.

ADA compliance specialist: Ensure compliance with the Americans with Disabilities Act by evaluating whether physical and employment access are available to disabled where reasonable accommodations can be made. Set up compliance time tables. Negotiate with department heads for reasonable accommodation to avoid litigation.

ADA investigator: Respond to complaints by employees or students of organization's failure to accommodate their disabilities by interviewing complainant and respondents, gathering other relevant information, comparing fact situation to law, working with the parties to resolve the complaint amicably.

adjunct (part-time) professor: Teach a specific area of law or a clinical education curriculum on a part-time or contract—as opposed to tenured or tenure track—basis.

administrative law judge (see hearing officer).

adoption lawyer: Facilitate the adoption process, either through a licensed agency or independently. Usually represent adoptive parents; occasionally represent birth parent or parents. Research possible legal problems and assure proper termination of parental rights. Occasionally represent biological parents in seeking to revoke an adoption that has already been finalized. Much of the work involves stepparent, grandparent and other intrafamily adoptions.

ADR specialist: Assist others to resolve conflicts in a timely, efficient, cost effective and non-litigious manner by encouraging discussion and honesty. Create an environment of information and empowerment so that adversaries shape the best possible resolutions for all concerned. Add to the parties' information and skill base for resolving future conflicts.

affirmative action director: Management training in EEO law and diversity issues. Develop programs to recruit and retain diverse employees. Assist in dispute resolution.

airline pilot: Determine route. Preflight check aircraft. Ensure proper maintenance and loading. Fly aircraft to destination. Open and close flight plan. Be prepared for and handle any emergency.

appellate lawyer: Research and write appeals of decisions from one court level to the next. Analyze and interpret court record. Research law. Write brief in accordance with rules for format and content. Argue appeal. May also coordinate preparation for appeal in terms of preserving record and keeping abreast of new decisions.

assistant editor, collegiate dictionary: Determine word meaning, usage, origin. Monitor new words. Oversee entire content of dictionary.

associate director, Center for Law and Entrepreneurship (excerpted from actual job announcement): Provide leadership and vision for the center, with a goal of educating lawyers to create value for their

365

entrepreneurial clients. Develop an advisory board. Explore and develop new educational programs and degrees. Initiate and coordinate regional and national symposia. Manage the center's staff. Administer the professional externship program. Raise funds through grants and contributions. Teach one or more courses related to the center's mission. Build strong linkages with the state's business and legal community. Coordinate the center's activities with other law school and university programs.

associate publisher of children's newspaper: Handle the day-to-day business management of the newspaper including supervising classified and other ad sales, budgeting, circulation, and customer relations.

audio and videotape course instruction: Design, create and market instructional courses on audio or videotape. Analyze needs of target buyer or user. Develop program. Stage production.

automation consultant: Review the needs and goals of a law office in terms of document production and telecommunications. Know the most up-to-date technology and prices. Understand the office's financial capacity. Advise the law office of its options to automate. Teach others about opportunities and help them get over their fear of new and changing technology.

bank fraud investigator: Investigate possible incidences of fraud, forgery, misrepresentation and other banking infractions within banking environment. Collect facts and figures and document findings.

bank probate administrator: Collect information on all assets and debts in estate. Contact resources and coordinate efforts to settle estate. Inform and negotiate with heirs, creditors and debtors. Attend court proceedings.

bank regulation analyst: Interpret and analyze federal banking regulations. Audit banking activities. Determine whether operations of the bank comply. Take steps to assure compliance with the law. Most common activity involves savings and loan debt to equity ratios, i.e. insuring proper amount of reserve cash. Interpret complex accounting procedures.

bank trust department consultant (petroleum): Advise and assist bank trust offices in negotiating and dealing with oil and gas companies concerning trust oil and gas assets. Evaluate properties for asset maximization.

bar review course administrator: Oversee administration of bar review courses. Find and negotiate contracts for lecture sites and lecturers. Organize and oversee preparation of study materials and all updates. Market, or oversee marketing of courses to law students.

bioethicist: Help hospitals, medical schools, government agencies and the public define and resolve ethical issues in medicine. Gather facts, confer with doctors and patients, review literature and apply moral reasoning and common sense to offer education and advice on such issues as genetic engineering, fetal research, right to die, right to suicide, frozen embryo storage, use of fetal tissue for research, artificial maintenance of brain dead infants to preserve organs for transplantation, notification of AIDS infection, genetic screening for jobs, euthanasia and animal experimentation. Offer guidance and recommendations rather than decisions and action.

business agent for import/export company: Research legal regulations and business feasibility of importing or exporting products or services in order to recommend or select particular markets. Advise as to the legal requirements to implement transactions in foreign markets. Negotiate prices and terms of sale.

business law instructor: Instruct students at the community college, undergraduate and graduate school levels in case, statutory and administrative law relevant to business organizations and transactions.

business valuations expert: Calculate the value of different kinds of businesses for use in purchase and sale transactions, divorce, estate settlement and damage calculations. Present opinions in court about value.

campaign manager: Walk with candidate to set the tone and pace of the campaign. Advise candidate on dealing with press. Verbalize positions on political issues. Oversee public appearances and meetings. Coordinate, plan, schedule fundraising and campaign events. Budget.

career consultant for lawyers: Work with law students and lawyers to identify areas of interest and barriers to change. Assist them with matching skills to possible career alternatives. Inform them of the opportunities available in traditional and nontraditional career paths. Help them present their assets in the job market to best effect.

central research staff: Field legal research questions from staff attorneys and appellate court judges. Research and prepare research memos. Survey how other jurisdictions have ruled on cases of first impression.

circuit mediator: Preside at mediation conferences in selected appellate court cases. Lead discussions of the procedural and substantive legal issues involved. Conduct economic analyses of a case's settlement value. Encourage settlement by creating and exploring options other than continued litigation.

city manager: Supervise the day-to-day operations as well as long-term planning for a municipality. Oversight includes departments of administration, logistics, personnel, finance, budget, and security. Serve as focal point for provision of information to political leadership of municipality. Serve as conduit for implementation of political leadership.

city or county council legal advisor: Advise members of the city council about legality of proposed actions. Determine whether actions comply with state and federal laws and regulations. Assist council in drafting or redrafting proposed legislation in a way that does comply with existing laws. Suggest revisions in laws.

claims adjuster: Review insurance claims for determination of liability and damage. Estimate amount of company reserves to set aside to cover claim. Investigate claims to determine settlement or litigation potential. Negotiate settlements by working directly with insured or with attorneys.

claims examiner: Review medical, property and other loss claims and compare them to statutory and policy provisions to determine coverage and benefits allowable. Investigate and document claims.

client services manager: Liaison between law firm management and clients. Listen to clients to determine their overall needs and evaluate how the law firm can best serve those needs. Conduct surveys of law firm performance. Introduce clients to law firm department representatives. Recommend updates in technology to encourage compatibility with clients. May resolve billing disputes and organize marketing activities like baseball games between client and firm.

client support specialist for legal publisher: Make contact with law firms, law schools and other purchasers of publishing services and products to educate and encourage use of products. Troubleshoot difficulties. Train law firm staff in usage. Answer questions by telephone.

code research analyst: Research and analyze municipal codes to determine compliance with current state and federal law. Recommend legislative changes to bring code into compliance. Incorporate public comment about problems with code into suggested revisions. Occasionally attend committee hearings and speak on changes that need to be made.

code reviser (see code research analyst).

commercial property manager: Ensure high occupancy rates and low operating costs for commercial properties either as independent or in-house employee. Negotiate and administer leases. Resolve disputes with tenants and service providers. Collect rents. Negotiate vendor, maintenance and repair contracts. Monitor condition of facilities.

commercial real estate broker: Represent sellers or lessors of commercial property in transactions. List and market properties. Match buyers with sellers. Assist in putting together financing packages. Monitor and supervise sale through closing.

commercial voice-over talent: Speak background commentary in radio, television or film productions, commercials and public service announcements. May dub lines for an actor whose voice is not appropriate for a particular role or for foreign language films or cartoons.

community relations coordinator: Responsible for working with the city, local governments, community groups, organizations and individuals to create, develop, implement and evaluate policies, procedures and programs that eliminate discrimination or remove the effects of past discrimination, as well as to promote positive community relations and mutual respect. Establish trust, build consensus and work effectively with diverse groups and individuals to develop and implement programs that overcome discrimination.

computer systems analyst: Develop new computer software systems. Troubleshoot computer system glitches. Customize systems for particular customers, environments or markets. See also description at beginning of Chapter 13.

computer-aided legal research trainer: Work with law students and lawyers to familiarize them with computer research resources. Attend programs and seminars to keep abreast of new developments. Work with employer to develop changes in products to make them more responsive to the needs of the users.

computer-aided trial exhibits designer: Design graphic representations of products, accidents, or injuries for presentation at mediation, settlement conference, or trial. Use consulting skills to identify potential exhibits. Brainstorm possibilities with clients and coworkers.

conference planner: Coordinate logistics for conferences. Research facilities and location; determine space, meal, hotel and equipment requirements. Handle registrations and contract with speakers.

congressional aide: Assist an individual congressman with issue analysis, problem-solving, and consensus building. Sometimes entails research and writing on policy issues. Often requires good organizational and networking abilities.

construction lawyer: Legal counsel for construction and real estate development companies. Manage legal issues arising in construction projects, including contractual disputes, and employment and other personnel matters. Ensure that federal and state labor and safety laws are followed. Represent the firm in discrimination and safety violation suits. Draft and enforce agreements with sub-contractors. File and collect on liens.

consulting lawyer: Hired by other lawyers or law firms to provide advice and consultation in a particular area of legal specialty on a project basis.

contract compliance administrator: Oversee details of contract execution. Ensure compliance with terms of contracts. Negotiate disputes over performance.

contract lawyer placement specialist: Interview potential contract lawyers and hiring lawyers to determine talent and needs. Match lawyers and law firms for short-term projects. Research employer needs and attorney skills. Present options to potential hiring lawyer. Negotiate rate. Oversee collection.

contract lawyer: A lawyer who provides legal services for another lawyer on a temporary, freelance, project, hourly or intermittent basis.

contract negotiator (government or corporation): Negotiate purchase or sales contracts for large organizations, dealing mostly in bulk sales or customization of products.

convention planner: Plan conventions for nonprofit organizations, political and professional associations from start to finish including negotiating and contracting for convention facilities, catering, transportation, events planning, educational programming and entertainment. Market program to potential attendees. Find and hire speakers. Manage facilities and logistical details at the convention itself. Follow up after the convention with accounting and other details.

copy editor: Edit articles, books, lists, or compilations submitted by other writers to a legal publication. Verify the content and check cites. Research varied aspects of law and write or rewrite articles.

corporate communications specialist: Coordinate information flow among corporate divisions, and to employees, customers, investors and the general public. Write annual reports, newsletters, brochures, press releases. Brainstorm new ways of communicating the corporation's message.

corporate director, federal affairs: Responsible for management and oversight of all federal government policy issues. Provide policy direction on key issues in international trade, regulation, technology and competitiveness. Represent the company with federal agencies, Congress and states.

corporate marketing: Identify, maximize and satisfy consumer demand for a company's products. Anticipate changes in demand through market research and analysis. Ensure quality, availability and price meet needs of market. Conduct focus groups to evaluate the product or the promotion of the product.

course designer for a CLE provider: Primary responsibility for developing course content of programs presented by the organization. Arrange for speakers. Solicit and monitor submitted written materials. Evaluate feedback on the course and redesign future programs.

court commissioner/magistrate: Preside over and decide preliminary legal disputes or lower level matters like guardianship, probate and family law.

court interpreter: Translate court proceedings (depositions, hearings, etc.) for those who communicate in a language or form (i.e. sign language) other than that used by the court.

crisis PR for law firms: Create and implement a media plan to minimize the negative impact of a law firm crisis like a large settlement against the firm or a firm client, or an entire department leaving the firm. Coordinate communication with the media. Instruct law firm in correct handling of media questions.

dance critic: Attend performances of local and visiting dance troupes and individual artists. Write critical reviews of the performance. Research the performers' repertoire, choreography, score, etc. Work on-staff or freelance for newspapers, magazines, arts publications, television or radio.

DEA agent: Investigate drug smuggling, manufacturing, selling and related criminal activity in order to arrest perpetrators and build a case against them.

dean of students: Responsible for academic counseling of law school students, organizing the faculty advising program, and international exchanges. Liaison with student organizations. Plan orientation and commencement programs. Oversee administration of financial aid, arranging academic accommodations for students with disabilities, supervision of law school registrar and direction of academic support program for non-traditional students.

department legal advisor: Advise a particular corporate department on legal matters related to day-to-day activities. Research and write memoranda on particular questions regarding tax, real estate, labor relations, contracts, finance, and acquisitions. Draft necessary documentation.

deputy general counsel, US Sentencing Commission (excerpted from an actual job announcement): Provide legal advice and counsel in sentencing issues pertaining to economic crimes. Perform legal research. Prepare legal memoranda and analytical reports. Provide information and analysis to Congress. Respond to inquiries. Lead or participate in staff working groups. Train practitioners and draft proposed amendments related to the federal sentencing guidelines.

development officer (see fund-raiser).

direct mail marketing company founder: Contact varying businesses and design and coordinate their marketing efforts through direct mailings to the general public. Review clients' products and services. Identify those who utilize this type of product or service. Determine purchasers' reasons for buying. Draft letters and other marketing information that communicates why and how the product or service is worth buying right now.

director of admissions (law school): Recruit students and analyze applications for admission. Work under supervision of Dean of law school. Travel to undergraduate colleges to present programs and answer questions relating to law school and the admissions process. Counsel potential students. Prepare budget. Supervise clerical staff and admissions committee.

director of alumni affairs: Serve as liaison between alumni of a university or professional school and the existing faculty and students. Encourage donation and participation in current activities of the school. Plan events and network facilitation services to alumni to encourage them to contribute financially and refer new students to the school.

director of business development (law firm): Coordinate, develop, and assist in implementation of a law firm's public relations, marketing strategies, and client relations. Develop and implement plans to develop new clients. Organize law firm functions like seminars to attract new clients or new business from current clients.

director of career services: Develop and manage programs, resources and activities to assist law school students in developing research skills and familiarizing themselves with legal practices and employers, career paths and the legal employment market. Develop and maintain contacts with employers throughout the country in order to market the law school, its students and its programs. Organize programs and counsel students individually on such matters as résumé preparation, identification of employment prospects and interviewing skills. Develop and maintain a comprehensive resource center, write and edit an up-to-date career services handbook, conduct seminars and workshops.

director of human relations commission: Responsible for organizing, implementing, directing and maintaining the administrative and enforcement activities and responsibilities of the human relations commission. Supervise support staff in the investigation of EEO, housing and public accommodation complaints. Implement programs dealing with social problems in the community.

director of legal information services: Coordinate resources, such as computer databases for legal research, for use by legal staff of a law firm. Instruct staff on use of research tools. Monitor latest technology regarding dissemination of legal information.

director of office of technology transfer: Responsible for developing and expanding a program which seeks to commercialize university research technologies and increase university/industry collaboration. Primarily concerned with bioengineering, medical-biotechnology and instrumentation. Initiate industry and faculty database used for marketing and licensing technologies. Improve program marketing materials and develop new marketing programs. Organize a symposium on technology transfer for researchers in the schools of medicine, public health, dentistry, nursing and bioengineering. Reorganize program's caseload administration and record system. Streamline university process for commercialization of technologies. Negotiate licenses valued from 15 million to over 2 billion dollars.

director of planned giving: Meet with wealthy individuals to assist them in donating money or property to a charitable organization in a way that minimizes tax liability and maximizes the benefit to both donor and donee. Help client combine and coordinate charitable-giving goals with personal financial planning needs. Educate potential donors about the benefit of leaving their assets to the organization before or upon their death.

director of planning, community redevelopment project: Coordinate a committee that will develop the master plan. Create sub-committees to address execution of the plan, i.e. budget, time frame for completion. Identify developers, architects, engineers, attorneys, community members who will carry out the plan. Establish review dates to determine the progress of the program.

director of professional development: Develop programs and resources for new associates at a law firm. Track CLEs. Organize and present seminars geared toward the special needs of the law firm. Anticipate problem areas and provide risk management. Maintain a brief bank.

director of the NCAA awards program: Meet with college coaches nationwide to set up and run programs that award high standards in athletic departments and among athletes.

director of training for judicial district: Supervise overall design, development and evaluation of continuing education curriculum for judicial and nonjudicial court personnel. Assess needs, determine methods, evaluate training programs, and make recommendations on goals and priorities.

Director/supervising attorney of clinical education program: Set up and administer legal practicum for current law students. Teach students how to listen, interview, advise clients, draft pleadings. Make court appearances with and without student support. Supervise legal interns.

disciplinary proceedings prosecutor: Prosecute other attorneys who have committed violations of disciplinary rules or code of ethics. Evaluate complaints. Interview and investigate witnesses, complainant and lawyer being charged. Present evidence at hearing. Write proposals to disciplinary board.

dispute resolution trainer: Instruct employees of corporation in resolving both internal and external disputes without the intervention of lawyers. Design and facilitate programs that help work teams, departments, managers, executives and others improve communication within the organization.

elder law lawyer: Assist senior citizen clients and their families with planning for issues related to old age including nursing home placement, Medicaid and Medicare planning, guardianship, estate planning, probate, pension claims. Mediate family disputes.

employee assistance program (EAP) counselor: Assist employees of a corporation with personal problems, usually by meeting with them to define the problem and then referring them to outside providers. May provide these services as an employee of the corporation or as part of an outside consulting firm.

employee benefits analyst: Analyze benefits provided to employees, both in specific industries and for different levels of employees (staff, executives, management).

Conduct statistical analysis of programs, offerings and cost and the matching of benefits to fit certain goals and objectives.

employee grievance mediator: Provide a forum for employees to express grievances against their supervisor, employer or workplace. Assist both sides in working out an amicable resolution to the problem.

employee relations officer or manager: Act as liaison between employees and management. Responsible for promulgating and monitoring compliance with employment laws, regulations and standards. Interpret rules for employees. Communicate employee concerns to management. Negotiate and resolve discrimination and harassment cases. Develop training programs.

environmental consulting: Investigate real properties to determine presence of environmentally hazardous substances. Interpret applicable federal, state and local laws to determine if property is in substantial compliance. Prepare written reports. Determine if further investigation is necessary. Deal with governmental agencies to determine remediation plan.

environmental protection specialist: Provide specialized, particular knowledge on compliance with environmental protection regulations, either in-house with the government or a corporation, or on a consulting basis.

ethics officer: Review government, university or corporate standards and practices for ethics violations. Train managers in rules of ethics. Problem solve with department managers when ethical issues arise.

executive director of a nonprofit agency: Coordinate and administer projects. Work with and implement goals of board of directors. Explain goals and purpose of agency and persuade people to donate money and services. Investigate available grants. Write grant proposals. Speak to groups. Plan and oversee budgeting for

agency. In smaller agencies, handle all of these tasks. In larger organizations, may only oversee these responsibilities.

executive search consultant: Headhunter for sales and management positions in well-established companies. Network nationwide to find well-qualified applicants for open positions, usually at upper management or sophisticated sales levels.

family law lawyer (see matrimonial lawyer).

FBI agent: Responsible for investigating white collar and violent crimes for the federal government. Subject matters may include financial/bank fraud, environmental crime or interstate criminal activity. Turn over information to the US Attorney General.

fee arbitration program director: Oversee and coordinate fee disputes between lawyers and clients. Solicit and sometime train volunteer arbitrators. Report to board. May mediate some disputes.

field education director: Coordinate the implementation and measurement of training services for multiple office operations.

financial plans sales director: Develop markets and find buyers for investment products. Supervise and consult with outside sales representatives. Set department goals and monitor results.

forensic psychologist: Evaluate lawsuits from the psychological perspective in child custody determinations, personal injury damage evaluations, employment claims, and criminal law matters. May be appointed by the court as a neutral evaluator or hired by either side for expert opinion. Meet with persons under evaluation. Write reports. Testify in court and in depositions.

fund-raiser (a.k.a. development officer) for a non-profit organization: Generate funds for health-care institutions, educational establishments, social-service groups, the arts, environmental causes, advocacy groups and political campaigns through donor research, special events planning, major gifts, corporate and foundation relations and planned giving. Research funding sources. Prepare written proposals. Generate ideas for fundraising projects. Organize and coordinate fundraising events. Meet with individual donors to request their contributions. Meet with existing donors to encourage their solicitation of donations from their associates.

general counsel: Give legal advice to officers, directors and employees of corporation to fulfill the goals and objectives of the corporation. Recommend action on new business ventures. Write and rewrite contracts and other legal documents. Review and sometimes draft employment and benefits documents. Assign more complex or larger legal matters to outside counsel. Oversee work of outside counsel.

government relations assistant: As employee of association, monitor federal legislation, write column and newsletter, organize lobbying and networking activities, and advise regarding government and law-related activities.

grant writer: Formulate and draft grant proposals to be reviewed by funding sources. Locate funding sources. Research funding sources to determine how to tailor grant. Entails knowledge of potential grantors, limitations, requirements, and special considerations applicable with respect to each potential grantor.

guardianship lawyer: Work on behalf of children, the disabled or the elderly in managing their affairs, or arguing for their rights. File guardianship or conservator actions to transfer decision-making authority from an incompetent person or child to a responsible adult. Counsel families. Interview doctors and others concerned with the alleged incompetent person.

hearing officer (administrative law judge): Hear and decide cases involving governmental administrative matters. Conduct hearings with the greatest degree of informality consistent with fairness and the nature of the proceeding. Issue proposed or final decisions, including findings of fact and conclusions of law. May travel to different locations to hear cases. Assignments may vary widely or be limited to subject matters like social and health services, workers' compensation, environmental regulation or immigration.

heir finder: Locate and contact individuals who have inherited tangible and intangible property so estates can be closed. Obtain information through genealogical or historical research.

human resources manager: Oversee development of employee policies including benefits, compensation, sexual harassment, management issues, and training programs. Often responsible for hiring and firing, resolving employee disputes and operating the employee assistance program.

human services consulting: Work with nonprofit organizations or government agencies on a project basis to evaluate the effectiveness of current programs, design and implement new programs or coordinate services among competing or cooperative organizations.

immigration lawyer: Interpret and apply immigration laws to assist clients in compliance. Facilitate corporate clients' needs to transfer foreign employees to US-based jobs for specialized tasks. Provides legal counsel to individuals seeking US citizenship. Help political refugees prove that they are entitled to refuge in the US. Help economic refugees show that they fit within the quota.

independent insurance adjuster: Assist insurance and corporate clients in investigating and evaluating claims. Hired to supplement the work of the claims office of an insurance company, or to act on behalf of a self-insured company.

industry newsletter editor: Decide content and themes of the newsletter. Solicit, write and edit articles. Work on layout of newsletter. Plan distribution, pricing and marketing.

in-house editor: Edit briefs, memos, correspondence and other documents created by law firm members before being released to the public. Train others in writing skills. May also submit articles to a local or national law journal or magazine on behalf of the firm.

insurance broker: Serve as the middle person between the insured and the insurance agency. Represent the insured in obtaining the best insurance for their particular needs.

insurance defense lawyer: Represent insurance companies in resolving claims filed by or against insureds. Conduct intensive research and fact-finding. Report frequently to claims adjusters and managers. Negotiate, mediate or arbitrate settlements. Try cases that can't be resolved outside court. Handle appeals.

insurance regulation analyst: Work for Insurance Commissioner. Analyze cost effectiveness and compliance issues in potential or existing insurance policies. Resolve disputes. Sometimes oversee controversies as hearing examiner.

intellectual property auditor: Inspect patent portfolios for any registered trademarks. Determine if the company owns the assets, and if so, look at the files related to the patent prosecution. Evaluate where the company's intellectual property can be sold or licensed to others. Review freelance agreements and policy regarding works created by employees to find defects in the chain of title in the ownership of copyrights or potential infringements or sales. Work according to an outline from management defining the areas of inquiry, the scope of the audit, the time frame, the documents to be reviewed, and the personnel to be interviewed.

intellectual property protection systems design: Design office procedures that protect patent, trademark, property rights, etc. Monitor patent applications, trade journals, and media. Identify infringements and alert owner(s). Prevent products from being copied by competing manufacturers.

international trade relations specialist: Apply public relation skills, usually to benefit a government entity or large business. Develop international market contacts. Promote the state, country or company in foreign markets. Assist those interested in importing and exporting goods and related services in making connections at home and abroad.

investigation and resolution specialist: Investigate and analyze internally- and externally-filed complaints asserting violations of university policies and complaints of discrimination, retaliation and harassment. Author and disseminate investigation reports which include factual determinations and analysis. Identify complaint trends and lead efforts to intervene appropriately. Lead cross-departmental resolution teams in devising, refining and implementing appropriate and creative approaches to dispute resolution. Educate departments about potential impacts of workplace actions, particularly with respect to avoidance of retaliation.

investment analyst: Analyze finances, operations, and management of corporations and partnerships for purposes of possible investment and financing by underwriters, brokerages, mutual funds, commercial bankers, or venture capitalists.

investment banking: Create and administer financial plans for clients wishing to invest for profit usually as an employee of a large financial organization like a major bank or investment company. Analyze investment opportunities. Negotiate purchases and sales on behalf of institutional clients.

investment strategist: Analyze investment opportunities and design a portfolio and strategy for the savings and other assets of a major corporation that minimizes risks and maximizes returns.

IP lawyer: Protect clients' intellectual property rights in patents, trademarks, copyrights, and trade secrets through US and foreign recordation and through litigation against infringements. Develop a system to recognize and protect clients' intellectual property interests.

IRS compliance analyst: As employee of corporation, review company accounting procedures and policies to assure compliance with current tax laws and regulation. Audit departmental accounting.

judge advocate general: Practice all types of law, but mainly criminal and family law, on behalf of any branch of the military, members of the armed services or their families.

labor negotiator: Represent management or labor in negotiations involving union contracts, employee salaries and benefits, or employee discipline or termination. Counsel union on federal and state labor-law issues, such as strikes and collective bargaining.

land use examiner: Analyze whether land use is in compliance with existing government zoning and planning requirements to meet community goals. Examine how particular land areas are currently being utilized or may be utilized in the future.

landman: Determine who owns real estate, what they own, and how it can be acquired, usually on behalf of a utility or energy company. Point out defects in title and advise on how to correct title. Advise on best way to use real estate resources. Come up with alternative uses of real property resources.

law enforcement legal advisor: Assist chief of police and other officers with day-to-day problems and crises arising from the work of the agency. Advise on workers compensation, job safety, prisoner issues, accidents and policy conduct.

law firm administrator: Organize and administer the business aspects of running a law firm. Carry out policies determined by partners re: hiring procedures of non-legal staff, advertising the firm, automation and office space decisions. Develop a business plan. Track benefits and office expenses. Organize retreats for partners or entire legal staff. Track

client and professional development as well as staff improvement. Troubleshoot and resolve management problems.

law librarian: Order and update library publications. Assist lawyers and law school professors with their legal research. Instruct on location of reference materials. Work in a law firm, law library or corporation.

law-related education director: As employee of bar association, coordinate programs in which volunteer lawyers teach elementary and secondary education students the basics of law. Serve as goodwill ambassador for the legal community.

lawyer referral service telephone intake attorney: Listen to problems of callers by phone, and refer them to lawyers in that specialty area or to other service providers. Sometimes match need with immediate solution. Must be aware of community resources in and outside of the law. Deal calmly with emotional people.

lawyers' assistance program director: Manage (and sometimes initiate) a bar-association sponsored service for lawyers with drug or alcohol problems, depression, or career dissatisfaction. Counsel individual lawyers. Conduct workshops, support groups and other meetings. Supervise and train volunteer lawyers. Educate bar members about these issues and how to confront them.

legal compliance manager: Manage a corporate legal compliance program. Monitor its impact to make sure it is working. Identify and recommend compliance policies, programs and procedures. Investigate reports of violations, and conduct compliance audits. Provide training and education to ensure employee awareness of and compliance with legal compliance program. Keep abreast of prevailing legal issues and requirements, regarding USDA, FDA, FTC, OSHA, OFCCCP.

legal correspondent: Investigate and research the law and facts and present it to lay persons and lawyers alike in a form (either oral or written) that is easily understood, helpful, and practical.

legal information answer line coordinator: Recruit and coordinate scheduling for answer line volunteers. Coordinate public service announcements and media handouts. May do grant writing, negotiate lease for office space and do other "business-related" tasks.

legal outreach program developer: Facilitate the delivery of pro bono or low cost legal services to the community. Solicit and train volunteers. Work with existing programs.

legal research and writing specialist: Responsible for conducting research in specific areas of law, often regarding complicated, obscure, or disputed issues, and then committing findings to proper written form.

legal studies professor (at the university level): Teach substantive areas of law or about the legal profession and legal process at the undergraduate level.

legal trivia game designer: Review case opinions, newspapers and other sources for stories about legal events. Extract interesting aspects to form into questions. Create game board, scoring mechanism, game rules. Market game to publishers.

legal writing instructor: Teach legal writing, legal research, and legal analysis. Often responsible for four hours of classroom teaching per week plus individual student tutorials. Critique and grade written assignments.

literary agent: Represent authors to publishers in an effort to publish their books, articles or stories. Seek out new authors. Negotiate contracts. Critique works.

litigation avoidance consultant: Advise corporations in the new product development phase on potential areas of litigation as to avoid litigation. Conduct seminars on the effectiveness of various methods of dispute resolution. Consult with lobbyists on possible legislation regarding the requirements of using alternative dispute resolution techniques prior to filing a lawsuit.

litigation management: Assist law firms or companies on a project basis to collect, organize and index documents produced in complex matters. Supervise teams of paralegals, data processing experts and lawyers.

loan administrator: Take custody of loan after approval. Keep track of performance. Focus primarily on loans which have past-due payments, and initiate process to restore payments or default. Ensure that proper notice and other procedural steps are taken to exercise bank's right to foreclose or collect.

lobbyist: Represent interests of a particular constituency in an attempt to influence legislation at the local, state or national level. Meet with legislators to educate them about the issues of the constituency to get voting support for measures supported by the constituency. Build coalitions with groups that share interests to increase influence.

managed care attorney: Provide legal advice and assistance to management on the legal, regulatory and business issues affecting managed care operations including relationships with participating providers, employers, members, employees, accreditation bodies and regulatory agencies.

manufacturer's representative: Sell products to retail establishments, wholesalers, and commercial users for resale to consumers. May represent more than one manufacturer at a time, for example a wide variety of sports products. Resell to current customers while developing new markets.

marketing manager (a.k.a. marketing coordinator): Design and manage image, promotion and client-development work for a law firm. Organize informational seminars and special events. Arrange speaking engagements for attorneys with industry groups. Assess firm's marketing database capabilities and recommend software purchases to enhance business development activities. Support business development programs for practice areas and individuals. Coordinate work proposal preparation, mailing list development, seminars, newsletters and brochures.

matrimonial (a.k.a. family law) lawyer: Counsel and advise clients in matters involving the marital relationship, including pre-marital agreements, post-marital agreements, divorce, child custody, child support and visitation issues. Represent clients in litigation involving any of these issues.

membership services director: Analyze the needs of bar association members to propose programs to meet those needs. Coordinate and implement membership benefits such as group insurance, travel and purchasing programs. Communicate with members about their issues and areas of concern.

ombuds: A neutral liaison between the general public or employees and a corporation, public agency or employer. Talk to citizens about their complaints. Investigate facts. Attempt to resolve complaints by acting as a mediator. At times advocate for citizens against the government. Create more access for citizens/employees. Help citizens navigate complex governmental bureaucracies. If complaint is not resolved, keep records of nature of complaint for long range planning. Recommend changes to the system to prevent future complaints.

planned giving director: Secure donations through bequest expectancies, life-income gifts and gifts of life insurance. Provide a strategic vision for planned giving. Provide advice, assistance and technical support to development officers for solicitation of planned and deferred gifts. Supervise a professional planned giving staff. Work with the business and finance functions of the foundation and the university to assure adherence to gift acceptance standards and policies and develop an outreach program to volunteers and allied professionals.

policy and legislative affairs director or staff:

Establish and maintain professional relationships with members of the legislature and administration. Identify and analyze legislation significant to the industry and the development and promotion of the company's position on legislative issues.

political consultant: Advise candidates on choice of issues important to the public, how to frame issues, and how to sell their position to voters. Advise on marketing and packaging. Focus on election strategies, management, public relations, damage control.

postal inspector: Gather information concerning mail fraud. Investigate criminal activity. Work with federal law.

prepaid legal plan administrator: Oversee legal HMO plan where people pay a monthly/annual fee to have coverage for basic legal services (i.e. wills, family matters, criminal).

pro bono foundation administrator: Coordinate review of requests for money to pro bono projects. Manage budget and employees. Coordinate fundraising efforts. Recruit volunteer lawyers to serve on board.

professional development training officer: Teach lawyering skills such as effective speaking and presentation, negotiation and client management techniques, and legal writing. Develop further aspects of and train personnel in elements of the law firm's quality management program.

professional speaker: Identify issues of concern or interest to targeted markets. Design keynote addresses, seminars, workshops and break-out sessions that address those issues at conventions, meetings, corporate retreats or other gatherings. Usually also publish books, booklets, tapes and other materials for purchase by attendees at the program.

program advisor: Review a specific government agency's programs to determine whether they are in compliance with applicable legislation. Answer legal questions asked by employees of the department. Design and present training programs in applicable areas of law. Advise regional offices in administration of programs.

program developer: Identify community legal service needs of poor on behalf of a legal aid organization. Develop plan for service delivery, including resources to support services. Know and draw on community financial and talent resources.

public affairs director: In charge of corporate relations with the media and the community. Develop corporate or governmental responses to public controversy. Spokesperson for organization, especially in high profile or crisis situations. Coordinate corporate involvement in community and national matters impacting its operations.

public affairs producer: Identify issues of public concern for a television or radio station. Initiate and coordinate community-involvement programming or projects that deal with those concerns.

public disclosure commission director: Review and disseminate information submitted to or collected by the government. Responsible for drafting and approval of dissemination standards and procedures. Coordinate storage and retrieval of public information.

publications manager: Responsible for overseeing and coordinating the solicitation, writing, editing, publishing, pricing and distribution of bar association CLE materials and other substantive publications.

purchasing agent: Purchase supplies and equipment for a corporation or government agency after determining the best products and negotiating the best price and quality. Budget. Converse with suppliers. Identify negotiating tricks.

real estate developer: Locate and buy land and buildings to develop into office buildings, malls, residential areas, condominiums, hotels, apartments, commercial areas. Locate investors and funding for projects. Oversee construction projects. Budget and monitor expenses.

real estate licensing course instructor: Provide instruction to individuals seeking to obtain real estate license. Prepare potential realtors for state exam.

recruiting administrator: Screen résumés on behalf of a law firm for associate positions, and organize on-campus interviews. Arrange advertisements for associate and partner-level positions. Supervise travel arrangements and interview schedules for applicants. Draft and finalize employment contracts. Stay current on employment law regulations that apply to hiring. Promote the law firm's reputation in the general employment market.

recycling coordinator: Gather information about existing recycling programs in a region. Contact all programs and attempt through mediation to prevent the duplication of services. Suggest the initiation of new programs to meet existing needs.

reporter for legal newspaper: Research, investigate, interview, write, and edit articles on legal issues. Interview legal scholars, attorneys. Travel to different courthouses. Develop creative ideas for future articles.

residential remodel contractor: Coordinate with home owners and architects to bid out a plan. Sometimes actually design the remodel. Obtain building permits. Contract with and supervise subcontractors. Supervise construction work throughout the process. Collect.

restaurant owner/operator: Conduct market research to develop a successful concept. Get funding. Hire and supervise chefs, wait staff, accountants, and others. Mediate disputes. Create menu. Market restaurant to the public and to corporations for group events.

restaurant reviewer: Visit restaurants. Sample food and drinks. Rate quality of food, service, and atmosphere. Analyze information and writes reviews. Arrange for publication in magazines, newspapers, journals, etc.

risk management advisor: Advise decision-makers within a business, hospital, or government agency about business practices that could subject the organization to liability and to what degree. Recommend steps to avoid risk.

risk management consultant: Advise businesses of any size, or government, on legal issues and risks inherent in company policies, procedures, activities, prospective projects, and litigated matters.

sales representative (legal publisher): Contact law firms, corporations, libraries and solo practitioners to promote and sell legal books, computer research programs, CD-ROM collections and other publications.

screenwriter: Write original screenplays, or adapt books or other written materials, stories or ideas for presentation on screen. When dealing with legal subject matters, act as a consultant on legal issues, courtroom presentation, and other aspects of the practice of law to ensure realism in the presentation.

SEC compliance examiner: Examine potential public offerings, prospectuses, and corporate information to ensure compliance with federal and state securities laws.

self-help law book publisher: Solicit, write, edit, design, arrange for printing of and market books containing ready-to-use forms and instructions to assist non-lawyers with legal matters, including how to draft a contract, draft a will, research a trademark, etc.

sexual harassment avoidance training: Design and present interactive seminars designed to educate management and employees of corporations and government about the elements of sexual harassment, how to avoid it, and how to deal with problems as they arise.

software designer: Research and outline a software package that meets the specific needs of a customer base. Interview customers about their needs. Compare existing systems. Set up cost-effective balance between power, flexibility, hardware compatibility, expandability, and human factors. Troubleshoot.

staff attorney for appellate court: Read, analyze, research and write draft opinions. Prepare judges for oral argument. Analyze legal arguments, issues, case law. Coordinate and implement research plan for appellate matters.

staff lawyer for municipal research service: Research and write reports for city attorneys on issues of law. Research laws for contracting municipalities. Answer telephone inquiries. Codify city ordinances.

stockbroker: Act as a sales agent between investors and publicly traded corporations, bonds, real estate investment trusts and other securities/investments.

strategic planning consultant: Provide counseling services for long-term strategic planning for law firms, businesses and governmental units. Advise clients regarding market conditions in their field. Identify organizational goals. Facilitate planning retreats.

supervising attorney, volunteer legal services: Coordinate the provision of legal services to persons unable to afford it otherwise. Oversee staffing, budgeting, fundraising, matching people with resources, etc. Provide supervision to second and third-year law students at university-sponsored legal aid clinics. Provide advice to low-income individuals.

supervisor of public trust accounts: Manage and administer trust funds of governmental entities, including making prudent investments.

tax lawyer: Research current internal revenue code policies. Evaluate compliance. Educate and explain policies. Advise and counsel clients on the tax ramifications of their past or potential actions and how to operate in a way that minimizes negative tax repercussions.

technical writer: Write instructional or explanatory manuals for products, or take technical data and express it in a way that makes it accessible to a lay audience.

telecommunications fraud consultant: Advise companies on how to detect and prevent fraud using telephones, computers or online services. Ascertain areas of fraudulent use, and turn over to government agencies or corporations.

television broadcast sales: Sell commercial air time to national and local businesses. Negotiate deals for multiple ads. Maintain good customer relations for repeat business.

title examiner: Research state of title to real property. Identify encumbrances, anomalies and claims. Report findings to parties to the transaction.

trainer: Educate employees in skills needed to achieve goals of the corporation. Teach "hard" skills like computer usage or customer service techniques or "soft" skills like leadership, team-building and dealing with change. May design programs or be certified to present programs designed by others. Design measurement tools to evaluate the effectiveness of training programs.

training administrator: Oversee training programs for large organizations to make certain they are in compliance with the most recent federal, state and local labor regulations. Research new laws, communicate with training departments impacted by changes in laws, and coordinate interests of competing training groups to create uniformly revised programs.

union representative: Represent union members in contract negotiations. Act as liaison between the company and a union member when complaints are filed by either against the other.

university administrator: In charge of leading or managing a department, division or specific function of a university. Responsible for compliance with rules and performance of individuals within that unit.

US trustee in bankruptcy: Appointed for each federal judicial district. Supervise the administration of bankruptcy cases. Oversee intake and pay-out of assets of an entity in bankruptcy. Assign auditing and oversight to other lawyers and accountants on a contract basis.

victim's compensation investigator or advocate: Review applications for government compensation programs, or investigate claims for private firms or insurance companies. Interview victims, and determine extent of claimant's injuries.

VP, community relations: Represent a corporation in the community. Create partnerships with nonprofit organizations and governmental agencies to improve the quality of life in the area as well as the company's public image. Investigate and respond to complaints from members of the community about such issues as noise, pollution, construction, expansion.

waste management planning: Study current waste management system usually for a city or county government. Develop understanding of different types of waste and their impact on the environment. Propose new plans for more efficient disposal of waste. Instigate and participate in public hearings. Work with representatives of all waste management providers in the area, including labor unions, to get approval of any changes in the system.

waste reduction and recycling supervisor: Implement countywide recycling program, including increasing public commitment to recycling. Oversee public relations campaign directed to business and households. Ensure compliance of municipalities and businesses with state/federal laws.

worker's compensation lawyer: Evaluate and pursue claims for work-related injuries under state administrative procedures almost always after an initial denial of the claim. Explain the process to the client. Request and review medical evaluations. File and argue appeals before an administrative tribunal and in court.

zoning and short-platting specialist: Review applications for exceptions to current zoning regulations. Compare to current laws and regulations. Issue recommendations for approval or denial.

INDEXES

Subject Matter Index

Subject Matter Index

A

accomplishments, see self-assessment
ADR, see alternative dispute resolution
advertisements, see classified ads
advertising, see communications
age discrimination: 17-18, 185-86; see also older worker
alternative career options: overview of, 115-121, 283; nontraditional law practice alternatives, 116, 262; working within law as a non-practitioner, 117, 344-345; providing legal information to the general public, 117-118; see also specific subject matters
alternative dispute resolution: options, 283-285; resources, 285-287; success stories, 71, 152, 174; mediation, 18, 19, 117, 284, 367; ombuds, 284-285, 377; grievance investigator, 285, 365, 374
alternative work schedules: overview, 151-155; part-time jobs, 152,154, 256, 262-263; commuting, 152-153, 257; how to negotiate, 154; project work, 159-160, 175-176, 189; working at home, 152, 257; resources, 262, 271; contract lawyering, 153-155, 175-176, 257, 346; temporary work, 11, 13, 14, 175-176
anger, letting go of, 255
appearance: importance of personal, 238, 254; of resume, 207
aptitude testing, see Johnson O'Connor Research Foundation
aptitudes, see skills
articulation, 176-177, 210, 236-237
arts and entertainment: options in, 287, 289; resources re, 289-292; success stories, 129-130, 288-289
associations: for salary information, 240; for research, 128, 283; building credibility through, 159, 196-197. See also alphabetical index, and individual listings by field.
attitude: and burnout, 42-43; destructive, 10, 29, 20, 24, 29, 37, 59-61, 177-178, 280, 218; importance of, 7, 15, 62, 64, 201; stressing in interview, 235, 238-239; toward enjoyment, 17, 33-37, 38-39; entitlement mentality, 169-170; glory-seeker, 182; impatience, 7-9; limitations, 61; respect, 26, 72, 83; self-esteem, 53, 165; self-reliance, 15
autonomy, 26, 83, 109

B

balance: 23, 24, 33-36; lack of & burnout, 42; success stories, 34, 150, 205, 262-263
banking, see corporate
bar associations: 120; value of participation, 159; options in, 291; resources re, 291-292; success stories, 4, 160
bar examination: need to take, 20; resources, 262
barriers to change, see change
benefits: in salary negotiations, 241; calculating value of, 241; health insurance, 247, 254
billable hour: 13, 27, 150; & burnout, 42
boredom, 17, 32, 33, 42
budgeting: for transition, 141, 142, 144, 145-146, 150; while unemployed, 254, see also income, money
burnout: attitudes that create, 42-43; causes of, 42-44, 260-261; definition of, 40-41; symptoms of, 40; v. dissatisfaction with work, 44; resources about, 259, 261, 270
business, see small business, entrepreneurial ventures, corporate

C

career change, see transition
career counseling: choosing, 261; determining need for, 233; finding, 261-263; free sources, 259; identifying good counselors, 272; need for career, 233, 273-274; nonprofit career programs for lawyers, 259; obtaining, 273-274; promises, 261-262; resources, 274-275
career development: 8, 24; phases of, 29-31
career strategies: self-defeating, 10; for the new workplace, 14
change: barriers to, 55, 50-53, 86-87,137; changing legal profession, 12-14, 259; changing workplace, 269-270; discomfort of, 47-49, 64-65; job, 149-151; facts about, 48; financial change resources, 270-271; formula for, 55; general resources, 269; of location, 20, 232, 262; overcoming resistance to, 54-56; process, 148; resistance to, 45-49, 54-55; the world, 25; where you are, 45, 149-151; see also transition, workplace
children: as barriers to change, 17, 47, 52; job involving, 63
classified ads: answering, 169, 191-193; in journals & websites, 283; placing, 193; reasons employers place, 193; self-assessment exercise using, 81; use and effectiveness, 191-193
COBRA, 254
communications: exploding myths about writing, 293; jobs in, 120, 292-293; resources re, 293-297; success stories, 159, 171, 293; advertising resources, 294; broadcasting resources, 294-295; entertainment resources, 295; public relations resources, 295; speaking career resources, 295-296; writing/editing resources, 296-297
compensation: amount to request, 231; history, 241; law firm partnership, 242; negotiations, 173, 240-243; researching, 240-241; research resources, 240; see also salary surveys listed under individual subject areas in Appendix 4
competition, 7, 13-14, 25-26, 27, 28, 31, 34-35, 90, 169, 174, 182
conflicts: leaving the law, 72-73; money v. meaning, 73; resolving, 74-75; work v. family, 73-74
consulting: 171, 205, 231; options in, 297-298; resources re, 298-299; success stories, 159-160, 230
contacts: as research aids, 199, 200, 201; being prepared for, 132, 201-203; establishing, 201; first approaches to, 129-130, 204; following up with, 204; importance of, 18, 128-129, 233; questions to ask, 131, 193;

referrals from, 133; resistance from, 131-132; see also family & friends, networking, implementation

contract lawyering, see alternative work schedule arrangements

corporate: attitudes towards lawyers, 181-182; options in, 19, 116, 117, 118, 300-303; resources re, 303-307; success stories, 156, 175, 181, 193, 196, 198, 230, 301; financial services resources, 304; human resources, 304-305; marketing & sales resources, 305; organizational development resources, 305; training resources, 305-306

counseling: options in, 121, 307-308; resources re careers, 308-309; educational background for, 157-158; need for psychological, 56; success stories, 56, 201, 260-261; see also career counseling

cover letters, see letters

creativity, 35, 83-84, 97, 106, 119

credentials: 231; as foundation of credibility, 62; value of law degree as, 4

credibility, 62-63

D

data-related skills developed by lawyers, 91

depression, 4, 41, 166

directories, see index to directories

disabilities, 189

dissatisfaction: among lawyers, 28-29; evaluating, 39; job v. career, 35, 37-39; roots of, 23-39; statistics, 28; & burnout, 44, 48; traits of contented lawyers, 39

E

education: 83, 118, 121; need for more, 155-156, 157, 161-162; qualification for, 157-158; options in, 117-118, 199, 120, 309, 311-312; resources re, 302-305; success stories, 184-185, 202-203, 310-311; law school administration, 118, 310-311

employers: demonstrating skills to, 93, 175-177, 180-181, 210, 213, 235-236; change in employer/employee

relationship, 11-12; evaluating needs of, 170, 171-189; informational interviewing, 129; expectations in job interviews, 134; why they hire, 171-178

employment contracts, 243, 364;

entrepreneurial ventures: 83, 120, 161; options re, 119, 120, 315, 317-318; resources re, 318-320; success stories, 120, 230, 293, 317, 353-354; suitability for, 319; tips, 317-318

environment: options in, 320; resources re, 321; success stories, 3, 34, 158, 171

ethics: options in, 321-322; resources re, 322; bioethicist, 366; ethics officer, 372

exercises: calculating the real costs of change, 86-87; classified ads review, 81-82; creating ideal job grid, 96-98; fantasy-job-a-week game, 85; figuring out your passions, 79-80; newsmagazine review, 81; quick-and-easy self assessment, 77-78; reasons to maintain status quo, 50-51; setting your priorities, 87-88; show and tell, 80-81; things I really love to do, 81; ; transferable skills analysis, 93-95; what do you value?, 84-85; what makes work meaningful to you, 82-84; writing a classified ad for your ideal job; 85; your fantasy employment, 86; your history of achievement, 79; your lasting contribution, 86; see also self-assessment, preferences

expectations: of others, 4, 36, 47, 52, 163; unreasonable, 23, 24-27, & burnout, 42; & dissatisfaction, 24, 29, 30, 35; v. reality, 26-27

F

failure, feelings of, 4-5, 9, 16-17, 165, 183-184

family, see friends & family

fatigue, 40-41

fear: moving past, 129-130; exercise to identify, 50-51; of change, 50-54, 173; of contacting others, 129; of disclosure, 4, 9, 129; of saying no, 36; of self-assessment, 6-7, 61; of phone, 129; of the unknown, 51

federal jobs, special help for, 331

financial concerns, see money

flexibility: as employee, 12, 14; in job hunt, 170, 173, 229-233

foundations, see nonprofits

freelance work, see alternative work schedule

friends & families: reaction of, 9, 10, 163-164, 166, 249; help from, 201,202; see also contacts, networking

G

golden handcuffs, 4, 9, 31, 40, 52, 65, 73, 140-141

government: options in, 118, 325-329; resources re, 329-332; special application rules, 219; federal jobs, 331; finding out about vacancies, 329; success stories, 181

guilt: easy work, 67; not being productive, 152; not liking work, 164

H

headhunters, 37, 177, 194-195, 205, 346, 350

health insurance, see benefits

healthcare: how to get into, 333; options in, 332-333; resources re, 333-334; success stories, 174, 198

helping others, 25, 83

I

Ideal Job Grid: purpose of, 69, 96; blank, 99; samples, 100-101; working with, 122-124; completing, 96-98; using, 122-124, 127, 149; sample entries, 103, 105, 108, 109, 110

identity, loss of, 51, 72-73, 152, 163-166

implementation: 7-9, 169-243; course corrections, 231, 233; general resources, 268; job hunt resources, 264-265, 276-279; tracking contacts, 228, see also classified ads, informational interviewing, marketing, networking, resumes

income, expectations of high, 25. See also money.

independent general counsel or part-time in-house counsel, 301

Information Age, 12, 172

informational interviewing: 128-133; defined; 128-129;

etiquette of, 130-133; getting started w/, 129-130; questions in, 131; persisting w/, 133
intellectual challenge: desire for, 25, 46, 68; decreased, 33
interests: 14, 66; defined, 97; list of, 103
international: analyzing preference for, 78; options in, 335; resources, re, 335-337; working abroad, 336; success stories, 3-4, 34, 151-152
Internet, 128, 204-205, 269-270
interviews: 173, 181, 234-239; common questions, 237; dressing for, 238; handling negatives in, 237-238; preparing for, 234-235; purpose of, 234, 239; questions to ask in, 238-239; selling points in, 236; storytelling in, 235-236; resources, 268; ten selling points, 236; see also informational interviewing

J
job: descriptions, 89, 209, 278-279, 292, 365-380; end of the, 11; listings for lawyers, 270-271; opening for growth, 172-174, 228; opening for maintenance, 172; security, 9, 15, 26, 32, 46, 83
job hunt, see implementation, marketing, networking, resumes, letters
job market: state of, 11-12, 169; hidden, 198-199
job search, see implementation, marketing, networking, resumes, letters
Johnson O'Connor Research Foundation 275
journalism, preparation for career in, 19, 159, see also communications
judiciary: options in, 337, 339; resources re, 339-340; success story, 152, 338-339

K
knowledge workers, 12

L
labor unions: options in, 340; resources re, 340-341
law degree: reasons for obtaining, 59-60, 63-64; value of, 4, 6, 7, 63-64, 157-158, 177, 217;

placement on resume, 217
law enforcement: options in, 341; resources re, 341
law firms: options in, 117, 342, 344; resources re, 344-346, 348-350; success stories, 205, 229, 343-344; summer clerkships, 20; law office management resources, 344-345; partnership negotiations, 242; partnership resources, 349; directories of, 349-350
law practice: trying out, 19-20; reality of, 25, 27; good things about, 27; downsides of, 27; specialties in, 115-116, 345-346; nontraditional alternatives, 117; closing an active, 244-245; selling a, 245-246; resources on changing, 259; litigation resources, 348-349
lay-off: avoiding, 66, 361; environment for, 361; recognizing signs of impending, 361; responding to, 137, 361-362; tips for handling, 362-364
leading: value in job hunt, 205-206
leaving the law: adjusting to, 163-166; bar association membership and, 247-248; drawbacks, 72-73; benefits, 73; steps to take when, 244-248
legal background: stereotypes about, 177, 179, 181-183; value of, 4, 5, 7, 17, 183
legal education: impact on creativity, 60-61; impact on ability to risk, 60-61; skills developed through, 90, 177
legal information science: options in, 350; resources re, 350-351
legal profession; downsizing in, 13; history of, 12-14; reasons for entering, 60; resources on changing, 259; resources on job announcements for, 264-265
legal search consultants, see headhunters
letters: broadcast, 195; cover, 178, 183, 195, 220-226, 231; effective, 220-222; follow-up to, 228; introductory, 223-224; mail campaigns, 195; mass mailings, 63, 169, 195; purpose of effective, 220; thank you, 204, 226, 231; to reply to ad, 225
LLM, value of, 157, 161
lobbying & public affairs: options

in, 351; resources, 351-352
long-distance job hunt: how to conduct, 232; international, 322; resources for, 262

M
mail campaigns, see letters
malpractice insurance, 14, 156, 246-247; tail policies, 247
marketing grid, 192
marketing: 170, 190-226; conventional techniques, 190; grid, 192; list of techniques, 192; elements of effective, 190-191; mail campaigns, 195; volunteering, 195-196; affiliating, 196; classified advertisements, 191-192; headhunters, 194-195; following up, 195, 197, 204, 228; record-keeping, 228; see also implementation
mediation, see alternative dispute resolution
megafirms, 13
midlife issues, 17-18, 31-32, 46, 185-186; resources, 269, 276-277
Minnesota study, 72-73, 119, 164, 179
minorities, 188-189
money: amount needed for transition, 141, 144, 145-146; as a red herring, 141; as motivation for change, 73, 180; changing relationship to, 143, 144-145; concerns in transition, 52, 138, 139, 140-147, 166, 184-185; evaluating needs, 142, 144, 150; resources re, 256-257; success stories, 140-141, 146, 155, 184-185; see also income
motivation, 3, 7, 15, 48, 55, 63-64, 65, 69-71
Myers-Briggs Personality Type Indicator, 275

N
negotiation, see compensation
networking: 199-205; at a meeting, 197; defined, 200; following up, 204; for shy people, 197; how employers use, 199-200; how to, 200-201; identifying contacts, 201; meeting with contacts, 204; online, 204-205; questions to pose, 203; small talk, 197; success stories, 198,

199-200, 201, 202-203, 205; see also friends & family

new graduates, 14, 19, 24, 30, 180, 185

nonprofits: 120, 158, 160; options in, 120, 322-324; resources re, 324-328; success stories, 4, 72, 151-152, 171, 174, 196, 206, 323-324

O

objections: overcoming, 19, 20, 179-189; no experience, 180-181; no lawyers wanted, 17, 181-183; loser lawyer, 16, 72, 183-184; too expensive, 184-185; too young, 185; overqualified, 185; too old, 185-186; fired, 186-187; time gap, 187; gender, 187-188; minority, 188-189; disability, 189; lack of commitment, 189

older workers, 17-18, 32, 180, 185-186

ombuds, see alternative dispute resolution

options: in ADR, 283, 285; in arts & entertainment, 287, 289; in bar associations, 291; in communications, 292-293; in consulting, 297-298; in corporate, business, banking, 300-303; in counseling, 307-308; in education, 309, 311-312; as an entrepreneur, 315, 317-318; in the environmental field, 320; in ethics, 321-322; in foundations & nonprofits, 322, 324; in government, 328-329; in healthcare, 332-333; in international work, 335; in the judiciary, 337, 339; in labor unions, 340; in law enforcement, 341; in law firms, 342, 344; in legal information science, 350; in lobbying & public affairs, 351; in publishing, 352; in real estate, 355, 357; in sports, 358; in technology, 361

overwork, 27, 33-34, 40, 41, 51, 73-74, 111, 150, 152-153

P

passion: as key to success, 3, 15, 61, 62, 64; figuring out your, 79-80, 81

people contact: 15, 67-68, 83; defined, 97; list of preferences

re, 109

people skills developed by lawyers, 92

persistence, 3, 8-9, 63-64, 170, 227-228, 233

predictions, 12, 15, 115-116, 127

preferences: 65-69, 152, 177; analyzing your preferences, 16-17, 38-39, 68-69; see also environmental, interests, people contact, self-assessment, skills, values

prejudice, see disability, minorities, older worker, objections, stereotypes

prioritizing, 65-66, 71-75, 87-88

procrastination, 67, 77, 78

project work, 189, 231

public affairs, see lobbying & public affairs

public relations, see communications

publishing: options in, 117, 119, 352; resources re, 352, 354-355; success stories, 120, 293, 353-354

Q

questions: for information interviewing, 131; asked in job interviews, 237; to ask in job interviews, 239

R

real estate: options in, 120, 355, 357; resources re, 357-358; success stories, 120, 356-357

recent graduate, see new graduate

references, 187, 209

research: 7, 107, 127-133, 170; written, 128; oral, 128-133, 174, 176, 180, 209; general resources for, 272-273

resistance to change, see change, resistance to

resources: on change, 269; on the changing legal profession, 259; on the changing workplace, 269-270; on stress and burnout, 259-260, 270; on financial change, 270-271; on alternative work schedules, 262, 271; on changing locations, 262; on self-assessment, 271-272, 274-276; on career counselors, 274-275; on testing, 285-276; on the job search, 264-266, 276-279; on resumes & cover letters, 211,

277; Internet, 211, 264-265, 277-278; for older workers, 276-277; on ADR, 285-287; on arts & entertainment, 289-291; on bar associations, 291-292; on communications, 293-297; on consulting, 298-299; on corporate business, banking, 303-307; on counseling, 308-309; on education, 312-315; on entrepreneurial ventures, 318-320; on environmental careers, 321; on ethics, 322; on foundation & nonprofits, 324-328; on government, 329-332; on healthcare, 333-334; on international opportunities, 335-337; on the judiciary, 339-340; on labor unions, 340-341; on law enforcement, 341; on law firms, 344-346, 348-350; on legal information science, 350-351; on lobbying & public affairs, 351-352; on publishing, 352, 354-355; on real estate, 357-358; on sports, 358, 360-361; on technology, 361-362

resumes: 157, 169, 176, 178, 183, 187, 190, 195, 207-218, 227, 229; purpose of, 207-208; preparation for, 208-209; writing services, 209-210; guidelines, 208; writing an effective, 210-212; scannable, 211; chronological, 178, 212, 214; functional, 212-213, 215; targeted, 213, 216; law degree and, 217; evaluating effectiveness, 218; affiliations and, 218; length, 218; resources, 267, 269

retirement, 32-33, 137

risk taking, 32, 47, 173

S

sabbatical, 46, 151-152, 165, 187

salary negotiations, see compensation

salary, see compensation

sales careers, 104, 179, 181

sample: interview questions, 131, 237, 239; letters, 223-226; resumes, 214-216

self-assessment: value of, 7, 44, 59-64, 170, 179-180, 184; process, 65-111, 149; time required for, 76; in current job, 149; quiz, 39; exercises, 68, 77-88; resources, 271-276; personality

preference quiz, 39; achievements, 79, 209; see also exercises, preferences, skills, interests, values, people contact
self-employment, 11, 305-308
selling, aversion to, 104
senior lawyers, see older worker
severance pay, 362-363, 364
skills: as key to satisfaction, 38; used in law, 125-126; developed in law practice, 91-92; developed in law school, 90; most preferred, 106-108; competency, 94-95; lists of, 105; develop rapport, 107; observe, 108; advise, 106-107; speak, 107; analyze, 106; organize, 106; persuade, 107; plan, 107; problem solving, 106; sample skills evaluation, 95; write, 106; manage, 107
small business, 172-173, 189, 233
solo practice: resources, 318-319; & part-time work, 152
small business, 172-173
specialization, 19, 32, 33, 115-116
sports: options in, 358; resources re, 358, 360-361; success stories, 156, 160, 178, 187
statistics: 25, 26, 28, 36-37, 48, 73, 127, 172, 186, 187-188, 190, 197, 199
status quo, reasons to maintain, 46-47, 50-53
stepping stones: another degree, 161-162; bridge jobs, 146; building a business, 161, changing things where you are, 149-151; consulting, 159-160; finding, 148-162; freelancing, 159; interim jobs, 160; internships, 159; non-degree course work, 161; switching to alternative work schedule, 152-153, 154; taking a step in the wrong direction, 155-156; taking some time off, 151-152; working as a contract lawyer, 153-155; volunteering, 158-159
stereotypes: about lawyers, 177, 179, 181, 182; see also overcoming objections
story-telling in interviews, 185, 235-236
strategies, see career strategies
success: definition of, 31, 71; effect of, 40; key to, 23; stories, 3-4, 34, 47, 63, 67, 71, 72, 118, 121, 120, 140-141, 143, 146,

148, 150, 151-152, 155-156, 158-160, 161, 162, 171, 175, 178, 179, 181, 184-185, 187, 196, 198, 199-200, 202-203, 205, 206, 229, 230, 260-261, 262-263, 273-274, 288-289, 293, 301, 310-311, 316-317, 323-324, 338-339, 343-344, 353-354, 356-357, 359-360
suitability: for law, 39, 347-348; for line of work, 38-39
support: from others, 9-10, 15, 44, 46, 76-77, 149, 165-166, 233; lack of, 45
systems, see implementation

T

tail policies, see malpractice insurance
teaching, see education
teamwork, 35, 110, 182
technology: options in, 361; resources re, 361-362; success stories, 3, 47, 67, 161, 230, 359-360
telecommuting, see alternative work schedules
temporary work, see alternative work schedules
time off, see sabbatical
timing, 51, 137-139, 147; see also stepping stones, transition
transferable skills analysis: 89-95, 176-177, 209; taking deposition analyzed, 93-94
transition: compared to lawsuit, 6; keys to successful, 6-10, 54; process, 148-149; readiness for, 138; spiraling circles of, 227; temporary work while exploring, 153-155,159; see also stepping stones
travel, preference for, 78, 102

U

unemployment, 17-18

V

values: as key to satisfaction, 38; defined, 67, 69-71, 97; expressed in law, 67; & burnout, 42-43; exercises for defining, 82-88; list of, 108; independence v. autonomy, 109; recognition, 26; versatility, 26
volunteering, 158-159, 195-196; and resume writing, 213, 217

W

websites: as research tool, 283; resources, 277-278. See also index to websites.
withdrawing from the profession, 163-166, 244-250
women, 187-188
work environment: defined, 36-38, 68; evaluating, 68; list of, 110; preferred, 97, work hours, 111; see also overwork
work hours, 111; see also overwork, work environment
workplace: changes in, 11-15, 127-128; understanding today's, 11-15, 169; rules of new, 14, 210; resources on today's, 254

Y

youth, as objection, 185

Index to Directories

ABA Awards and Grants Listing, 324
ABA Guide to Foreign Law Firms, 335
ABA-Approved Law Schools, 313
ALJ Handbook, 339
Almanac of American Employers, 278
American Lobbyists Directory, 351
America's New Foundations, 326
Annual Directory of Grant Support, 326
Associate Salary Survey, 349
Association of American University Presses Directory, 296
Associations Yellow Book, 326
ASTD's Buyer's Guide and Consultant Directory, 306
Attorneys and Agents Registered to Practice Before the US Patent & Trademark Office, 361
Attorney's Guide to State Bar Admission Requirements, 262
Best's Directory of Recommended Independent Insurance Adjusters, 304
Biographical Directory of Legal Administration Professionals, 344
BNA's Directory of State and Federal Courts, Judges and Clerks, 339
Business & Finance Career Directory, 304
Business Organizations, Agencies and Publications Directory, 278
Business Phone Book USA, 306
Congressional Staff Directory, 331

Congressional Yellow Book, 331
Consultants and Consulting
    Organizations Directory, 299
Corporate Foundations Profile, 326
Corporate Giving Yellow Pages, 326
Corporate Yellow Book, 306
County Directory, 331
Cyberhound's Guide to Associations
    and Nonprofit Organizations on
    the Internet, 326
Directories of Major Employers, 279
Directory of American Firms
    Operating in Foreign Countries,
    336
Directory of Appellate Central Staff
    Counsel, 339
Directory of Bankruptcy Attorneys,
    346
Directory of Corporate Affiliations,
    306
Directory of Corporate Counsel,
    303
Directory of Entertainment & Sports
    Lawyers, 359
Directory of Environmental
    Attorneys, 321
Directory of Federal Jobs &
    Employers, 331
Directory of Intellectual Property
    Attorneys, 346
Directory of Law School ADR
    Courses & Programs, 286
Directory of Lawyer Assistance
    Programs, 308
Directory of Lawyer Disciplinary
    Agencies and Client Protection
    Funds, 322
Directory of Lawyer Referral
    Services, 291
Directory of Lawyers Assistance
    Programs, 259
Directory of Legal Aid and Defender
    Offices in the US, 325
Directory of Legal Employers, 266,
    349
Directory of Litigation Attorneys,
    349
Directory of Opportunities in
    International Law, 335
Directory of Paralegal Training
    Programs, 313
Directory of Public Interest Law
    Centers, 325
Directory of Publications &
    Broadcast Media, 297
Directory of Subscribers to the AFL-
    CIO Lawyers Coordinating
    Committee. 340
Directory of US Labor

Organizations, 341
Encyclopedia of Associations, 279,
    296
Encyclopedia of Business
    Information Sources, 279
Environmental Law Careers
    Directory, 321
Federal and State Judicial Clerkship
    Directory, 339
Federal Regional Yellow Book, 332
Federal Regulatory Directory, 332
Federal Yellow Book, 332
Financial Yellow Book, 304
Foundation Directory Part 2, 327
Foundation Directory, 327
Gale Environmental Sourcebook,
    321
Goodworks: A Guide to Careers in
    Social Change, 327
Government Affairs Yellow Book,
    351
Government Job Finder, 332
Guide to US Foundations, 327
Harvard Business School's Career
    Guide for Finance, 304
Hudson's Subscription Newsletter
    Directory, 296
Human Rights Organizations and
    Periodicals Directory, 336
International Directory of Little
    Magazines and Small Presses,
    296
International Directory of Marketing
    Research Companies and
    Services, 305
International Jobs Directory, 337
Job Seeker's Guide to Private and
    Public Employers, 279
JobBank Guide to Health Care
    Companies, 334
Judicial Yellow Book, 340
Law and Legal Information
    Directory, 266
Law Books & Serials In Print, 354
Law Firms Yellow Book, 349
Legal Newsletters in Print, 294
Legal Researcher's Desk Reference,
    266, 291, 354
Literary Market Place, 296
Management Consulting, 299
Martindale-Hubbell Dispute
    Resolution Directory, 286
Martindale-Hubbell International
    Law Directory, 335
Martindale-Hubbell Law Directory,
    350
Medical & Health Information
    Directory, 334
Military Facilities Directory, 332

Million Dollar Directory, 306
Municipal Directory, 332
Municipal Yellow Book, 332
NAPIL Public Interest Career
    Resources Guide, 325
National Directory of Corporate
    Giving, 327
National Directory of Corporate
    Public Affairs, 352
National Directory of Law Schools,
    312
National Directory of Minority-
    Owned Business Firms, 306
National Directory of Nonprofit
    Organizations, 327
National Directory of Prosecuting
    Attorneys, 341
National Directory of Women-
    Owned Business Firms, 307
National Job Bank, 307
News Media Yellow Book, 297
Newsletters in Print, 279
Newspapers Career Directory, 296
NLJ 250, 350
National Trade and Professional
    Associations of the US, 279
O'Dwyer's Directory of Public
    Relations Firms, 295
Of Counsel 700, 350
Official Congressional Directory, 332
Official Museum Directory, 290
Plunkett's Entertainment & Media
    Industry Almanac, 295
Plunkett's Financial Services
    Industry Almanac, 304
Plunkett's Healthcare Industry
    Almanac, 334
Plunkett's Infotech Industry
    Almanac, 362
Professional's Job Finder, 279
Public Service and International
    Law, 336
Publishers Directory, 355
Realtors National Membership
    Directory, 359
Research Centers Directory, 351
Songwriter's Market, 290
Sports Market Place Directory, 360
Sports Summit Sports Business
    Directory, 360
Standard Directory of Advertising
    Agencies, 294
Standard Periodical Directory, 279
State Directory, 332
State Yellow Book, 332
Telecommunications Directory, 362
The Am-Law 100, 350
The Environmental Career Guide,
    321

Index to Organizations

The Forbes 500, 307
The Fortune 500, 307
The Insider's Guide to Law Firms, 350
The Job Seeker's Guide to Private and Public Companies, 307
The Job-Seeker's Guide to Socially Responsible Companies, 307
The Wall Street Journal Guide to Who's Who and What's What on Wall Street, 304
Trade Shows Worldwide, 305
Training and Development Organizations Directory, 315
Ulrich's International Periodicals Directory, 279, 337
US Industrial Directory, 307
Want's Federal-State Court Directory, 340
Ward's Business Directory of US Private and Public Companies, 307
Washington Representatives, 352
Who's Who in Association Management, 326
Who's Who in Professional Speaking ,295
Who's Who in Training and Development, Training & Development, 306
Who's Who, 279
Writer's Guide to Book Editors, Publishers & Literary Agents, 296
Writer's Guide to Hollywood Producers, Directors, and Screenwriter's Agents, 297
Writer's Market, 297
Yale Law School Public Interest Fellowships Guide, 325

Index to Organizations

ABA Section of Dispute Resolution, 285
Academy of Family Mediators, 285
Academy of Legal Studies in Business 312
American Academy of Matrimonial Lawyers, 308
American Academy of Medical Administrators, 334
American Association for Adult and Continuing Education, 314
American Association for Employment in Education, Inc., 314
American Association for Higher Education (AAHE), 314

American Association for Paralegal Education, 313
American Association of Advertising Agencies 294
American Association of Attorney-CPAs, 345
American Association of Community Colleges, 314
American Association of Health Plans, 334
American Association of Law Libraries, 350
American Association of Law Schools, 313
American Association of Museums, 289
American Association of Nurse Attorneys, 346
American Association of Professional Landmen, 321
American Association of Public Welfare Attorneys, 329
American Bankers Association, 304
American Bar Association, 291, 345
American Civil Liberties Union (ACLU), 324
American College of Healthcare Executives, 334
American College of Real Estate Lawyers, 358
American College of Trust & Estate Counsel, 346
American Compensation Association, 304
American Corporate Counsel Association, 303
American Counseling Association, 308
American Health Lawyers Association, 333
American Immigration Lawyers Association, 335
American Intellectual Property Law Association, 361
American Library Association, 351
American Management Association International, 305
American Marketing Association, 305
American Medical Group Association, 334
American Society for Information Science, 351
American Society for Training and Development, 306
American Society of Association Executives, 325
American Society of International Law, 335

Association for Multimedia Communications, 361
Association for Practical and Professional Ethics, 322
Association for Quality and Participation, 306
Association of Continuing Legal Education, 313
Association of Family and Conciliation Courts, 286
Association of Legal Administrators, 344
Association of Professional Responsibility Lawyers, 322
Association of Trial Lawyers of America, 341, 348
Career Planning and Adult Development Network, 308
Chamber of Commerce, 278, 306
Christian Legal Society, 349
Commission on Lawyers Assistance Programs, 308
Computer Law Association, 361
Council of Appellate Staff Attorneys, 339
Council on Foundations, 326
Council on Governmental Ethics Laws, 322
CPR Institute for Dispute Resolution, 286
Defense Research Institute, 348
Employee Assistance Professionals Association, 309
Healthcare Financial Management Association, 334
Institute of Certified Financial Planners, 299
International Alliance of Holistic Lawyers, 349
International Association of Business Communicators, 295
International Interactive Communications Society, 362
International Platform Association, 295
International Trademark Association, 361
Law Practice Management section of the American Bar Association, 344
Lawyer-Pilots Bar Association, 345
Meeting Professionals International, 305
Military Lawyers Conference, 330
NASPA, Inc., 362
National Academy of Elder Law Attorneys, Inc., 346
National Association for Law Placement, 266, 314

National Association for Public Interest Law, 325
National Association of Administrative Law Judges, 340
National Association of Bar Executives, 291
National Association of Bond Lawyers, 345
National Association of Broadcasters, 294
National Association of College and University Attorneys, 314
National Association of Communicators, 297
National Association of Criminal Defense Lawyers, 341
National Association of Hearing Officials, 340
National Association of Social Workers, 309
National Association of Student Personnel Administrators, 315
National Association of Temporary & Staffing Services, 305
National Association of Women in Construction, 359
National Board for Certified Counselors, 309
National Committee on Planned Giving, 327
National Conference of Appellate Court Clerks, 340
National Conference of Bar Foundations, 325
National Contract Managers Association, 303
National Council for International Health, 337
National Employment Lawyers Association, 346
National Institute for Dispute Resolution, 286
National Law Firm Marketing Association, 344
National Legal Aid & Defender Association, 325, 341
National Organization of Bar Counsel, 292
National Society of Fundraising Executives, 327
National Speakers Association, 295
National Writers Association, 296
Newsletter Publishers Association, 355
NSBA Council of School Attorneys, 314
Organizational Development Network, 305

Public Relations Society of America, 295
Radio-Television News Directors Association, 294
Society for Human Resource Management, 305
Society for Marketing Professional Services, 359
Society for Nonprofit Organizations, 327
Society for Technical Communication, 296
Society of Professional Journalists, 297
Society of Professionals in Dispute Resolution, 286
Software Publishers Association, 362
Sports Lawyers Association, 359
The Foundation Center, 328
The Ombudsman Association, 287
Toastmasters International, 295
Transportation Lawyers Association, 346
Volunteer Lawyers for the Arts, 289

Index to Websites
(organizations excluded)

ABA Job Opportunities, 291
Academic Employment Network, 314
Actor's Equity Association Hotlines, 290
Altman Weil Pensa Website, 344
America's Job Bank, 277
American Banker Online, 304
Applied Ethics Resources on WWW, 322
Army Civilian Personnel Online, 330
Attorneys@Work, 264
Back Stage Online, 290
BarPlus, 262
Bourque Newswatch, 296
Business Job Finder, 277
Cal Law, 264
Career Magazine, 277
Career Path, 277
CareerMosaic, 277
CareerOpps: Association/Nonprofit Jobs, 326
Careers in Intellectual Property Law, 361
CBS Sportsline, 360
CompLaw, 265
Counsel Connect, 294
Directory of Trust Institutions, 303
Econet, 321
Editor and Publisher's Classified Page, 296

Education World, 314
Emplawyernet,. 265
Envirolink, 321
E-Span's Job Options, 278
Essential Information, 326
Federal Judiciary Home Page, 340
FedWorld Information Network, 332
Find Satisfaction in the Law, 264
Forum on Communications Law, 293
Goodworks, 327
GovBot, 332
Great American Website, 279, 332
Hieros Gamos Legal Employment Classifieds, 265
Hoover's Online, 279
International Career Employment Center, 337
Job Bank USA, 278
JobTrak, 278
Largest Newspaper Index on the Web, 296
Law Guru.com, 266
Law Info, 266
Law Journal Extra!—Law Employment Center, 265
LawJobs WWW, 265
Lawjobs-L., 265
LawMatch, 265
Lawyers Weekly Classifieds, 265
Legal Employment Search Site, 265
Mining's Private School Listings, 315
Monster Board, 278
Most Frequently Asked Questions about the Navy Judge Advocate General Corps, 330
National Clearinghouse for Legal Services, Inc. Website, 325
National Educators Employment Review, 315
NationJob, 278
Office of Personnel Management Website, 332
Online Career Center, 278
PR Opportunities, 295
Public Service JobNet, 325
PursuitNet, 278
Recruiter Online Network, 278
Recruiting Links, 278
Seamless Legal Job Center, 265
Switchboard, 279
Teacher Job Links, 315
The Riley Guide, 278
United Nations Website, 337
Virtual Job Fair, 278
Web 100, 307
Working Solo Online, 320

About the Author

Deborah Arron, JD, has devoted herself to helping law school graduates achieve greater career satisfaction and success since 1988. In the last eleven years, she has reached well over 100,000 lawyers and law students through her books, seminars and consulting sessions.

Arron is the author of three popular career books for law schools graduates, *What Can You Do with a Law Degree?*, *Running from the Law: Why Good Lawyers Are Getting Out of the Legal Profession* and the *Complete Guide to Contract Lawyering: What Every Lawyer and Law Firm Needs to Know About Temporary Legal Services*. All three books have been praised by the National Association for Law Placement, *Law Practice Management Magazine* and other law journals across the country. Arron also wrote the chapter on nontraditional careers in the last two editions of the ABA's *Changing Jobs: A Handbook for Lawyers*. She is currently working on a new book about the growing threat of professional career obsolescence.

Arron speaks nationwide on the subject of professional career development. Sponsors of her programs for lawyers include law schools, bar associations and university alumni associations in over two dozen states across the country. She also presents practice development and stress management programs for law firms, and job-hunting and alternative career programs exclusively for law students.

Arron is frequently quoted as an expert on professional careers in well-known publications like *Time, Money, Fortune, Working Woman, Newsweek,* the *ABA Journal, USA Today* and the *National Law Journal.* Her work has also been cited in such respected career-related publications as *The Occupational Outlook Quarterly* and the *Career Planning and Adult Development Journal.*

Arron obtained her BA degree magna cum laude and Phi Beta Kappa from the University of Washington in 1971. She earned her JD from UCLA Law School in 1975, where she was on the staff of the UCLA Law Review.

Arron began her ten-year legal career in 1976 as the first female associate of a large insurance defense firm in Seattle. From 1978 to 1984, she was managing partner of a small civil litigation law firm, and then worked as a solo practitioner for an additional year. Her legal practice included a diverse mix of real estate purchase and sale, dissolution of marriage, guardianship, consumer protection, elder law and other property-related matters. She was also elected to the Board of Trustees of the (Seattle-) King County Bar Association after leading its Young Lawyers Section.

In the summer of 1985, Arron closed her practice to take a one-year sabbatical—from which she never returned! At first, she engaged in substantial self-assessment and travel. Then, she began the long process of researching and writing her first book, *Running from the Law.* In 1988, she founded an information-and-support group for Seattle lawyers considering job or career change. That program provided direct and referral services to over 1,200 participants before it was incorporated into the Washington State Bar Association three years later.

Arron is now a professional member of the National Speakers Association, and belongs to the Career Planning and Adult Development Network, the Washington State Bar Association and the California Bar.

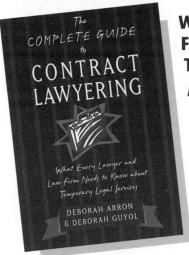

WHAT EVERY LAWYER & LAW FIRM NEEDS TO KNOW ABOUT TEMPORARY LEGAL SERVICES

by Deborah Arron, Deborah Guyol

320 pages $34.95

All indicators point to temporary work as the fastest growing category of American employment today. Although lawyers have been among the last to turn to temporary employment, the *Wall Street Journal* says the use of contract legal help "has gone mainstream." Today thousands of lawyers are taking advantage of this flexible new work arrangement. In this first comprehensive guide to contract lawyering, there are chapters on rate-setting and marketing . . . ethical, malpractice and insurance considerations . . . the myths and realities of contract lawyering . . . and how to find the nation's best placement agencies. 320 pages in all. Here's what the critics say:

> "This book is a must for any attorney—novice or seasoned veteran—who is considering contracting."
>
> —*Women Lawyers Journal*

> "This practical book has all the answers."
>
> —*Ohio Lawyer*

> "Thorough and detailed information. This book is worth buying."
>
> —*Lawyers Weekly USA*

> "Every law office should own a copy of this book. For $42.95, it is a steal."
>
> —*Legal Information Alert*

> "No one involved in contract lawyering should be without this thorough and timely resource."
>
> —*ABA Law Practice Management*

Turn to the next page for ordering information.

LEGAL CAREER SERIES
O R D E R   F O R M

3 EASY WAYS TO ORDER (SEE BELOW)

■ ## WHAT CAN YOU DO WITH A LAW DEGREE?
A Lawyer's Guide to Career Alternatives Inside, Outside & Around the Law
By Deborah Arron   (392 pages, 4th edition 1999; $29.95)

■ ## THE COMPLETE GUIDE TO CONTRACT LAWYERING:
What Every Lawyer & Law Firm Needs to Know About Temporary Legal Services
By Deborah Arron, Deborah Guyol   (320 pages, 2nd edition 1999; $34.95)
(Turn to the previous page to read more about this title.)

❶ **THREE EASY WAYS TO ORDER**

▶ To order by check or money order, send payment to:
Niche Press, P.O. Box 99477R, Seattle WA 98199.

▶ To order by credit card, call the For Counsel catalog at (800) 637-0098, or
the National Association for Law Placement at (202) 667-1666.

▶ To order by computer, go to this website: www.Amazon.com.

❷ **FOR TITLES ORDERED DIRECTLY FROM NICHE PRESS**   **Total**

What Can You Do With a Law Degree ($29.95)   _____
The Complete Guide to Contract Lawyering ($34.95)   _____
Washington State residents, add 8.6% sales tax   _____
    Shipping/handling $4 per book for U.S zip codes   _____
    For International shipping rates, inquire before ordering
    ✔ If you wish FedEx overnight or FedEx 2nd Day,
    circle one, and write your Acct #_____

Payment enclosed (U.S.$) _____

❸ **SHIPPING INFORMATION**

Name _____

Address _____

Phone (   ) _____

City _____ State _____ ZIP _____

✔ **For more information about ordering or**
Deborah Arron's national speaking schedule,
call us at (800) 359-9629 from 9 AM - 5 PM PST,
or e-mail us at nichemj@aol.com.